A Behavior System

Publications of the Yale University Press by the same author

Essentials of Behavior

Mathematico-Deductive Theory of Rote Learning
(*With others*)

A BEHAVIOR SYSTEM

An Introduction to Behavior Theory

Concerning the Individual Organism

BY CLARK L. HULL

Sterling Professor of Psychology

Yale University

New Haven: YALE UNIVERSITY PRESS, 1952

London: Geoffrey Cumberlege, Oxford University Press

Foreword

To the completion of this book Professor Hull gave all the energy that he could muster during the last three years of his life. Owing to declining health he was permitted to work only a few hours a day. Visits to his office and laboratory and attendance at scientific seminars and discussions were drastically curtailed. Despite these handicaps he won the race. On May 10, 1952, he died, with the satisfaction of having finished a major portion of a program of research and writing that he had set for himself years earlier as his contribution to the efforts of the Institute of Human Relations to develop a basic science of behavior.

The manuscript was turned over to the Yale University Press upon its completion early in February 1952. The galley proofs were ready shortly before he died. He did not see them. They were read for typographical errors and inconsistencies by his assistant and secretary, Ruth Hays. Throughout the reading of both the galley and page proofs Frank A. Logan gave invaluable assistance in matters requiring technical knowledge. Had Professor Hull lived to read the galley proofs, he would no doubt have made some last minute changes in technical details and would have detected any major alterations that needed to be made. He was keenly aware that in this rapidly growing field no volume can long remain completely up to date.

The subject index and glossary of symbols were prepared by his research assistant, John A. Antoinetti.

In the preface Professor Hull gives generous acknowledgment to all who aided him in the preparation of the manuscript. We, in turn, now desire to honor him for his generosity in making freely available to all of us such a rich reservoir of original ideas.

May, 1952   MARK A. MAY, *Director*
                                              Institute of Human Relations

v

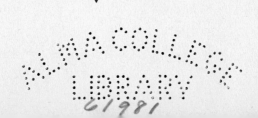

Preface

A decade or more ago I drew up a plan which proposed the writing of three volumes intended to cover in an elementary manner the range of ordinary mammalian behavior. This book is the second in that series. The first volume, *Principles of Behavior* (1943), was designed in the main to state the more important primary behavior principles considered necessary to mediate the deductions of a natural-science theory of behavior. A small supplementary volume, *Essentials of Behavior* (1951), presents these principles in a revised and nearly up-to-date form. The present work is intended primarily to show the application of the principles to the deduction of the simpler phenomena characterizing the behavior of single organisms. According to my original plan the third and final volume would apply these same principles to the deduction of the elementary phenomena of social behavior, i.e., of behavior manifested when the interacting objects are mammalian organisms of the same species. I greatly regret that in all probability I shall not be able to write the third volume.

In the following pages I have made a serious attempt to give a quantitative, systematic account of some of the more important forms of non-social behavior. I make no pretense of having said the last word on any of them. I trust that the quantitative methodology employed will readily make apparent to all serious students the errors which presumably have eluded our scrutiny and insight; hidden fallacies may seriously delay the advancement of a young science.

I am glad to take this occasion to thank the many persons who in one way or another have contributed to this volume. John M.

Felsinger, Arthur I. Gladstone, and Harry G. Yamaguchi performed a major task in experimentally quantifying reaction potential ($_sE_R$). William J. Arnold, Arthur I. Gladstone, Allen J. Sprow, and Charles B. Woodbury made necessary empirical quantitative determinations of various sorts of behavior chaining. Dr. Yamaguchi and John A. Antoinetti performed the computations upon which many of the theoretical graphs are based, and Mr. Antoinetti also prepared the subject index. Frank A. Logan read and gave an expert criticism of the entire manuscript during the final stages of its preparation. Frederick S. Cates made most of the line drawings for the various figures. In a different category are Professors Carl I. Hovland, Neal E. Miller, and Irvin L. Child; these men have given moral support and other aid whenever it was needed. Professor Kenneth W. Spence, through his unfailing interest in and understanding of the problems here discussed, and through criticisms, suggestions, and relevant experiments which he and his students have performed, has contributed to a degree feebly expressed by these few lines. In still another category are many workers, some of them personally unknown to me, who have done experiments bearing on the problems considered here, or who have subjected my theories to searching criticism. Both empirical and theoretical-critical investigations are, at bottom, cooperative searches for the truth which we all seek. I have learned from all these people, and I take this occasion to thank them. I wish to thank Ruth Hays, now rounding out more than a score of years as my secretary, for contributing her genius in effective scientific expression. I thank Professor Mark A. May, Director of the Institute of Human Relations, for vigorous and continuous support in this difficult and sometimes discouraging task. And finally, I am deeply grateful to Yale University and the Institute of Human Relations for the freedom from routine academic duties which has made the completion of this task possible.

C. L. H.

New Haven
January, 1952

Contents

Foreword   v

Preface   vii

1. Introductory Considerations   1

2. Simple Trial-and-Error Learning   15

3. Discrimination Learning   59

4. Behavior and the Molar Stimulus Trace (s')   100

5. Fractional Antedating Goal Reactions   124

6. Simple Behavior Chains   156

7. Learning Within the Individual Behavior Link   192

8. Behavior in Relation to Objects in Space   215

9. Multidirectional Maze Learning   275

10. The Problem-Solving Assembly of Behavior Segments   308

11. Value, Valuation, and Behavior Theory   327

12. Concluding Considerations   347

Glossary of Symbols   357

Index of Names   361

Index of Subjects   363

1. Introductory Considerations

Science has two essential aspects—the empirical and the explanatory. The empirical aspect is primarily concerned with the facts of the science as revealed by observation and experiment. The explanatory or theoretical aspect, on the other hand, consists in a serious attempt to understand the facts of the science, and to integrate them into a coherent, i.e., a logical, system. From these observations and integrations there are derived, directly or indirectly, the basic laws of the science. Since in a young science a certain amount of uncertainty naturally surrounds these basic laws, especially as to whether they are really basic, i.e., primary or underivable, their validity is temporarily assumed. It is for this reason that we have here called *postulates* what we assume to be laws. Once a set of presumptively basic laws has been isolated, the way is opened for the development of a natural-science theoretical system. That is primarily the task of this volume. It will present in a certain amount of detail an elementary theory of behavior.

The specific task of the present chapter is to prepare the reader in a rather general way for the chapters which are to follow. Perhaps we can best show what our purpose is by contrasting this volume with *Principles of Behavior*, which was written earlier. That work was designed in the main to present the more important presumptive elementary laws of mammalian behavior, together with relevant explanatory considerations so that they would be provisionally understood. Because of the novelty of this approach to behavior theory at that time, we felt it desirable to give a number of fairly elaborate examples of the deductive use of the principles in the logical derivation of secondary laws (or explanations) of more complex behavior phenomena. For this reason many readers of *Principles of Behavior* have mistakenly considered that work as presenting a completed system. Actually it contained merely some preliminary illustrative examples of what the ultimate system was intended to be.

The chapters which follow Chapter 1 are designed to set forth in some detail a genuine portion of the developing system—that portion concerned with non-social behavior. Paralleling the presentation of the theoretical conclusions there will be given, from time to time, a summary of the agreements and disagreements between the deductions from the postulates and the corresponding empirical facts. In this way the reader will be reminded not only of the necessity of continuously checking the results of theoretical implications, but of the current defects as well as the modest successes of the system as so far developed.

Another incidental factor which may be noted in this connection is the surprising extent to which experimentation has not yet covered in a quantitative way the fields already broached in systematic theory, and *vice versa*. Thus experiments continuously call for new theories to explain their findings, and theories continuously call for new experiments to test the validity of their theorems. The two are truly inseparable.

Perhaps the reader of the following chapters will be aided in his understanding of our efforts if he recalls that the development of a systematic science of molar behavior is just beginning. What appear to be basic laws present themselves as the system grows. Also, occasionally a principle previously considered true is found to be in error; it is then dropped out of the postulate set or is changed. But when you change a postulate in a logical system some of the conclusions in the system as a whole, e.g., a section or so written three or four years earlier, should be changed, because the different parts of a scientific work are all expected to be consistent with one another. If this is not done, the portions written earlier and those containing the later developments may not entirely agree. But if publication is ever to occur there comes a time when new developments must simply be recorded and consistency be trusted to later manuscript revisions. It is probably too much to hope that all such inconsistencies have been found and rectified in the present work.

In this connection it must be understood that behavior consists in an exceedingly complex mass of interrelations. On the other hand, exposition is essentially linear, and a linear presentation of behavior complexities inevitably distorts the reality. One of the most obvious distortions arising from this fact lies in over-simplification. To arrive at a genuine understanding of the multidimensional relationships of behavior is a personal achievement requiring a lifetime. Our effort to present some of the true richness of behavior reality in this exposition is seen scattered through the text in the frequent references to other related parts. The hurried reader may ignore these references, but the serious student with time for thought will find them helpful.

Strictly speaking, the body of a scientific system consists of the mathematical derivations of the theorems which correspond to the empirical facts of the science. The deductions presented in this volume are all of a relatively simple concrete form, and are mostly quite informal. At one time a few of us worked out for a limited range of behavior a strict system to explore its possibilities (3). It is probably too early to do this on a large scale, though the rare persons qualified for such a task should before very long attempt to do it at least for the field covered by the present volume.

Then there is the question of the numerical values of the different constants or parameters which appear in the mathematical derivations. Not one of these is really known at present except as the roughest approximation. The most conspicuous example of this is found in the field of individual and species differences, the values of which are believed to be based almost entirely on differences in constants. The same limitation holds in regard to the equations representing many of the functions stated in the postulates. Naturally the lack of this knowledge places great limitations on the range of theoretical predictions and on comparisons with empirical fact. Sometimes, otherwise significant potential theorems are not even mentioned because of the magnitude of these uncertainties. In other situations, however, where the probability seems to favor a given outcome a theoretical interpretation is attempted mainly as a means of calling attention to the problem and our general approach to the solution.

But clearly, before he can follow intelligently the deductions of the behavior phenomena presently to be discussed, the reader must know the substance of the postulates upon which the reasonings are based. Whether he has some familiarity with the system as a whole or whether he is coming to it for the first time, he probably will have occasion to return to these principles more than once for thoughtful scrutiny; their implications are no more obvious at first sight than are those of the axioms of Euclid. For this reason the postulates are assembled in the present chapter, and to facilitate easy reference and identification they are listed in sequence, each postulate being given an upper-case Roman numeral.

Also assembled in the present chapter are the formulations of certain major implications of the postulates, here called *corollaries*. These are placed in sequence with the postulates, each corollary following the postulate upon which it mainly depends; they are identified by lower-case Roman numerals. We shall find some of these corollaries to be of considerable use in the deductions of certain theorems which will appear in the body of this work.

The reasoning underlying the formulations of most of the postulates and corollaries has been published previously (*1; 2*); the reasoning in support of others is given in the present work. The reader may locate these logical considerations by consulting either the reference numbers attached to certain postulates and corollaries or the footnotes indicating where they may be found in the following chapters. It may be added that most of these postulates have been based on the behavior of lower organisms, particularly the rat, in the belief that the behavior of all mammals operates according to the same primary laws. Humans have the added capacity of speech, symbolic behavior, with its accompanying advantages to the higher mental processes. Whether this introduces any primary behavioral laws remains to be determined.

We must note that this set of postulates and corollaries differs in some respects from any previously put forward. For example, the delay-in-reinforcement principle (J) is changed from a postulate to a major corollary (iii). Also, where the substance of a principle is expressible as a provisional numerical equation, the latter is now given as the best available approximation. For purposes of convenient reference to and identification of the more important equations presented throughout this and the following chapters, a sequential number placed within parenthesis accompanies each, on the right-hand margin.

A glossary of signs as used in this volume will be found on pages 357 ff. For the most part these symbols are the same as those used in *Principles of Behavior* and *Essentials of Behavior*, though there are a few changes, additions, and withdrawals.

Here follow the behavior postulates and major corollaries, set up in bold-faced type and italics, respectively, to distinguish them clearly from the body of the text.

Postulate I. Unlearned Stimulus-response Connections ($_sU_R$) (*1*, p. 47; *2*, p. 4)

Organisms at birth possess receptor-effector connections ($_sU_R$) which under combined stimulation (S) and drive (D) have the potentiality of evoking a hierarchy of responses that either individually or in combination are more likely to terminate a need than would be a random selection from the reactions resulting from other stimulus and drive combinations.

Postulate II. Stimulus Reception (S and s)[1] (*2*, pp. 7 ff.)

A. When a brief stimulus (S) impinges upon a suitable receptor there is initiated the recruitment phase of a self-propagating molar afferent trace impulse ($\dot{s}'$), the molar stimulus equivalent ($\dot{S}'$) of which rises as a power function of time ($\underset{.}{t}$) since the beginning of the stimulus, i.e.,

$$\dot{S}' = 465{,}190 \times t^{7.6936} + 1.0, \tag{1}$$

$\dot{S}'$ reaching its maximum (and termination) when $\underset{.}{t}$ equals about .450″.
B. Following the maximum of the recruitment phase of the molar stimulus trace, there supervenes a more lengthy subsident phase ($\underset{.}{s}'$), the stimulus equivalent of which descends as a power function of time (t'), i.e.,

$$\underset{.}{S}' = 6.9310(t' + .01)^{-1.0796}, \tag{2}$$

where $t' = \underset{.}{t} - .450″$.
C. The intensity of the molar stimulus trace (s') is a logarithmic function of the molar stimulus equivalent of the trace, i.e.,

$$s' = \log S'. \tag{3}$$

Postulate III. Primary Reinforcement (*2*, pp. 15 ff.)

Whenever an effector activity (R) is closely associated with a stimulus afferent impulse or trace (s) and the conjunction is closely associated

[1] For the derivation of Postulate II see Chapter 4, pp. 101 ff.

with the rapid diminution in the motivational stimulus (S_D or s_G), there will result an increment (Δ) to a tendency for that stimulus to evoke that response.

Corollary i. Secondary Motivation (2, pp. 21 ff.)

When neutral stimuli are repeatedly and consistently associated with the evocation of a primary or secondary drive and this drive stimulus undergoes an abrupt diminution, the hitherto neutral stimuli acquire the capacity to bring about the drive stimuli (S_D), which thereby become the condition (C_D) of a secondary drive or motivation.

Corollary ii. Secondary Reinforcement (2, pp. 26 ff.)

A neutral receptor impulse which occurs repeatedly and consistently in close conjunction with a reinforcing state of affairs, whether primary or secondary, will itself acquire the power of acting as a reinforcing agent.

Postulate IV. The Law of Habit Formation ($_sH_R$) (1, pp. 102 ff.; 2, pp. 29 ff.)

If reinforcements follow each other at evenly distributed intervals, everything else constant, the resulting habit will increase in strength as a positive growth function of the number of trials according to the equation,

$$_sH_R = 1 - 10^{-.0305\dot{N}}, \tag{4}$$

where $\dot{N}$ is the total number of reinforcements from Z.

Postulate V. Primary Motivation or Drive (D) (1, pp. 226 ff.; 2, pp. 33 ff.)

A. Primary motivation (D), at least that resulting from food privation, consists of two multiplicative components: (1) the drive proper (D′) which is an increasing monotonic sigmoid function of h, the number of hours of food privation; and (2) a negative or inanition component (ϵ) which is a positively accelerated monotonic function of h decreasing from 1.0 to zero, i.e.,

$$D = D' \times \epsilon. \tag{5}$$

where

$$D' = 37.824 \times 10^{-27.496\frac{1}{h}} + 4.001,$$

and

$$\epsilon = 1 - .00001045h^{2.486}.$$

B. The functional relationship of drive (D) to one drive condition (food privation) is: during the time from $h = 0$ to about $h = 3$, drive rises in a linear manner until the function abruptly shifts to a near horizontal, then to a concave-upward course, gradually changing to a convex-upward course reaching a maximum of 12.3σ at about $h = 59$, after which it gradually falls to the reaction threshold $({}_s L_R)$ at around $h = 100$.

C. Each drive condition (C_D) generates a characteristic drive stimulus (S_D) which is a monotonic increasing function of this state.

D. At least some drive conditions tend partially to motivate into action habits which have been set up on the basis of different drive conditions.

Postulate VI. Stimulus-intensity Dynamism (V) (*2*, pp. 41 ff.)

Other things constant, the magnitude of the stimulus-intensity component (V) of reaction potential $({}_s E_R)$ is a monotonic increasing logarithmic function of S, i.e.,

$$V = 1 - 10^{-.44 \log S}. \qquad (6)$$

Postulate VII. Incentive Motivation (K) (*1*, pp. 124 ff.; *2*, pp. 47 ff.)

The incentive component (K) of reaction potential $({}_s E_R)$ is a negatively accelerated increasing monotonic function of the weight (w) of food or quantity of other incentive (K') given as reinforcement, i.e.,

$$K = 1 - 10^{-a\sqrt{w}}. \qquad (7)$$

Postulate VIII. The Constitution of Reaction Potential $({}_s E_R)$ (*1*, pp. 178 ff.; *2*, pp. 57 ff.)

The reaction potential $({}_s E_R)$ of a bit of learned behavior at any given stage of learning, where conditions are constant throughout learning and response-evocation, is determined (1) by the drive (D) operating during the learning process multiplied (2) by the dynamism of the signaling stimulus trace (V_1), (3) by the incentive reinforcement (K), and (4) by the habit strength $({}_s H_R)$, i.e.,

$$_s E_R = D \times V_1 \times K \times {}_s H_R. \qquad (8)$$

Corollary iii. Delay in Reinforcement (J) (*1*, pp. 135 ff.; *2*, pp. 52 ff.)[2]

A. *The greater the delay in reinforcement of a link within a given behavior chain, learning and response-evocation conditions remaining*

---

[2] The derivation of this corollary is presented in Chapter 5, pp. 126 ff.

constant, the weaker will be the resulting reaction potential of the link in question to the stimulus traces present at the time.

B. *The greater the delay in the receipt of the incentive by groups of learning subjects, learning and response-evocation conditions remaining constant, the weaker will be the resulting learned reaction potentials* ($_s E_{R_d}$), *the shape of the gradient as a function of the respective delays being roughly that of decay with the lower limit of the extended gradient passing beneath the reaction threshold, i.e.,*

$$J = {}_s\underline{E}_{R_d} = D \times V_2 \times K \times {}_s H_R \times 10^{-.15d} \times V_1, \quad (9)$$

where,

$$d = \log \dot{S}' \text{ of } V_1 - \log \dot{S}' \text{ of } V_2.$$

Corollary iv. The Summation ($\dotplus$) *of Habit Strengths (2, pp. 60 ff.)*

If two stimuli, S' and S, are reinforced separately to a response (R) *by $\dot{N}'$ and $\dot{N}$ reinforcements respectively, and the $_{s'} H_R$ generalizes to S in the amount of $_s H'_R$, the summation* ($\dotplus$) *of the two habit strengths at S will be the same as would result from the equivalent number of reinforcements at S, i.e.,*

$$_s H_R \dotplus {}_s H'_R = {}_s H_R + {}_s H'_R - {}_s H_R \times {}_s H'_R. \quad (10)$$

Corollary v. The Summation ($\dotplus$) *of Reaction Potentials (2, pp. 64 ff.)*

If two stimuli, S' and S, are reinforced separately to a response (R) *and $_{s'} E_R$ generalizes to S in the amount of $_s E'_R$, the two reaction potentials will summate at S as would the equivalent number of reinforcements in an original learning, i.e.,*

$$_s E_R \dotplus {}_s E'_R = {}_s E_R + {}_s E'_R - \frac{_s E_R \times {}_s E'_R}{M}, \quad (11)$$

where M is the asymptote of $_s E_R$ by distributed trials.

Corollary vi. The Withdrawal ($\dotdiv$) *of Habit Strength (2, pp. 66 ff.)*

If a smaller habit strength ($_s H'_R$) *is to be withdrawn* ($\dotdiv$) *from a larger habit strength* (C), *the result will be:*

$$C \dotdiv {}_s H'_R = {}_s H_R = \frac{C - {}_s H'_R}{1 - {}_s H'_R}. \quad (12)$$

Corollary vii. The Withdrawal ($\div$) of Reaction Potential (2, pp. 68 ff.)

If a smaller reaction potential ($_s\underline{E}'_R$) is to be withdrawn ($\div$) from a larger reaction potential (C), the result will be:

$$C \div {_s}\underline{E}'_R = {_s}E_R = \frac{M(C - {_s}\underline{E}'_R)}{M - {_s}\underline{E}'_R}. \tag{13}$$

Corollary viii. The Problem of the Behavioral Summation ($\dotplus$) of Incentive Substances (K) (2, pp. 70 ff.)

If two incentive substances, f and a, have $A\sqrt{w}$ and $B\sqrt{m}$ as the exponential components of their respective functional equations, the second substance will combine ($\dotplus$) with the first in the production of the total K according to the following equation:

$$K_{f+a} = 1 - 10^{-A\sqrt{w + m \times \frac{B^2}{A^2}}}. \tag{14}$$

Postulate IX. Inhibitory Potential (1, pp. 258 ff.; 2, pp. 73 ff.)

A. Whenever a reaction (R) is evoked from an organism there is left an increment of primary negative drive (I_R) which inhibits to a degree according to its magnitude the reaction potential ($_sE_R$) to that response.
B. With the passage of time since its formation, I_R spontaneously dissipates approximately as a simple decay function of the time (t) elapsed, i.e.,

$$I'_R = I_R \times 10^{-.018t}. \tag{15}$$

C. If responses (R) occur in close succession without further reinforcement, the successive increments of inhibition (ΔI_R) to these responses summate to attain appreciable amounts of I_R. These also summate with $_sI_R$ to make up an inhibitory aggregate ($\dot{I}_R$), i.e.,

$$\dot{I}_R = I_R \dotplus {_s}I_R. \tag{16}$$

D. When experimental extinction occurs by massed practice, the $\dot{I}_R$ present at once after the successive reaction evocations is a positive growth function of the order of those responses ($\dot{n}$), i.e.,

$$\dot{I}_R = 1.84(1 - 10^{-.0434\dot{n}}). \tag{17}$$

E. For constant values of superthreshold reaction potential ($_s\bar{E}_R$) set up by massed practice, the number of unreinforced responses (n) producible by massed extinction procedure is a linear decreasing function of the magnitude of the work (W) involved in operating the manipulanda, i.e.,

$$n = 3.25(1.1476 - .00984W).$$ (18)

Corollary ix. Conditioned Inhibition (2, pp. 74 ff.)

Stimuli and stimulus traces closely associated with the cessation of a given activity, and in the presence of appreciable I_R from that response, become conditioned to this particular non-activity, yielding conditioned inhibition ($_sI_R$) which will oppose $_sE_R$'s involving that response, the amount of Δ_sI_R generated being an increasing function of the I_R present.

Corollary x. Inhibitory Potential ($\dot{I}_R$) as a Function of Work (1, pp. 279 ff.; 2, pp. 81 ff.)

For a constant value of n, the inhibitory potential ($\dot{I}_R$) generated by the total massed extinction of reaction potential set up by massed practice begins as a positively accelerated increasing function of the work (W) involved in operating the manipulandum, which gradually changes to a negative acceleration at around 80 grams, finally becoming asymptotic at around 110 grams.

Corollary xi. Inhibitory Potential ($\dot{I}_R$) as a Function of the Number of Responses (1, pp. 260 ff.; 2, pp. 84 ff.)

For a constant value of the work (W) involved in operating the manipulandum, the inhibitory potential ($\dot{I}_R$) generated by the total massed extinction of reaction potential set up by massed practice is a negatively accelerated increasing function of the total number of reactions (n) required.

Postulate X. Stimulus Generalization ($_s\overline{H}_R$, $_sE_R$, and $_sI_R$) (1, p. 183; 2, pp. 86 ff.)

A. In the case of qualitative stimuli, S_1 and S_2, the effective habit strength ($_s\overline{H}_R$) generates a stimulus generalization gradient on the qualitative continuum from the simple learned attachment of S_1 to R:

$$_{S_2}\overline{H}_R = {_{S_1}}H_R \times 10^{-.0135d},$$ (19)

where d represents the difference between S_1 and S_2 in j.n.d.'s, and

$$_{S_2}E_R = D \times K \times V_2 \times {_{S_2}}\overline{H}_R,$$ (20)

and where $D \times K \times V_2$ is constant.

B. A stimulus intensity (S_1) generalizes to a second stimulus intensity (S_2) according to the equation,

$$_{S_2}\bar{H}_R = {}_{S_1}H_R \times 10^{-bd} \times V_1, \tag{21}$$

where d represents the difference between S_1 and S_2 in log units and

$$_{S_2}E_R = D \times K \times V_2 \times {}_{S_2}\bar{H}_R, \tag{22}$$

and where ($D \times K$) is constant and V_2 is the stimulus-intensity dynamism at S_2.

C. In the case of qualitative stimulus differences, ordinary conditioning and extinction spontaneously generate a gradient of inhibitory potential ($_{S}I_R$) which is a negative growth function of $_{S}I_R$ and d, i.e.,

$$_{S_2}I_R = {}_{S_1}I_R \times 10^{-ad}, \tag{23}$$

and in the case of stimulus-intensity differences,

$$_{S_2}I_R = {}_{S_1}I_R \times 10^{-bd} \times V_2. \tag{24}$$

Corollary xii. The Generalization of $_{S}H_R$ and $_{S}E_R$ on S_D as a Continuum (1, pp. 235 ff.; 2, pp. 89 ff.)

When a habit is set up in association with a given drive intensity (S_D) and its strength is tested under a different drive intensity, there will result a falling gradient of $_{S}\bar{H}_R$ and $_{S}\underline{E}_R$.

Postulate XI. Afferent Stimulus Interaction (1, pp. 216 ff.; 2, pp. 93 ff.)

All afferent impulses (s's) active at any given instant, mutually interact converting each other into š's which differ qualitatively from the original s's so that a reaction potential ($_{s}E_R$) set up on the basis of one afferent impulse (s) will show a generalization fall to $_{š}E_R$ when the reaction (R) is evoked by the other afferent impulse (š), the amount of the change in the afferent impulses being shown by the number of j.n.d.'s separating the $_{s}E_R$'s involved according to the principle,

$$d = \frac{\log \frac{_{s}E_R}{_{š}E_R}}{i}. \tag{25}$$

Postulate XII. Behavioral Oscillation ($_{S}O_R$) (1, pp. 304 ff.; 2, pp. 96 ff.)

A. A reaction potential ($_{S}E_R$) oscillates from moment to moment, the distribution of behavioral oscillation ($_{S}O_R$) deviating slightly from the

Gaussian probability form in being leptokurtic with β_2 at about 4.0; i.e., the distribution is represented by the equation (*4*, p. lxiii),

$$ y = y_0 \frac{1}{\left(1 + \dfrac{x^2}{a^2}\right)^m}. $$

B. The oscillation of $_sE_R$ begins with the dispersion of approximately zero at the absolute zero (Z) of $_sH_R$, this at first rising as a positive growth function of the number of subthreshold reinforcements to an unsteady maximum, after which it remains relatively constant though with increasing variability.

C. The oscillations of competing reaction potentials at any given instant are asynchronous.

Corollary xiii. Response Generalization (1, pp. 316, 319)[3]

A. *The contraction of each muscle involved in a habitual act varies its $_sE_R$ from instant to instant ($_sO_R$) about a central reinforced region of intensity which is approximately normal (leptokurtic) in distribution; this constitutes* response-intensity generalization.

B. *Where several muscles jointly contract to produce a given habitual act, the contraction of each muscle varies more or less ($_sO_R$) independently of the others, producing a qualitative deviation from the central tendency of the joint result of the muscular contractions originally reinforced; this constitutes* qualitative response generalization.

Postulate XIII. Absolute Zero of Reaction Potential (Z) and the Reaction Threshold ($_sL_R$) (1, pp. 322 ff.; 2, p. 101)

A. The reaction threshold ($_sL_R$) stands at an appreciable distance (B) above the absolute zero (Z) of reaction potential ($_sE_R$), i.e.,

$$ _sL_R = Z + B. \tag{26} $$

B. No reaction evocation (R) will occur unless the momentary reaction potential at the time exceeds the reaction threshold, i.e., unless,

$$ _s\dot{\bar{E}}_R > {_s}L_R. \tag{27} $$

Corollary xiv. The Competition of Incompatible Reaction Potentials ($_s\bar{E}_R$) *(1, pp. 341 ff.; 2, p. 104)*

When the net reaction potentials ($_s\bar{E}_R$) to two or more incompatible reactions (R) occur in an organism at the same instant, each in a

---

[3] The derivation of this corollary is presented in Chapter 2.

magnitude greater than $_sL_R$, *only that reaction whose momentary reaction potential* $(_s\dot{E}_R)$ *is greatest will be evoked.*

Postulate XIV. Reaction Potential ($_sE_R$) as a Function of Reaction Latency ($_st_R$) (1, pp. 336 ff.; 2, p. 105)

Reaction potential ($_sE_R$) is a negatively accelerated decreasing function of the median reaction latency ($_st_R$), i.e.,

$$_sE_R = 2.845(_st_R)^{-.483}. \tag{28}$$

Postulate XV. Reaction Potential ($_sE_R$) as a Function of Reaction Amplitude (A) (1, pp. 339 ff.; 2, p. 108)

Reaction potential ($_sE_R$) is an increasing linear function of the Tarchanoff galvanic skin reaction amplitude (A), i.e.,

$$_sE_R = .02492A. \tag{29}$$

Postulate XVI. Complete Experimental Extinction (n) as a Function of Reaction Potential ($_sE_R$) (1, pp. 227 ff.; 2, p. 110)

A. The reaction potentials ($_sE_R$) acquired by massed reinforcements are a negatively accelerated monotonic increasing function of the median number of massed unreinforced reaction evocations (n) required to produce their experimental extinction, the work (W) involved in each operation of the manipulandum remaining constant, i.e.,

$$_sE_R = 4.0(1 - 10^{-.0110n}) + .46. \tag{30}$$

B. The reaction potentials ($_sE_R$) acquired by quasi-distributed reinforcements are a positively accelerated monotonic increasing function of the median number of massed unreinforced reaction evocations (n) required to produce their experimental extinction, the work (W) involved in each operation of the manipulandum remaining constant, i.e.,

$$_sE_R = .1225 \times 10^{.0647n} + 2.114. \tag{31}$$

Postulate XVII. Individual Differences (2, p. 115)

The "constant" numerical values appearing in equations representing primary molar behavioral laws vary from species to species, from individual to individual, and from some physiological states to others in the same individual at different times, all quite apart from the factor of behavioral oscillation ($_sO_R$).

Corollary xv. Secondary Reinforcement by Fractional Antedating Goal Reaction ($r_G \rightarrow s_G$)[4]

When a stimulus (S) or a stimulus trace (s) acts at the same time that a hitherto unrelated response (R) occurs and this coincidence is accompanied by an antedating goal reaction (r_G), the secondary reinforcing powers of the stimulus evoked by the latter (s_G) will reinforce S to R, giving rise to a new S --> R dynamic connection.

REFERENCES

1. Hull, C. L. *Principles of behavior.* New York: D. Appleton-Century Company, 1943.
2. Hull, C. L. *Essentials of behavior.* New Haven: Yale Univ. Press, 1951.
3. Hull, C. L., Hovland, C. I., Ross, R. T., Hall, M., Perkins, D. T., and Fitch, F. B. *Mathematico-deductive theory of rote learning.* New Haven: Yale Univ. Press, 1940.
4. Pearson, K. *Tables for statisticians and biometricians,* Part I (3rd ed.). England: Cambridge Univ. Press, 1930.

[4] The derivation of this corollary is presented in Chapter 5, pp. 124 ff.

2. Simple Trial-and-Error Learning

We shall begin our elementary account of systematic behavior theory with the consideration of trial-and-error learning, one of the less complex, more common, and better known of the behavior processes.

A Concrete Example of Simple Trial-and-Error Learning

Consider the following. A hungry but very tame albino rat, about three months of age, is placed in a small rectangular cage; the cage is made of rather coarse wire screen so that the animal's behavior may be clearly observed. A small brass rod with a short crosspiece at its end projects through one of the meshes of the screen a half inch or so into the cage. A short distance outside the cage this rod is pivoted on an easily moved bearing in such a way that the crosspiece within the cage can be moved freely up and down. A weak spring outside the cage holds the portion inside, upward against a restraining shoulder. However, a slight pressure on the crosspiece will depress the end of the rod a few millimeters, thereby closing an electric circuit which activates an electromagnet; this in turn releases from a magazine into a food-cup placed on the floor of the cage a small cylinder of food much relished by the rat.

When first placed in the cage the rat remains quiet for a time, looking about from a somewhat crouching posture suggesting fear. Gradually he relaxes from the fear posture and sniffing about begins to examine his surroundings, pausing frequently to wash his face or just sit for a time, and then resuming his exploration. At length he approaches the food-cup, which, having the odor of food about it from previous use, focuses his attention on its vicinity.

He rears on his hind legs to sniff the cage wall above the food-cup, and his paws chance to press lightly on the crossbar of the rod. This at once closes the electric circuit, a food pellet drops into the cup, and presently the rat finds and eats the pellet. The random exploratory activity then is resumed much as before except that it is confined more closely to the region of the food-cup. This of course increases the probability of the chance pressure of the bar, and after some minutes, much sniffing, and considerable face-washing the rat touches the bar again and eats the resulting food.

The learning process continues for fifteen minutes or so. As practice goes on, the amount of random sniffing and exploration grows less and less, and the time required to secure each succeeding pellet diminishes, on the whole, until practically all irrelevant activity has disappeared and the rat spends the time between operations of the bar exclusively in eating the pellet he has secured by his immediately preceding pressure. After two or three such practice sessions the animal has, by a process of *trial-and-error*, fully learned to secure food from the apparatus.

With the exception of the originally very feeble tendency to press the bar, the various movements which the experimental cage situation in conjunction with the animal's need of food originally evoked have all disappeared. This process of the differential strengthening of the one reaction tendency in relation to the competing reaction tendencies is known as trial-and-error *selection*. The responses which resulted in a reduction of the need will be known as *appropriate, correct,* or *right* responses (R_+), whereas those which did not do this will be known as *inappropriate, incorrect,* or *wrong* responses (R_-).

An Elementary Theoretical Analysis

With a picture of simple trial-and-error learning before us we proceed to a statement of the more obvious theoretical questions demanding explanation and a preliminary examination of the explanations themselves—the postulates utilized in the deductions and a notion of how the deductions are effected. The tracing through of this simple reasoning (6) will give a certain amount of preliminary qualitative understanding and perspective useful for the comprehension of the more technical quantitative deductions which make up the bulk of this chapter.

1. Why are the false or inappropriate reactions (R_-), such as sniffing in a given corner, gradually abandoned? The answer is that R_- abandonment occurs to a considerable extent because of experimental extinction (IX A; ix).[1] It is also due in part to the strengthening of R_+ which competes with R_-.

2. Why are erroneous reactions (R_-'s) often repeated many times before being abandoned? Experimental extinction is a cumulative process and numerous repetitions are required to generate enough internal inhibition (I_{R_-} and sI_{R_-}) to diminish the initially dominant reaction tendency or potential (sE_{R_-}) to a strength less than that of the next strongest reaction potential (IX C).

3. What determines the order in which the several responses are tried by the organism? This is partly determined by the stimuli which chance to impinge upon the organism at any given time, but mainly by the relative strength of the several competing reaction potentials in the hierarchy of sE_R's possessed at that time by the organism.

4. Why does one organism follow a different sequence of reaction from that followed by another organism, the stimulation given being parallel? This is mainly because the previous history of an organism differs considerably from that of other organisms in the relevant hierarchy of the reaction potentials laid down in each.

5. When the correct reaction (R_+) finally occurs, what strengthens this response tendency? The answer to this is in accordance with the principles of reinforcement (III; IV).

6. Why does the organism often return to R_-'s after one or more successes (R_+'s)? This is in part because of behavioral oscillation (sO_R) (XII A, C) and in part because of recovery from preceding experimental extinction (IX B).

7. How can we be sure both that the R_+'s increase in strength following reinforcement and that the R_-'s decrease in strength through failure of reinforcement? This is revealed by changes in the respective response latencies. The implication is that the R_+ responses decrease in reaction time and the R_- responses increase (XIV).

---

[1] Upper-case Roman numerals in parenthesis (i.e., IX A) here and elsewhere throughout the text indicate postulates relevant to the subject being discussed at that point. Similar insertions in lower-case Roman numerals (i.e., ix) indicate relevant corollaries.

There are many more questions which we shall need to ask and attempt to answer about simple trial-and-error learning, and some of the briefly stated answers to those above will need to be elaborated in considerable quantitative detail. Nevertheless, if the reader has really understood the seven explanations just given he will be well on his way to a comprehension of the more detailed quantitative explanations now to begin.

Conditions Antecedent to Simple Trial-and-Error Learning

From the preceding considerations a number of the essential conditions of simple trial-and-error learning are evident. One of these is that the situation in conjunction with the need or needs of the organism at the time (*11*, pp. 226 ff.) will produce a variety of more or less persistent tendencies to action. The origins of these tendencies are various. The process of organic evolution, through inheritance, provides the organism with a considerable variety of innate reaction tendencies ($_sU_R$) at the very outset of life; this furnishes an adequate basis for genuine trial-and-error learning. The process of antecedent trial-and-error learnings in a great but miscellaneous series of situations selects, joins, and molds the inherited tendencies to action so that one stimulus combination will evoke one movement or muscular-contraction combination, another partially different stimulus combination will evoke a different reaction combination, and so on. Since the number of different types of receptors is distinctly limited, it necessarily comes about that at a relatively early stage in the life of the organism all the receptor types have been connected in various combinations to one reaction or another. As a result, when a "new" situation is encountered by the organism, i.e., one involving a combination of receptor activations and intensities different from any previously adapted to, it is inevitable that the stimulus components of the "new" situation will, through the principle of stimulus generalization (*11*, pp. 185, 186; X A), tend to evoke with greater or less intensity *all* of the reactions and reaction sequences hitherto learned. Thus, after life has gone on for a considerable period, the stimulus components of a "new" situation are *not* new; the novelty consists almost entirely in the fact that the stimulus elements come in a new *combination*.

Moreover, the muscles whose contractions will be necessary to bring about a state of affairs which will reduce the organism's need will all have been used in adaptations to other situations, so their use in an unfamiliar problem situation will not be new either. The novelty here, again, will be in the combination of the muscles and the combinations of the reaction intensities required of each to produce the reinforcing state of affairs. It is evident that when encountering any novel situation an organism at a fairly early stage of life has the potentiality of an almost limitless variety of reaction tendencies, consisting of inherited tendencies overlaid and modified by those acquired through all the learning of its preceding life.

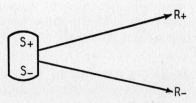

On the basis of the above preliminary analysis we may represent more precisely the origin and precipitating conditions of simple trial-and-error learning for the present expository purposes as follows. A correct reaction, R_+, is connected to a stimulus aggregate, S_+, in conjunction with other accidentally accompanying stimuli or stimulus aggregates. Similarly, an incorrect reaction, R_-, is connected to a largely different stimulus aggregate, S_-.

FIGURE 1. Diagrammatic representation of the divergent reaction potentials arising from the conjunction of two stimuli connected to incompatible responses. R_+ represents pushing a small brass bar to the left, and R_- represents pressing downward a bar similar in appearance but placed in a horizontal, rather than vertical, position. (See Figure 13, p. 50.)

Finally, S_+ and S_- are presented simultaneously, together with one or more chance stimuli or stimulus aggregates novel to each. The resulting formula is shown diagrammatically in Figure 1. An experimental situation representing an opportunity for the subject to make the responses separately may be seen in Figure 13 (p. 50). Reinforcement always follows R_+, but never follows R_-.

A not unusual complication of such situations is that either S_+ or S_-, or both, will not be exactly the same as the stimuli directly conditioned to R_+ and R_- respectively, but will fall on a generalization continuum more or less remote from the stimuli $\dot{S}_+$ and $\dot{S}_-$ which were originally connected to the respective reactions. Under these conditions, S_+ and S_- will tend to evoke their respective reaction potentials $(_sE_R)$ if not too remote on the generalization continuum. But since R_+ and R_- by assumption cannot be performed simultaneously, only the one of the two which is at the moment the stronger will be performed (xiv).

Quantitative Assumptions

A theoretical analysis of behavior phenomena is fairly complex even when the simplest possible conditions are assumed. Accordingly we shall begin our analysis with a radical simplification that will limit our competing reaction potentials, which are superthreshold in magnitude (XIII B; *11*, pp. 304 ff.), to two responses. Secondly, in order to eliminate the complications inherent in perseverational stimulus traces in those experimental extinction effects (IX A; *11*, pp. 258 ff.) which are susceptible to spontaneous recovery (IX B; *11*, pp. 258 ff.), we shall assume that an interval of 24 hours occurs between successive trials. This means that in case of an erroneous reaction no further or correctional choice is permitted on that trial (*12*). We shall assume further (X A) that at every reinforcement of R_+ there is not only a direct gain to R_+ in the increment (Δ) in ${}_sE_{R_+}$ but there is a positive generalization transfer from $\Delta {}_sE_{R_+}$ to ${}_sE_{R_-}$; and at every lack of reinforcement of the occurrence of R_- there is not only a loss in the reaction potential from $\Delta {}_sI_{R_-}$ to R_-, but a generalized loss transfer of $\Delta {}_sI_{R_-}$ to ${}_sI_{R_+}$.

Finally we shall assume that the statement of the competing reaction potentials utilized in the deductions represents the state of affairs after external inhibition (*11*, p. 217), incidental to the presentation of stimuli in combinations different from those under which original reinforcement occurred, has already taken place. Because of the wide separation of the trials here assumed we shall call this *distributed-trials simple trial-and-error learning*. This situation is in contrast to one involving closely successive repetitions, which is known as *massed-trials simple trial-and-error learning*. The distributed-trials analysis will occupy us throughout the next two sections, after which we shall take up massed-trials simple trial-and-error learning.

There are certain quantitative conditions which are so central to the trial-and-error process utilized in our exposition that they cannot possibly be eliminated. One of these is the amount of reaction potential (${}_sE_R$) characteristic of each of the competing reaction tendencies, from which there follows the question of whether the positive or the negative reaction potential (if either) is initially greater, and the magnitude of the difference between them in case any difference exists. In order to have available a convenient means of reference to the reaction potential characteristics of the two competing response tendencies, we shall represent that of the "correct" reaction by the symbol $_sE_{R_+}$, and that of the "incorrect" reaction by the symbol $_sE_{R_-}$.

The above considerations lead to the need for a statement of a number of quantitatively distinguishable combinations of antecedent conditions or cases assumed at the beginning of the trial-and-error process. These are as follows:

$$\begin{array}{lll}
\text{Case I} & _sE_{R_+} = 2.5\sigma; & _sE_{R_-} = 2.5\sigma. \\
\text{Case II} & _sE_{R_+} = 4.5\sigma; & _sE_{R_-} = 4.5\sigma. \\
\text{Case III} & _sE_{R_+} = 5.0\sigma; & _sE_{R_-} = 2.0\sigma. \\
\text{Case IV} & _sE_{R_+} = 2.0\sigma; & _sE_{R_-} = 5.0\sigma. \\
\text{Case V} & _sE_{R_+} = .856\sigma; & _sE_{R_-} = 5.0\sigma.
\end{array}$$

Cases I and II Where $_sE_{R_+}$ and $_sE_{R_-}$ Are Equal

We have before us at this point the task of tracing quantitatively the characteristic events of distributed-trials simple trial-and-error learning under two related sets of conditions, i.e., Cases I and II where $_sE_{R_+} = {_sE_{R_-}}$ and both may be relatively weak or relatively strong. Proceeding directly to the consideration of Case I, we take $_sE_{R_+}$ and $_sE_{R_-}$ at the comparatively low level of 2.5σ each. This means that the probability of each reaction occurring will at the outset be .5 or 50 per cent. Let us first consider the 50 per cent of organisms which respond to stimulation with R_+ and so receive reinforcement. According to the present system, the value of $_sE_{R_+}$ after one reinforcement is given by the equation (11, p. 120):

$$\Delta_sE_{R_+} = M - {_sE_{R_+}} - (M - {_sE_{R_+}})10^{-i} \tag{32}$$

where,

$\Delta_sE_{R_+}$ is the increment to the reaction potential from a single reinforcement under the stated conditions;

M is the reaction potential at the limit of practice under the conditions of reinforcement obtaining, here taken as 6.0σ;

$_sE_{R_+}$ is the reaction potential just *previous* to the reinforcement under consideration, here taken as 2.5σ; and i is the exponential constant characteristic of the particular organism under the given conditions of learning, here taken as .091.[2]

Substituting appropriately in equation 32, we have,

$$\Delta_s E_{R_+} = 6.0 - 2.5 - (6.0 - 2.5)10^{-.091}$$
$$= 3.5 - \frac{3.5}{1.2333}$$
$$= 3.5 - 2.8386$$
$$\therefore \Delta_s E_{R_+} = .6614.$$

It follows that the $_sE_{R_+}$ *after* the reinforcement must be,

$$_sE_{R_+} + \Delta_s E_{R_+} = 2.5 + .6614 = 3.1614.$$

At this point we must introduce the action of stimulus generalization (*10*, X A). In the trial-and-error situation assumed here there are in common for the evocation of R_+ and R_- the explicit stimuli, S_+S_-. There are also the stimuli within the body of the organism together with many external environmental stimuli. These make up a considerable number of common stimuli conditioned to the response. In the interest of expository simplicity these will be neglected for the present.

On the other hand, R_+ consists in the pushing of a small brass vertical bar (S_+) to the left (Figure 13, p. 50), whereas R_- consists in the pressing downward of a horizontal bar (S_-) of the same size but situated about two inches away. These objects considered separately are rather different sets of stimuli. Actually, during the trial-and-error process both S_+ and S_- are presented at the same time. In short, it is evident that so far as the stimuli are concerned there will be a considerable, though by no means complete, stimulus generalization.

Moreover, we have here a complication in that R_+ and R_- often involve the use of practically the same muscles, though in a more or less different way; in the case of an occasional animal, however, one bar would be moved with the paw and the other with the side

---

[2] This is about five times the empirical value of .018 found in an experiment (*11*, p. 347) which approached the conditions here assumed the most closely of any known to the author. This large value is taken in order to shorten the rather tedious computations necessarily involved in the working out of the example. The decrement ($\Delta_s I_{R_-}$) resulting from an unreinforced evocation of R_- has been taken arbitrarily from the same experiment.

of the head. This usually near identity of the responding organs for R_+ and R_- gives the two responses much in common with most animals, though by no means complete identity of response. If they were identical, generalization would of course be very high. As things stand in regard to the responses it is clear that there is bound to be less stimulus generalization than the marked similarity of the stimulus combinations would produce.

Generalizing on the preceding considerations, we arrive at the following major corollary:

Corollary xvi

A. *When an organism acquires two reaction potentials, $_sE_{R_+}$ and $_sE_{R_-}$, the two stimuli of which are very similar and the responses of which are different though they often involve substantially the same muscles, there will be in addition to a gain in $_sE_{R_+}$, also a generalization of reaction potential from $\Delta_sE_{R_+}$ to $_sE_{R_-}$.*

B. *When one of the habits ($_sE_R$) undergoes partial or complete experimental extinction, there will be, in addition to the loss in $_sE_{R_-}$, also a generalization of $\Delta_sI_{R_-}$ from this false reaction tendency to the other or correct one ($_sE_{R_+}$)*

Evidence has been found verifying both part A and part B of the above corollary. This is as follows:

Part A. Holland, using the apparatus shown in Figure 13 (p. 50), trained 115 albino rats on one manipulandum alone for 20 trials. This bar was then retracted and the second manipulandum was extended into the animal's chamber. The results showed that the training on the first bar greatly facilitated the learning on the second bar. For example, the latency of the twelfth and thirteenth trials on the first bar was the same as that of the third and fourth trials on the second bar (*3*, pp. 28–29). Thus Corollary xvi A finds empirical confirmation.

Part B. In a somewhat similar experimental situation four comparable groups of 25 albino rats each showed on the average only 47.66 per cent as many trials to the experimental extinction on one habit immediately *after* the other habit had been extinguished as they did when the same habit was extinguished first, thus demonstrating marked perseverative generalization of extinction effects (*9*, p. 247) and substantiating Corollary xvi B.

We shall accordingly assume (xvi A) that each $\Delta_s E_{R_+}$ generalizes 20 per cent to $_s E_{R_-}$. This means that in the present case,

$$\Delta_s \underline{E}_{R_-} = .6614 \times .2 = .1323.$$

Therefore the $_s E_{R_-}$, as an indirect result of the reinforcement of $_s E_{R_+}$, *also* undergoes a gain, i.e.,

$$_s \overline{E}_{R_-} + \Delta_s \underline{E}_{R_-} = 2.5 + .1323 = 2.6323.$$

As a result of the preceding computations, those subjects which respond correctly on the first trial should have for the two competing reaction potentials *after* the response (and its reinforcement),

$$_s E_{R_+} = 3.1614; \qquad _s E_{R_-} = 2.6323.$$

We turn now to the change in the reaction potentials in those organisms which respond to R_-. Here we assume that the maximum conditioned inhibition possible of generation from a reaction potential undergoing experimental extinction equals the $_s E_{R_-}$ in question. We also tentatively assume, though without adequate evidence, that $\Delta_s I_{R_-}$ follows the same law with the same constants as $\Delta_s E_{R_+}$. Accordingly,[3]

$$\Delta_s I_{R_-} = {}_s I_{R_-} - {}_s I_{R_-} \times 10^{-.091}$$
$$= 2.5 - \frac{2.5}{1.233}$$
$$= 2.5 - 2.0276$$
$$\therefore \Delta_s I_{R_-} = .4724.$$

As before, we assume that for these subjects 20 per cent of this inhibitory increment also generalizes to the competing correct response (R_+). Therefore the generalized inhibition will be,

$$.4724 \times .2 = .0945.$$

This added to the R_+ of these subjects, since inhibition is inherently negative, is

$$_s E_{R_+} + \Delta_s I_{R_+} = 2.5 + (-.0945) = 2.4055.$$

[3] These computations were performed before Corollary vii and equation 13 became available. This would change the absolute value of some of the results but it is not believed that it would change any of the theorems.

Moreover, the new $_sE_{R_-}$ will be,

$$_sE_{R_-} + \Delta_sI_{R_-} = 2.5 - .4724 = 2.0276.$$

It follows that after the false response (R_-) has been made, the respective reaction potentials of this second group of subjects will be,

$$_sE_{R_+} = 2.4055; \qquad _sE_{R_-} = 2.0276.$$

Now because of the fortuitous nature of the oscillation function, it would be quite impracticable to trace out in arithmetical detail the consequences of all of the various possible combinations of correct $(+)$ and incorrect $(-)$ responses as they might occur in a particular organism, to say nothing of all the organisms. We shall accordingly resort to an approximation to this. This is suggested by the practice among experimentalists of pooling the response scores of all the organisms within a given experiment which are regarded as comparable in learning rate. Specifically, we shall calculate a weighted average of the first-trial $_sE_{R_+}$ scores of the two groups of subjects calculated above; this will be taken as the $_sE_{R_+}$ value of the group as a whole at the beginning of the next trial, and the same will hold for the $_sE_{R_-}$ value. This amounts to adding together the products of the two $_sE_{R_+}$ values, each multiplied by the proportionate chance of occurrence, .50. Accordingly, at the beginning of the second trial,

$$\begin{aligned}_sE_{R_+} &= 3.1614 \times .50 + 2.4055 \times .50 \\ &= 1.5807 + 1.2027 \\ &= 2.7835.\end{aligned}$$

Similarly for $_sE_{R_-}$, we have:

$$\begin{aligned}_sE_{R_-} &= 2.6323 \times .50 + 2.0276 \times .50 \\ &= 1.3162 + 1.0138 \\ &= 2.3300.\end{aligned}$$

Thus at the beginning of the third trial we have the competition between these two means:

$$_sE_{R_+} = 2.7835 \qquad \text{and} \qquad _sE_{R_-} = 2.3300.$$

Now the probability of the responses of the organisms as represented by these two means would evidently be substantially the same as would be the probability of the dominance of one of any other two events represented by means in ordinary statistical practice.[4] Assuming that the standard deviation of the respective means alike is 1.0, the standard deviation of the difference (σ_d) between the two means (XII C) therefore becomes:

$$\sigma_d^2 = \sigma_+^2 + \sigma_-^2$$
$$= 2\sigma^2$$
$$\therefore \sigma_d = \sigma \sqrt{2} = 1.414. \tag{33}$$

Accordingly we may write the following equation, using x in place of d to conform with statistical usage:

$$\frac{x}{\sigma_d} = \frac{d}{\sigma_d} = \frac{{}_sE_{R_+} - {}_sE_{R_-}}{\sigma_d}. \tag{34}$$

Substituting,

$$= \frac{2.7835 - 2.3300}{1.414}$$
$$= \frac{.4535}{1.414}$$
$$\therefore \frac{x}{\sigma_d} = .3207.$$

Looking up the probability corresponding to .3207 in an appropriate table of the probability function, e.g., Guilford (1, p. 538), we find that,

$$p_+ = .126 + .500 = .626,$$
and that
$$p_- = 1.00 - .626 = .374.$$

By successively repeating the process just described, each time using in the weighted-mean process the p_+ and p_- values secured in the preceding computations, we obtain the theoretical results appearing in Table 1 and Figures 2 and 3. An inspection of the table and figures shows that:

[4] In strict consistence we should here utilize the leptokurtic distribution which we have been at some pains to postulate (XII A), rather than the normal probability function customary in statistics. It is believed that the small difference in the outcome would not, at the present time, repay the difficulties involved, especially in view of the present imperfect knowledge of the constants necessarily utilized and of the leptokurtic function itself.

TABLE 1. A table showing the theoretical progress of distributed-trials simple trial-and-error learning where the asymptote (M) of the primitive $_SE_{R_+}$ learning curve is taken as 6σ, and where the competing reaction potentials begin equal at the relatively low level of 2.5σ (Case I).

Trial number	Reaction potential ($_SE_R$) in σ		$\dfrac{d}{\sigma_d}$	Reaction probability (p)	
	R_+	R_-		P_+	P_-
1	2.5	2.5	.00	.50	.50
2	2.784	2.330	.321	.626	.374
3	3.131	2.241	.629	.735	.265
4	3.507	2.209	.918	.821	.179
5	3.879	2.212	1.179	.881	.119
6	4.222	2.232	1.407	.920	.080
7	4.524	2.260	1.601	.945	.055
8	4.783	2.290	1.763	.961	.039
9	5.001	2.317	1.898	.971	.029
10	5.182	2.341	2.009	.978	.022
11	5.331	2.361	2.100	.982	.018
12	5.454	2.378	2.175	.985	.015
13	5.554	2.392	2.236	.987	.013
14	5.636	2.403	2.287	.989	.011
15	5.703	2.411	2.328	.990	.010

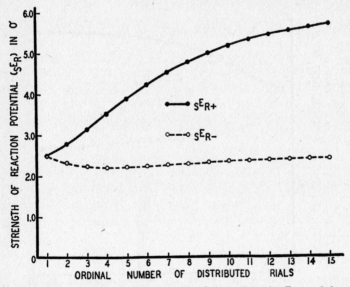

FIGURE 2. Graphic theoretical representation of the increase in $_SE_{R_+}$ and the general decrease in $_SE_{R_-}$ as the distributed trials of a simple trial-and-error learning progress (Case I). Each trial is counted as one, regardless of whether the response is R_+ or R_-. Note the inflected form of the $_SE_{R_+}$ curve and the slight rise in the $_SE_{R_-}$ curve after trial 4. Plotted from values presented in Table 1.

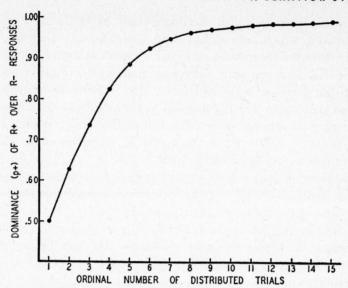

FIGURE 3. Graph representing the probability curve of the dominance of $_sE_{R+}$ in the theoretical distributed-trials simple trial-and-error learning as a function of the number of trials where the two competing reaction potentials begin with equal values (Case I). Plotted from values appearing in Table 1.

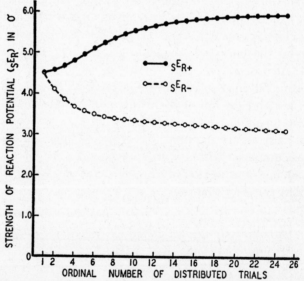

FIGURE 4. Graphic representation of the theoretical increase in $_sE_{R+}$ and the decrease in $_sE_{R-}$ (Case II). Note the relatively smaller rise in the $_sE_{R+}$ curve, the relatively greater fall in the $_sE_{R-}$ curve, and that $_sE_{R-}$ shows no rise at any time as compared with Figure 2.

The $_sE_{R_+}$ increases with successive trials, at first with a positive acceleration which later inflects into a negative acceleration. This differs from the theoretical primitive curve of learning (IV).

The $_sE_{R_-}$ decreases with successive trials, with a negative acceleration, the decrease between trials 4 and 5 changing to an actual though slight gain which continues as far as calculated, ultimately recovering two-thirds of the $_sE_{R_-}$ lost during the first four trials. This paradox is due to the fact that R_+ reinforcements ($\Delta_sE_{R_+}$) generalize (XVI A) appreciably to R_-.

The curve of learning shown as Figure 3, a probability function, is not dependent upon either primary learning function alone ($_sE_{R_+}$ and $_sE_{R_-}$, Figure 2), but upon the *difference* between them. This means that when the probability learning curve reaches its maximum or 100 per cent + responses, $_sE_{R_+}$ has by no means reached its asymptote nor has $_sE_{R_-}$ nearly reached zero. This probability curve of learning approaches the conventional "curve of learning" in form (*16*, p. 575), though a curve fit shows that despite a very close approximation it fails systematically.[5]

We turn next to Case II, where at the outset $_sE_{R_+} = {_sE_{R_-}}$ and both values have a magnitude of 4.5σ. The computational procedure is exactly the same as that given above which generated Table 1. The results for Case II are not particularly different except as to the curves of $_sE_{R_+}$ and $_sE_{R_-}$. These are presented in Figure 4. An inspection of this figure shows the same rise in $_sE_{R_+}$ and the same fall in $_sE_{R_-}$ as appears in Figure 2 except that the rise of $_sE_{R_+}$ is less and the fall of $_sE_{R_-}$ is greater. Moreover the curve of $_sE_{R_-}$ has no terminal rise, as it does in Figure 2. The computations show that 25 trials are required to reach a .978 per cent dominance of $_sE_{R_+}$, as compared with 10 trials for Case I.

Generalizing on the preceding considerations we now proceed to formulate our first theorem:

THEOREM 1. *In distributed-trials simple trial-and-error learning where there are only two superthreshold competing reaction potentials, and where at the beginning $_sE_{R_+} = {_sE_{R_-}}$:*
A. *There are evolved two primary curves of learning ($_sE_{R_+}$ and $_sE_{R_-}$) as a function of the number of trials (N).*

[5] The fitted equation obtained is,

$$p = .755(1 - 10^{-.159N}) + .245.$$

B. *The proportion of reinforcement (+) trials increases as trial and error continues, whereas that of the non-reinforcement (−) trials progressively decreases.*

C. *The curve of $_sE_{R_+} = f(N)$ in both Case I and Case II at first rises with a positive acceleration and later becomes negatively accelerated.*

D. *The curve of $_sE_{R_-} = f(N)$ in Case I at first falls with a negative acceleration and later rises slowly but continuously, with a positive acceleration, then with a negative acceleration.*

E. *The greater the initial values of $_sE_{R_+}$ and $_sE_{R_-}$, the smaller will be the relative rise in $_sE_{R_+}$ as a result of the trial-and-error process, and the greater the fall in $_sE_{R_-}$.*

F. *The probability curve of learning is a function of the amount of difference between the two primary curves of learning, $_sE_{R_+}$ and $_sE_{R_-}$.*

G. *At the first trial the probability of occurrence of the respective reactions approaches equality, i.e., it is .50, .50.*

H. *The course of the probability curve of learning is a negatively accelerated rise approaching the conventional learning function in shape.*

We have found no experimental material regarding distributed trial-and-error learning where $_sE_{R_+} = {}_sE_{R_-}$ at the beginning of the process. In a situation where $_sE_{R_+}$ and $_sE_{R_-}$ were nearly equal, however, Holland (3) reported that the $_sE_{R_-}$ latency changed from 1.4 seconds at the first trial to 1.2 seconds at the one-hundredth trial, thus showing a slight gain; and the $_sE_{R_+}$ changed from 4.8 seconds at the first trial to .8 second at the one-hundredth trial, thus showing a marked gain. This constitutes a partial empirical verification of Theorem 1 A.

No adequate evidence has been found regarding Theorems 1 B, C, D, E, F, and G, though the latency values of Holland's trial-and-error series, if preserved, would validate Theorems 1 C and 1 D.

A probability curve of $_sE_{R_+}$ evocation by distributed-trials simple trial-and-error learning is represented in the upper graph of Figure 8 (p. 37), though $_sE_{R_-}$ was on the whole a little the stronger at the outset since the p_+ on the first trial was around .30. However, between the third and fifth trials it rose to .50. Thus from that point on, Theorem 1 H finds rough empirical verification.

Cases III, IV, and V, Where $_sE_{R_+}$ and $_sE_{R_-}$ Are Not Equal

As stated above (p. 21), in Case III $_sE_{R_+} = 5.0$ and $_sE_{R_-} = 2.0$. Pursuing the method of computation already explained, we formulate Table 2 according to these assumptions. An inspection of this table shows that the two primary learning curves naturally begin at quite separate points. Their course is so brief to the 99 per cent

TABLE 2. A table showing the theoretical progress of distributed-trials simple trial-and-error learning where the asymptote of the $_sE_R$ learning potentiality is taken as 6.0σ and where the competing reaction potentials are initially: $_sE_{R_+} = 5.0\sigma$ and $_sE_{R_-} = 2.0\sigma$ (Case III).

Trial number	Reaction potential ($_sE_R$) in σ		$\dfrac{d}{\sigma_d}$	Reaction probability (p)	
	R_+	R_-		p_+	p_-
1	5.0	2.0	2.122	.983	.017
2	5.184	2.031	2.230	.987	.013
3	5.338	2.056	2.231	.990	.010

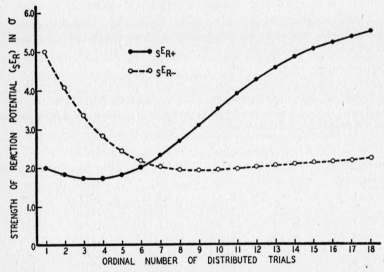

FIGURE 5. Graphic representation of the theoretical curves of the courses of $_sE_{R_+}$ and $_sE_{R_-}$ during a simple trial-and-error process by distributed trials, where $_sE_{R_+}$ originates at 2.0σ and $_sE_{R_-}$ at 5.0σ (Case IV). Note that the $_sE_{R_+}$ curve begins with a period of fall (through generalized $\Delta_sI_{R_+}$), and that the $_sE_{R_-}$ curve terminates with a period of rise (through generalized $\Delta_sE_{R_-}$). Plotted from values shown in Table 3.

level of $_sE_{R_+}$ that they have no theoretical significance, except as to methodology. Accordingly we present no graphs of this case.

We next proceed to the consideration of Case IV, where $_sE_{R_+}$ = 2.0σ and $_sE_{R_-}$ = 5.0σ. Table 3 is based on the same computational methods as those used in Tables 1 and 2, and from this

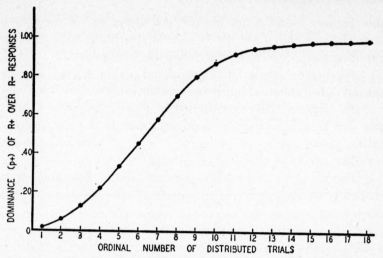

FIGURE 6. Graph representing the theoretical course of a probability-of-reaction curve of learning derived from the competition of the two reaction potentials shown in Table 3 and Figure 5. Note the markedly sigmoid shape of this curve.

TABLE 3. Table showing the theoretical progress of distributed-trials simple trial-and-error learning where the asymptote of the $_sE_R$ learning potential is taken as 6.0σ and the competing learning potentials are initially: (Case IV): $_sE_{R_+} = 2.0\sigma$ and $_sE_{R_-} = 5.0\sigma$. This represents probably the most interesting and significant case of simple trial-and-error learning.

Trial number	Reaction potential ($_sE_R$) in σ		$\dfrac{d}{\sigma_d}$	Reaction probability (p)	
	R_+	R_-		p_+	p_-
1	2.0	5.0	−2.122	.017	.983
2	1.827	4.074	−1.589	.056	.944
3	1.726	3.356	−1.153	.124	.876
4	1.715	2.821	− .782	.217	.783
5	1.807	2.438	− .446	.328	.672
6	2.005	2.181	− .124	.451	.549
7	2.300	2.023	.196	.578	.422
8	2.672	1.942	.516	.697	.303
9	3.088	1.919	.827	.796	.204
10	3.511	1.932	1.117	.868	.132
11	3.910	1.966	1.375	.915	.085
12	4.265	2.006	1.597	.945	.055
13	4.571	2.048	1.784	.963	.037
14	4.828	2.085	1.940	.974	.026
15	5.042	2.118	2.068	.981	.019
16	5.218	2.146	2.173	.985	.015
17	5.362	2.169	2.258	.988	.012
18	5.480	2.188	2.328	.990	.010

table Figures 5 and 6 are plotted. An inspection of these figures shows at once that Case IV is radically different from the three preceding cases. We derive the following conclusions:

1. $_sE_{R_+}$ begins with a fairly protracted period of loss (from generalized $\Delta_sI_{R_-}$), after which it rises rather rapidly.

2. $_sE_{R_-}$ follows fairly consistently a negatively accelerated loss, after which it shows a fairly protracted period of gain (from generalized $\Delta_sE_{R_+}$).

3. The curves of $_sE_{R_+}$ and $_sE_{R_-}$ cross.

4. The curve of correct-response probability follows a characteristically sigmoid course with a positively accelerated rise at first which later turns to a negatively accelerated rise.

We now proceed to Case V, where $_sE_{R_-} = 5.0\sigma$ and $_sE_{R_+} = .856\sigma$. It must be noted that since the reaction threshold is $.356\sigma$, this leaves $.856\sigma - .356\sigma$, or $.5\sigma$ as a superthreshold $(_s\ddot{E}_{R_+})$ value. By computations exactly analogous to those employed in the four preceding cases, the outcome represented in Table 4 has been

TABLE 4. A table showing the early details of the trial-and-error process where $_sE_{R_+} = .856\sigma$ and $_sE_{R_-} = 5.0\sigma$ (Case V). Note that the reaction threshold $(_sL_R)$ is taken as $.356\sigma$, which leaves as the superthreshold value of $_sE_{R_+}$, $.856\sigma - .356\sigma$, or $.5\sigma$, which is represented by the symbol $_s\ddot{E}_{R_+}$. Note also that as far as carried $_sE_{R_+}$ and $_sE_{R_-}$ grow progressively less.

Trial number	Reaction potential ($_sE_R$) in σ			$\dfrac{d}{\sigma_d}$	Reaction probability (p)	
	R_+	$_s\ddot{E}_R$	R_-		$p+$	$p-$
1	.856	.5	5.0	−3.182	.001	.999
2	.812	.312	4.056	−2.648	.004	.996
3	.664	.164	3.294	−2.214	.013	.987
4	.555	.055	2.682	−1.858	.032	.968
5	.396	−.007	2.199		.000	1.000
6	.266	−.090	1.783		.000	1.000

obtained. As the trials go on practically only R_- responses occur, and the generalization of the $\Delta_sI_{R_-}$'s resulting from these unreinforced responses very soon brings the already weak $_sE_{R_+}$ to a negative, i.e., subthreshold, value which grows less and less with each trial. But (XII B) the range of oscillation $(_sO_R)$ in this region approaches zero as $_sE_{R_+}$ approaches absolute zero. There are several consequences of this, though none is fully represented in Table 4.

One is that σ_d will grow progressively smaller as the trials continue, which will make $\dfrac{d}{\sigma_d}$ increase and this *taken alone* would make p_+ decrease. A second result is that whenever the reaction potential falls below the reaction threshold ($_sL_R$) no response based on that momentary reaction potential can take place. This means that as $_sE_{R_-}$ approaches $_sL_R$ a progressively larger proportion of the $_sE_{R_+}$ values will fail to compete with $_sE_{R_-}$, which will tend to decrease the p_+ values as the number of trials continue. And, finally, when the value of $_sE_{R_+}$ (median) becomes negative (below the reaction threshold, $_sL_R$) this will still further decrease the competition of $_sE_{R_+}$ with $_sE_{R_-}$ until p_+ will ultimately become zero and p_- will become 1.000. That is the main point in the consideration of Case V. In Table 4 this is symbolized by an abrupt transition to $p_+ = .000$, as soon as $_s\ddot{E}_{R_+}$ shows a negative value, though strictly speaking this would not be the case until the negative value of $_s\ddot{E}_{R_+}$ became greater than half the range of the diminishing $_sO_R$ dispersion.

Generalizing on the preceding considerations, we arrive at the following theorems:

THEOREM 2. *When trial-and-error learning begins with $_sE_{R_+}$ = 5.0σ and $_sE_{R_-}$ = 2.0σ (Case III), the learning process up to p = .99 is brief and follows essentially the general course described in Theorem 1 H.*

THEOREM 3. *When trial-and-error learning begins with $_sE_{R_+}$ = 2.0σ and $_sE_{R_-}$ = 5.0σ (Case IV), the curve of $_sE_{R_+}$ begins with a brief but fairly marked loss followed by a rapid rise; and that of $_sE_{R_-}$ begins high, falls with a negative acceleration, and later rises perceptibly.*

THEOREM 4. *The curve of response probability in Case IV follows a characteristic positively accelerated rise to 50 per cent, when it shifts to a slower negatively accelerated rise toward 100 per cent, making in all a sigmoid figure.*

THEOREM 5. *When trial-and-error learning begins with $_sE_{R_+}$ = .856σ, or thereabouts, and $_sE_{R_-}$ = 5.0σ (Case V): the $_sE_{R_+}$ progressively falls to negative values below the response threshold, the momentary oscillation values almost never exceeding those of $_sE_{R_-}$; positive reinforcements will almost never occur; and in general the learning process will be a biological failure.*

Proceeding to the empirical evidence concerning these theorems, we find nothing specifically relevant to Theorems 2 and 3. There is, however, a certain amount of continuous-trials trial-and-error[6] evidence on Theorems 4 and 5. It was found in hitherto unpublished data of an otherwise published study (9) that 72 albino rats carried out this latter type of learning, with 39 trials by the median animal. These results were manipulated according to the equally weighted Vincent method and the per cent of R_+ reaction evocations at each of the 39 trials was calculated. These data were then

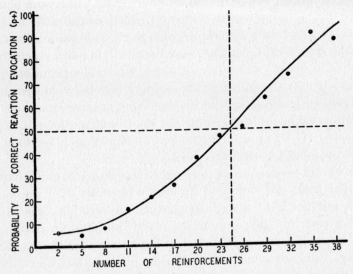

FIGURE 7. Vincent curve of the empirical probability of correct (R_+) reaction evocation in the course of simple trial-and-error learning by the continuous-trials method. Note the similarity to Figure 6, which represents the results of a theoretical analysis of the same case of learning but by distributed trials.

averaged by threes. The resulting values are represented graphically in Figure 7. There the initial portion of the empirical curve corresponds closely to the theoretical one (Figure 6), but the latter portion does not, probably because the training was not continued through enough trials to show the final slowing effect.

In regard to Theorem 5, it has been reported (9) that out of 83 subjects submitted to trial-and-error learning by continuous trials under conditions substantially like those of Case IV (or Case V), seven animals responded with complete failure of R_+ responses.

[6] See a subsequent section (p. 38) devoted to this subject.

Yet when tested 52 hours later, after I_R would have been completely dissipated (IX B), they responded with 37, 4, 0, 1, 1, 2, and 4 reactions respectively, showing that the $_sE_R$ was even then existent to a small but superthreshold amount in all but one animal (*9*, p. 249). These results accordingly give a fair empirical substantiation to Theorem 5.

Simple Trial-and-Error Learning by Massed Trials

The distinction between massed and distributed trials in learning is one of degree. If a period of 24 hours should intervene between trials the learning would surely be called distributed, and if a period of 30 seconds should intervene the learning would be called massed. However, there comes an intermediate point at which it is difficult to decide which term is more applicable. From one point of view it may be said that the dividing line between distributed and massed learning is found where the trials are separated by a time-interval of sufficient length for the stimulus trace (s') to have decreased (II B) to a functional zero. Unfortunately we do not yet know the length of this interval.

In our present context it is only important to note that distributed trials are separated by longer intervals than are massed trials, but not long enough to produce appreciable forgetting. It follows from this that more of the reactive inhibition (ΔI_R) generated by each reaction (IX A) will have time to dissipate (IX B) during distributed trials than during massed. It follows further that during and at the termination of massed learning more I_R will be present than during and at the termination of distributed trials. From this and IX B, Theorem 6 follows at once:

THEOREM 6. *Tests made after the termination of simple trial-and-error learning will show a greater spontaneous increase (reminiscence) in reaction potential if the material is learned by massed trials than if it is learned by distributed trials.*

By logic analogous to the preceding it is clear that more I_R will be present throughout learning by massed trials than by distributed or less-massed trials. From this and Corollary ix it follows that by massed trials more conditioned inhibition ($_sI_R$) will be generated than by distributed trials. But,

$$\dot{I}_R = I_R + {_sI_R}.$$

From these considerations we arrive at our next theorem:

THEOREM 7. *Tests made during the simple learning process will show that distributed trials will be more efficient than massed trials.*

But since (ix) conditioned inhibition ($_sI_R$) has much the status of an ordinary habit and so does not dissipate appreciably with time, and since,

$$_s\bar{E}_R = {_sE_R} - {_sI_R},$$

there follows our next theorem:

THEOREM 8. *Tests applied 24 hours after the completion of a given amount of learning will show, other things equal, that distributed-trials learning is more efficient than massed-trials learning, though the advantage is not as great as will appear during the learning processes.*

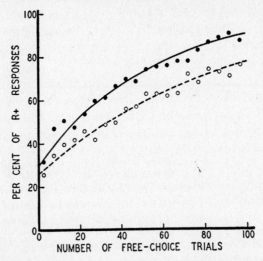

FIGURE 8. Probability learning curves of simple trial-and-error learning by distributed trials (above) and by massed trials (below). Adapted from Holland (*3*, p. 39).

Unfortunately there is not very much empirical evidence bearing directly on the theorems of the present section, so far as simple trial-and-error learning is concerned, though there is a great deal of pertinent evidence from other types of learning:

1. There is a wealth of evidence regarding the matter of reminiscence in rote and other forms of learning (*13*, pp. 263–270) which substantiates Theorem 6.

2. Holland (3) gave simple trial-and-error training to 45 albino rats by distributed trials, and similar training to 45 rats by massed trials. The advantage of the distributed-trials group is evident from an inspection of Figure 8. This gives empirical substantiation to Theorem 7.

3. Kimble (14) trained 50 human subjects on an upside-down printing task by massed practice, and 46 comparable subjects on the same task by spaced practice. Six other groups of about 60 subjects each were trained for 5, 10, 15, 20, 25, and 30 minutes by massed practice, after which they were given 10 minutes' rest

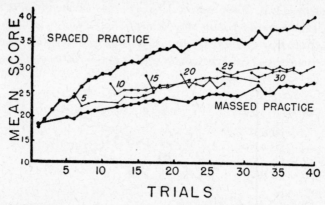

FIGURE 9. Graph showing the learning curves of between 50 and 60 human subjects in an upside-down copying test by spaced and by massed practice. The light lines show the scores of an equal number of control subjects for five trials each after ten minutes' rest following the completion of different stages of massed practice. Note that the first trial after rest shows the reminiscence effect but it does not equal the score of the distributed-practice group after the first such case. After Kimble (14, p. 19).

and then practice was resumed for five more minutes. Kimble's graph, reproduced as Figure 9, shows not only the great superiority of the spaced-practice group over the massed-practice group, but also that as a rule the first trial after each ten-minute rest given a massed-practice control group yielded a smaller performance score than did the trial given the spaced-practice group. This last fact substantiates empirically the point of Theorem 8.

Simple Trial-and-Error Learning by Continuous Trials

Perhaps the most common form of experimental procedure in simple trial-and-error learning is neither of the above-mentioned methods, but that which we shall call *continuous trials* simple trial-

and-error learning, a special form of learning by massed trials. By this procedure the organism remains continuously in the presence of the competing manipulanda. For this reason the timing of the reaction evocations is more or less irregular since they depend upon the changing conditions within the animal's body as manifested by behavioral oscillation (XII A) and other factors. Let us now examine the problem of how trial-and-error learning can occur under such conditions.

The question is a historical one. A number of earlier writers, such as Hobhouse (2, p. 174), Holmes (4, p. 166), Thorndike (17, pp. 188 ff.), Watson (18, p. 262), and Koffka (15, pp. 158 ff.) have struggled with it. Posed most sharply by Watson, Thorndike, and Koffka, the situation is presented by our Case IV except that under the conditions here considered learning occurs by *continuous* trials. We assume that in this case $_sE_{R_+} = 1.0\sigma$ and $_sE_{R_-} = 5.0\sigma$ at trial 1. Now it is evident that under such conditions R_- ordinarily will occur without reinforcement quite a number of times before R_+ takes place and receives its reinforcement. Let us assume five continuous repetitions of R_-, after which R_+ occurs, i.e.,

$$R_- \quad R_- \quad R_- \quad R_- \quad R_- \quad R_+.$$

Watson argued that because R_+ occurred at the last of the series immediately preceding reinforcement it would receive stronger reinforcement than would R_-; Thorndike and Koffka argued truly that in a situation such as we have assumed, R_- would really occur more times than R_+, and that by the supposed "law of use" would receive a greater increment to its learning.

This condition requires us to make use of a principle not hitherto cited in this chapter, namely, the *gradient of reinforcement* (iii B). According to this principle, the greater the time which intervenes between an act and its reinforcement, the smaller will be the $\Delta_s E_R$ which results from the reinforcement. We may represent this roughly by the equation,

$$J = 10^{-jt}, \tag{35}$$

where j has a tentative value, here taken as .163. From these considerations and equation 35, it follows that,

$$J = {}_sE_{R_d} = 6.0\sigma \times 10^{-.163t}, \tag{36}$$

where $_sE_{R_d}$ represents reaction potential due to delay in reinforcement.

Assuming that each of the above listed R_'s requires an average of two seconds for its performance, there would be delay intervals of 2, 4, 6, 8, and 10 seconds before the several erroneous reactions would receive reinforcement. Substituting the t values one at a time in equation 36 and solving, we secure the following reaction potential values for the several R's at the limit of practice:

Delay in reinforcement in sec.	10″	8″	6″	4″	2″
$_sE_{R_-}$ at the limit of practice	.1404	.2982	.6311	1.3368	2.8326
$\Delta_sE_{R_-}$ at the first trial	.0044	.0094	.0199	.0421	.0892

Substituting one-sixth of these values (since $_sE_{R_-}$ already has 5.0 of its possible 6.0σ) one at a time as M's in equation 37,

$$\Delta_sE_R = M(1 - 10^{-.091}), \qquad (37)$$

we have the bottom line of values in the above table.

Now these Δ_sE_R's combined (+) in succession, according to our provisional reaction-potential summation equation (v), amount to .155σ.

But the five non-reinforced responses coming in close succession also generate $\Delta \dot{I}_R$'s according to IX D, i.e.,

$$\Delta \dot{I}_R = 5.0(1 - 10^{-.091 \times 5})$$
$$= 3.246.$$

Also by the generalization principle utilized above, 20 per cent of this, combined with the .100 due to work (W), amounts to .658 and generalizes to $\Delta_sE_{R_+}$.

On the other hand, the reinforcement (at t = 0) of $_s\dot{E}_{R_+}$ amounts to .945, 20 per cent, or .172, of which generalizes to $\Delta_sE_{R_-}$. In addition, a small amount of $\dot{I}_R$, say .100σ, results from the work (W) of executing R_+.[7] Summarizing these various increments, observing appropriate signs, and performing the algebraic behavioral summations (+ and ÷) (see Corollaries v and vii), we find the following:

[7] This work-produced $\dot{I}_R$ theoretically should have been included in the trial-and-error computations given in the preceding sections, but in view of our ignorance regarding all of the constants involved and in the interest of expository simplicity it has hitherto been ignored. The remainder of the $\dot{I}_R$ in experimental extinction is assumed to be due to the failure of incipient anticipatory reaction of its realization.

	Original $_8E_R$	Summated J's	Δ proper	Generalized Δ	Net result ($+$), ($-$)
$\Delta_8E_{R_-}$	$+5.0$	$+.155$	$-.100, -3.246$	$+.172$	$+3.903$
$\Delta_8E_{R_+}$	$+1.0$	......	$-.100, + .945$	$-.658$	$+1.188$

A glance at this table will show that the erroneous tendency ($_8E_{R_-}$) has in this trial alone shifted from 5.0σ downward to 3.903σ, a learning gain of around 1.1σ; and that the correct response tendency ($_8E_{R_+}$) has shifted from 1.0 upward to 1.188σ, a gain of around $.19\sigma$. Thus on both counts the organism will be better prepared to survive, especially if tested again before the I_R dissipates. In this connection we hasten to point out that owing to the complexity and novelty of the above computations, together with our lack of knowledge of the numerous parameters involved, no special significance should be attached to the values secured, though the procedure should explain in a concrete manner the general nature of the theory. Actually, of course, if we count each of the false responses here involved as a separate trial the gain is not so very much more than was yielded by the same number of acts (Table 3, p_+ column) by the distributed-trials procedure in a somewhat similar situation.

Generalizing on the above considerations, we arrive at the following theorem:

THEOREM 9. *Simple trial-and-error learning by the continuous-trials procedure will eventuate in positive learning, the end result being much the same as by the distributed-trials procedure.*

That continuous-trials simple trial-and-error learning really occurs without difficulty has long been known empirically. The only question historically is how to explain, i.e., deduce it. It would appear that Watson was on the right track with his observation that reinforcement is associated with the last response of each response series, though at that time without the knowledge of the gradient of reinforcement and especially of the accumulation of $\hat{I}_R$ it was impossible to perform the deduction.

Response Alternation in General Where Two Reaction Potentials Are in Repeated Competition

The preceding pages have had much to say concerning the momentary oscillation of reaction potentials. But the momentary oscillation principle does not prevent the occurrence of appreciable sequences of one reaction to the exclusion of the other.

Preliminary to the study of these phenomena as related to simple trial-and-error learning, it will be well to explain the employment of certain useful terms. Perhaps the most fundamental concept in this complex of relationships is that of *response alternation*. An alternation is said to occur when one type of response shifts to the other, R_, on the next occasion. For example, in the response-sequence fragment:

$$\ldots \; R_- \,|\, R_+ \;\; R_+ \;\; R_+ \,|\, R_- \;\; R_- \,|\, R_+ \ldots$$

there are three alternations, each marked by a short, vertical line. Our second concept, flowing directly from the first, is that of the *alternation phase;* this includes the number of reactions falling between two successive response alternations. Thus in the above example, the first complete alternation phase represented contains three R_+'s. Our third concept is that of the *alternation cycle*. An alternation cycle is the succession of responses comprised in two successive alternation phases. In the above example, an alternation cycle of 3 + 2, or five reactions, is enclosed between the two heavy vertical lines. Finally, there is the concept of the *asymmetry* of the response cycle; this term refers to the fact that in a behavior cycle there may be more reactions in one alternation phase than in the other. Thus in the above example of an alternation cycle, asymmetry is indicated by the fact that the first phase contains three responses, whereas the second phase contains only two.

In the theory of chance it is customary to represent the complete certainty of the occurrence of an event by 1.00, and any known probability less than certainty by a decimal. Thus the chance of heads on any single coin toss is .50, and that of tails is $1.00 - .50$ or .50 also. In cases of this sort where two events are involved in the chance, the probability of one event is usually called p, and that of the other event is usually called q. Thus,

$$p + q = 1.00. \tag{38}$$

Now, it may be shown that the mean number (F') of one phase of two alternative events (p) which in the long run will occur without an alternation in an infinite number of continuous trials is $\frac{1}{q}$, i.e.,

$$F'_p = \frac{1}{q}, \qquad (39)$$

and

$$F'_q = \frac{1}{p}.$$

From equations 38 and 39 we have,

$$F'_p = \frac{1}{1.00 - p}. \qquad (40)$$

For example, if the probability of the occurrence of R_+ is .75, then,

$$F'_p = \frac{1}{1.00 - .75}$$
$$= \frac{1}{.25}$$
$$= 4.00.$$

Similarly,

$$F'_q = \frac{1}{1.00 - .25}$$
$$= \frac{1}{.75}$$
$$= 1.333.$$

In this case the total mean alternation cycle (B') would be,

$$B' = F'_p + F'_q$$
$$= 4 + 1.333$$
$$= 5.333.$$

At this point it must be noted that the formulae so far considered yield the mean number of p or q events in uninterrupted sequences such as occur in dice throws where (1) the number of throws involved is assumed to be infinite, and (2) the values of p and q remain constant throughout the series. Neither of these conditions is found in empirical trial-and-error learning situations. Such series rarely exceed one or two hundred trials, and usually do not exceed fifty; the theoretical example worked out for Table 5 (p. 46) has only 18 trials, and the median N in the empirical investigation discussed above (Figure 7) was 39. It is evident that a sequence of alternative events which is short will not have as great a mean value of F' as a sequence which is longer, because a marked

limitation in the length of the series as a whole will necessarily
exclude from the values to be averaged some very long uninterrupted sequences of both p and q events. The mean number of
uninterrupted p events (F_p) in a limited series of N events is given
by the provisional equation,[8]

$$F_p = F_p' \left[1 - \frac{(F_p' - 1)^{N+2} - 1}{(F_p' - 2)F_p'^{N+1}} \right]. \tag{41}$$

Let it be supposed, for example, that p = .95 and N = 18. By
equation 40,

$$F_p' = \frac{1}{1.00 - .95}$$
$$= \frac{1}{.05}$$
$$= 20.$$

An F_p' value of 20 would, of course, be quite impossible in the
assumed situation since there are only 18 events in the entire series,
i.e., N = 18. Next, by substituting these values in equation 41, we
have,

$$F_p = 20 \left[1 - \frac{(20 - 1)^{18+2} - 1}{(20 - 2)20^{18+1}} \right]$$
$$= 20 \left[1 - \frac{19^{20} - 1}{18 \times 20^{19}} \right]$$
$$= 20(1 - .3982)$$
$$= 20 \times .6018$$
$$= 12.036.$$

It will be recalled that equations 40 and 41 are based on the
supposition that p does not change. This means that a theoretical
mean alternation phase calculated for the outset of a simple trial-
and-error process really represents the mean length of such a phase
if the reaction-evocation process should continue unchanged for a
very considerable number of trials, as at that single point. Actually
p does change, and rather rapidly under certain conditions as
shown in Tables 1 and 3. It follows that a value of F_p calculated
from equation 41 bears only an approximation to the true F_p.
As yet this function is not known, though it is possible to state

[8] This and other formulae employed in the present section were derived for use here
by Alfred W. Jones, in August, 1943.

certain things about it. This all means that until a more adequate mathematical analysis of the purely chance situation is attained, only rather general conclusions may be drawn concerning the behavior of organisms in actual simple trial-and-error learning situations. However, no radical error should result in our tentative examination; at least it will serve to open the problem to theoretical analysis.

A convenient index of the nature and degree of response-cycle asymmetry (Y) is the quotient obtained by dividing the difference between the number of reactions in the respective phases of the response cycle by the total number of responses in the cycle; to this quotient is affixed the sign of the phase containing the greater number of responses. Stated formally, this index becomes,

$$Y = \frac{F_p - F_q}{F_p + F_q}. \tag{42}$$

Thus in the example considered above (p. 43), assuming that p represents probability of the correct reaction, we have,

$$Y = \frac{4 - 1.333}{4 + 1.333}$$
$$= + \frac{2.667}{5.333}$$
$$\therefore Y = +.50.$$

The meaning of the above concepts may be further illustrated by the well-studied laws of the outcome of the successive tosses of a single coin. The theory of chance shows that in the long run the average number (F) of successive heads before a reversal is two, and the same is true of tails. This of course yields a mean cycle, where the number of throws is unlimited, of $2 + 2 = 4$ reactions. Finally, since the two phases are equal, the asymmetry (Y) will be:

$$Y = \frac{2 - 2}{2 + 2}$$
$$= \frac{.00}{4}$$
$$= .00;$$

i.e., the theoretical head-tail cycles in coin tossing are perfectly symmetrical.

Response Alternation Characteristics of Simple Trial-and-Error Learning

With the preliminary analysis of the phenomena of the alternation of purely chance events in general before us, we may now proceed to its use in the theory of simple trial-and-error learning. Since the theoretical data of Table 3, when taken together, display practically the whole range (i.e., from beginning to end) of a typical case of simple trial-and-error learning, we shall take for our present purpose the probability values appearing in the last two columns of that table. These values are reproduced as the second and third columns of Table 5.

TABLE 5. A table showing the progressive changes in the theoretical mean number of uninterrupted sequences (F) of R_+ and R_- respectively in a case of distributed-trials simple trial-and-error learning, the changes in the length of the mean alternation cycle (B) and in the asymmetry index (Y).

Trial number	Reaction probability		Theoretical mean number responses per alternation phase, N = ∞		Theoretical mean number responses per alternation phase, N = 18		Theoretical mean number responses per alternation cycle, N = 18	Theoretical asymmetry of alternation cycle, n = 18
ber	p_+	p_-	F'_+	F'_-	F_+	F_-	B	Y
1	.017	.983	1.02	58.82	.266	15.612	15.878	−.966
2	.056	.944	1.06	17.86	.680	11.507	12.187	−.888
3	.124	.876	1.14	8.06	1.035	7.305	8.340	−.752
4	.217	.783	1.28	4.61	1.260	4.547	5.807	−.566
5	.328	.672	1.49	3.05	1.486	3.046	4.532	−.344
6	.451	.549	1.82	2.22	1.821	2.217	4.038	−.098
7	.578	.422	2.37	1.73	2.370	1.730	4.100	.156
8	.697	.303	3.30	1.43	3.294	1.432	4.726	.394
9	.796	.204	4.90	1.26	4.816	1.234	6.050	.592
10	.868	.132	7.58	1.15	6.969	1.060	8.029	.736
11	.915	.085	11.76	1.09	9.367	.870	10.237	.830
12	.945	.055	18.18	1.06	11.593	.673	12.266	.890
13	.963	.037	27.03	1.04	13.292	.507	13.799	.926
14	.974	.026	38.46	1.03	14.504	.391	14.895	.947
15	.981	.019	52.63	1.02	15.353	.292	15.645	.963
16	.985	.015	66.67	1.02	15.860	.238	16.098	.970
17	.988	.012	83.33	1.01	16.258	.195	16.453	.976
18	.990	.010	100.00	1.01	16.520	.166	16.686	.980

Next, each of these values is substituted in equations 39 and 40 in order to determine the theoretical mean number of the R_+ responses and the R_- responses in the respective alternation phases at the different stages of the learning process on the simple chance assumptions based on an unlimited series of trials. These are shown in the fourth and fifth columns of Table 5. The values are then converted by means of equation 41 to chance values based on the assumption of only 18 trials; these are shown in the sixth and seventh columns of Table 5. They are represented graphically in Figure 10. There it may be seen that the value of F_+, beginning at .31, rises very slowly at first, then with great rapidity, after which

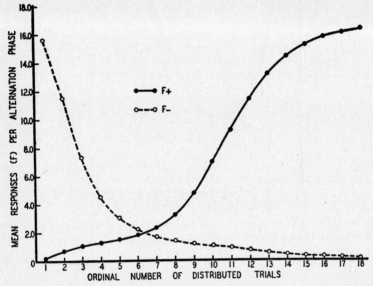

FIGURE 10. Graphs showing the theoretical mean number of responses (F) per alternation phase as a function of the number of trials in distributed-trials simple trial-and-error learning for p_+ and p_- respectively. Plotted from columns 6 and 7 of Table 5.

the rate of rise considerably lessens. On the other hand, F_- begins with a large value and falls rapidly at first, after which its rate of fall becomes nearly linear.

The values of the alternation cycles (the sum of the values in columns 6 and 7) as a function of the number of reinforcements are shown in the next-to-last column of Table 5. They are represented graphically in Figure 11. A glance at this figure shows that at the beginning and end of a complete simple trial-and-error process where R_- is decidedly dominant at the outset, the alternation cycles are relatively protracted, the minimum being reached at a point somewhat anterior to the middle of the reinforcements where

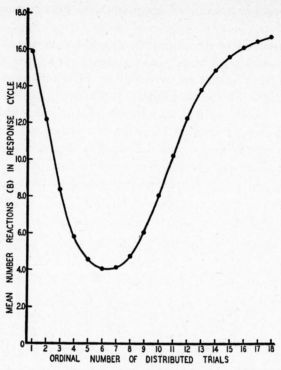

FIGURE 11. Length of theoretical mean response cycle as a function of the number of reinforcements. Plotted from the next-to-last column of Table 5.

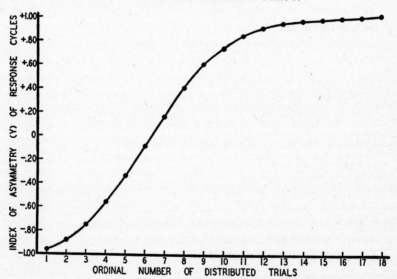

FIGURE 12. This figure represents the index of theoretical asymmetry of the alternation cycle as a function of the number of reinforcements in distributed-trials simple trial-and-error learning. Plotted from the last column of Table 5.

the cycle reaches a value of approximately four responses, as do coin tosses.

The asymmetry of the alternation cycle has been calculated by means of equation 42 from values appearing in columns 6 and 7 of Table 5; the Y values are presented in the last column. They are represented graphically in Figure 12. There it may be seen at a glance that the theoretical asymmetry of a complete simple trial-and-error process begins in the negative phase and rises with a positive acceleration to a zero value, after which it passes into a positive phase through which it rises with a negative acceleration, the whole presenting a characteristic sigmoid picture.

Generalizing from the preceding considerations, we arrive at the following theorem:

THEOREM 10. *In simple trial-and-error learning where* R_+ *is fairly strong but several σ's weaker than* R_-:

A. *The mean* R_+ *alternation phase* (F_p) *will be minimal at the outset of practice but will gradually increase with a negative acceleration to a maximal value as practice is indefinitely continued.*

B. *The mean* R_- *alternation phase* (F_q) *begins with a maximal value and falls at a positively and then a negatively accelerated rate to a minimal value.*

C. *The alternation cycle* (B) *begins with a relatively large value, falls at first with a positive and then with a negative acceleration to a minimal value near 4, after which it rises again, at first with a positive and then with a negative acceleration, to a relatively large value.*

D. *The index of asymmetry* (Y) *in Case IV of the complete simple trial-and-error learning process begins with a value approaching* -1.00 *according to the magnitude of the difference between* R_+ *and* R_-, *and then rises through zero to* $+1.00$, *following a sigmoid course.*

Comparison of Theoretical with Empirical Phenomena of Response Alternation

We may now proceed to the consideration of the empirical validity of certain of the theorems derived above regarding the response alternation aspect of simple trial-and-error learning. The empirical evidence, for the most part, comes from a single experiment on continuous-trials learning of this type (9). In this experiment albino rats were given one day's training in operating the vertical bar shown in Figure 13, the horizontal bar being retracted. The animals were allowed to make only 15 reactions, each reaction being reinforced by a small cylinder of hard but appetizing food. Twenty-four hours later the vertical bar was retracted and the horizontal bar was introduced. Sixty manipulations were evoked on the horizontal bar, each being followed by the same type of

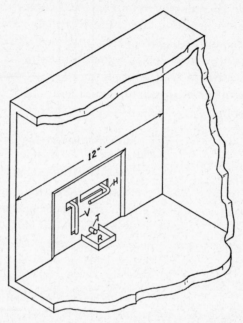

FIGURE 13. Diagrammatic representation of the apparatus side of the rat's compartment of the experimental box which was employed in the experiment concerned with simple trial-and-error learning by continuous trials. The vertical bar was positive and the horizontal bar was negative, i.e., when the vertical bar was pushed to the left during the trial-and-error process a small cylinder of food fell through the tube, T, into the food-dish, R, but when the horizontal bar was pressed downward, no food was delivered (9, p. 237).

reinforcement as was given for the vertical bar. The following day the already strong horizontal-bar habit was given four more reinforcements, and then the animal was presented with *both* bars, as shown in Figure 13, the apparatus being set so that the operation of the vertical bar would give food the same as during the original training. This is substantially the situation represented above as Case IV (pp. 31ff.). A total of 159 animals were employed in one group or another in this experiment.

From this procedure the following empirical facts were reported:

Of 76 animals which mastered the trial-and-error learning (9), all displayed one or more response-alternation cycles, the median animal responding in three and the extreme animal in 15 alternation cycles. This is in general accord with Theorem 10 C.

Of these 76 animals (9), 25 gave a total of four, five, or six complete response-alternation cycles. The scores of each of the first and last four alternation phases of these 25 records were averaged to secure a somewhat exaggerated effect. The results of this operation are shown graphically in Figure 14. There may be seen a fair approximation to the theoretical Figure 10, in that as practice continues (1) R_ shows a progressive and generally negatively accelerated fall, and (2) R+ shows a progressive and generally positively accelerated rise. This is in substantial agreement with Theorem 10 A and B, though there may be seen some discrepancy at the upper level of each curve. It is believed that this discrepancy is due to the fact that the trial-and-error process did not begin at an early enough stage and also was not carried far enough to show its full effect.

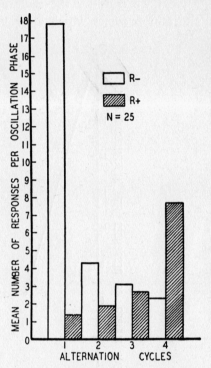

FIGURE 14. Graph showing the mean number of reactions in each alternation phase of four alternation cycles made by 25 animals, each of which gave four or more response-alternation cycles during a single simple trial-and-error learning process by continuous trials. Plotted from data from Hull (9, p. 252).

The data represented in Figure 14 have been combined into alternation cycles and plotted as Figure 15. This shows a clear tendency for the alternation cycles to be high at the beginning and the end of the simple trial-and-error learning process, though due to the fact that the trial-and-error learning was not carried to an advanced stage the data for these figures do not give much opportunity for the long cycles at the posterior end of the process to manifest themselves. Thus the theory as presented in Theorem 10 C and Figure 11 is confirmed in the main, though not in complete detail.

Next we consider the asymmetry of the four mean empirical alternation cycles which appear in Figure 15. These asymmetry

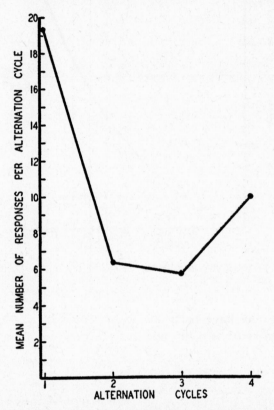

FIGURE 15. Graph showing the mean number of reactions per alternation cycle as reported by an empirical study of simple trial-and-error learning where R_- is initially stronger than R_+. Plotted from calculations made from the data represented in Figure 14.

values are shown graphically in Figure 16, where the graph is relevant to Theorem 10 D and the theoretical curve shown in Figure 12. Here again the agreement is substantial as to the general course of the curve, but some of its proportions differ. In this connection it is to be noted that the point where the rise changes from a positive to a negative acceleration does not appear in Figure 16,

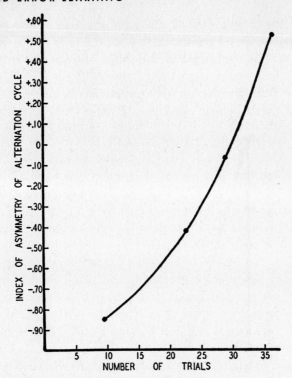

FIGURE 16. Empirical graph showing the rise in index of asymmetry of mean alternation cycles. Calculated from the data represented in Figure 14.

though this may have been due in part at least to the fact that the trial-and-error process was not carried far enough in the experiment.

Summary

This chapter presents two deductions of very general application. One deduction is to the effect that increments of both $_sE_R$ and $_sI_R$ generalize to situations having stimuli which are relatively similar and *responses which usually involve substantially the same muscle combinations*. Recently, empirical evidence to this effect has become known. The other theorem states the deduction that massed trials in simple trial-and-error and similar learning are less effective than are distributed trials, a fact long known empirically.

Simple trial-and-error learning itself takes place in normal mammalian organisms when they are presented with a stimulus situation that either through the organism's inheritance or previous learning, or both, tends to evoke two or more distinguishable reactions, of which only one receives reinforcement. In case the competing reaction potentials are two, and both are weak but equal in strength (Case I) there will be first a more or less irregular alternation between them, the erroneous one gradually becoming weakened by experimental extinction and the successful one being gradually strengthened by reinforcement. The increase in strength of the correct reaction potential is generally sigmoid in nature, beginning with a positive and ending with a negative acceleration. The erroneous reaction potential falls with a negative acceleration followed by a mild rise due to the generalization of the reinforcements which are occurring. These processes jointly generate a rather steep, negatively accelerated probability-of-reaction-evocation curve of learning which begins with each R at about 50 per cent and reaches perfection (100 per cent) without the correct reaction potential rising anywhere near its physiological limit and without the erroneous reaction potential at the end standing very much below its original level.

When simple trial-and-error learning begins with two equal reaction potentials which are both relatively strong (Case II), the same general situation as that just described results, though there is a reduction in the amount of growth of the correct tendency, an increase in the amount of fall in the erroneous tendency, and more trials are necessary for the correct tendency to attain complete dominance.

Perhaps the classical form of simple trial-and-error learning is found where the erroneous reaction potential is strongly dominant at the outset of the process and where the correct reaction potential is much weaker but well above the reaction threshold (Case IV). The course of the correct reaction potential is at first slightly downward as the result of generalized extinction effects; at length, however, from the increase in the proportion of the reinforced trials it begins to rise with a positive acceleration. This rise near the end of the process tends to pass over into a negative acceleration. As in Cases I and II, the fall of R_- is negatively accelerated at the beginning and this fall is about the same in extent as the rise of the correct reaction potential. Late in the process the fall gives place to a slight rise due to generalized $\Delta_s E_{R_+}$'s. The probability of correct reaction evocation which results from the competition of the two processes in this case shows a very clearly marked sigmoid curve of learning. It is thus evident that the probability "curve of learning," even in the same type of learning process, is not constant but that the form is dependent upon the conditions under which the learning occurs, in this case the $_s E_{R_-}$ points at which learning begins.

In Case V, which is the same as Case IV except that R_+ is only a little above the reaction threshold, the generalization of extinction effects from R_- may depress the correct reaction potential below the reaction threshold before the two potentials get close enough together for the oscillation tendency to bring about any evocation of R_+. In such an event, of course, R_+ ordinarily will never be evoked and the organism will fail in adapting to the situation.

The theory of probability shows that dominance alternation in the case of two competing reaction potentials in a simple trial-and-error situation contains longer or shorter runs of one reaction potential to the exclusion of the other. Analysis reveals that at the outset of Case IV, our most general form of simple trial-and-error learning, (1) the negative phase of each alternation cycle is, on the average, considerably longer than the positive phase; (2) as the learning progresses the two become about equal; and (3) as the learning approaches perfection the positive phase becomes much the longer. In a parallel manner, at the outset of such learning the mean alternation cycle as a whole is relatively long; it falls to a minimum near the middle of the process, after which it rises to indefinite heights with continued practice.

A comparison of the theorems derived from the present system with the empirical evidence now available reveals an extensive amount of rough approximation which tends to support at least the main features of the postulates employed. However, there is a notable lack of empirical evidence regarding the separate learning curves of R_+ and R_-, though this could easily be supplied (XIV) by the latencies of these responses if accurately taken under the distributed-trials technique. Careful quantitative work in this field should lead to a precise determination of the "constants" involved in the equations as dependent on various conditions, and may lead to important revisions in the theory itself.

TERMINAL NOTES

ADDITIONAL FORMS OF TRIAL-AND-ERROR LEARNING

In addition to the forms of trial-and-error learning discussed above, there may be mentioned three others. The first of these occurs in the situation where the amount of reinforcement of the negative reaction is not negative but is positive, though less than that yielded by the positive reaction. An incidental treatment of this type of learning has been given elsewhere (*11*, p. 146) in connection with a consideration of the effect of differential delays in reinforcement. A second form of simple trial-and-error learning which has a rather similar mechanism and outcome is observed in case a differential amount or quality of the reinforcing agent is yielded by each of two competing reactions.

A third form of simple trial-and-error learning occurs where each of two competing reaction potentials receives exactly the same reinforcement, but the work (W) involved (*11*, p. 294), or the punishment received, incidental to the performance of one of the reactions is less than that incidental to the performance of the other. In this case there develops a greater amount of inhibition in connection with the reaction involving the greater amount of work, which neutralizes at least a portion of the potential leading to this reaction and thus leaves a differential advantage in effective reaction potential in favor of the reaction involving the less work (*11*, pp. 293 ff.).

HISTORICAL NOTE CONCERNING THE CAUSE OF
    ALTERNATION CYCLES

The first discussion of the alternation cycle seems to have appeared in 1917, the mechanism at that time being conceived as a fairly regular wave phenomenon superposed upon the learning process as the increasing strength of the habit gradually crosses a static reaction threshold with increased trials (*5*). This hypothesis yielded both the phenomenon of alternation itself and the characteristic changes in the asymmetry of the alternation cycle. However, that approach implied an alternation cycle of constant mean length, whereas we have seen that the cycle actually shows a marked tendency to become minimal at the point of zero asymmetry.

In 1935 there appeared a second study of the subject (*7*), in the field of rote learning, in which the number of oscillation cycles was investigated in their relation to the influence of caffeine citrate. No new phenomena specifically concerned with the length or the asymmetry of the alternation cycle were reported, though it was found that the cyclic phenomena extended over a wider range in the central part of the series than at the ends.

In 1939 an empirical study of animal trial-and-error learning (9) showed for the first time the progressive fall in the negative (extinction) alternation phase of the alternation cycle and the progressive rise in the positive (reinforcement) phase of the cycle, and, by implication, the tendency to a minimal value of the cycle length in the region of zero asymmetry.

The second theoretical attempt in this connection was published in 1930 (6). This explanation of the phenomenon of behavioral alternation in trial-and-error learning was derived solely from the extinction of R_- to a point such that R_+ could be evoked. The recurrence of R_- later was attributed to the spontaneous recovery of R_- from this extinction. In 1936 substantially the same hypothesis was presented, though in a somewhat more formal manner (8, p. 20, Theorem IV).

In 1940 a still different hypothesis was put forward as to the nature of behavioral alternation in connection with a general theoretical consideration of rote learning (13). By this hypothesis, behavioral oscillation was postulated to be a function of varying resistance to reaction evocation at the reaction threshold.

In connection with a detailed behavioral systematization (11, pp. 304 ff.), there was presented in 1943 a modification of the 1940 hypothesis as to the nature of behavioral oscillation; namely, that it is a function of habit strength, that all habit strengths oscillate independently, and that the reaction threshold is static. No specific application was made at that time to alternation cycles as such.

REFERENCES

1. Guilford, J. P. *Psychometric methods*. New York: McGraw-Hill Book Co., 1936.
2. Hobhouse, L. T. *Mind in evolution*. London: Macmillan and Co., 1926.
3. Holland, G. Trial-and-error learning: massed and distributed trials with habits of unequal initial strength. Ph.D. thesis on file in the Yale Univ. Library, 1947.

---

4. Holmes, S. J. *The evolution of animal intelligence.* New York: Henry Holt, 1911.
5. Hull, C. L. The formation and retention of associations among the insane. *Amer. J. Psychol.*, 1917, 28, 419–435.
6. Hull, C. L. Simple trial-and-error learning: a study in psychological theory. *Psychol. Rev.*, 1930, 37, 241–256.
7. Hull, C. L. The influence of caffeine and other factors on certain phenomena of rote learning. *J. Gen. Psychol.*, 1935, 13, 249–274.
8. Hull, C. L. Mind, mechanism, and adaptive behavior. *Psychol. Rev.*, 1937, 44, 1–32.
9. Hull, C. L. Simple trial-and-error learning—an empirical investigation, *J. Comp. Psychol.*, 1939, 27, 233–258.
10. Hull, C. L. The problem of stimulus equivalence in behavior theory. *Psychol. Rev.*, 1939, 46, 9–30.
11. Hull, C. L. *Principles of behavior.* New York: D. Appleton-Century Co., Inc., 1943.
12. Hull, C. L., and Spence, K. W. "Correction" vs. "non-correction" method of trial-and-error learning in rats. *J. Comp. Psychol.*, 1938, 25, 127–145.
13. Hull, C. L., Hovland, C. I., Ross, R. T., Hall, M., Perkins, D. T., and Fitch, F. B. *Mathematico-deductive theory of rote learning.* New Haven: Yale Univ. Press, 1940.
14. Kimble, G. A. An experimental test of a two-factor theory of inhibition. *J. Exper. Psychol.*, 1949, 39, 15–23.
15. Koffka, K. *The growth of the mind.* New York: Harcourt, Brace and Co., Inc., 1925.
16. Ladd, G. T., and Woodworth, R. S. *Elements of physiological psychology.* New York: Charles Scribner's Sons, 1911.
17. Thorndike, E. L. *The original nature of man.* Educational psychology series, Volume I. New York: Teachers College, Columbia Univ., 1913.
18. Watson, J. B. *Behavior.* New York: Henry Holt and Co., 1914.

3. Discrimination Learning[1]

At the outset of our consideration of the subject of discrimination learning it will be well to clarify our use of certain terms. It is especially important to distinguish simple discrimination learning from simple trial-and-error learning,[2] which was discussed in some detail in the preceding chapter.

The distinction can be made perhaps most effectively on the basis of the stimulus-response relationships involved. Let it be supposed, for example, that each of two stimuli, S_1 and S_2, has the capacity to evoke a particular reaction, R_1, as shown in Figure 17. Because S_1 and S_2 are dynamically equivalent in so far as the evocation of R_1 is concerned, this relationship

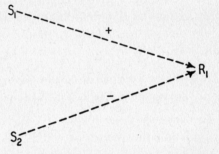

FIGURE 17. Diagram showing the type of stimulus-response situation which precipitates simple discrimination learning. Because the reaction potentialities at the outset converge from S_1 and S_2 upon R_1, this is called the convergent S ⇢ R situation. For a contrasting diagram of the divergent S ⇢ R situation which is basic to simple trial-and-error learning, recall Figure 1, p. 19.

may be said to be that of *stimulus equivalence*. Let it be supposed further that when R_1 is evoked by S_1 (S_2 being absent) the situation will be such that reinforcement will follow, but that when R_1 is

[1] A portion of Chapter 3 appeared nearly *verbatim*, in the *Psychological Review*, 1950, *57*, 303–313.

[2] This distinction has been emphasized by Spence (*17*, pp. 429–430). The present chapter is essentially the writer's interpretation of Spence's extension and formalization (*17*; *18*; *19*) of Pavlov's analysis (*15*, pp. 117 ff.) of discrimination learning.

evoked by S_2 (S_1 being absent) reinforcement will in no case follow. Under these conditions $S_1 \dashrightarrow R_1$ will be progressively strengthened by reinforcement, and $S_2 \dashrightarrow R_1$ will be progressively weakened by experimental extinction, until at length S_1 will uniformly evoke R_1 and S_2 never will; this latter constitutes the state of perfect *simple discrimination*.

In summarizing the contrast of the two types of learning just considered we may say that they are alike in that they involve the selective strengthening of one (the adaptive) receptor-effector connection rather than some other (the unadaptive) receptor-effector connection. They are distinguished by the fact that in simple discrimination learning the receptor-effector connection selected differs on the *stimulus side* from the one eliminated, whereas in simple trial-and-error learning the receptor-effector connection selected differs on the *response side* from that which is eliminated. By extending the meaning of the word *selection* a little, we may say that *simple discrimination learning involves primarily stimulus selection, whereas simple trial-and-error learning involves primarily response selection.*

A Concrete Example of Simple Separate-Discriminanda Presentation Discrimination Learning

In order that the reader may secure an appreciation of the phenomenon the theory of which we are about to consider, we now present a simple concrete case of such learning. This consisted, first, in the associative connection of a locomotor and door-lifting response to the stimulus of a black card (S_1) which constituted the main portion of the door (D) of Figure 18, as seen by an albino rat approaching it from the chamber beneath lid L. The response to black was always followed by food reinforcement. A curve of this portion of the learning from its beginning approximately up to its asymptote through days I to VII appears in Figure 19. The $_sE_R$ values on the graph were secured by the determination of the median response latency of a group of eight animals and then the calculation of the equivalent reaction potential by the substitution of the $_st_R$'s in equation 28.

When the animals had learned to respond to the black card they were presented with an irregular alternation between the black (S_1) and a white card (S_2). When the door-opening response (R_1) followed the presentation of the black card, food reinforcement resulted as usual, but when R_1 followed the presentation of the white card, no food was ever given. This *differential reinforcement*, as it is called, gradually caused a differentiation in the response intensities to the two stimuli, as shown in Figure 19, beginning at day 1 and continuing up through day 48. This represents the

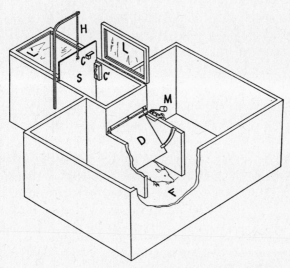

FIGURE 18. A drawing of the apparatus utilized in the study of simple white-black discrimination. The albino rat is placed in the chamber beneath the transparent lid marked L′, which is shown as closed. When the animal is facing the shutter (S) ready to go into the next chamber, the experimenter lifts S somewhat more than enough for the rat easily to pass through into the chamber beneath the lid, L, shown as open, the shutter being suspended in this position by the hooked rod, H. Just as the shutter rises high enough for the animal to pass through, the shoulder C depresses the spring contact C′, starting an electric laboratory clock recording time in hundredth seconds. Next, the animal pushes beneath the sloping cardboard door (D) to get the food, F. When the door is raised one inch the microswitch (M) stops the clock, which then shows the response time of the subject. The white or black stimuli to be discriminated were placed on the side of the door faced by the rat when in the chamber beneath lid L. Reproduced from Wilcoxon, Hays, and Hull (22).

peculiarly discriminatory learning. It should be observed that on and around day 45, S_1 (black) evoked a reaction potential of approximately 4.5σ. In this connection we note that the reaction potential evoked by S_2 first increased with S_1, then fell very gradually as differential reinforcement progressed.

But how is this differentiation between black and white distributed among the five shades—black, dark gray, middle gray,

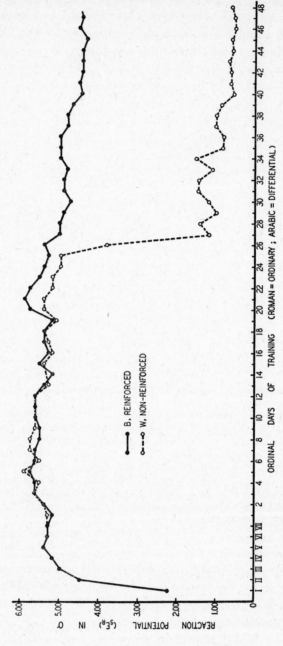

FIGURE 19. Graphic representation of the original learning (days I to VII) and of the results of the differential reinforcements (days 1 to 48). Note that despite the fact that black (S_1) was frequently reinforced and never received a nonreinforcement, it ended with a considerably lower sE_R than was displayed on day VII. Reproduced by permission of John A. Antoinetti (1).

light gray, and white? In order to determine this experimentally Antoinetti tested a group of eight rats, which were similar but had been trained somewhat differently, for their reaction potentials on the five shades of the series. To do this the differential-reinforcement procedure was continued in the main except that among each subject's sixteen daily response-evocation trials there were given on each of six consecutive days two "test" trials on dark gray, middle gray, and light gray. This technique yielded from each

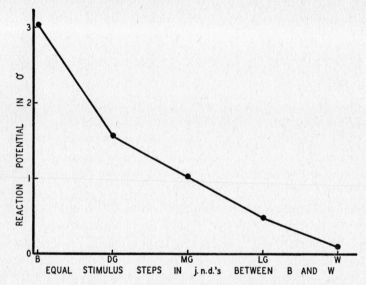

FIGURE 20. A rough average post-discrimination generalization gradient secured by Antoinetti on the black-white continuum after differential reinforcement, in terms of a human j.n.d. scale of brightness. The animals differed considerably in their learned powers of discrimination. Reproduced by permission of John A. Antoinetti (7).

subject two scores on each gray; in addition, of course, several additional scores on black and white were obtained on these days. The order of presentation of the six critical test trials was varied with the different subjects in such a way that no shade would, on the average, be presented earlier or later than the other two. Since none of the special test stimuli was reinforced, it is assumed that all three of them would be slightly depressed by the incidental non-reinforcement.

We note also that the Munsell coated papers which Antoinetti used as stimuli are very carefully graded psycho-physically so as to have equal differences in terms of "just noticeable differences" (j.n.d.'s) as seen by the human eye. This may be called the "qualitative" or subjective scale of brightness which is the traditional approach. In addition we shall later (p. 78) consider the quantitative or objective scale of brightness in terms of per cent physical reflectance of the papers. The resulting post-discrimination generalization gradient of this psychophysical scale is shown in Figure 20.

We shall now proceed to derive a theoretical account of the empirical phenomena just presented as an illustration of the qualitative approach.

The Special Role of Incidental Stimuli (S₃) in Discrimination Learning

The most important type of discrimination learning is based on stimulus generalization (*10*; *6*; *5*). Present available evidence indicates that the gradient of stimulus generalization takes the general form graphically represented in the lower portion of Figure 21. The phenomenon of stimulus generalization as employed by Pavlov and many other writers (*15*; *11*; *18*) is based on a continuous series of potential stimuli, and for this reason this series potentiality is called a stimulus continuum. Such a continuum could be the series of sound (pitch) vibrations varying from high to low; of colors ranging from deep red to orange; of light intensities extending from a strong illumination to one near zero in amount; or of cutaneous vibrations at a constant rate varying from a strong intensity to a weak one. The continuum utilized by Antoinetti in the example given above included Munsell coated papers ranging from a white having 78.66 per cent of the reflectivity of magnesium oxide to a black having 1.21 per cent.

During learning days I to VII in Antoinetti's experimental situation, it is obvious that in addition to the blackness of S_1 (i.e., of the generalization continuum), many additional or incidental stimuli become conditioned to R_1. These include other stimuli which consistently impinge on the organism's sensorium during the repeated reinforcements; for example, the sound of the click when the sheet-metal shutter (S) is lifted, the lights and shadows of the chamber which the animal passes through from shutter to door (D), any odors that may have been consistently present, and the infinitely complex stimuli coming from the animal's own body.

We shall call these non-continuum stimulus elements the *incidental* stimuli. They will be represented as a whole by S_3. The learned attachment of S_3 to R_1 obviously sets up a separate reaction potential which operates wherever S_3 occurs, and S_3 always accompanies

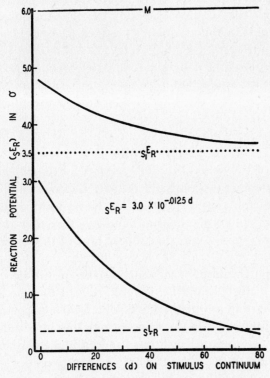

FIGURE 21. The lower portion of this figure shows a graphic representation of a theoretical generalization gradient on a qualitative stimulus continuum plotted in terms of j.n.d. differences. Above is shown the same gradient after it has been combined (+) with a reaction potential of 3.5σ (dotted horizontal line) assumed to be caused by incidental stimuli (S_3). Note that this summation greatly distorts the generalization gradient (a) by moving it upward leaving its asymptote at the level of 3.5σ, and (b) by greatly reducing its slope. The value of M is represented by the upper horizontal line at 6.0σ, and that of the reaction threshold is represented by the broken line at $.355\sigma$.

the generalization continuum as used in the experiment. This means that the S_3 stimuli by themselves will evoke R_1 whenever S_1 or S_2 are presented, quite apart from the latter. Thus, so far as S_3 is concerned, this combination of circumstances gives a superficial appearance of 100 per cent generalization.

Now since both sets of stimuli, S_1 and S_3, involve the same response their reaction potentials must combine $(+)$ with each other (*11*, pp. 222 ff.). Let us assume (IV) that the irrelevant (S_3) habit strength ($_sH_R$) taken by itself amounts to .58333, whereas the habit strength of $S_1 \rightarrow R_1$ taken by itself amounts to .50. Assuming that M equals 6.0σ and (VIII) multiplying, we find that the reaction potential controlled by S_1 directly is $.50 \times 6.0$, or 3.0σ, and that controlled by S_3 is $.5833 \times 6.0$, or 3.5σ. Combining this constant incidental reaction potential of 3.5σ with each point of the generalization gradient by means of summation equation 11, we secure the displaced and distorted gradient shown in the upper portion of Figure 21.

Let us compare these two manifestations of the same gradient. The addition of the irrelevant $_{s_8}E_R$ of 3.5σ artificially raises the asymptote of the generalization gradient by that amount. At the same time, summation greatly flattens the gradient, though the fractional amount of fall toward the asymptote of each gradient at each increment of d is constant and exactly equal in both, in the present case approximately 56.23 per cent of the preceding point. However, if the value of M were reduced from 6.0σ to 5.0σ, the upper gradient would appear much less steep still, i.e., it would be even more distorted, and if M were reduced to 3.6σ the gradient would be so flat as to be practically horizontal; empirically it would hardly be detectable. At bottom this is because near the asymptote in ordinary learning (*4*) additional practice adds little to the strength of the habit.

From the preceding considerations, we arrive at our eleventh theorem:

THEOREM 11 A. *The stimulus generalization gradient as produced on a stimulus continuum by simple learning is summated $(+)$ with the reaction potential based on the incidental stimuli present during the learning.*

B. *This summation $(+)$ artificially raises the apparent asymptote of the gradient and progressively flattens the gradient. As the incidental reaction potential approaches the magnitude of M, the gradient approaches the horizontal.*

Theorem 11, as illustrated by Figure 21, finds substantial corroboration in the gradients reported by Hovland (*8*; *9*). Incidentally this may explain why Pavlov's (*15*, p. 118), Hovland's, and Brown's (*2*) generalization gradients were approximately horizontal on the first unreinforced trial utilized in the tests for generalization (see Figure 22, first trial). As a matter of fact, practically the same thing is shown by Antoinetti's graph (Figure 19) at days 1 to 19 by the near equality of the S_1 and S_2 values, even though these are each based on eight differential reinforcements each day.[3]

Next there arises a question of how, in case the incidental $_sE_R$ nearly equals the value of M, the generalization gradient can ever become manifest. The answer is that its appearance results from the gradual removal of the incidental $_sE_R$ by experimental extinction. Frequently, however, $S_3 \rightarrow R_1$ cannot be extinguished without the non-reinforced presentation of the stimulus continuum in some form. For example, in the Antoinetti experiment a door is required, and any door must be of some shade. We shall accordingly neglect for the present the $_sE_R$ connected by stimulus generalization to S_2, and concentrate on the $_sE_R$ based on S_3.

At the outset of differential reinforcement, the incidental reaction potential of $S_3 \rightarrow R_1$ presumably is well along toward its asymptote (Figure 19) from the training of days I to VII. This implies that the extinction portion of the differential reinforcement training will start from near zero and presumably (*22*) will be advancing relatively rapidly. It follows that during differential reinforcement the $_{s_3}I_R$ will tend gradually to overtake the $_{s_3}E_R$ and the superthreshold portion of the $_{s_3}\bar{E}_R$ will gradually approach zero, i.e., there will be a tendency toward,[4]

$$_{s_3}\ddot{E}_R \doteq {}_{s_3}I_R = 0. \tag{43}$$

This means that the effective reaction potential under the control of the incidental stimuli will for most purposes gradually become relatively neutral and unimportant in the determining of overt

[3] The relative slowness of Antoinetti's S_2's in developing inhibitory potential from the differential reinforcement employed appears, from a comparison of his results with data reported by Raben (*16*), to be due in part to the number of non-reinforcements given with each reinforcement. It is customary to give a half dozen or more non-reinforcements to S_2 for a single reinforcement to S_1; and in general the more non-reinforcements to S_2, relatively the more prompt will be the differentiation. This fact, in turn, may be due in part to the short time-intervals between trials (see terminal note, Chapter 4) and, in addition, to the fact that S_2 and S_3 became secondary reinforcing agents during the original seven days of training when all stimuli were reinforced.

[4] $_s\ddot{E}_R = {}_s\dot{E}_R \doteq {}_sL_R.$

action. However, it may be added that many stimuli which are present nearly all the time are believed to be neutralized early in life for most responses by the process just described, and therefore do not undergo the further neutralization.

In terms of our equations as applied to Figure 21, we simply reduce the values of the summated ($\dot{+}$) but distorted gradient shown above by 3.5σ less the value of $_sL_R$. This amounts to a reversal of the summational procedure which produced the gradient

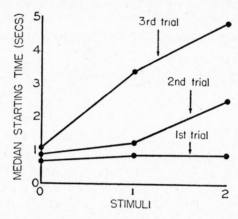

F I G U R E 22. Graphic representation of the gradual appearance of the stimulus generalization gradient during the process of differential reinforcement. Note that the gradient is here based on response latency and that when so represented it rises, instead of falling as it does when plotted in reaction potentials. Reproduced by permission of J. S. Brown (2, p. 218).

in the first place. The symbolical reversal (withdrawal, or $\dot{-}$) is performed for us by equation 13. This of course substantially reveals the true gradient in its proper position as represented at the bottom of the figure with which we began our analysis.

Generalizing on these considerations, we arrive at our twelfth theorem:

THEOREM 12. *As the differential reinforcement trials of the discrimination learning process take place one by one, leading as they do to the practical neutralization of* $S_3 \dashrightarrow R_1$, *the generalization gradient based on the stimulus continuum must gradually emerge with a progressively steepened gradient, standing in substantially its true form and position at the end of the process except that its level at* S_2 *must necessarily be at the reaction threshold* ($_sL_R$).

While not duplicating the conditions of the theorem, two independent studies, one by Hovland (8) and one by Brown (2), show a clear increase in the steepness of the generalization gradient as the extinction incidental to testing for the presence of the gradient progresses. The Brown results are reproduced as Figure 22. Note the progressive increase in the slope of the gradients as the ordinal number of trials increases. Incidentally the level rises at the point conditioned, showing that $_sE_R$ is being withdrawn all along the generalization gradient. To be wholly convincing, of course, such an experiment must remove only the $S_3 \dashrightarrow R_1$, whereas Brown's and Hovland's experiments, since the testing trials were not reinforced, presumably removed a portion of $S_1 \dashrightarrow R_1$ as well.

Differential Reinforcement Applied to S_1 (+) and S_2 (−) on the Stimulus Continuum Only

With the theoretical elimination of the influence of the incidental reaction potential (S_3) by having it reduced in strength to a practical threshold value, we may now consider the effects of differential reinforcement on the stimulus continuum without this complication. This is in a sense the heart of discrimination theory. *This analysis will be made by the use of the qualitative or subjective (j.n.d.) scale traditional in the treatment of stimulus-intensity discrimination.*

It will be recalled that the stimulus continuum of our example was the range from black (S_1) through the series of intervening grays down to white (S_2), the response (R_1) being originally connected to black by simple reinforced association. Now by the principle of stimulus generalization, the reaction potential of $S_1 \dashrightarrow R_1$ would extend in diminishing amounts toward white. Unfortunately we do not know to what low values this gradient spontaneously falls, i.e., without the influence of the extinction effects of $S_2 \rightarrow R_1$. Indeed, strictly speaking we do not know whether it spontaneously falls at all. This is because, up to the present time, when an empirical test for the gradient is made it is done with the responses which are evoked to the various test stimuli on the continuum always non-reinforced, which naturally introduces a certain amount of extinction all along the continuum tested for generalization. This sometimes has been considered (12, p. 125) to indicate that the parts of the continuum remote from the point positively reinforced may be more susceptible to the influence of experimental extinction than are those which are closer, and that this differential resistance to extinction may be an indispensable contributing cause producing the gradient.

However this may be, one thing is clear: the conditioning of R_1 to S_1 at one point of a stimulus continuum in fact sets up the potentiality of a generalization gradient which becomes manifest either (a) by differential resistance to extinction, or (b) by the

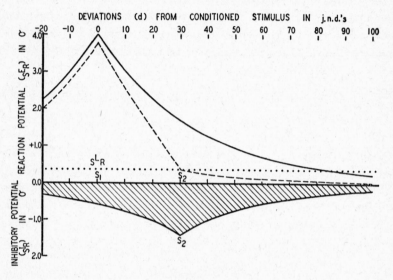

FIGURE 23. Graphic representation of the theoretical interaction ($\div$) of the gradients of the stimulus generalization of reaction potential (upper solid curves) and of conditioned inhibition (lower solid curves) which produce the discrimination gradients (broken-line curves) between. By sighting along the section of this latter line from S_1 to S_2, it may be seen that this discrimination gradient proper still has a slight curvature remaining from the primary stimulus generalization gradient from which it was derived. Note also that its maximum ($_s\dot{E}_R$) lacks a little of the original maximum ($_sE_R$). This same value appears in Figures 24 and 27 at d = 30 (*10*, p. 25).

removal of a distorting reaction potential attached to incidental stimuli (S_3). Until this uncertainty is removed by appropriate experiment the present writer is ready to gamble that the dominant mechanism in the development of the generalization gradient is the removal of the incidental ($S_3 \dashrightarrow R_1$) reaction potential. The existence of incidental stimuli in most situations of this nature is an obvious fact. Moreover, this deduction explains at the same time the steepening of the gradient and the lowering of its asymptote.

On the other hand, the hypothesis of differential resistance to experimental extinction is purely *ad hoc*.

The upper gradient in Figure 23 is accordingly constructed on this hypothesis, S_1 necessarily falling on a d value of zero. The values of this gradient are calculated by means of the equation,

$$_s\underline{E}_R = 4.0 \times 10^{-.0125d}.$$

In the differential reinforcement process in this case the S_2 is assumed to fall at d = 30, which reduces the reaction potential at that point to the reaction threshold, taken as .355 (*4*). Now this reduction in reaction potential is due in the main to the accumulation of conditioned inhibition. Moreover, conditioned inhibition generalizes on the stimulus continuum substantially as does reaction potential (X C). The slope of neither gradient is known with precision, but they evidently do not differ very much. We shall accordingly here assume them to be equal.

But in order to calculate the generalization gradient of $_s I_R$, we must know the amount that is to be withdrawn from the $_s E_R$ at d = 30. Now this $_s E_R$ value is 1.6868σ, and this withdrawal must be of the $\doteq$ variety which requires the use of equation 13. In this equation, therefore,

$$C = 1.6868\sigma.$$
$$_{s_1}E_R = _s L_R = .355\sigma,$$
$$M = 6.0\sigma,$$

and

$$_{s_2}E_R = _s I_R.$$

Substituting in equation 13, we have,

$$
\begin{aligned}
_s I_R &= \frac{M(C - _{s_1}E_R)}{M - _{s_1}E_R} \\
&= \frac{6.0(1.6868 - .355)}{6.0 - .355} \\
&= \frac{6.0 \times 1.3318}{5.645}
\end{aligned}
$$
$$\therefore \; _s\underline{I}_R = 1.4156.$$

Accordingly the generalization gradient of conditioned inhibition is calculated on the equation,

$$_s\underline{I}_R = 1.4156 \times 10^{-.0125d}.$$

It is plotted as the shaded double-winged gradient at the bottom of the figure, inverted as it must be when plotted against the negative scale at the left.

Next the generalized conditioned inhibition must be withdrawn ($\div$) at each point from the corresponding reaction potential by the repeated use of equation 13. A graphic representation of these differences is shown as a broken line between the two basic gradients. The portion of this difference function falling between S_1 and

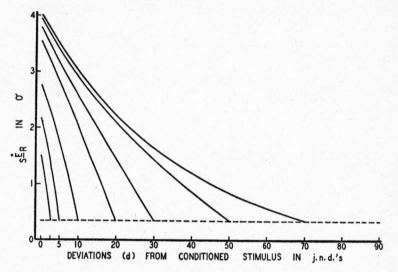

FIGURE 24. Graphic representation of the theoretical discrimination gradients resulting from the differential reinforcement of discrimination learning at progressively smaller differences (d's) between S_1 and S_2.

S_2 will be called the *discrimination* gradient. It is evident from a glance at Figure 23 that this discrimination gradient is much more nearly linear than an ordinary stimulus generalization gradient, and that its maximum height, the *net discriminatory reaction potential* ($_s\dot{\bar{E}}_R$), is appreciably less than the original stimulus generalization gradient above it.

Consider now the results of the application of the differential reinforcement procedure to S_1 and S_2 when the latter falls at $d = 90$. In this case the $_{s_2}\bar{E}_R$ already stands below the reaction threshold, which means that the maximum $_sI_R$ at that point will be zero and there will be no $_sI_R$ to be withdrawn anywhere from the stimulus generalization gradient. Accordingly, on these assumptions this discrimination gradient will be the stimulus generalization gradient without change. If we move S_2 up to a d of 80 or 70, it is evident to inspection that the maximum amount of $_sI_R$ will be so small that its generalization will not change the stimulus generalization gradient appreciably. However, as we move S_2 up to d = 60 and especially to 50, it is clear that the curvature of the discrimination gradient will grow less, its slope will grow more steep, and its height, $_s\dot{E}_R$, also will grow less, ultimately becoming zero when d is 0. Various theoretical discrimination gradients of this type,

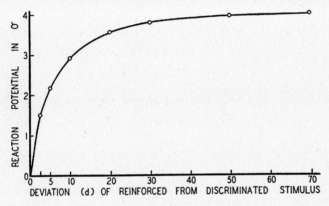

FIGURE 25. Graph representing the theoretical net discriminatory reaction potential ($_s\dot{E}_R$) as a function of the difference (d) between the reinforced and the discriminated stimulus.

as computed on the above assumptions, are represented in Figure 24. The d value involved in each is indicated by the lowest level ($_sL_R$) reached by each.

Because of the theoretical importance of the relationship, we have also plotted the net discriminatory reaction potential ($_s\dot{E}_R$) remaining after complete differential reinforcement as a function of d. This is shown in Figure 25. There it may be seen that the $_s\dot{E}_R$ begins falling very slowly as d decreases, and falls progressively more rapidly as d approaches zero.

Finally it may be stated that the ratios of $_s\dot{E}_R$ to d were calculated for the values represented in Figures 24 and 25. They were found to increase progressively as d approaches zero.

Generalizing on the preceding considerations, we arrive at our thirteenth theorem:

THEOREM 13 A. *When differential reinforcement is applied to*
S_{1+} *and* S_{2-}, *with d practically the entire range of the stimulus continuum, discrimination between the two will be learned by the average
rat.*

B. *The gradient of* $_sE_R$ *evocable by the stimulus continuum as a whole
becomes markedly concave upward, with an asymptote which is the
reaction threshold* $(_sL_R)$.

C. *As the range of d is decreased, the discrimination gradient connecting* S_1 *and* S_2 *becomes less concave upward, passing into a slightly
convex upward form after d = 30.*

D. *As the range of d is decreased, the more nearly vertical will be a
straight line drawn from the reaction potentials of* S_1 *and* S_2.

E. *As the range of d is decreased, the smaller will be the net discriminatory reaction potential attached to* S_1, $_s\dot{E}_R$ *equalling zero when
d equals zero.*

F. *As the range of d is decreased, the ratio of the* $_s\dot{E}_R$ *to d at* S_1
increases with a positive acceleration.

Up to the present time reports of experimental work on the
extremely simple form of discrimination learning which is the basis
of the preceding analysis have appeared in only three published
studies (*3*; *5*; *16*). So far as reported, none of these studies disagrees
noticeably with Theorem 13. Frick (*3*, p. 119) presents results
which tend to substantiate 13 A and 13 B, and Raben reports data
(*16*, p. 267) which are also in general harmony with 13 A and 13 B,
and to some extent with 13 E and 13 F. In addition we have in the
still more recent work of Antoinetti, incomplete as this is being
written, detailed evidence on 13 A and 13 B, as well as other
portions of the theorem.

We may take this occasion also to consider the learning curves
shown in Figure 19. The curve of the first seven days (designated
by Roman numerals) is evidently the ordinary growth curve of
simple learning (IV). With the onset of differential reinforcement
the distinctive sort of curve characteristic of discrimination learning
begins. After some days of differential reinforcement the extinction
effects $(_sI_R)$ on S_2 begin to produce a fall in the "white" curve.
And since the "black" curve must also gradually lose the $S_3 \rightarrow R_1$
component (Figure 21) at the beginning of the differential reinforcement, this also should fall. In addition, the extinction effect

($_sI_R$) on S_2 generalizes to some extent to S_1, which also contributes to the fall of the "black" curve, though not so much. But S_1 is reinforced at every response in which it is involved. It follows that the "white" curve falls practically to its reaction threshold as differential reinforcement continues, whereas the "black" curve remains fairly high.

Simple Discrimination with Three Discriminanda Presented Separately

Our discussion of discrimination learning up to the present has usually been concerned with the use of two discriminanda (20) or stimuli, one of which is positive or reinforced (+), and the other of which is negative or nonreinforced (−); the formula in this case is, therefore + −. The next most common number of discriminanda used experimentally has been three. Of these, the combination which has been utilized most is that where one stimulus is reinforced (+) and the stimuli at each side on the stimulus continuum are not reinforced (−). The formula for this type of triple discriminanda is − + −. We proceed now with the quantitative theoretical analysis of this type of discrimination. It is somewhat more complex than that for two stimuli just described, but the principles are at bottom the same.

Let it be supposed that we have a learning situation substantially like that represented in Figure 23 except that the two negative stimuli are placed at 10 d units on each side of the reinforced stimulus (Figure 26). We first calculate the generalization where $d = 10$.

$$_sE_R = 4.0 \times 10^{-.0125 \times 10}$$
$$= 3.0.$$

From this we withdraw (÷) the reaction threshold of .355 by using equation 13. Substituting, we have,

$$\frac{6.0(3.0 - .355)}{6 - .355} = \frac{15.87}{5.645} = 2.811,$$

which is the amount of $_sI_R$ which must be developed at $d = 10$ to reduce the $_sE_R$ at that point to the reaction threshold.

At this stage we must determine the amount of conditioned inhibition which is generated in connection with each of the two negative stimuli. They are separated by twice $d = 10$, or $d = 20$.

Substituting in the usual generalization equation, we have,

$$_S\underline{I}_R = {_SI}_R \times 10^{-.0125 \times 20}$$
$$\therefore {_S\underline{I}}_R = .5624 {_SI}_R.$$

This means that there will be combined the full $_SI_R$ at each discrimination point, and the generalized $_SI_R$ from the other point,

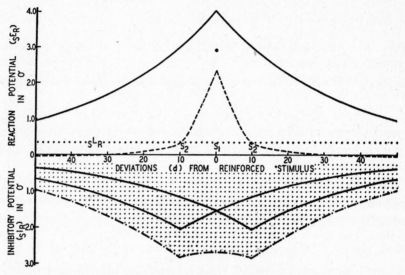

FIGURE 26. Diagrammatic representation of the interaction of the gradient of reaction potential ($_SE_R$, the solid line above) with the two gradients of conditioned inhibition ($_SI_R$, the two crossed solid lines through the stippled region below) which combine ($\dotplus$) to produce the total $_SI_R$ (dot-dash line below). The withdrawal ($\dotdiv$) of these latter values from the $_SE_R$ values above yields the discriminatory reaction potential represented by the broken line between. The isolated circle above the maximum of the broken line representing the net discriminatory reaction potential ($_S\dot{E}_R$) shows, for comparative purposes, the net discriminatory reaction potential yielded by two discriminanda at d = 10, as shown in Figure 25. The figure as a whole represents the dynamics of the − + − type of triple-discriminanda discrimination.

which together make up 2.811σ of conditioned inhibition. Substituting appropriately in the summation equation 11, we have,

$$_SI_R \dotplus .5624 {_SI}_R = {_SI}_R + .5624 {_SI}_R - \frac{_SI_R \times .5624 {_SI}_R}{6}$$
$$= 1.5624 {_SI}_R - .09373 {_SI}_R^2 = 2.811.$$

Solving this equation and taking the negative root, we have,

$$_SI_R = 2.052,$$

as the value of the conditioned inhibition at each of the two points of differential inhibition.

We next calculate the generalized conditioned inhibition at the point of intersection of the two generalized inhibitory gradients midway between them (d = 10),

$$_{s}\underline{I}_{R} = 2.052 \times 10^{-.0125 \times 10}$$
$$= 1.538.$$

But since there are two of these values at this point they must be summated by equation 11,

$$1.538 + 1.538 - \frac{1.538 \times 1.538}{6} = 2.682,$$

which is the value of a typical point on the dot-dash line immediately beneath. This line represents the summation ($\dot{+}$) of the two generalized $_{s}I_{R}$ gradients throughout the range represented.

The final step of the determination of the discriminatory reaction potential is to withdraw ($\div$) this 2.682 of $_{s}I_{R}$ from the maximum reinforcement at the top, 4.0σ. Once more using equation 13, we have,

$$_{s}\dot{\underline{E}}_{R} = \frac{6(4.0 - 2.682)}{6 - 2.682} = 2.383.$$

This is represented by the high point of the broken line above S$_1$ and is to be compared with the $_{s}\dot{\underline{E}}_{R}$ yield by the two discriminanda (see Figure 25), which amounts to 2.91 σ, represented by the isolated dot directly above.

Generalizing from the preceding considerations, we arrive at our fourteenth theorem:

THEOREM 14. *Discrimination learning with three discriminanda in the form* − + − *is possible, but is more difficult than is comparable discrimination learning with two discriminanda,* + −, *because in the* − + − *form the conditioned inhibition* ($_{s}I_{R}$) *generalizes upon the reinforced reaction potential from both sides, summating at* S$_1$, *the slope of this summation gradient being much less steep than would be a single* $_{s}I_{R}$ *gradient from the same maximum.*

No experiments involving the separately presented stimuli discrimination analyzed above in the use of the − + − form of triple discriminanda have been found. However, several studies have been reported which used the more complex form of simultaneous presentation or comparison of three different-sized visual objects. Lashley (*14*, p. 164) used three white circles on a black ground and found that rats did not learn to choose the middle-sized circle within the amount of training given, though in the + − − form this same amount of training was sufficient to yield the choice of either the largest or the smallest circles. Spence (*19*), working with chimpanzees and using squares of 100, 160, and 256 sq. cm. in area made of white enameled sheet-iron clamped to separate food boxes, found that the problem concerned with the intermediate-size of square was learned on the average in 145 trials, whereas the problem concerned with two such discriminanda was learned in a mean of only 80 trials. Thus the empirical evidence on this type of discrimination learning agrees substantially with the results of the theoretical analysis of the separate presentation form. Moreover, an examination of the analysis represented in Figure 26, which follows substantially Spence's analysis (*19*, pp. 259 ff.), indicates that the essential reason for the greater difficulty of the discrimination problem involving intermediate size is that in the latter the $_sI_R$ generalizes from two directions, converging upon S_1 where it summates, this summation being much greater than would be the ordinary generalization gradient from the maximum conditioned inhibition at S_2. This is shown by the gentle slope from S_2 to S_1 of the $_sI_R$ (dot-dash) line at the bottom of Figure 26.

The Generalization of Reaction Potential ($_sE_R$) Based on Stimulus Intensities

In a preceding section of this chapter we observed the role that qualitative or subjective stimulus generalization (j.n.d. scale) plays in the determination of reaction potential. It is now our task to consider how this operates in the case of quantitative or objective stimulus intensity as measured by a physical scale.

Here the determination of $_sE_R$ is based on equation 20,

$$_{s_2}\underline{E}_R = D \times K \times V_2 \times {_{s_2}}\bar{H}_R, \qquad (20)$$

where V_2 represents the response evocation conditions. In our treatment of qualitative stimulus generalization earlier in the chapter, all values on the right-hand member of this equation were held constant except $_s\bar{H}_R$, the product of $D \times V_1 \times K$ being 4.0σ on the assumption that $D = 6.0\sigma$, $V_1 = .939$, and $K = .71$. However, in the quantitative or stimulus-intensity aspect of stimulus generalization of reaction potential, *two* components of this equation are varied, viz., $_s\bar{H}_R$, and V_2, the product of the other two $(D \times K)$ being held constant at 4.0572σ. But here we must note a striking fact: not only are V_1 and V_2 dependent upon stimulus intensity (S), but $_s\bar{H}_R$ is also. The novelty is found especially in the derivation of $_s\bar{H}_R$, which we now proceed to consider. In the present situation the equation for generalized habit strength is,

$$_{s_2}\bar{H}_R = {}_{s_1}H_R \times 10^{-.15d}, \tag{44}$$

where d, instead of being the difference between S_1 and S_2 in j.n.d.'s as in qualitative stimulus generalization, is the difference between the logarithms of S_1 and S_2.

To make this and its role in stimulus-intensity generalization quite clear we shall present a typical derivation of a theoretical generalized reaction potential. The assumed conditions are that the habit was set up to a visual stimulus of 1010 units (e.g., milli-lamberts), and that it generalized to, i.e., the response was evoked by, a stimulus of 10 units of intensity. The logarithms of these two stimulus intensities are, respectively, 3.00432 and 1.00000 (see Table 6). The difference between the two logarithms is 2.00432, which equals d. Substituting this value in equation 44, we have,

$$_{s_2}\bar{H}_R = {}_{s_1}H_R \times 10^{-.15\times2.00432}$$
$$= {}_{s_1}H_R \times 10^{-.30065}.$$

Assuming that the original habit strength was at its maximum, i.e., that

$$_{s_1}H_R = 1.0,$$

we have,

$$_{s_2}\bar{H}_R = 1.0 \times \frac{1}{2.0255}$$
$$= 1.0 \times .4937$$
$$\therefore {}_{s_2}\bar{H}_R = .4937,$$

which appears as the fourth entry of column 1, Table 6.

We next substitute log S, as always in equation 6,

$$V_2 = 1 - 10^{-.44 \log S}, \tag{6}$$

and solve for V_2, securing .6391, which appears as the fifth entry of column 1, Table 6. We now use equation 20 in the form,

$$\text{s}\underline{E}_\text{R} = V_2 \times \text{s}\bar{H}_\text{R} \times 4.0572\sigma.$$

Substituting in this equation from Table 6, we have,

$$= .6391 \times .4937 \times 4.0572$$
$$\therefore \text{s}\underline{E}_\text{R} = 1.279,$$

which appears as the bottom entry in column 1, Table 6.

The $\text{s}\underline{E}_\text{R}$ values in the other columns of this table were calculated in an exactly analogous manner. They are represented graphically

TABLE 6. Table showing the derivation of a theoretical generalized reaction potential ($\text{s}\underline{E}_\text{R}$) gradient based on stimulus generalization from a strong (S_1) to a weak (S_2) stimulus intensity.

Stimulus intensity (S)	10	100.5	210	410	610	810	1010
Log S	1.00000	2.00216	2.32222	2.61278	2.78533	2.90849	3.00432
d from strong to weak stimulus intensity	2.00432	1.00216	.68210	.39154	.21899	.09583	.00000
Generalized habit strength ($\text{s}\bar{H}_\text{R}$)	.4937	.7075	.7901	.8735	.9153	.9676	1.0000
Stimulus-intensity dynamism (V)	.6391	.8623	.9052	.9292	.9405	.9475	.9524
Generalized reaction potential ($\text{s}\bar{H}_\text{R} \times V_2 \times 4.0572 = \text{s}\underline{E}_\text{R}$)	1.279	2.475	2.902	3.293	3.538	3.720	3.864

in the continuous-line curve of Figure 27. The corresponding reaction potential values where the generalization extends in the opposite direction, i.e., from 10 units to 1010 units, were calculated by exactly the same principle but are not shown in the table. These results are also presented in Figure 27, but by the broken line.

Generalizing on the preceding considerations as represented in Figure 27, we arrive at our fifteenth theorem:

THEOREM 15 A. *When a reaction potential ($\text{s}\underline{E}_\text{R}$) generalizes from a stronger to a weaker stimulus intensity (in the lower range of magnitude), the gradient is relatively steep in its downward slope and its curvature is convex upward.*

B. *When a corresponding reaction potential ($_s\underline{E}_R$) generalizes from a weaker to a stronger stimulus intensity (in the lower range of magnitude) the gradient is relatively gentle in its downward slope and its curvature is for the most part concave upward.*

C. *The gradient originating at the weaker stimulus intensity has a markedly lesser $_s\underline{E}_R$ at $d = 0$ than the one originating at the stronger stimulus intensity.*

We are fortunate in having empirical evidence bearing directly on the soundness of this theorem in an experiment reported by

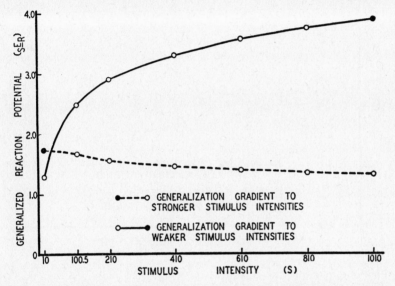

FIGURE 27. Graphs representing theoretical stimulus generalization reaction potential gradients starting at opposite extremes of the same range of stimulus intensities and extending to the other extreme. They are plotted on the basis of ordinary stimulus-intensity units. The points of origin are represented by solid black circles.

Judson Brown (*2*). But before considering Brown's results let us note a striking change which takes place in the curvature of the two theoretical gradients when they are plotted on the basis of log S, only three of the data points being used—the first, last, and that which falls at the mean of these two log values. In order to show this we have replotted the three points in question as Figure 28. There it may be seen at once that the gradient of generalization from a strong to a weak stimulus extreme now has a slight but clear concave-upward curvature, whereas the gradient generalizing from a weak to a strong stimulus extreme has a definite convex-upward curvature, an exact reversal of the direction of curvature in each case from that shown in Figure 27.

With this relationship in mind we turn to Brown's stimulus-intensity generalization investigation. He trained two groups of rats to go to food on a straight runway. During the learning the food reward was associated with screens which were illuminated by a very weak light with one group, and by a very strong light

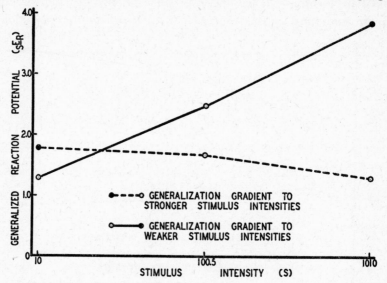

FIGURE 28. Three-point graphs representing theoretical stimulus generalization reaction potential gradients plotted on the basis of log stimulus intensity. Note that the three values of each gradient here represented are exactly the same as the corresponding values represented in Figure 27 but that the difference in the manner of plotting reverses the curvature of both gradients.

with the other group. After the learning, Brown secured a quantitative measure of the strength of the rats' tendency to go to screens with different illumination. As the measure of this reaction potential he utilized the mean magnitude of the pull of the animals when put in a little rubber harness halfway down the runway from the screen. The test lights placed on the screen were: the extreme weak illumination, the extreme strong illumination, and an illumination corresponding approximately to the mean log of the intensity of the two extreme illuminations. Thus each group of animals produced a different generalization gradient. These gradients are both represented in Figure 29, after the manner of the theoretical Figure 28.

A comparison of Figure 29 with Figure 28 shows that *when plotted against log intensities:*

1. The generalization gradient from strong toward weak agrees in having a relatively steep fall with a concave-upward curvature.

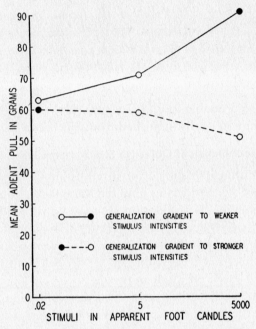

FIGURE 29. Graphic representation of empirical reaction potential as modified by stimulus-intensity generalization and stimulus-intensity dynamism, corresponding roughly to Figure 28. Plotted from data published by Brown (*2*) as represented in a previous publication by the present author (*13*).

2. The generalization gradient from weak to strong agrees in having a relatively gentle fall with a convex-upward curvature.

3. The origin of the weak-to-strong gradient is considerably lower than that of the strong-to-weak gradient.

Thus all three points of Theorem 25 appear to be substantiated.

At this point we note an implication of Theorem 15 and Figure 27 which arises from the fact that stimulus generalization logically extends in two directions from an intensity to which a response has been reinforced. Thus if the two gradients shown in Figure 27 originated at the same point, i.e., at S = 1010 units, and extended over a total range from 10 to 2010 units, the broken-line gradient would have its point of origin increased to 4.057σ (through the increase in V_1) and would extend to S = 2010, falling appreciably less than it does in Figure 27. From these considerations we arrive at our sixteenth theorem:

THEOREM 16. *Stimulus generalization reaction potentials ($_s\underline{E}_R$) extend in both directions along a stimulus-intensity continuum from a single point of reinforcement, the wing extending toward increasing stimulus intensities on the whole having much higher reaction potentials for given deviations from the reinforcement point, especially as d increases.*

We have been unable to find any empirical data bearing directly upon Theorem 16 as distinguished from Theorem 15.

The Simple Discrimination of Objective Stimulus Intensities

We shall continue the subject of stimulus-intensity generalization in this section by considering how the same factors operate jointly in simple stimulus discrimination. It may be recalled that in the discrimination considered above (Figure 23) the data dealt with were treated as non-quantitative, i.e., they were treated as qualitative in nature, since the value of V was held constant and the d values were based on j.n.d.'s.

Let us now consider the theoretical discrimination of two light intensities in the lower range: 4 units and 24 units (millilamberts). The d in this case is therefore the difference between the logarithms of 4 and 24 respectively, i.e.,

$$1.38021 - .60206 = .77815.$$

As in stimulus-intensity generalization of reaction potential considered in the immediately preceding section, we shall assume that D $\times$ K = 4.0572σ, and that $_s H_R$ = 1.0; also, that the generalization exponent is $-.15$ (equation 44).

The various major steps of the computation of this discrimination are entered in the first data column of Table 7. V_1 and V_2 are calculated by equation 6 where, as stated above, the S_1 is 4 units and the S_2 is 24 units. This yields a V_1 value of .4568 and a V_2 value of .7530. These values appear as the second and third entries of the first number-column of Table 7.

Next, reaction potential at S_1 is calculated by equation 20,

$$_sE_R = D \times V_2 \times K \times {_sH_R}. \tag{20}$$

But here the S_2 (of response evocation) is the same as the S_1 (of original learning). But since,

$$D \times K \times {_{s_1}H_R} = 4.0572,$$

and

$$V_1 = .4568,$$

it follows that,

$$_{s_1}E_R = 4.0572 \times .4568$$
$$= 1.8533,$$

which appears as the fourth entry in the first number column of Table 7.

TABLE 7. The major steps in the computation of the theoretical discriminatory reaction potential ($_s\dot{E}_R$) at the intensity stimuli of reinforcement for two adjacent pairs of stimuli (S_1 and the contrasted stimulus, S_2) in millilamberts.

		From 4 (S_1) to 24 (S_2) milli-lamberts	From 24 (S_1) to 4 (S_2) millilam-berts	From 24 (S_1) to 44 (S_2) millilam-berts
1	Stimulus intensities (S) in discrimination			
2	Stimulus-intensity dynamism (V_1)	.4568	.7530	.7530
3	Stimulus-intensity dynamism (V_2)	.7530	.4568	.81082
4	Reaction potential at S_1 ($V_1 \times 4.0572 = {_{s_1}E_R}$)	1.8533	3.0551	3.0551
5	Generalized habit strength ($_s\bar{H}_R$)	.76435	.76435	.91308
6	Generalized reaction potential ($_s\underline{E}_R$) at S_2 ($_s\bar{H}_R \times V_2 \times 4.0572$)	2.3351	1.4166	3.0037
7	$_sL_R$ withdrawn ($\div$) from $_s\underline{E}_R$ (at S_2) = $_{s_2}I_R$	2.1046	1.1284	2.8153
8	Generalized $_sI_R$ (at S_1) i.e., $_{s_2}I_R \times {_s\bar{H}_R} = {_{s_1}I_R}$	1.6087	.8624	2.5706
9	$_{s_1}I_R$ withdrawn ($\div$) from $_{s_1}E_R$ at S_1 = $_{s_1}\dot{E}_R$	.3342	2.5608	.8477

At this point we calculate the generalization of the $_s\bar{H}_R$ from S_1 to S_2:

$$_{s_2}\bar{H}_R = {_sH_R} \times 10^{-.15 \times .77815}$$
$$= 1.0 \times .76435$$
$$_{s_2}\bar{H}_R = .76435.$$

This value appears as the fifth entry in the first number column of Table 7. From this we secure the generalized reaction potential:

$$_{S_2}\underline{E}_R = {_{S_2}}\bar{H}_R \times V_2 \times 4.0572$$
$$= .76435 \times .7530 \times 4.0572$$
$$= 2.3351,$$

which appears as the sixth entry in the first number column of Table 7.

Now this value is extinguished by differential reinforcement to the reaction threshold, which as usual is taken as $.355\sigma$. We accordingly withdraw $(\div)$ $.355\sigma$ from 2.3351 to determine how much $_sI_R$ will be generated in the process. This is done by means of equation 13. Substituting appropriately in this equation and solving, we find that $_sI_R$ will be 2.1046, which is the seventh entry in the first data column of Table 7. Next, this $_sI_R$ generalizes back from S_2 to S_1. There is considerable uncertainty concerning the role of V in the generalization of $_sI_R$. Considerations of an *a priori* nature fail us here and, as always in such cases, resort ultimately must be had to experiment. In the provisional computations given below the V is not used; the $_sI_R$ as such has disappeared, though the habituation aspect of $_sI_R$ remains. Because of this and other uncertainties the computation is given in detail:

$$_s\underline{I}_R = 10^{-.15 \times .77815} \times 2.1046$$
$$= .76435 \times 2.1046$$
$$= 1.6087.$$

This appears as the eighth entry in the first number column of Table 7. Finally, this generalized inhibition $(_s\underline{I}_R)$ must be withdrawn $(\div)$ from the reaction potential originally at S_1, which is 1.8533. Substituting in equation 13, we have,

$$_s\dot{E}_R = \frac{6.0(1.8533 - 1.6087)}{6.0 - 1.6087}$$
$$= \frac{1.4676}{4.3913} = .3342.$$

Solving, we secure .3342, which appears as the ninth and last item in the first number column of Table 7. Thus it appears that discrimination between two stimulus intensities has been deduced from our postulates with a reaction-potential reduction from 1.8533 to .3342, the outcome being in this respect much like the qualitative discrimination considered above (pp. 69 ff.).

Generalizing on the preceding considerations, we arrive at part A of our seventeenth theorem:

THEOREM 17 A. *Simple stimulus-intensity discrimination can be learned, with a reduction in reaction potential as an inverse function of d, much as is the case with qualitative discrimination.*

Our next problem concerns the theoretical effectiveness of discriminatory learning as dependent on whether the reinforced stimulus is the more or the less intense of a pair of stimuli which are identical except that one is reinforced and the other is not. In the case represented in number-column 1 of Table 7, the intensities were 4 and 24; the stimulus of less intensity, 4 units, was reinforced, and the one of greater intensity, 24 units, was extinguished. We accordingly proceed to calculate the possible net reaction potential $(_s\dot{E}_R)$ of the opposite case, where the stimulus of greater intensity, 24 units, is reinforced and the one of less intensity, 4 units, is not. Employing the same principles of determination as before, we secure the results which appear in number-column 2 of Table 7; row 9 of this column shows that the final net reaction potential is 2.5608, as distinguished from the .3342 of the reverse situation.

Generalizing from the preceding considerations, we arrive at part B of Theorem 17:

THEOREM 17 B. *When the simple discrimination of two stimulus intensities occurs, the difference between the intensities remaining constant, the process is more effective in terms of the net reaction potential $(_s\dot{E}_R)$ yield when reinforcement is given to the more intense rather than to the less intense of the two discriminanda.*

Our final problem here concerns the theoretical influence on discriminatory learning effectiveness resulting from an increase of the stimulus intensities while the difference between them is kept constant. In the two cases just considered the difference was that between 4 and 24, or 20 units. Let us now examine the discriminatory effectiveness of the intensities when they are increased to 24 and 44 units respectively. The derivation of $_s\dot{E}_R$ in this case is presented in the third number-column of Table 7. A comparison of the last item in number-columns 1 and 3 shows that

$$.3342 < .8477,$$

i.e., the $_s\dot{E}_R$ for discriminating an intensity of 24 units from one of 44 units is greater than that for discriminating one of 4 units as compared with 24 units. This, however, is probably contrary to empirical expectation.

Generalizing on these considerations, we arrive at part C of Theorem 17, even though it may be contrary to empirical expectation:

> THEOREM 17 C. *When the simple discrimination of two stimulus intensities occurs, the difference between the intensities remaining constant, the effectiveness of the discriminatory process in net reaction-potential ($_s\dot{E}_R$) yield increases as the intensities of the two discriminanda increase.*

A small amount of evidence bearing directly on all three parts of Theorem 17 is found in Antoinetti's unpublished experimental results. These indicate that the type of discrimination learning there shown, with the more intense of the discriminanda reinforced, was successful. The reflectance difference between the two papers used as visual objects was 77.45 per cent. The $_s\dot{E}_R$ was 4.36σ. Thus part A of Theorem 17 finds partial empirical verification.

Regarding the validity of part B of Theorem 17, Antoinetti's results show that in the reverse case from that just considered, where the less intense stimulus of the pair was reinforced, the $_s\dot{E}_R$ yielded was only 2.65σ. But,

$$4.36\sigma > 2.65\sigma.$$

This difference is significant at the five per cent level of confidence. Accordingly part B of Theorem 17 finds apparent empirical verification.

Finally we consider in detail the validity of part C of Theorem 17. As already indicated, this theorem is probably contrary to empirical fact. But the false implications of a system must be exhibited along with the true ones if the system is to advance the science adequately. Actually part C is opposed by what is probably the most firmly established empirical relationship in the whole field of behavior. This relationship is that in simultaneous or closely successive stimulus-presentation discrimination, the net discrimination efficiency ($_s\dot{E}_R$) grows less as the intensity of the two discriminanda is increased, the absolute difference between the stimuli remaining constant. This is neither Weber's law nor Fechner's law, though it is closely related to both.

This long-known relationship is apparent, though in a somewhat indirect manner, in the very specialized type of discrimination involving the separate presentation of the discriminanda already considered in this chapter. After Antoinetti's animals had about reached the limit of discrimination learning between black and white, he proceeded gradually to decrease the difference between the discriminanda of his two groups of animals in such a way that one group was discriminating between two discriminanda at the lighter extreme (near white) and the other group at the darker extreme (near black) of reflectance intensity yielded by the Munsell coated papers. At the darker stimulus extreme the stimuli were 1.210 per cent and 6.555 per cent respectively, with a reflectance difference of 5.345 per cent. This yielded an $_s\dot{E}_R$ value of 1.23σ. At the lighter stimulus extreme the two stimuli were 78.66 per cent and 43.06 per cent respectively, with a reflectance difference of 35.60 per cent. This large difference yielded the comparatively small $_s\dot{E}_R$ of $.90\sigma$. But,

$$1.23\sigma > .90\sigma,$$

which is the exact reverse of Theorem 17 C. This difference is not significant.

The above results are complicated by the fact that in the case of the weak stimulus discriminanda the weaker stimulus of the pair was the one reinforced, whereas in the case of the strong discriminanda the stronger stimulus of the pair was the one reinforced. As shown by Theorem 17 B and related evidence, this would have favored the apparent discrimination power of the more intense pair of discriminanda. Even so, the inverse relation of discrimination power to the intensity of the two discriminanda is very marked. We accordingly conclude that Theorem 17 C is *not* valid.

This obviously implies a serious defect somewhere in the postulate set, or in the analysis of the process, or in both. Nevertheless we are of the opinion that this or any other system of behavior theory if thoroughly sound must be able to deduce the fact that discrimination efficiency grows less, other things equal, as the stimulus

intensity of the discriminanda grows greater, even though this
deduction has never been made.

Simple Single-Stimulus Presentation Discriminatory Trial-and-Error Learning

While a certain amount of the simple discriminatory learning of
the sort analyzed above has been reported (*3; 16*), the greater part
of the work done in this field has been combined with trial-and-
error learning in one form or another. It will be convenient at this
point to introduce this combination of processes in a simple form.
Let it be assumed that the albino rat is in an apparatus something
like that shown above in Figure 13, except that there is only one
manipulandum. This projects straight into the experimental
chamber through a slit in the metal panel. It can be moved a
little to right or left, one or the other movement automatically
releasing a pellet of food into the food-cup according to the stimulus
being presented and the response made. At once after the response,
whichever it is, the manipulandum is automatically withdrawn
through the panel to a point inaccessible to the animal so that no
further manipulation on that trial will be possible. The critical
stimuli to be discriminated in this case are buzzer sounds, let us
say, which are presented one at a time. The two stimuli chosen are
a loud sound (S_1), an intensity of 100 decibels, and a less intense
sound (S_2) of 50 decibels. Finally, the apparatus is so arranged
that when the 100-decibel sound is presented and the manipulandum is moved to the right a pellet of food always drops into the
cup, but if the movement is to the left no pellet is found; and when
the 50-decibel sound is presented and a movement to the left
occurs, a pellet of food drops into the cup, but not if the movement
is toward the right. In case of either false movement, the withdrawal of the manipulandum of course prevents any second choice
on that trial. The task of the subject, then, is to associate the loud
sound (S_1) with the choice of the right-hand movement (R_1)
+ food, and to associate the moderate sound (S_2) with the choice
of the left-hand movement (R_2) + food. The selection (R_1 or R_2)
of the movements is the trial-and-error aspect of the learning, and
the power of making this choice correctly on the basis of the
respective sound signals (S_1 or S_2) is the discriminatory aspect of
the learning.

Let us say that the manipulandum is presented at the very

beginning of the experiment without the buzzer stimuli, and the apparatus is set so that a movement to the right will give a pellet, then a movement to the left will give a pellet, and so on in an irregular alternation up to a total of ten pellets. After this preliminary training the manipulandum is carefully cleaned and the apparatus is set to give the reward only while the particular sound is being presented as described above. At this stage, but one trial will be given per day and the sound stimuli will be alternated, one at each trial, in an irregular manner so that in the course of forty days, twenty sounds will be of loud and twenty will be of moderate intensity.

It is to be expected that the "incidental" stimuli of the apparatus, and so on, will be associated about equally with both R's. As in simple discrimination, these stimuli (S_3) will receive reinforcement and non-reinforcement to approximately the same extent after the preliminary training. This will tend to equalize their strengths as the $_{s_3}E_R$ and the $_{s_3}I_R$ approach their respective asymptotes so that in time differential reinforcement will approximately neutralize the incidental reaction potential involved. But the primary theoretical problem here is the discrimination of the strong from the moderate sound intensity of the stimulus continuum; i.e., to generate conditioned inhibition to the generalized tendencies from each sound intensity to the response proper to each. This means that there are four stimulus-response combinations:

1. When S_1 is followed by R_1, that combination generates $_{s_1}E_{R_1}$.
2. When S_1 is followed by R_2, that combination generates $_{s_1}I_{R_2}$.
3. When S_2 is followed by R_2, that combination generates $_{s_2}E_{R_2}$.
4. When S_2 is followed by R_1, that combination generates $_{s_2}I_{R_1}$.

It is evident from the above description that the theoretical problems of both simple discrimination and simple trial-and-error learning are involved here. In terms of associative connection analogous to that represented in Figures 1 and 17 with two connecting lines each, one right and one wrong, we now have the situation represented by Figure 30, with four connecting lines, two right (reinforced) and two wrong (non-reinforced).

So far as we can now see this presentation of S_1 and S_2 by an irregular alternation will produce a type of learning at each stimulus substantially like that represented in Figure 23, with the additional factor of response generalization between R_1 and R_2

as discussed in detail in the description of simple trial-and-error learning (Chapter 2, especially pp. 22 ff.). With the reduction of the superthreshold reaction potential ($_s\dot{E}_{R-}$) of $S_2 \rightarrow R_1$ and of $S_1 \rightarrow R_2$, each to near zero, there will remain portions of $S_1 \rightarrow R_1$ and $S_2 \rightarrow R_2$ after the withdrawal from them respectively of the

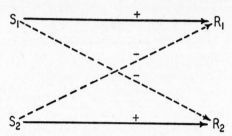

FIGURE 30. Diagrammatic representation of the reinforced (+) and non-reinforced (−) connections between the respective continuum stimuli and responses in a simple discriminatory trial-and-error situation in which either S_1 or S_2 is presented at a given trial. The broken lines in this diagram represent generalized but maladaptive (−) reaction potentials ($_s\underline{E}_R$).

generalized $_{s_1}I_{R_2}$ and $_{s_2}I_{R_1}$. These will be the discriminatory reaction potentials $_{s_1}\dot{\underline{E}}_{R_1}$ and $_{s_2}\dot{\underline{E}}_{R_2}$, the net end product of the learning activity.

Joint-Stimulus Presentation Discriminatory Trial-and-Error Learning

In concluding our analysis of the various forms of simple discrimination learning, we now take up the form of discriminatory trial-and-error learning which involves the simultaneous presentation of two stimuli to be discriminated. Typical examples of such empirical investigations are found in Spence's experiments with chimpanzees (17), Lashley's jumping experiments employing rats (14), and Köhler's transposition experiments with chickens. Actually this procedure corresponds to the great mass of experiments performed on humans in connection with the Weber-Fechner law.

In Spence's experiment chimpanzees learned to identify two separate food boxes on which white squares of different size had been placed. The box with the larger square could be opened, and contained a bit of food, whereas the box with the smaller square was locked. If the animal chanced to try the lid of the latter box it was permitted no second choice and got no food on that trial. Under such conditions these organisms soon learn to scrutinize the cues closely, looking first at one and then at the other before lifting the lid of one of the boxes (*18*, p. 432, footnote 3).

The movements involved in examining the cues, i.e., in exposing the receptors to the relevant stimuli in such a problem situation, will be referred to as *receptor adjustment acts*. The detailed theory of the evolution of this type of habit will be presented later (Chapter 6) in connection with an account of compound trial-and-error learning, of which it is a small-scale example.

In Lashley's experiment a rat was placed on a stand separated some inches from two doors on each of which was a circle of white cardboard, one larger than the other. When the rat leaped against the large circle, say, the door would swing open easily and in the compartment beyond would be found a bit of food; the door with the small circle, on the other hand, would in such case be locked so that if the animal leaped against this circle it received a punishing blow from the impact against the unyielding surface, fell a short distance into a net, and received no food on that trial. In the course of a few hundred trials, the number depending upon the differences in the areas of the two circles, the rat would gradually learn to look first at one of the cards and then at the other before jumping, and to jump only to the larger circle.

In Köhler's experiment hens were presented with kernels of grain on two sheets of gray paper, one sheet darker than the other. The hens were permitted to secure the grain from one shade of gray, but not from the other. After many trials the hens learned to attempt to eat only the grain which lay on the paper from which it could be secured.

From a casual consideration of the three cases of simultaneous-stimuli presentation discrimination learning just cited, in the light of the preceding analysis, it is evident that we have to do here with a considerably more complex process than that of simple discrimination learning. In addition to discrimination itself and the response selection of trial and error already considered in the preceding sections of the chapter, we have the phenomena of *comparison* which results from the receptor adjustment acts. These acts themselves result, in the first place, from the oscillation ($_sO_R$) of $_sE_R$ as manifested by the organism's moving its head from side to side—Muenzinger and Tolman's "vicarious trial and error." The reinforcement of such movements occurs when they chance to be followed by a successful instrumental act which itself is reinforced. In such a situation the receptor adjustment act is reinforced according to the delay-of-reinforcement principle (iii). The reception of the patterns of the stimuli in close succession by the eye, say, constitutes the comparison.

The effectiveness of comparison itself depends upon two principles. The first is the principle of the stimulus trace (II), which allows the stimulus first received to persist until the second or comparison stimulus is received. These impulses thereupon undergo an interaction (XI) which changes each to some extent but not entirely. This afferent interaction change in turn, through the principle of stimulus generalization (X A), has two effects: first, the degree to which the stimulus trace remains unchanged produces a tendency to generalization of the ordinary sort based on its original nature; i.e., the reaction potential primarily based on this stimulus trace, through previous habit formation, will tend to be evoked by other stimuli, with the amount of reduction depending on the difference (d) between the two stimuli involved. This gives rise to responses based on the *absolute* nature of stimuli. The second effect resulting from the afferent interaction change is the degree to which interaction has changed the stimulus; i.e., the degree and nature of the afferent shift from the trace of the preceding stimulus to the stimulus which follows will tend to generalize to other transitions with the usual fall in $_sE_R$ as the two transitions differ. This calls forth the *relations* type of responses.

Grice's recent experiment (5) indicates that there is little difference in the ease of learning between the simultaneous-stimuli presentation method and the single-stimulus presentation method. However, older studies (*18*; *19*) suggest that the method of simultaneous comparisons probably favors the "relations" type of response in transposition tests.

Summary

Discrimination learning in simple form is the acquisition of the power of responding differentially to stimuli, S_1 and S_2, which originally are more or less equivalent to each other in response (R_1) evocation. The process of differentiating the response-evocation potentiality of S_1 and S_2 is complicated by certain active stimuli (S_3) which are present with *both* S_1 and S_2. This would produce the appearance of a generalization between S_1 and S_2 even if the latter completely lack this tendency.

The primary process which gives rise to the discrimination of the stimulus complex is differential reinforcement. In the course of time with an equal number of occurrences of S_1 and S_2, both $_{S_2}E_{R_1}$ and $_{S_2}I_{R_1}$ tend to approach their asymptotes, which will reduce $_{S_2}E_{R_1}$ toward its reaction threshold. Moreover, since the rates of both learnings are reduced as the asymptotes are approached, presumably S_3 loses much of its capacity to acquire not only response R_1 but also other responses employing to different degrees the same effectors. This should produce extensive transfer-of-learning effects wherever S_3 is involved.

Along with the process of neutralizing S_3 to R_1, the differential reinforcement gradually builds up $S_1 \dashrightarrow R_1$. But this reaction potential generalizes to $S_2 \dashrightarrow R_1$, which is never reinforced, giving rise to $_{S_2}I_{R_1}$ which generalizes back upon $S_1 \dashrightarrow R_1$ and reduces the latter appreciably. The net result of this double generalization of $_SE_R$ and $_SI_R$ is the marked loss by S_2 of the power to evoke R_1 and the retention of a considerable though reduced power of S_1 to evoke R_1. This seems to be the essence of discriminatory learning.

Discrimination learning may involve numerous discriminanda, and their combinations may vary widely as to the stimuli which are reinforced and those which are not reinforced. For example, in the case of three stimuli there may be the formulae $+ - +$, or $+ + -$, or $- - +$, or $- + -$. Of these four we have analyzed only the last. It is believed that the same general methodology could be adapted to the remaining three, as well as to many other possible forms. Theoretical analysis reveals that $- + -$ had an appreciably weaker yield of net $_S\dot{E}_R$ at the limit of learning than $+ -$.

Stimulus intensities show stimulus generalization much as do qualitative stimulus similarities, but with differences. The d is believed to be based on log S, which produces an asymmetry in the gradients extending toward increasing intensities as contrasted with decreasing intensities. This introduces certain differences in the theory of quantitative discrimination as distinguished from qualitative discrimination. The theory in its present state yields a fair deductive agreement with both intensity generalization and discrimination empirical facts, but in each there is a rather clear indication of defect somewhere in the postulates involved. The false implications of the postulates are presented along with those agreeing with fact because it is believed that the progress of behavior science at its present stage is best served by presenting the defects as well as the virtues of a system.

A simple form of discrimination learning combined with trial-and-error learning is found in a situation permitting on a given occasion only one or the other of two responses, R_1 and R_2, say, and presenting only one or the other of the stimuli S_1 and S_2. The detailed analysis of this type of learning was not performed. No report of separate-stimuli presentation discriminatory trial-and-error learning has been found in the empirical literature.

The detailed analysis of joint or simultaneous stimuli presentation trial-and-error learning, also, was not performed. It is evident, however, that in this type of learning three new factors enter: (1) the learning of a receptor-adjustment act, (2) the trace of the first stimulus persisting until the second stimulus is received, and (3) the interaction of the two afferent processes. It is believed that the response on transposition tests will be governed in part by the generalization of the absolute values of the original stimuli (21; 23). But since the interaction of S_1 and S_2 is usually appreciable, this interaction effect will generalize more or less to other interaction effects produced in transposition tests, which presumably will give rise to what has been called a *relational* response (7).

TERMINAL NOTES

A PROPOSED METHOD OF QUANTIFYING DIFFERENTIALLY
THE $S_1 \dashrightarrow R_1$ AND THE $S_3 \dashrightarrow R_1$ REACTION POTENTIALS

Let it be supposed that we wish to determine empirically the reaction potential to sound intensity of $S_1 \dashrightarrow R_1$, uncomplicated by $S_3 \dashrightarrow R_1$ values. We will begin by setting up a reinforced connection between a 100-decibel sound and the response to the apparatus shown in Figure 18, on 100 albino rats. After this habit has reached its asymptote, the median reaction latency ($_st_R$) of the group will be determined and this converted into reaction potential by equation 28 (4). This should be the summation ($\dotplus$) of the reaction potentials evoked by S_1 and S_3.

Then the 100-decibel sound stimulus component will be removed from the stimulus complex and the response latency noted and converted into reaction potential. This would be the $S_3 \dashrightarrow R_1$ magnitude except for possible interaction effects (XI). It should also be appreciably less than that before the sound removal. This $S_3 \dashrightarrow R_1$ value withdrawn ($\div$) from the original total reaction potential should yield the approximate value of $_{s_1}E_{R_1}$.

A useful checking approximation to the above values with the same subjects could be secured by extinguishing the $S_3 \dashrightarrow R_1$ reaction by massed trials. Substituting this $\dot{n}$ in an appropriate equation, $_s\ddot{E}_R = f(n)$, the equivalent $_{s_3}\ddot{E}_{R_1}$ value could be secured. Then by restoring the sound and extinguishing again, substituting the new $\dot{n}$ in the equation $_s\ddot{E}_R = f(n)$, the $_{s_1}E_{R_1}$ value (except for interaction effects) presumably would be secured.

THE DETERMINATION OF THE EXPONENT OF THE GENERALIZATION GRADIENT IN THE CASE OF STIMULUS INTENSITIES

The splitting up of the causal factors of the stimulus generalization gradient ($_s\bar{\underline{E}}_R$) into two components ($_s\bar{H}_R$ and V) in the case of stimulus intensities raises the question of how the functions of the separate factors can be determined. A proposed procedure, which further illustrates the theory, is as follows.

First, five or more groups of organisms would be taught a habit by the Hays procedure described above (p. 60 ff.), with the use of critical stimuli which increase by equal log intensities (millilamberts) starting at extremely weak values. The median response latencies of each of these five learning curves would be converted into $_s E_R$'s by equation 28, and learning equations fitted. The coefficients of these equations would then be plotted as a function of log S and a separate equation fitted to them. This would be the equation of the particular stimulus-intensity dynamism involved.

The equation for V, uncomplicated by stimulus generalization, would be used in connection with equation 20 in the interpretation of stimulus generalization ($_s\underline{E}_R$) gradients both (1) toward increasing and (2) toward decreasing stimulus intensities analogous to those of Brown (2) and Hovland (9), the gradients being stated in objective physical units such as millilamberts. Each $_s E_R$ value secured would be divided by the V value of the corresponding stimulus intensity. These quotients would then be plotted separately

from increasing and decreasing intensities as a function of the log
stimulus intensity difference (d) producing each; these should be
generalization gradients in terms of $_8\bar{H}_R$ multiplied by a constant
which would be D × K × J. The present analysis anticipates that
the resulting equations would, except for sampling limitations, be
identical, and that they would represent the true generalization
gradient of habit strength uncomplicated by the circular considerations involved in the use of the j.n.d. units hitherto employed.

REFERENCES

1. Antoinetti, J. A. The effect of discrimination training upon
   generalization. 1950, unpublished.
2. Brown, J. S. The generalization of approach responses as a
   function of stimulus intensity and strength of motivation.
   J. Comp. Psychol., 1943, *33*, 209–226.
3. Frick, F. C. An analysis of an operant discrimination. *J.
   Psychol.*, 1948, *26*, 93–123.
4. Gladstone, A. I., Yamaguchi, H. G., Hull, C. L., and Felsinger,
   J. M. Some functional relationships of reaction potential
   ($_8E_R$) and related phenomena. *J. Exper. Psychol.*, 1947, *37*,
   510–526.
5. Grice, G. R. Visual discrimination learning with simultaneous
   and successive presentation of stimuli. *J. Comp. and Physiol.
   Psychol.*, 1949, *42*, 365–373.
6. Grice, G. R., and Saltz, E. The generalization of an instrumental response to stimuli varying in the size dimension.
   J. Exper. Psychol. 1950, *40*, 702–708.
7. Gulliksen, H., and Wolfle, D. L. A theory of learning and transfer: I. *Psychometrika*, 1938, *3*, 127–149.
8. Hovland, C. I. The generalization of conditioned responses: I.
   The sensory generalization of conditioned responses with
   varying frequencies of tone. *J. Gen. Psychol.*, 1937, *17*,
   125–148.
9. Hovland, C. I. The generalization of conditioned responses: II.
   The sensory generalization of conditioned responses with
   varying intensities of tone. *J. Genet. Psychol.*, 1937, *51*,
   279–291.
10. Hull, C. L. The problem of stimulus equivalence in behavior
    theory. *Psychol. Rev.*, 1939, *46*, 9–30.

11. Hull, C. L. *Principles of behavior*. New York: D. Appleton-Century Co., Inc., 1943.

12. Hull, C. L. The problem of primary stimulus generalization. *Psychol. Rev.*, 1947, *54*, 120–134.

13. Hull, C. L. Stimulus intensity dynamism (V) and stimulus generalization. *Psychol. Rev.*, 1949, *56*, 67–76.

14. Lashley, K. S. The mechanism of vision: XV. Preliminary studies of the rat's capacity for detail vision. *J. Gen. Psychol.*, 1938, *18*, 123–193.

15. Pavlov, I. P. *Conditioned reflexes* (trans. by G. V. Anrep). London: Oxford Univ. Press, 1927.

16. Raben, M. W. The white rat's discrimination of differences in intensity of illumination measured by a running response. *J. Comp. and Physiol. Psychol.*, 1949, 42, 254–272.

17. Spence, K. W. The nature of discrimination learning in animals. *Psychol. Rev.*, 1936. *43*, 427–449.

18. Spence, K. W. The differential response in animals to stimuli varying within a single dimension. *Psychol. Rev.*, 1937, *44*, 430–444.

19. Spence, K. W. The basis of solution by chimpanzees of the intermediate size problem. *J. Exper. Psychol.*, 1942, *31*, 257–271.

20. Tolman, E. C. *Purposive behavior in animals and men*. New York: Century Co., 1932.

21. Warden, C. J., and Rowley, J. B. The discrimination of absolute versus relative brightness in the ring dove, Turtur risorius. *J. Comp. Psychol.*, 1929, *9*, 317–337.

22. Wilcoxon, H. C., Hays, R., and Hull, C. L. A preliminary determination of the functional relationship of effective reaction potential ($_s\bar{E}_R$) and the original number of Vincentized extinction reactions (ṅ). *J. Exper. Psychol.*, 1950, *40*, 194–199.

23. Wolfle, D. L. Absolute brightness discrimination in the white rat. *J. Comp. Psychol.*, 1937, *24*, 59–71.

4. Behavior and the Molar Stimulus Trace (s')

The notion of the stimulus trace was originally put forward by Pavlov (*16*), but he left it in an essentially qualitative state. The present chapter is designed to open the field definitely to the quantification of this concept, because this must be accomplished before much significant systematization can occur. The great importance of the role of the stimulus trace in systematic adaptive dynamics makes this necessary at the present time even though much basic experimentation is still lacking. This means that the chapter must be essentially pioneering in nature, with the presumptive associated roughness in its trial-and-error approximations.

We shall mean by the expression *stimulus trace* the molar after-effects (s') following the termination of a brief stimulation such as the sound of a single click. This concept has a possible neurophysiological aspect—namely, the primary mechanism may lie in the neural response (s) of the receptor when stimulated (*7*, pp. 42 ff.), or, on the other hand, in the gradual weakening of some accessory muscular contraction. However, these physiological aspects are not our present primary concern. Here we shall consider only that aspect called molar. The molar stimulus trace is never observed as such, i.e., it is a theoretical construct. From this fact it follows that its empirical determination must be indirect. This naturally causes considerable difficulty. We shall first attempt to give a general exposition of the nature of the molar stimulus trace. This can best be done by describing the methods employed in the formulation of Postulate II.

The Derivation of the Stimulus-Trace Postulate (II)

Reynolds (*17*) conditioned the blinking of the human eyelid to various ages of the stimulus trace initiated by a single click. A puff of air was delivered at varying intervals following the click to four different groups of human subjects. All groups acquired the conditioned-reflex blink after 90 trials separated by periods varying from one to two minutes. This clearly means that the stimulus trace at various ages can be conditioned to a response with distinctly different resulting reaction potential strengths. Reynolds' results showed that his several delay groups gave characteristically different per cents of overt blinking responses to the conditioned stimulus. These varying susceptibilities to conditionability of stimulus traces of various ages are themselves believed to be due to differential stimulus trace intensities at those ages. On the ten trials from 81 to 90 the four groups gave the results shown in the second line of Table 8.

At this point we proceed to a theoretical analysis of these and related data with a view to the preliminary formulation of a

TABLE 8. The derivation of equivalent stimulus trace intensities (S) on Reynolds' subsident stimulus trace gradient (*17*), on the basic assumption that at the maximum, Ṣ must equal approximately 1000.0 units of stimulus intensity.

Age of trace (t)	.250″	.450″	1.150″	2.250″
Per cent overt responses	68	98	70	31
Corresponding reaction potentials	3.0435	4.6295	3.1002	2.0799
Stimulus-intensity dynamism (V_1)		.952155	.637622	.427776
Calculated equivalent stimulus trace intensity ($\dot{S}'$)		1000.8	10.048	3.558

quantified postulate. The first step is the conversion of these per cent responses into σ values. Using the ordinary probability table we secure the equivalent reaction potential values, shown in the third line of Table 8, which presumably represent approximations to corresponding $_sE_R$'s. These values appear graphically as part of Figure 1 of *Essentials of Behavior*. Of the four $_sE_R$ values we are especially concerned with the final three, which represent approximations to the reaction potentials occurring at .450″, 1.150″, and 2.250″; i.e., on the falling or subsident range of the stimulus trace. Now, these reaction potentials are evidently set up under very different trace values (V_1) at the several delay times, though the evocations are presumably in the same general temporal region.

This means that the V_2 value for the responses conditioned in this region must be approximately constant at $t = .45''$.

Next we proceed to estimate from the $_sE_R$ values, as they stand, the corresponding V_1's of the *learning* process, which are carefully to be distinguished from the *evocation* processes (V_2's). By equation 8',

$$_sE_R = D \times V_2 \times K \times _{s_1}H_R \times V_1 \tag{8'}$$

We now shall assume that $D \times V_2 \times K \times _{s_1}H_R = 4.862128.$[1] It follows that if the several $_sE_R$ values in Table 8 are divided by 4.862128, the quotients will be V_1's. Performing these divisions for the three values Reynolds found in his subsident gradient, we have the V_1 values which appear in the fourth row of Table 8.

With the V_1 values available we may substitute them one at a time in equation 6,

$$V_1 = 1 - 10^{-.44 \log S}, \tag{6}$$

and solve for S, which we have been seeking.

Substituting the first V_1 value of the fourth row, Table 8, we have,

$$.952155 = 1 - 10^{-.44 \log S}.$$

Solving for S,

$$.047845 = 10^{-.44 \log S}$$

$$10^{.44 \log S} = \frac{1}{.047845} = 20.9008$$

$$.44 \log S = \log 20.9008 = 1.32016$$

$$\log S = \frac{1.32016}{.44} = 3.00036$$

$$S = \text{antilog } 3.00036$$

$$\therefore S = 1000.8.$$

This value appears in the last row of Table 8. The other two values in this row were calculated by means of equation 6 in a similar manner.

With a sufficient number of S values available it should be possible to fit an equation to the corresponding t' values where,

$$t' = t - .450''.$$

---

[1] The 4.862128 was a value deliberately chosen to yield about 1000.0 units of stimulus intensity at $t = .45''$.

Unfortunately there are only three pairs of such values. But in an emergency we do the best we can with what is available. At the same time we change S to S′ because there is no actual stimulus intensity here, and because the stimulus trace is in its subsident phase. The resulting fitted equation is:

$$\dot{S}' = 6.881(t' + .01128)^{-1.1104}. \tag{45}$$

There remains the question of the recruitment gradient characteristics of S′. Kimble (12) has published some empirical results in this range more or less comparable to those of Reynolds. Kimble's results are given in the first, second, and third lines of Table 9.

TABLE 9. The derivation of the equivalent recruitment stimulus trace intensities (S′) from Kimble's stimulus trace gradient (12).

Age of trace (t)	.100″	.200″	.225″	.250″	.300″	.400″
Per cent overt responses	45	51	54	77	87	95
Corresponding reaction potentials	2.4501	2.6009	2.6762	3.3146	3.7022	4.2207
Stimulus-intensity dynamism (V_1)	.50392	.53493	.55042	.681721	.76144	.86808
Equivalent stimulus intensities ($\dot{S}'$)	4.92	5.70	6.15	13.49	25.98	99.83

From these values are calculated the equivalent V_1 values and the presumably corresponding $\dot{S}'$ values shown respectively in the fourth and fifth lines of the table. Fitting an equation to the pairs of values in the first and last rows of Table 8, we have:

$$\dot{S}' = 9967.6t^{5.0485} + 3.0. \tag{46}$$

Freely adapting equations 46 and 45 to each other to eliminate inconsistencies presumably due to limitations in the size of the empirical samples and various artifacts (since they must be identical at their maximum point), we arrive at tentative equations 1 and 2:

$$\dot{S}' = 465,190t^{7.6936} + 1.0; \tag{1}$$
$$\dot{S}' = 6.9310(t' + .01)^{-1.0796}; \tag{2}$$

which form the basis for Postulate II, parts A and B respectively (p. 5). It will be observed that these equations are so written that the maximum equivalent stimulus intensity (S′) amounts to a conventional 1000 units. This means that real light units (milli-lamberts) would sometimes greatly exceed that amount.

The necessarily indirect nature of the above determinations of equations 1 and 2 should give the reader a realistic comprehension of the two major aspects of the molar stimulus trace.

Reaction Potential ($_s\underline{E}_R$) on the Stimulus Trace as a Generalization Continuum

The next step in our analysis will be to determine in a preliminary manner the theoretical stimulus generalization characteristics of reaction potential ($_s\underline{E}_R$) throughout the molar stimulus trace. With equations 1, 2, and 6, and those of Postulate X B available, we are now able to calculate this throughout *both* phases, given the point of reinforcement. As in the first empirical case considered, we shall assume that the place of reinforcement occurs at the optimum point, i.e., .45″ after the presentation of the conditioned stimulus. We first calculate the equivalent stimulus intensity (S′) of the stimulus trace by means of equations 1 and 2. The values for the subsident phase of the stimulus trace are shown in the second line of numbers in Table 10. With those values available we calculate the equivalent stimulus-intensity dynamism values (V_2) at various ages of the trace by means of equation 6. These V_2 values are presented as the third row of numbers in Table 10.

Our next task is to calculate the generalized $_s\bar{H}_R$ throughout both trace phases. Assuming that habit strength has reached its maximum (1.00) at the point of reinforcement ($t = .45″$, i.e., $\dot{t}′ = 0″$), from which it generalizes, we find by means of Postulate X B that,

$$_{s_2}\bar{H}_R = {}_{s_1}H_R \times 10^{-.15d},$$

where d is the difference between the logarithm of the conditioned stimulus (S_1) and that of the evoking stimulus (S_2). These $_s\bar{H}_R$ values for the subsident phase of the trace are shown in the fourth row of Table 10.

Finally, we substitute in Postulate X B, i.e.,

$$_{s_2}\underline{E}_R = ({}_{s_2}\bar{H}_R \times V_2)(D \times K \times V_1).$$

Assuming that ($D \times K \times V_1$) = 4.862128, V_1 in this case being .95214, $_{s_2}\bar{H}_R$ as shown in line 4, and V_2 as in line 3, we have the values of $_{s_2}\underline{E}_R$ as in line 5. These values represent superthreshold

T A B L E 10. The derivation of reaction potentials at various points on the subsident stimulus trace as a generalization continuum, when reinforcement occurs at $\dot{\mathrm{t}}$ = .45".

	0.00	0.05	0.2	0.5	1.0	1.5	2.0	2.5	3.0	3.5	4.0	5.0
Time since maximum of trace ($\dot{\mathrm{t}}'$)												
Equivalent of stimulus intensity ($S'_{\dot{\mathrm{t}}}$)	1000.0	144.51	37.371	14.339	6.8571	4.4419	3.2619	2.5664	2.1093	1.7868	1.5476	1.2169
Stimulus-intensity dynamism (V_2)	.95214	.88789	.79672	.69016	.57135	.48111	.40561	.33946	.27992	.22540	.17482	.08274
Habit strength ($s_2\bar{H}_R$) as generalized on the stimulus trace as a continuum	1.00000	.74815	.61077	.52902	.47361	.44375	.42366	.40870	.39685	.38709	.37884	.36542
Generalized suprathreshold reaction potentials ($s_2\underline{E}_R$) in σ	4.6294	3.2298	2.3660	1.7752	1.3157	1.0380	.8355	.6746	.5401	.4242	.3220	.1470

reaction potentials, i.e., they are based on actual responses. Gladstone *et al* (2) have shown with rats that the threshold stands $.426\sigma$ above the absolute zero of reaction potential (Z). Values corresponding to row 5 were calculated for the *recruitment* phase of the stimulus trace (ţ = $0''$ to $.45''$) by strictly analogous procedures.

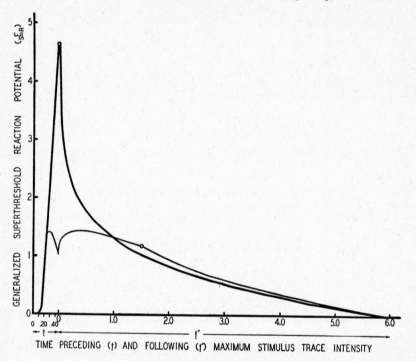

TIME PRECEDING (ţ) AND FOLLOWING (ţ') MAXIMUM STIMULUS TRACE INTENSITY

FIGURE 31. Graphs representing the theoretical superthreshold generalization reaction potentials ($s'E_R$) as conditioned to ţ' = $0''$ (heavy circle) and ţ' = $1.5''$ (light circle), and generalized on the recruitment and subsident phases of the respective stimulus traces. It is to be noted that the two recruitment gradients are so close together from t' = $0''$ to around $.23''$ that they could not be represented by separate lines; also that the $_sE_R$ conditioned at ţ' = $1.5''$ rises for the most part as it generalizes toward the origin of the trace, falling quite sharply near ţ' = $0''$, then rising very sharply again, and then falling to zero.

The results of these computations for the two phases of this trace are represented graphically by the respective wings of the heavier curve of Figure 31, where the reinforcement is assumed to occur at ţ' = $0''$. Completely parallel computations based on the assumption that reinforcement (V_1) had occurred at ţ' = $1.5''$ are represented graphically by the lighter curve in Figure 31.

Some Tentative Theorems Regarding the Stimulus Trace

The examination of Postulate II and Figure 31, together with the considerations of the preceding section, gives rise to the following generalizations:

THEOREM 18 A. *The stimulus trace* (s') *reaches a maximum at about .450''.*

B. *Both the recruitment phase and the subsident phase of the stimulus trace are power functions of time.*

C. *The subsident phase of the stimulus trace has a much longer duration than the recruitment phase.*

D. *The recruitment phase of the stimulus trace must always alternate in occurrence with the subsident phase.*

Turning to the heavy graph of Figure 31, we observe that according to the present theory when reinforcement occurs at the point of maximum intensity on the stimulus trace $(t = .45'')$ the following generalizations may be made:

THEOREM 19 A. *The recruitment phase of the generalized super-threshold reaction potential* $(_s\underline{E}_R)$, *when reinforcement occurs about .45'' after stimulation, rises steeply in a slightly concave-upward manner to the point of reinforcement, after which it falls sharply but much more slowly in a decelerated manner toward a zero value.*

B. *The recruitment phase of* $_s\underline{E}_R$ *rises appreciably above the reaction threshold at about .15 seconds after stimulation.*

C. *The recruitment phase and the subsident phase of reaction potential pass through exactly the same sequence of reaction potentials on each stimulus occasion but in a reverse order and at a markedly different rate.*

Our next principle follows from 19 B and C, and from Postulate X:

THEOREM 20 A. *Reaction by generalized evocation must take place between relatively similar stimulus intensities of the two phases of the stimulus trace, particularly from the subsident phase (conditioning) to the recruitment phase (subsequent evocation), and from a part of one phase to a different part of the same phase.*

But since the superthreshold reaction potential associated with a portion of the recruitment phase of such stimulus traces must always precede any superthreshold portion of the subsident section, it follows that:

> B. *There will be a strong tendency for* S → R *connections set up during both phases of the stimulus trace to be evoked by an earlier portion of a subsequently occurring recruitment phase.*

When a response is evoked earlier in the stimulus sequence than the point corresponding to the circumstances of its original reinforcement, we have a case of *antedating reaction*. Now when a response antedates the conditions of its reinforcement, the subject is said anthropomorphically to *anticipate* the reinforcement. This has given rise in some quarters to the use of the term *expectancy (3)*. It follows from Theorem 20 B that the basic objective principle underlying the notion of "expectancy" as such has here been formally derived as a bit of integrated behavior theory. Therefore, the notion of "expectancy" appears now as a *secondary* principle *(20)* rather than as a primary one as is sometimes assumed.[2]

The essence of $_sO_R$ is the variation in intensity of $_sE_R$. Now if $_sO_R$ chanced to have a low value at the occurrence of a stimulus conditioned to a response, but a high value a moment later, the response *could* take place later than the conditions of original reinforcement and presumably would occasionally do so. Therefore it follows that:

> C. *There will be a weak tendency (probability) for responses conditioned to the recruitment phase of a stimulus trace to be evoked by a later portion of a subsequently occurring stimulus trace.*

Turning now to the consideration of the more lightly plotted graph in Figure 31, jointly with the more heavily plotted graph, we arrive at the following generalizations:

> THEOREM 21 A. *When an* S → R *connection is set up on the subsident portion of a stimulus trace below the maximum trace intensity, the reaction potential when evocation occurs at the point reinforced (other things equal) is weaker than when reinforcement and evocation occur at a stronger trace point.*
>
> B. *The later on the subsident phase of the stimulus trace that reinforcement occurs (other things equal), the more any subsequent response evocation is likely to antedate in time the conditions of its reinforcement.*

[2] See Chapter 5, especially the first terminal note.

It will be noticed that the reaction potential reinforced at $t' = 1.5''$ on the subsident trace, when generalized from $1.5''$ to $0''$ is much greater than when generalized from $1.5''$ to $6.0''$. Generalizing from this consideration, we arrive at part C of Theorem 21:

> C. *Generalized reaction potential for comparable time deviations from the point of reinforcement toward the maximum stimulus intensity on the subsident phase of a stimulus trace is definitely greater than when generalization from the same point of reinforcement occurs on the weaker extreme of the same stimulus trace.*

But sometimes the manipulandum as well as much of the external stimulus pattern does not become available to the subject until a point has been reached on the stimulus trace later than the point of reinforcement. From this, together with a consideration of both graphs in Figure 31, we have:

> D. *On the subsident trace, the farther down below any given point of reinforcement the response is evoked, the weaker the response will be.*

But if the phases of the stimulus trace posterior to the point of reinforcement (s'_e) are able to evoke reactions, as is implied by Theorem 20 C, does this mean that the reaction will be repeated continuously as long as the stimulus trace retains any appreciable strength? In considering this question it should be recalled that (1) when a stimulus trace evokes a reaction, proprioceptive and other stimuli impinging on the various receptors as the result of the reaction may be expected by the principle of afferent interaction (XI) to change somewhat the nature of the stimulus trace, thereby reducing that habit's reaction evocation powers; (2) the I_R produced by the act itself will tend for a short time to inhibit the act; and (3) in the case of successful flight reactions the evocation of the act and the consequent primary reinforcement of its connection with the trace of the proprioceptive stimuli arising from a preceding flight evocation will rarely or never occur.

Generalizing from these considerations, we arrive at our twenty-second theorem:

> THEOREM 22. *If one phase of a perseverative stimulus trace (s') evokes a reaction (R), a subsequent phase of that individual trace will not be likely to do so unless the conditions of the situation are*

such as directly to condition the repetition to that phase along with the proprioceptive stimulus traces left by a preceding reaction of the same kind.

The Adaptive Significance of Antedating Reactions Mediated by the Perseverative Stimulus Trace

The occurrence of events in the external environment to which the organism must react in order to survive is lawful. Thus if event B follows event A under certain circumstances on one occasion, it will do so on subsequent occasions of the same kind. Now, if event A activates some of an organism's receptors as it occurs, and event B through its stimuli evokes a reaction which reduces a need created by event B, this reaction will be conditioned to the perseverative stimulus traces left in the organism by event A. After the conditioning process has raised a reaction potential ($_s E_R$) to a value greater than the reaction threshold ($_s L_R$), as we have seen above, reaction R will begin to antedate its original occurrence in the event-sequence involving the organism and its environment. In case event B is the impact or onset of some sort of injury or other need of that type, and the reaction (R) is a defense reaction taking the form of flight or withdrawal from the neighborhood, it is clear that if the withdrawal reaction takes place before the occurrence of the injurious situation the organism will not be there to receive the injury and the antedating reaction will have been an effective defense reaction. In a world filled with predatory organisms, where flight is frequently very desirable, the added time for such flight made possible by the antedating conditioned trace reaction must obviously be of immense survival value. Indeed, a more effective adaptive mechanism could hardly be imagined. From these considerations we arrive at part A of our twenty-third theorem:

> THEOREM 23 A. *Organisms capable of having their reactions conditioned to perseverative stimulus traces will be able to execute successful defense reactions* (6, p. 22, Theorem VIII).

On the side of positive motivation such as that produced by food need, it is generally true that the shorter the duration of a need, the better is the organism's chance of survival. Thus any mechanism which hastens the attainment of a goal, other things equal, favors survival. This principle of adaptive dynamics, while less dramatic in its action than the avoidance of tissue injury, applies both to approach or *adient* reactions (e.g., seizure of prey) and to flight or *abient* reactions.

But where a continuing stimulus operates there must be a competition among the responses conditioned to it. It follows from Theorem 20 B that in this competition the responses evoked by the recruitment phase of the trace will tend to eliminate by a "short-circuit" responses which were originally in the behavior sequence, because there will not remain in the series any proprioception adequate to evoke the chain in question. Therefore we have part B of Theorem 23:

> B. *Organisms capable of having their reactions reinforced to stimulus traces will manifest the phenomenon of "short-circuiting" behavior sequences* (5, pp. 520, 522).

The theory of the short-circuiting of reactions will be taken up in considerable detail in a subsequent chapter (see pp. 278 ff.). But before we leave this subject even temporarily we must point out that the stimulus trace is by no means the only mechanism which mediates adaptively antedating reactions. One of the more obvious of the additional mechanisms is found in the persisting of *external* stimuli, such as the stimuli arising from the apparatus in conditioning situations. This mechanism brings about antedating reactions in a manner even more obvious than that of the perseverative stimulus trace (7, p. 74). Still a third important mechanism which mediates antedating reactions is the persisting *internal* stimulus associated with a continuing, though diminishing, need (S_D); the practical outcome in this case is substantially the same as that of the continuing external stimulus.

The Dilemma of the Conditioned Defense Reaction

To superficial view the conditioned defense reaction leads to a kind of biological paradox (4, p. 509). In the case of a response leading to food consumption, the act will always be followed by reinforcement and so the reaction potential will be kept up to full strength. In this respect the conditioned defense reaction differs radically. As pointed out above, for a conditioned defense reaction to be wholly successful the movement must occur so early in the sequence that the organism will completely escape injury.

But in case the organism succeeded in escaping the injury there would be no cessation of pain to serve as a reinforcing agent, and repeated reaction without reinforcement would generate experimental extinction (IX D). The consequent cessation or retardation of the reaction due to this weakening would cause a subsequent recurrence of the injury. This in turn would initiate a second cycle substantially like the first, which would be followed by others, a series of successful escapes always alternating with a series of injuries. As an adaptive mechanism such an arrangement clearly would not represent a very high degree of efficiency.

Actually the biological dilemma sketched above is only a half truth. It is probable that organisms under the assumed conditions may tend to go through a cycle or so of this type. Ordinarily, however, these cycles do not go on recurring indefinitely. The stimuli produced by the events uniformly associated with the original reinforcement process acquire the power of secondary reinforcement (ii, *10*). Each relapse tends to strengthen the power of secondary reinforcement until it becomes strong enough to neutralize whatever inhibition is generated by the work (W) involved in the performance of the reaction in question.

Generalizing upon the above considerations, we arrive at our twenty-fourth theorem:

> THEOREM 24. *Organisms which execute antedating defense reactions will tend to display a few escape-injury cycles, but through the support of accumulating secondary reinforcement the escape phases of these cycles will gradually become longer and the injury phases shorter, until soon the reaction tendency will become functionally autonomous* (7, p. 101).

Delay Learning as Discrimination on the Stimulus Trace Continuum

It has been intimated above that the problem of the adaptive timing of reactions is essentially that of synchronizing reactions to the tempo of events in the environment in such a way that the habits involved will receive the maximum amount of reinforcement. We have already seen that adaptation often requires very prompt reaction. There are situations, however, when a too prompt reaction will be unadaptive, i.e., situations that demand a delay in the reaction if it is to be reinforced. We must now consider this problem in some detail, particularly as related to reactions conditioned to perseverative stimulus traces.

Let it be supposed that a reaction (R) has been conditioned to the maximum intensity of 4σ to a perseverative stimulus trace (s′) which has an age of 2″; that all reactions occurring earlier than 2″ are unreinforced (7, p. 258); and that all reactions occurring later than 2″ will be reinforced. The unreinforced reactions will generate extinction effects where t < 2″ (7, pp. 277 ff.), which will generalize upon the excitatory tendencies produced by the reinforcements where t > 2″ (7, p. 264). It is evident from these considerations that we have here essentially a case of separate-presentation simple discrimination learning on the dimension of the perseverative stimulus trace.

Generalizing on the above considerations, we arrive at parts A and B of our twenty-fifth theorem:

THEOREM 25 A. *If the antedating reactions evoked during the setting up of trace conditioned reactions consistently are not followed by reinforcement even at the usual point of reinforcement, this phase of the perseverative stimulus trace will gradually cease evoking reactions, with the result that later phases of the trace will be free to evoke the reaction even though the response will be somewhat weakened; this will therefore be a true delayed trace reaction.*

B. *That phase of the perseverative stimulus trace which is subjected to extinction during the differential reinforcement involved in the setting up of a delayed conditioned trace reaction will acquire conditioned inhibitory characteristics (7, p. 281), resulting in the so-called "inhibition of delay"; and reactions normally evoked by other stimuli will suffer interference if these latter stimuli act during this period of delay.*

If a delayed conditioned trace reaction has been established, a certain amount of inhibition will be set up at that phase of the stimulus trace at which the non-reinforced reactions have occurred, the rise of this inhibition will be gradual, and so the amount of delay in reaction will increase gradually. This gives rise to part C of our theorem:

C. *Where a delay in the evocation of conditioned trace reactions is being set up, the amount of the delay will increase gradually.*

In case the trials are massed, a good deal of spontaneously dissipatible inhibition will be involved in the delay. From this follows part D of Theorem 25:

> D. *If an appreciable pause follows the setting up of a delay on a conditioned perseverative stimulus trace by massed trials, a test subsequent to the pause will show the delay to have partially or wholly disappeared.*

The postulates of the present system imply that if the primary drive is appreciably increased this will tend to over-ride moderate extinction effects (7, pp. 242, 250). Closely analogous effects are known to be produced by the action of caffeine citrate. From these considerations we arrive at our last two parts of Theorem 25:

> E. *If a delay on a conditioned stimulus trace has been achieved, it will be lessened or quite masked by an increase in the primary drive (16, p. 127).*
> F. *If a delay on a conditioned stimulus trace has been achieved, it will be lessened or completely masked by the action of certain substances such as caffeine and benzedrine (16, p. 127; 21).*

The Discrimination of Stimulus-Trace Patterns in Repeated Training Reversals

We now arrive at a fairly complex form of learning which has been known experimentally for a score or so of years but concerning the theory of which much uncertainty exists. Let it be supposed that albino rats are trained in a T-maze with food-reward in the right-hand alley for ten trials at one-minute intervals on the first day, then food reward in the left-hand alley for ten trials at one-minute intervals on the second day, and so on with training reversed each day for twenty or more days. No second choices are permitted the subjects. Several experiments of this general type have been reported (*14; 15*). They reveal a progressively decreasing number of erroneous choices in each block of trials after reversal. Sometimes an animal will perfect the discrimination (*14*), showing only one error after reversal, that on the first trial. How may this degree of reversal type learning be explained?

One reason why reversal learning is so puzzling is that at first sight it *appears* that *all* the bonds acquired one day are reversed the next, and so on indefinitely. This is not true. Moreover, as explained above in detail in a quite different connection (p. 67), and by North in the present connection (*15*, p. 443), as the reversals continue the two short-trace habits and *their opposing extinctions* all tend to become of maximal strength according to the present theory. But as the short-trace habits and their extinctions approach their maximum strengths the net $_s\bar{E}_R$'s of the respective turns will approach zero and the number of trials required to yield a given advantage to either short-trace habit after reversal must increase indefinitely. We are accordingly forced to dismiss the role of ordinary short-trace stimuli as involved in a possible explanation of reversal learning.

As stated above, it is not true that all *stimulus trace combinations* are reversed each day. A little thought on the reader's part will show him that in this experiment there are two combinations of *long* stimulus traces, one or the other of which if followed by a right-hand choice, say, *always* will be reinforced, and an analogous pair of relations *always* holding for the left-hand choice. These four specific cases are all shown in some detail in Table 11.Under the

TABLE 11. The combinations (1) of long stimulus trace conditions and (2) of responses which are always reinforced under the reversal assumptions stated in the text. The cases in Roman numerals at the left apply only to the trace combinations in the middle columns.

Case	One-minute stimulus-trace combination	Always reinforced if followed by the act of:
I	Right-hand turn + food (reinforcement)	a right-hand turn
II	Left-hand turn + no food (frustration)	a right-hand turn
III	Left-hand turn + food (reinforcement)	a left-hand turn
IV	Right-hand turn + no food (frustration)	a left-hand turn

present assumptions cases I or II occur on days 1, 3, 5, etc., and cases III or IV occur on days 2, 4, 6, etc.; cases I and III involve the perseverational stimuli resulting from reinforcement, and cases II and IV involve the perseveration stimuli resulting from reinforcement failures or frustrations.

Next, the reader will clearly understand that two additional principles must operate if this learning reversal is to succeed. The first principle is that the patterning of these stimulus traces depends on afferent interaction (XI). For example, the one-minute trace of a right turn in the maze coupled with the receipt of food (case I) is very different from the one-minute trace of a right turn coupled with no food (case IV). The second principle operating here is that of discrimination learning (Chapter 3). For example, the subject must be able to distinguish the implication of a short (2″) trace of a right turn from that of a long (1′) trace of a right turn; and to distinguish a long trace of a turn to the right coupled with food reinforcement from a long trace of a turn to the right coupled with the frustration of no food. These rather subtle differences are difficult for non-speaking animals to respond to successfully, and it is no wonder that rats and even apes learn the reversals slowly.

Generalizing on the preceding considerations, we arrive at our twenty-sixth theorem:

> THEOREM 26. *Organisms possessing normal afferent interaction and perseverative trace mechanisms and the usual mammalian discrimination powers will learn to reverse learned responses with a progressive saving of errors, with the initial error at a series of trials as the lower limit (cases II and IV).*

The Experimental Validity of the Preceding Theorems

Turning now to the question of the general empirical validity of the above theorems, we find that neurophysiology has not produced any relevant direct evidence regarding Theorem 18. However, there is considerable empirical data available regarding most of the other theorems.

The work of Wolfle (*22*), Reynolds (*17*), and Kimble (*12*) supports the general view that learning is optimal when reinforcement follows the conditioned stimulus by a short half second, and that the gradients at each side proceed by a concave-upward curvature. This fact tends to substantiate Theorem 19 A.

The approximate soundness of Theorem 19 B is shown by the minimum latency value of human reaction to visual stimuli if a little is added to the latency to provide for the time consumed by the physiological response itself. The truth of Theorem 19 C appears to be almost self-evident, even though the relationship seems never before to have been pointed out.

The strong tendency of learned responses to antedate the conditions under which reinforcement occurred has long been known. Rodnick (*18*) reports what purported to be a galvanic skin conditioned-reflex experiment; in this the reaction was conditioned primarily to the trace of a tactual-vibratory stimulus lasting only .18″, which was followed after an interval of 17.4″ by a reinforcing shock also lasting .18″. The modal latency of this rather sluggish response early in the training was 3.0″, though the distribution skewed off to the long latency side even up to 17.0″. The typical distribution of these latencies shows experimentally that almost all of the responses antedated the conditions of reinforcement. This may be seen in Figure 32. Thus Theorem 20, parts A and B, appears to find empirical verification.

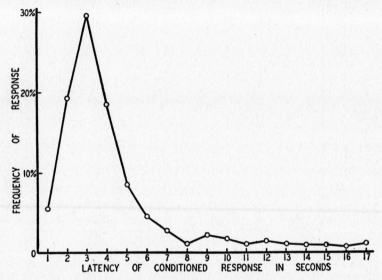

FIGURE 32. The distribution of the first third of the response latencies from five subjects based on what purports to be a trace conditioned galvanic skin reflex conditioned to the trace 17.4 seconds after its initiation. Note the antedating nature of the reactions and their distinctly skewed distribution. Adapted from Rodnick (18, p. 423).

In this connection we may note that at one time it was customary for psychologists working on the phenomena of rote learning (13, pp. 70 ff.) to speak of antedating reactions as *remote forward associations,* and of perseverative reactions as *remote backward associations.* This was before the Pavlovian concepts of stimulus traces and stimulus generalization on stimulus-trace continua as here used were introduced into the theory of rote and compound trial-and-error learning, which reduced both types of "remote" associations substantially to the generalization of *simultaneous* association.

Incidentally the above deduction of perseverative reaction tendencies (Theorem 20 C) serves to supply the lack which John A.
McGeoch pointed out in 1942 when he remarked (*13*, p. 92),
"Neither Hull nor Guthrie has worked out a systematic account of
backward associations in theoretical terms."

We have not been able to find any empirical data bearing directly
on Theorem 21, parts A and B. On the other hand, both forward
and backward generalizations in the case of compound trial-and-
error learning (*8*, p. 126; *9*, p. 21) support Theorem 21 C.

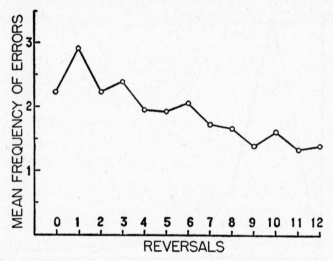

FIGURE 33. Mean frequency of errors in the original learning and on each of numerous reversals on a T-maze. Reproduced by permission of A. J. North (*15*).

In a somewhat similar manner Theorem 21 D is roughly substantiated by Czehura's results, which showed a falling concave-
upward shape (*1*). His "traces," however, sometimes seemed to last
for about a half-minute, and this suggests that some internal motor
response may have been persisting there instead of the trace as
ordinarily conceived. This may also explain why the logarithmic
curvature of Czehura's gradients does not agree with the present
theory.

The fact that ordinarily defense reactions are not repeated in a
clonic manner unless the type of reinforcement which has been
received involves the proprioception of previous responses tends to
substantiate Theorem 22.

The confirmation of Theorem 23, parts A and B, is found in everyday observation, which demonstrates its importance (*5*). Theorem 24 definitely needs a precise experiment to determine its validity in detail.

Theorem 25 A is a well authenticated experimental phenomenon reported by Pavlov (*16*, p. 93). Theorem 25 B is somewhat equivocally substantiated by an experiment reported by Rodnick (*19*). Theorem 25 C appears to be fully substantiated by an experiment reported by Rodnick (*18*), both for delayed and for trace conditioned reflexes. Theorem 25 E is well substantiated by Pavlov (*16*, p. 127). Theorem 25 F was empirically validated regarding the action of caffeine, by Switzer (*21*).

As already indicated, the fact that chimpanzees (*14*) and albino rats (*15*) can learn, though with difficulty, to discriminate repeated training reversals presents empirical verification of Theorem 26. This evidence is represented graphically in Figure 33. It is noteworthy, however, that the learning does not become perceptible until the fourth or fifth reversal.

Summary

Despite the fact that the molar stimulus trace is a theoretical construct, a fairly clear but tentative quantitative postulate regarding its nature has been derived from a few relevant learning data. From this postulate and in association mainly with the principles of stimulus-intensity dynamism and stimulus generalization there have been derived theoretically a number of important behavioral principles, most of which have long been known. Even so, without their theoretical derivation they could hardly be considered as fully understood.

Perhaps the most significant principle peculiarly dependent upon the stimulus trace is the fact that newly learned stimulus-response connections under ordinary circumstances almost invariably evoke the response in advance of the conditions of the reinforcement. This is a valuable biological device in defense reactions and in the seizure of prey. In addition, the movements which originally occurred in the interval thus shortened are dropped out of the behavior sequence, i.e., they are short-circuited. This is adaptive in that it reduces useless energy consumption.

On the other hand, if reinforcement is given by massed repetitions and continued for a considerable length of time with an appreciable and constant delay, inhibition (I_R and $_sI_R$) will develop which will produce a slowing of the reaction latency. Rodnick found that this retardation of the responses in trace galvanic reactions was very much slower in being brought about than in an experiment where the stimulus itself was continuous, i.e., in the delayed conditioned reaction. This may very well be due to the fact that there is a much greater relative fall (change or d) in the intensity of the trace (s′) than in that of the afferent correlate of the continuing stimulus (S).

Under certain circumstances, such as the temporary absence of the customary manipulandum, the response cannot take place completely until various periods of the stimulus trace have passed. In general the theory implies that for a given point of such evocation the more intense the trace, the stronger will be the response, though generalization presumably occurs along the trace as a continuum.

Perhaps our most striking achievement in the deduction of the stimulus trace mechanism is that it explains the ability of non-talking organisms, such as rats and chimpanzees, to learn repeated training reversals.

The trace thus accounts for response evocation by stimuli no longer acting, and largely for the ubiquitous anthropomorphic phenomenon of "expectation." Traces also probably are the main factors involved in the determination of the behavior normally attributed to the rather nebulous concept of "set."

TERMINAL NOTE

THE EXTINCTION OF RESPONSES BASED ON 50 PER CENT
    REINFORCEMENTS

Let it be supposed that a stimulus is conditioned in one group of organisms (*a*) to a response by 30 reinforcements at half-minute intervals and in a comparable group of similar organisms (*b*) by 30 similar reinforcements, interspersed at random by 30 non-reinforcements. At end of the above training both groups are submitted to experimental extinction with trials also at half-minute intervals. It is well known empirically that group *b* will resist experimental extinction better than group *a*. Why should this be?

Apparently the answer lies largely in the role played by the perseverative stimulus traces as presented in the above chapter. In the case of group *a* the response is conditioned to various after-effects of reinforcements, both immediate and remote. In the case of group *b* the response is conditioned to the mixed after-effects of both reinforcements and non-reinforcements, and there will be a tendency for the reinforcements actually to set up connections between the responses and 30-second traces of non-reinforcements themselves. This will naturally oppose the extinction effects of the non-reinforcements interposed among the genuine reinforcements.

Now, consider the extinction process proper: In group *a* it presumably will result in part from the loss of the trace effects of the regular reinforcements which are now replaced by the traces of non-reinforcements. In group *b*, however, the presence of non-reinforcement traces during extinction will not create a very radical change (loss) from the original conditioning; indeed the traces of non-reinforcement, being so closely associated with genuine reinforcements, probably have a mild secondary reinforcing power. On two counts, then, group *b* with its 50 per cent reinforcement should resist experimental extinction better than group *a* with its 100 per cent reinforcement.

On the other hand, if the conditioning of groups *a* and *b* is by trials separated by intervals long enough to permit the traces of the non-reinforcements to dissipate before the next following reinforcement takes place, the latter will not connect the non-reinforcement trace with the response. As a result we should not expect group *b* to resist extinction better than group *a*.

It may be added that since the differential reinforcement utilized in discrimination experiments may involve 50 per cent (or 12½) reinforcement exclusively, it follows that if this process is to be effective, the intervals between the trials should be long enough to permit the after-effects of the non-reinforcements largely to dissipate.

References

1. Czehura, W. S. The generalization of temporal stimulus patterns on the time continuum. *J. Comp. Psychol.*, 1943, *36*, 79–90.

2. Gladstone, A. I., Yamaguchi, H. G., Hull, C. L., and Felsinger, J. M. Some functional relationships of reaction potential and related phenomena. *J. Exper. Psychol.*, 1947, *37*, 510–526.
3. Hilgard, E. R. *Theories of learning.* New York: Appleton-Century-Crofts, Inc., 1948.
4. Hull, C. L. A functional interpretation of the conditioned reflex. *Psychol. Rev.*, 1937, *44*, 498–511.
5. Hull, C. L. Knowledge and purpose as habit mechanisms. *Psychol. Rev.*, 1930, *30*, 511–525.
6. Hull, C. L. Mind, mechanism, and adaptive behavior. *Psychol. Rev.*, 1937, *44*, 1–32.
7. Hull, C. L. *Principles of behavior.* New York: D. Appleton-Century Co., Inc., 1943.
8. Hull, C. L. Reactively heterogeneous compound trial-and-error learning with distributed trials and terminal reinforcement. *J. Exper. Psychol.*, 1947, *37*, 118–135.
9. Hull, C. L. Reactively heterogeneous compound trial-and-error learning with distributed trials and serial reinforcement. *J. Exper. Psychol.*, 1948, *38*, 17–28.
10. Hull, C. L. Behavior postulates and corollaries—1949. *Psychol. Rev.*, 1950, *57*, 173–180.
11. Hull, C. L. *Essentials of behavior.* New Haven: Yale Univ. Press, 1951.
12. Kimble, G. A. Conditioning as a function of the time between conditioned and unconditioned stimuli. *J. Exper. Psychol.*, 1947, *37*, 1–15.
13. McGeoch, J. A. *The psychology of human learning.* New York: Longmans, Green, and Co., 1942.
14. Nissen, H. W., Riesen, A. H., and Nowlis, V. Delayed response and discrimination learning by chimpanzees. *J. Comp. Psychol.*, 1938, *26*, 361–386.
15. North, A. J. Improvement in successive discrimination reversals. *J. Comp. and Physiol. Psychol.*, 1950, *43*, 442–460.
16. Pavlov, I. P. *Conditioned reflexes* (trans. by G. V. Anrep). London: Oxford Univ. Press, 1927.
17. Reynolds, B. The acquisition of a trace conditioned response as a function of the magnitude of the stimulus trace. *J. Exper. Psychol.*, 1945, *35*, 15–30.

18. Rodnick, E. H. Characteristics of delayed and trace conditioned responses. *J. Exper. Psychol.*, 1937, *20*, 409–425.
19. Rodnick, E. H. Does the interval of delay of conditioned responses possess inhibitory properties? *J. Exper. Psychol.*, 1937, *20*, 507–527.
20. Spence, K. W. Theoretical interpretations of learning. Chapter 18 in *Handbook of experimental psychology*, S. S. Stevens, editor. New York: John Wiley and Sons, 1951.
21. Switzer, S. A. The effect of caffeine on experimental extinction of conditioned reactions. *J. Gen. Psychol.*, 1935, *12*, 78–94.
22. Wolfle, H. M. Conditioning as a function of the interval between the conditioned and the original stimulus. *J. Gen. Psychol.*, 1932, *7*, 80–103.

5. Fractional Antedating Goal Reactions

We have shown that stimulus traces presumably serve as generalizing agents, and as such should strongly tend to evoke reactions antedating the conditions of the original action occurrence (Theorem 20, p. 107). We must now note two further related but rather different mechanisms which perform a somewhat similar function of generalization continua—namely, (1) the drive stimulus, S_D (5, pp. 519 ff.), and (2) the sequence of external stimuli, S_1, S_2, S_3, and so on.

Preliminary Considerations Regarding the Antedating Goal Reaction

Consider an organism which is presented with a sequence or chain of external stimuli, S_1, S_2, S_3, S_4, and S_G, and which makes a sequence of responses, R_1, R_2, R_3, R_4, and R_G, where S_G is the food stimulus and R_G is the consummatory response, e.g., that of eating. The organism is assumed to be hungry, so that S_{D_h} will accompany the R_{G_e} or eating response (6, pp. 495 ff.). Now, according to Postulate III, a goal response such as eating is assumed to initiate and accompany the process of diminishing S_D which produces reinforcement.

The preceding considerations show that R_G may be reinforced to the persisting S_D (6, p. 487) and to the rather differently persisting traces of S_1, S_2, S_3, S_4, and S_G. It follows that on a repetition of this sequence there will be a tendency for S_D, together with the traces of S_1, S_2, S_3, and so on, to evoke R_G at the outset of the sequence and more or less continuously throughout it except in so far as there may be a conflict between R_G and the necessary instrumental movements of the sequence, such as R_1, R_2, R_3, and R_4. Presumably in any such situation the instrumental acts would dominate the conflicting portion of the antedating generalized act, permitting the non-conflicting or fractional portion to persist in a covert form. We shall represent this non-conflicting part of R_G by r_G. For this reason such assumed persistence (r_G) is called the *fractional* antedating goal reaction.

There are several points to observe in regard to this fractional antedating goal-reaction concept. The first thing is that its origin requires r_G to be intimately associated with the attainment of goals, i.e., with reinforcements. But the association with reinforcements is known to set up the power of secondary reinforcements (ii).

Generalizing on the above considerations, we arrive at Corollary xv (already given in Chapter 1):

Corollary xv

> *When a stimulus (S) or a stimulus trace (s) acts at the same time that a hitherto unrelated response (R) occurs and this coincidence is accompanied by an antedating goal reaction (r_G), the secondary reinforcing powers of the stimulus evoked by the latter (s_G) will reinforce S to R, giving rise to a new S $\dashrightarrow$ R dynamic connection.*

The second point to observe in regard to r_G is that such a response presumably produces a continuous stimulus which is characteristic of the consumption of the goal substance (K) throughout the behavior series of which it is a part. We shall call this the *fractional goal stimulus* (s_G). A third point is that the different drive stimuli (S_D) differentiate the various needs and guide the behavior to their realization to some extent, but the goal stimuli (s_G), because of their infinite variety, constitute a wealth of stimuli leading to such guidance. A fourth important characteristic of such fractional antedating goal reactions is that in the behavior sequence here assumed, when the fractional goal reaction is evoked at S_4 it is called forth by generalization on four traces (from S_1, S_2, S_3, and S_4); at S_3 it is evoked by generalization on three traces (from S_1, S_2, and S_3); at S_2 it is evoked by generalization on two traces (S_1 and S_2); and at S_1 it is evoked by generalization on only one trace (S_1).

Reaction Potential as a Function (J) of the Delay in Receiving the Incentive[1]

When stimuli such as S_1, S_2, S_3, and S_4 are consistently followed by a reinforcing state of affairs (R_G), their traces will acquire the capacity to evoke r_G with its secondary reinforcing powers. This implies that S_1 will acquire the power to evoke R_1, i.e., $S_1 \dashrightarrow R_1$, $S_2 \dashrightarrow R_2$, $S_3 \dashrightarrow R_3$, $S_4 \dashrightarrow R_4$, and $S_G \dashrightarrow R_G$. But, as pointed out above (p. 125), the r_G decreases in strength from S_4 to S_1, in that order, which presumably means that its reinforcing power decreases from S_4 to S_1. It follows that $S_G \dashrightarrow R_G$, $S_4 \dashrightarrow R_4$, $S_3 \dashrightarrow R_3$, $S_2 \dashrightarrow R_2$, and $S_1 \dashrightarrow R_1$ will decrease in strength from the point of reinforcement backward to the beginning of the sequence. Now, the generalization on a subsident trace toward its maximum intensity is relatively horizontal on the whole, but with a sharp reduction as the maximum trace is approached (Figure 31, Chapter 4). But this progressive decrease of the relatively horizontal generalization effect in question will produce a gradient which slopes downward in intensity from S_G to S_1 with a marked concave-upward curvature. This is the substance of the principle of the *gradient of reinforcement within a given reaction chain* (type A) (*8*, p. 135).

Generalizing from the preceding considerations we arrive at part A of Corollary iii (already given in Chapter 1):

Corollary iii

> A. *The greater the delay in reinforcement of a link within a given behavior chain, the weaker will be the resulting reaction potential of the link in question to the stimulus traces present at the time.*

Corollary iii A shows that the delay in reinforcement within a continuous sequence of reactions tends to generate a chain of responses, which manifests a progressively diminishing reaction potential from the point of reinforcement back to the link farthest removed from the reception of the incentive. We must now note that there is a case roughly parallel to this in which (1) but a single $S \dashrightarrow R$ connection is involved, (2) the delay in primary reinforcement varies from one experimental situation to another, and (3)

---

[1] The symbol J was originally used to represent a postulate (*8*, p. 178), but it is now regarded as derivable from other postulates of the set. However, even though derived, the symbol is retained to represent the same general function of the effects of delay in receiving the incentive (K').

the organism does nothing in particular through chain reactions or otherwise during the delay. It is *this non-chaining case of the gradient of reinforcement* which we shall now consider in some detail.

As pointed out in the first part of this chapter, both S_D and the stimulus trace presumably become attached to r_G. We shall accordingly take up the stimulus-trace factor alone in this section. If later S_D is proved experimentally to have this sort of power to an appreciable extent, the theoretical consideration of the two may then be combined ($+$).

Since the detailed quantitative theory of the delay in reinforcement of single responses is both very new and very complex, we proceed to its elaboration with considerable uncertainty. The importance of opening the problem to the consideration of behavior scientists, however, is great enough to warrant the effort even at the risk of making some errors. Incidentally it is encouraging to observe that a few writers (*19*; *20*; *16*) have already suggested the general idea which we shall advance. Spence first proposed the basic notion that the fractional antedating goal reaction would generalize on the continuum of the stimulus trace. From this the present theory has been developed. First we shall sketch the theory in a preliminary qualitative manner and then proceed to a detailed quantitative derivation.

Let it be supposed that a hungry albino rat is presented at hourly intervals with a response-bar in a Skinner-box situation, and that each time the animal makes a bar-pressing response (R) to the smell of food on the bar a delay of 4″ elapses before it receives the food reward (K′). Simultaneously with the animal's reception of the food the goal reaction of eating (r_G) occurs and becomes primarily reinforced to the stimulus trace left by the apparatus and response stimuli. This trace appears after a brief recruitment phase of a short half second, and then proceeds abruptly into a relatively protracted subsident phase during which it decays to zero. In 4″ it will diminish to a comparatively small value. Our working hypothesis is that the strength of the associated r_G is a positive function of the magnitude of the stimulus trace to which it is attached. This is one factor in weakening the response (R) when the reward is delayed. Each time the apparatus is presented to the subject after its reinforcement to r_G the trace will tend to evoke the r_G throughout its earlier or stronger sections by stimulus-trace generalization, i.e., in close temporal proximity to R. This ante-dating evocation of r_G naturally produces an antedating s_G. Now since s_G is intimately associated with primary reinforcement, e.g., eating, it will acquire the power of secondary reinforcement (xvi). But the greater the delay in reinforcement, the weaker will be the generalized r_G, the weaker the s_G, and consequently the weaker the secondary reinforcement between S, the apparatus stimulus, and R, the response. Presumably the generalization is based on $_sH_R$ and the response, r_G, is evoked by the junction of $_s\bar{H}_R$ and the D which is always present. This is a rough qualitative outline of the theory of the present gradient of reinforcement of a response as a function of its delay.

Having before us the qualitative substance of the single-link gradient of reinforcement, we may now proceed to a more detailed development of the theory, this time in a numerical quantitative manner. Perhaps the best way to do this is to present at once the basic assumed equation,

$$J = {}_sE_{R_d} = D \times K \times V_2 \times {}_sH_R \times 10^{-.15d} \times V_1 \qquad (9)$$

where
$$D = 5.17142$$
$$K = .98745$$
$$V_2 = .95214$$
$${}_sH_R = .97$$
$$d = 2.81034$$
$$V_1 = .17482.$$

Now according to the present hypothesis two fairly distinct reaction potentials are involved here: (1) that of the goal reaction ($_sE_{r_G}$), and (2) that of the instrumental or bar-pressing reaction ($_sE_R$); D, K, and H are common to both reactions and function in both jointly to produce the J result. As an explanatory detail it may be stated that V_1 is supposed to operate only on the goal reaction potential ($_sE_{r_G}$) generalizing on the stimulus trace, and the V_2 is supposed to operate only in the production of the final or instru-mental act ($_sE_R$) of pressing the bar, though this makes no differ-ence in the result since the whole of equation 9 is multiplicative. The detailed theoretical computations of the entire gradient are shown in Table 12. In order that the reader may understand this table we shall now trace in some detail the computational process

TABLE 12. Theoretical derivation of the reaction potentials where the incentive (K′) reinforcement is delayed varying lengths of time following the coincidence of the response and the maximum of the stimulus trace. Rows 1, 2, and 6 are taken from Table 10.

	0.00	0.05	0.2	0.5	1.0	1.5	2.0	3.0	4.0	5.0
1 Time of wait since trace maximum (t') in seconds										
2 Stimulus trace intensity (S')	1000.0	144.51	37.371	14.339	6.8571	4.4419	3.2619	2.1693	1.5476	1.2169
3 Log S'	3.00000	2.15990	1.57253	1.15652	.83614	.64757	.51347	.32414	.18966	.08525
4 d	.00000	.84010	1.42747	1.84348	2.16386	2.35243	2.48653	2.67586	2.81034	2.91475
5 $10^{-.15d}$	1.00000	.74813	.61077	.52902	.47361	.44375	.42366	.39685	.37884	.36542
6 V_1	.95214	.88789	.79672	.69016	.57135	.48111	.40561	.27992	.17482	.08274
7 $J = s\bar{E}R_d$	4.49054	3.13280	2.29496	1.72196	1.27620	1.00687	.81043	.52395	.31235	.14257

where the delay in reinforcement is assumed to have been 4″ as already suggested.

One of the most complicated computations concerns the generalization of $_s\bar{E}_{r_G}$ along the stimulus trace. In the first place there are involved two stimulus traces: (1) that of the apparatus stimuli and (2) that of the proprioception of the response (R). The bar-pressing response must always follow the presentation of the apparatus stimuli by varying amounts of time, since R occurs more or less by chance. This means that the two stimulus traces will differ in strength by varying amounts on different occasions. Since we know very little quantitatively about stimulus-trace generalization we shall consider only one trace, or a kind of composite of the two. Both traces presumably reach their maximum strength a short half second after their respective physical stimulations. It follows that at 4″ after R occurs this trace is only about 3.5″ from its maximum, and the trace of the visual apparatus stimuli will have varying amounts of strength more than 3.5″ from *its* maximum. We shall accordingly assume that the maximum strength of the two traces will fall on the average at about the time R occurs, or 4″ from the time of the receipt of the incentive (K′).

The first time the food reinforcement occurs the apparatus trace will have fallen from 1000.0 units (Table 12, line 2, column 1) to 1.5476 units (Table 12, line 2, column 9). This means that the reaction potential thus set up will be between the goal reaction (r_G) of eating and the greatly enfeebled stimulus-trace element. On the next trial (one hour later) we may expect a *new* event to occur, namely, the generalization of the habit function involved. According to equation 21 this may be expressed as,

$$_{s_2}H_r = {}_{s_1}H_r 10^{-.15d} \tag{21}$$

where $d = \log \dot{S}_2'' - \log \dot{S}_1''$. By Table 12, line 3, $\log \dot{S}_2' = 3.00000$ and $\log \dot{S}_1' = .18966$. Accordingly

$$d = 3.00000 - .18966 = 2.81034.$$

Substituting this value for d in equation 21 and solving we have the function,

$$10^{-.15 \times 2.81034} = .37884,$$

which appears in line 5, column 9.

At this point we introduce V_1, which was computed from S' (at 4″ delay, column 9) by means of equation 6. This yields .17482 as shown in row 6, column 9. It is assumed that $_sH_{r_G}$ is dependent on the stimulus-intensity dynamism of the trace to which it is reinforced. This accounts for the presence of V_1 in equation 9.[2]

Finally, substituting in equation 9 the computed results shown in Table 12, we have

$$J = {_s\underline{E}_{R_d}} = 5.17142 \times .98745 \times .95214 \times .97 \times .37884$$
$$\times .17482 = .31235, \quad (47)$$

which is the theoretical amount of the reaction potential under conditions of delay. This is the value we have been seeking. In

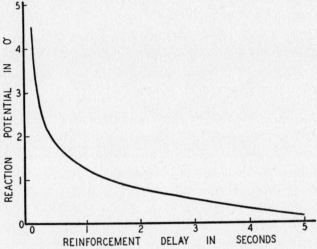

FIGURE 34. Graphical representation of a theoretical gradient as a function (J) of he delay in reinforcement. Plotted from the final line of values in Table 12.

Table 12 it appears in row 7, column 9. The remaining values in this table were calculated in an exactly analogous manner.

We secure a representation of the theoretical gradient of reinforcement as a function of the several delays, given in the first values of the ten columns in Table 12, by plotting the final values of the same columns. This is shown as Figure 34. It is particularly

[2] In case it is decided that V_1 does not belong in equation 9, the generalization of $_sH_R$ alone (row 5) will produce a delay-of-reinforcement gradient which agrees very well with empirical fact even though it may not be quite the same shape as Figure 34. One reason for assuming that $_sH_R$ has a characteristic such as $_sE_R$ is that it presumably comes from the act r_G, which itself involves its own reaction potential.

to be observed that each of these final delay values represents a determination with a distinct group of comparable subjects. This must be sharply distinguished from the situation considered in Corollary iii A in that the latter involves the dynamics of behavior chains (Chapter 6) in which each subject or each trial undergoes all the delays of the experiment; in the case involved here the subject supposedly does little or nothing but wait for food during a specific period of delay.

These and related considerations bring us to our next theorem, which, because of the great amount of use which it will serve, we shall call a corollary. (This also was given in Chapter 1.)

Corollary iii

B. *The greater the delay in the receipt of the incentive by groups of learning subjects, the weaker will be the resulting learned reaction potentials* ($_s\underline{E}_{R_d}$), *the shape of the gradient as a function of the respective delays being roughly that of decay with the lower limit of the extended gradient passing beneath the reaction threshold, i.e.,*

$$J = {}_s\underline{E}_{R_d} = D \times K \times V_2 \times {}_sH_R \times 10^{-.15d} \times V_1 \quad (9)$$

where

$$d = \log \underset{.}{S}' \text{ of } V_2 - \log \underset{.}{S}' \text{ of } V_1.$$

It happens that a great deal of excellent experimental work is available bearing on the validity of Corollaries iii A and iii B. The information regarding iii A comes from behavior chains (Chapter 6). This evidence suggests strongly that the chain gradients of delay in reinforcement presumably fall less as a maximum and are of much gentler slope than are those generated by single S $\dashrightarrow$ R delays. Corollary iii A accordingly has ample empirical verification. Studies by Wolfe (*25*), Perin (*14*), Perkins (*15*), and Grice (*3*), among others, show the limiting effect on the final reaction potential of the delay in reinforcement and the general shape of the curve. Accordingly it may be said that Corollary iii B also has received substantial empirical verification.

Even so neither theory has yet been verified in detail. Most of the type iii B delay-in-reinforcement gradients that have been published have a slightly different curvature from that shown in Figure 34; this is particularly noticeable at the lower extreme, which usually tends to become more horizontal at the asymptote. One of Perin's curves, however, has a shape much like Figure 34 (*8*, p. 139).

Recent experimental studies, especially several emanating from the University of Iowa laboratory, show that as greater care is taken to avoid secondary reinforcement from the apparatus situation the fall in the gradient becomes progressively more rapid; i.e., the length of the gradient is related to the amount of reinforcement which is present. For example, Wolfe's gradient (1934) was reported in terms of minutes, whereas the curves reported by Perin and by Spence's students (1946–1950) were in terms of a few seconds only as is the gradient shown in Figure 34. In this respect, also, the deduction is, accordingly, supported by recent experimentation.

As may easily be seen, there are in the foregoing situation (iii B) numerous postulated factors and many uncertainties yet to be clarified jointly by experiment and by systematic interpretation of theory; from which we conclude that these deductions must be considered no more than first approximations. Since the amount of $_sE_R$ (according to equation 9 as worked out in Table 12) involves the product of six different values, the detailed relationship is left uncertain. The author's previous writings on this subject suggest that the asymptote of each learning curve is limited by the amount of delay, and follows a course approximately according to that shown in Figure 34. On the other hand, certain investigators (e.g., Seward, *16*) seem to attribute the delay in reinforcement to motivation. Problems of this type are exceedingly difficult to solve experimentally because $_sH_R$ presumably can never be observed behaviorally apart from $_sE_R$, D, K, and the rest. Actually this may mean that it is impossible to determine just how each of the five values represented in equation 9 is related to the gradient of reaction potential as a function of the delay in reinforcement, because basically the question may turn out to be a false one.

The Realization of an Anticipation and Its Frustration

When $r_G \dashrightarrow s_G$ leads to $S_G \dashrightarrow R_G$, i.e., when the anticipation of food leads to the actual eating of the food, we have what we shall call the *realization of an anticipation*. It is evident that under these circumstances the strength of the connection between the trace and r_G, and that between s_G and the preliminary movements leading to R_G, will be further increased.

But what will happen if, after the habit is established, the anticipation is not realized; if the anticipated food is not found as
previously? Clearly, the absence of S_G, the major stimulus component, will eventually terminate the goal behavior formerly
evoked by s_G, and the acts involved in an effort to realize the
anticipation will generate I_R, which will tend to inhibit them.
This termination is what is known as *experimental extinction*. But
before the extinction may be considered complete, generalization
from somewhat similar situations which have been reinforced
after a little delay will produce a considerably stronger series of
the subgoal reaction with wider variations, such as those involved
in searching behavior. These more aggressive reactions will be
accompanied by internal (emotional) secretions, but in the end
they will receive no reinforcement and the inhibitions conditioned
to them will accumulate in amounts greater than the reaction
potential; the extinction may then be said to be complete. Since
the process of conditioning the inhibition to s_G is one of learning, the
resulting quantitative outcome of experimental extinction is shown
substantially as an ordinary learning curve, sometimes with a little
initial rise in $_sE_R$ due to emotion (D).

Generalizing on the preceding considerations, we arrive at our
next major conclusion:

Corollary xvii

> *On the abrupt cessation of the customary reinforcement of a previously
> learned act, the repeated presentation of the evoking stimuli will for a
> time (1) continue to evoke the act, (2) sometimes with at first a slight
> rise in reaction potential, (3) followed by a progressive fall in reaction
> potential, which (4) is the reverse of a positive learning curve.*[3]

Although the fact of experimental extinction has been known
in a common-sense way since time out of mind, Pavlov (*13*) was
the first to establish the phenomenon on an empirical level.

There is still another superficially paradoxical case which is
explained by the anticipatory mechanism. This is the fact that if
an animal is systematically and uniformly rewarded *after* the num-

---

[3] This corollary represents an attempt to derive a part of Postulates IX A and IX D.
The presence of postulates and a corollary concerning the same subject illustrates the
transitional stage in which behavior theory finds itself at present.

ber of unrewarded acts is gradually increased, it may be taught to do a great deal of work for quite a small reward. In this case the stimulus of repeated failure leads to an anticipated reward (r_G) which counteracts to a large extent the influence of the accumulating I_R. The point is that unless a very great deal of work (W) is involved the $_sI_R$ appears not completely to counteract the effect of the r_G which accompanies each non-reinforced response, because

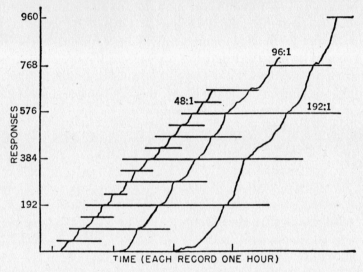

FIGURE 35. Graphic record of a rat trained to work on the basis of various ratios of unreinforced to reinforced acts. Plotted from Skinner's published data. Reproduced from Keller and Schoenfeld (*9*, p. 95).

the traces of these responses are always reinforced in a major way at the end of the sequence. Apparently the reason experimental extinction takes place so easily when non-reinforcement first begins to occur consistently is that r_G has not been given a chance to become attached to the traces of stimuli produced by non-reinforcement. This is of course a sound biological economy.

Generalizing on the preceding considerations, we arrive at our next theorem:

THEOREM 27. *In case an animal is taught an act through a given reinforcement and then is given a gradually increasing series of non-reinforced massed response evocations always followed at once by primary reinforcement, the* r_G *will become attached to the traces of these*

non-reinforcements in such a way as to reinforce them, largely neutral-
izing the I_R *accumulating and thus permitting very long primarily*
unreinforced behavior series to occur.

Experimental work bearing on the validity of Theorem 27 has
been reported, especially by Skinner (*18*). He states that a single rat
was gradually shifted from learning to give a series of eight unreinforced responses before receiving one reinforcement up to a maximum ratio of 192 unreinforced responses to one reinforcement! A
graphic record of this animal's behavior is shown in Figure 35. Theorem 27 appears to have found a convincing empirical verification.

It should be observed that the traces from the various responses
become reinforced to R_G at the end of a fixed number of acts. As
pointed out above (Corollary iii A), this gradient of generalization
slopes downward from the reinforcement to the beginning as a
concave-upward slope.

From the preceding considerations, we arrive at our next
theorem:

THEOREM 28. *When an organism has become accustomed to making
a number of unreinforced responses to one reinforcement in a fixed
ratio continuously, the responses will start out relatively slowly and
will increase in rapidity with a positive acceleration, reaching a maximum at the point of reinforcement.*

It happens that the Skinner data plotted as Figure 35 also
illustrates this theorem very nicely. Each of the three records presented consists of a series of these gradient-of-reinforcement curves
between the successive horizontal lines. Thus Theorem 28 appears
to find empirical verification.

Two Double-Drive Learning Situations

There is much reason to believe that the internal drive stimulus
(S_D) in hunger differs from that in thirst. For example, in the Hull-
Leeper experiments (*7; 12*) albino rats learned after varying
amounts of training to turn to the right, say (R_{Rt}), around a maze
rectangle when hungry (S_{D_h}) but not thirsty, and to turn the
opposite way (R_{Lt}) around the rectangle when thirsty (S_{D_t}) but not
hungry. The first situation may be represented fairly adequately
for this purpose by,

$$S_{D_h} \dashrightarrow R_{Rt}$$

and the second by,

$$S_{D_t} \dashrightarrow R_{Lt}.$$

The point is that each stimulus is associated with the evocation of a different turning response, and since only one of the stimuli was present at a time there should be a tendency for the associated response only to occur on any given test occasion. No doubt the antedating goal reaction enters into the situation but this expository complexity need not be considered at this time. (See p. 139.)

The above symbolic representation of the presumptive partial dynamics of the situation serves fairly well to explain the phenomena resulting from this particular experimental arrangement, but it would be an easy matter to set up an experiment which could *not* be explained in this simple manner. For example, let it be assumed that an albino rat when *both* hungry and thirsty is placed in a simple T-maze. If the animal turns right (R_{Rt}) to that arm of the maze, it finds food and eats; if it turns left (R_{Lt}) into that arm of the maze, it finds water and drinks. By analogy of the preceding analysis, S_{D_h} and S_{D_t} will *both* be attached to R_{Rt} and R_{Lt}. So far as this mechanism alone goes, when the animal later enters the maze hungry but not thirsty the S_{D_h} alone will tend to evoke both R_{Rt} and R_{Lt}. And similarly, when the animal is thirsty but not hungry the S_{D_t} alone will tend to evoke both R_{Rt} and R_{Lt}. The result will be:

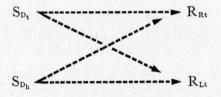

i.e., on this assumption alone both stimuli will evoke both responses. In other words, the preceding type of analysis furnishes no presumption that the hungry organism will tend to choose the right arm of the T more frequently than the left arm, or that the thirsty organism will tend to choose the left arm more frequently than the right arm.

However, Spence, Bergmann, and Lippitt (*20*) have made a rather different theoretical analysis of this experimental situation, which seems to avoid the above difficulties. They suggest that the fractional antedating goal reaction enters the situation, changing its dynamics quite radically:

1. The organism, both hungry and thirsty, turns into the right arm of the T, finds food there, and eats it.

2. As a result of this the stimulus traces of these events, notably of looking right at choice point x of the $T(s_{x_R})$ and beyond, will be reinforced to the eating or goal responses (r_{G_e}), i.e.,

$$S_{x_R} \dashrightarrow r_{G_e}.$$

3. On subsequent occasions the fractional antedating goal response (r_{G_e}) will be drawn forward to S_{x_R} and earlier.

4. Because of this the combination of the trace of S_{x_R} (i.e., s_{x_R} looking to the right) and s_{G_e} (eating) will always be reinforced to the right-turning response (R_{Rt}), i.e.,

$$\left. \begin{array}{c} s_{x_R} \\ s_{G_e} \end{array} \right\} \dashrightarrow R_{Rt}.$$

5. Similarly the trace of s_{x_L} (looking to the left at choice point x) and s_{G_d} (drinking) will be reinforced to the left-turning response (R_{Lt}), i.e.,

$$\left. \begin{array}{c} s_{x_L} \\ s_{G_d} \end{array} \right\} \dashrightarrow R_{Lt}.$$

6. Now during the past life of the organism, S_{D_h} and S_{D_t} have usually not been equal, and upon the whole the animal has been accustomed to eat when hungry and drink when thirsty.

7. By Corollary xii, responses will show a falling generalization from a great to a small or zero S_D, so that the effective reaction potential of each drive to its own consummatory goal reaction will be stronger than to that of the other drive.

8. Therefore, at the beginning of this experiment, $S_{D_h} \dashrightarrow r_{G_e} > S_{D_h} \dashrightarrow r_{G_d}$.

9. It accordingly follows that even though during this brief experiment S_{D_h} and S_{D_t} have been reinforced to both r_{G_e} and r_{G_d}, the effects of the previous inequalities will survive to some extent.

10. Therefore when on the test S_{D_h} alone is given,

$$S_{D_h} \dashrightarrow r_{G_e} > S_{D_h} \dashrightarrow r_{G_d},$$

i.e., under these test conditions,

$$S_{G_e} > S_{G_d}.$$

11. It follows from 4, 10, and Postulate VI that

$$\left.\begin{array}{c} S_{x_R} \\ S_{D_h} \\ S_{G_e} \end{array}\right\} \dashrightarrow R_{Rt} > \left.\begin{array}{c} S_{x_R} \\ S_{D_h} \\ S_{G_e} \end{array}\right\} \dashrightarrow R_{Lt},$$

i.e., under these conditions $R_{Rt} > R_{Lt}$.

12. Similarly, it follows from 5 and similar reasoning that,

$$\left.\begin{array}{c} S_{x_L} \\ S_{D_t} \\ S_{G_d} \end{array}\right\} \dashrightarrow R_{Lt} > \left.\begin{array}{c} S_{x_L} \\ S_{D_t} \\ S_{G_d} \end{array}\right\} \dashrightarrow R_{Rt},$$

i.e., under these conditions $R_{Lt} > R_{Rt}$.

13. From 11 and 12 it follows that the organism, after such train-ing and when subject to only one need (within the limits of the oscillation function), will tend to go directly to the arm of the maze where it has been accustomed to receive temporary release from the cravings it has at the time and so receive reinforcement.

Generalizing on the preceding considerations, we arrive at our next theorem:

THEOREM 29. *If an organism has two drives operating and is repeat-edly in a situation where one or the other drive stimulus may be rein-forced by a distinct series of movements, it will later, when only one of the drives is operating, at once tend to perform the movements which formerly led to the reduction of the S_D in question.*

There is a single experiment bearing on the theoretical deduction just given, that of Kendler (*10*). As a matter of fact, the present author used this experiment as a kind of target at which the theory was aimed. Actually the theoretical conclusion agrees very well with Kendler's empirical findings. He reports that on the test under each of the single drives his animals turned in the direction of the appropriate reinforcing agent a statistically reliable number of times.

And now, after the preceding discussion of the second double-drive problem, we may return to the first (Hull-Leeper) problem with our new analysis and a more adequate, though not a simpler, statement of the theoretical outcome. On the analogy of the inequality shown in step #11 of the preceding deduction, we can now state for the first double-drive problem:

$$\left. \begin{array}{c} S_{D_h} \\ S_{G_e} \end{array} \right\} \dashrightarrow R_{Rt} > \left. \begin{array}{c} S_{D_h} \\ S_{G_e} \end{array} \right\} \dashrightarrow R_{Lt},$$

i.e., in respect to $_sE_R$ under *these* circumstances.

$$R_{Rt} > R_{Lt}.$$

And on the analogy of the inequality #12 of the preceding deduction we may state:

$$\left. \begin{array}{c} S_{D_t} \\ S_{G_d} \end{array} \right\} \dashrightarrow R_{Lt} > \left. \begin{array}{c} S_{D_t} \\ S_{G_d} \end{array} \right\} \dashrightarrow R_{Rt},$$

i.e., in respect to $_sE_R$ under *these* conditions,

$$R_{Lt} > R_{Rt}.$$

The fact that both Hull's and Leeper's rats learned to discriminate hunger from thirst stimuli amply substantiates Theorem 29. Also it is likely that the more rapid learning by Leeper's technique was due to the reinforcing effect of $r_G \rightarrow s_G$ which presumably was evoked in a mild form by the animals' seeing the food when not hungry and seeing the water when not thirsty. This leads us to the consideration of latent learning.

Latent Learning in Theoretical Perspective

Among other scientific values which the fractional antedating goal reaction appears to have is the fact that it permits an understanding of some of the elusive phenomena concerned with latent learning. But before we go into that matter it may be well to consider as a useful background the theoretical aspects of the more general question of manifest and latent reaction potential. Let us take for expository purposes an earlier and simpler form of equation 8 (Postulate X),

$$_sE_R = D \times K \times {_sH_R}. \tag{48}$$

Suppose that in this situation (equation 48) $D = 0$, $K = .9$, and $_sH_R = .6126$. Substituting these values, we have:

$$_sE_R = 0.$$

The point is that the considerable learning represented by $_sH_R$ = .6126 would not be evident in the behavior of the organism as $_sE_R$, i.e., this $_sH_R$ would be *latent*. On the other hand, if D = 3.105 we should have:

$$_sE_R = 3.105 \times .9 = .6126$$
$$= 1.7119,$$

which is an appreciable reaction potential. Now the influence of the $_sH_R$ has become *manifest* as contrasted with its previous latency.

Or suppose we have the D and $_sH_R$ values as just assumed but K = 0, i.e.,

$$_sE_R = 3.105 \times 0 = .6126$$
$$= 0.$$

Once again, but for a quite different reason, the $_sH_R$ becomes latent, though when the K = .9 is restored it becomes manifest as in the computation presented just above.

The early experimental studies of latent learning tended to consider the modifications in learning curves caused by an abrupt shift from a relatively slight reward, what we would now call a secondary reinforcement, to a fairly large reward. As just shown it is an easy matter theoretically to represent these shifts of both the drive (D) and the incentive (K) functions. Because of their more central significance in the present historical problem, we shall here consider only shifts from smaller to larger incentives, rewards, or reinforcing (K') agents and the reverse. This is a complex process and must be elaborated.

In connection with the shift in the quantity of the incentive during or at the completion of the learning we note that there are at least three processes involved. The first is implicit in Postulate VII. In this process the permanent response intensity varies with the magnitude of the incentive according to equation 7. The second process may be called the *Crespi effect*, because it was Crespi who first clearly demonstrated its existence and general nature (2). Through this effect, when the incentive changes from that operative during the particular learning, the corresponding response intensity (or latency) not only shifts upward or downward as implied in equation 7, but both sorts of response shifts are in excess of the permanent response intensities called for by equation 7. The third effect associated with shifts in incentive is that the

permanent response change itself is a rather rapid asymptotic
learning process requiring about four trials for its approximate
completion. These points are shown with admirable clearness by
Crespi's graphs which are reproduced as Figure 36. Unfortunately
there are two matters which Crespi's experiment does not clarify:
the questions of (1) whether the excess shift effect is temporary or

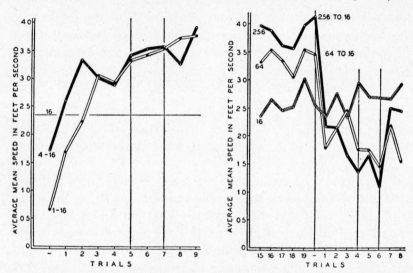

FIGURE 36. Curves showing the Crespi incentive-shift effects; left, the upward shift
to 16 units of food from still lower values and right, the downward shift to 16 units of
food from still higher values. The small numbers 1, 4, 16, 64 and 256 indicate the number of fiftieth grams of incentive involved. Note the positive incentive shift effect in
excess of the original 16-unit level at the left, and the negative effect falling below the
original 16-unit level at the right. Adapted from Crespi (2, p.508).

permanent, and (2) which shift effect the rapid supplementary
learning applies to. Following Crespi, we take the position that the
excess shift effect is an emotional response and therefore temporary.
We assume that this learning, both positive and negative, is at the
rate of 80 per cent on each trial,[4] whereas the ordinary rate of
maze learning is here assumed to be at the rate of 10 per cent on
each trial. This means that with continued stimulation the excess
shift effect will soon reverse itself, returning to the presumably
normal effect of equation 7. All of these conclusions are, of course,
subject to empirical verification.

[4] This assumption has the status of a distinct postulate. Through an oversight it was
not listed in Chapter 1.

Because of the foregoing considerations and the fact that Crespi's effect seems not to appear in maze learning, we shall now ignore this matter completely and proceed to the deduction of the permanent transition of the incentive upward at $N = 10$. The value of the lower incentive (K) is taken as .6, whereas that of the upper is taken as .9, the difference being .3. Multiplying this difference by .8 per trial, the new incentive factor on increase, we have .24. This added to the .6 previously used amounts to .6 + .24 = .84. In addition, the value of $_sH_R$ has shifted to .6862 at $N = 11$. It will be recalled that here the value of D is 3.105. Substituting all these values in our modified $_sE_R$ equation 48, we have *after* the tenth trial and *before* the eleventh trial,

$$_sE_R = 3.105 \times .84 \times .6862 \times 1.789.$$

Similarly, the next $_sH_R = .7176$ and the new K obtained by an analogous procedure amounts to .888. Substituting in equation 48 again we have, after the eleventh trial and before the twelfth trial,

$$_sE_R = 3.105 \times .888 \times .7176 = 1.977,$$

and after the twelfth trial but before the thirteenth,

$$_sE_R = 3.105 \times .8976 \times .7458 = 2.077.$$

This value of 2.077 deviates only $.0004\sigma$ from the value which would have resulted had an incentive value of .9 been used from the beginning, and is far too small a difference to be detected by empirical methods now available. Exactly analogous computations were made for a second shift of the incentive upward from .6 to .9 at $N = 20$, and with exactly analogous results. The theoretical results of these shifts are represented graphically in Figure 37.

The procedure in the case of the *downward* shifting of incentive, while exactly analogous, differs in some of its details because the learning in this case consists in a progressive *decrease* in the K value from .9 to .6. The difference in K as before is .9 − .6 = .3, and .3 × .8 = .24. This is *subtracted* from .9, i.e., .9 − .24 = .66. The value of $_sH_R$ at $N = 16$ is .8147, while D is the same as before. Substituting in equation 48, we have:

$$_sE_R = 3.105 \times .66 \times .8147 = 1.6696.$$

Similarly, where N = 17,

$$_sE_R = 3.105 \times .612 \times .8332 = 1.5834;$$

where N = 18,

$$_sE_R = 3.105 \times .6024 \times .8499 \times 1.5897;$$

and where N = 19,

$$_sE_R = 3.105 \times .60048 \times .8649 = 1.6126.$$

In this series of computations, despite the fact that the value of the K component progressively decreases, the $_sE_R$ values at N = 18 and 19 progressively increase because of the increase in N and so

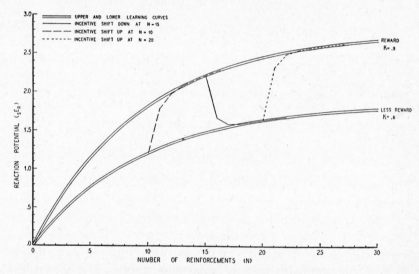

FIGURE 37. Graphs showing the theoretical permanent transition from one incentive to another, both upward and downward during the process of learning. The transitions at N = 10 and N = 20 show a shift upward; the one at N = 15 shows a shift downward. Other things constant, the larger the value of N at the time of the shift in K, apparently the greater will be the resulting change in reaction potential.

of $_sH_R$, though the approach to the standard reaction potential curve is still $.0004\sigma$ smaller than that resulting from the shift; this value is, of course, far smaller than could be secured by ordinary experimental procedures or graphical representation. The preceding computations are shown graphically in Figure 37.

Generalizing on these considerations, we arrive at our next theorem:

THEOREM 30. *Other things constant, an abrupt shift in the incentive used during a maze-learning process will be followed first by a major shift in reaction potential and then by two or more progressively smaller shifts on successive trials, the series constituting a rapid learning process of the exponential variety, culminating in the course that the $_sE_R$ would have followed had the new incentive been operating continuously from the beginning of the learning.*

We are fortunate in having several excellent empirical investigations bearing on the soundness of the present corollary. In a classical

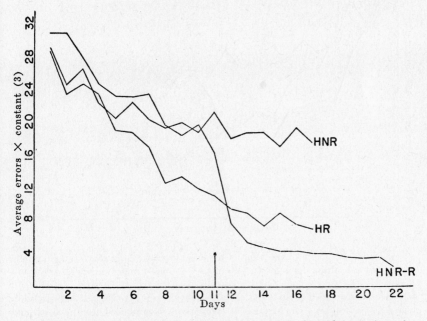

FIGURE 38. Graphic representation of the empirical effect of a shift in the incentive upward in terms of blind-alley entrances made on the maze shown in Figure 67. Here the increased incentive was added at the arrow. The curves HR and HNR are from control experiments, here inserted for purposes of comparison. Reproduced from Tolman and Honzik (*23*, p. 267).

study by Tolman and Honzik (*23*), two groups of 41 rats each were trained on the maze shown in Figure 67. One group received no reward in the food-box during the first ten days; they were retained there for two minutes and then returned to their living cages where after three hours they were given their regular feeding. On the eleventh day and thereafter, this group received food reward in the end box. The behavior of these animals is shown in the HNR-R curve of Figure 38, together with curves from two control groups. With the addition of increased incentive the experimental group at once began to reduce its error scores, reaching the permanent level in about three days. A few years earlier Blodgett (1) had reported an experiment similar to this, in which he secured analogous results.

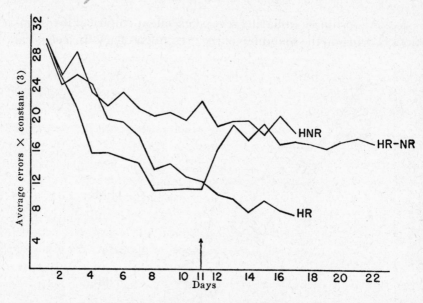

FIGURE 39. Graphic representation of the empirical effect of a shift in the incentive downward in terms of the number of blind-alley entrances made in the maze shown in Figure 67. The weaker incentive was substituted at the arrow. The curves of HR and HNR correspond to the two empirical curves shown in Figure 38, and are inserted in this figure as controls for purposes of comparison. Reproduced from Tolman and Honzik, (23, p. 262).

The animals of Tolman and Honzik's other group were trained with reward in the food-box during the first ten days, and thereafter with no reward; instead they were retained in the food-box for two minutes and then returned to the living cage where, after three hours, they were given their regular feeding. The mean behavior of this second group is shown in the HR-NR curve of Figure 39; the same control group curves as those appearing in

Figure 38 are included here also for purposes of comparison. Beginning with the withdrawal of the stronger incentive, a marked rise may be seen in the number of errors; about two days were required for this to reach the upper level. Moreover, in the original study as reported there are two parallel latency graphs both of which show at least three separate subordinate shifts tending, upon the whole, to decrease progressively in magnitude.

Of course the above facts have been well known for a considerable time, so that Theorem 30 is not a prediction but rather an explanation and a formulation. At all events, the deduction agrees substantially with empirical facts. Incidentally these facts were originally put forward by Tolman (*22*) as the major evidence for his concept of latent learning. Because the Tolman-Honzik data do not clearly show the Crespi incentive-shift effects (*2*, p. 508), we have made no attempt to incorporate these phenomena into the present formulation.

The reason why latent learning has attracted so much attention is not that it is of any obvious practical importance, at least at the present time, but because of its theoretical significance. This will be evident from a quotation from Tolman (*22*, pp. 363–364):

> But, as we saw at the beginning of the chapter, the Law of Effect also does not hold. The latent learning experiments indicate very definitely that just as much learning . . . goes on without differential effects, *or, at the most, with only very minor degrees of such effects*, as with strongly differential ones. . . . Differential effects are, that is, necessary for selective performance but are not necessary, *or at the most in only a very minor degree*, for the mere learning . . . which underlies such performance. [Italics added.]

The italicized portions of this quotation show that at the time it was written little distinction was made between a zero incentive or effect and a minor degree of incentive or effect. On the other hand, recent studies have shown that secondary reinforcement seems to have fairly strong reinforcing effects. For example, secondary reinforcement probably was the factor which caused the fall in the hunger-no-reward (HNR) curve shown in Figure 38. As a matter of fact its fall was almost half as great as that of the hunger-reward (HR) shown in the same figure. Such a large and consistent effect is not accidental and clearly must be reckoned with.

Moreover there is strong reason to believe that a great difference exists between a very small K', i.e., a little reinforcement, and no reinforcement at all. By the computations shown below it appears that if a habit amounts to .6126 and an incentive (K) amounts to .01, this would bring out the reaction potential at

$$_sE_R = 3.109 \times .01 \times .6126$$
$$= .1902.$$

But when the K rises to .9 the $_sE_R$ will rise in a few trials to 1.7119, as we saw above (p. 141).

Current Aspects of the Latent Learning Problem

In the thirty years or so which have passed since the original experiment on latent learning was performed a great deal of scientific work has taken place in this difficult field. The matters of secondary (static) reinforcement from the apparatus situation and the various drive motivations have been as carefully controlled as possible, so that in case presumably latent learning occurs the variable factor producing it may be identified. During this time those who are developing the reinforcement-theoretical approach have become interested in the possibility of deriving latent learning by way of the fractional antedating goal reaction. We propose to examine this possibility now.

Let it be supposed that an organism satiated with both food and water but motivated by a mild third incentive, such as a cage mate, is repeatedly run through a T-maze with food at the end of the right arm of the maze and water at the end of the left arm, in addition to a cage mate in each place. After an equal number of these mildly socially rewarded trials on each arm of the T, what should we expect to have theoretically, in the case of the right arm of the T?

1. We have seen reason to believe that even when the subject is fully fed the sight of food will mildly evoke $r_G \rightarrow s_G$, secondarily reinforcing (xv) a little the trace $s_{x_{Rt}}$ (looking toward the right) to R_{Rt} even though eating does not occur;

$$\left.\begin{array}{c} s_{x_{Rt}} \\ S_{\dot{D}} \\ s_{G_e} \end{array}\right\} \dashrightarrow R_{Rt}.$$

2. In an exactly similar manner the left turn to the water arm of the maze would yield a slight tendency to

$$\left.\begin{array}{c} S_{x_L} \\ S_{\dot{D}} \\ S_{G_d} \end{array}\right\} \dashrightarrow R_{Lt.}$$

3. Now as pointed out above, organisms usually eat when hungry and drink when thirsty. Therefore,

$$S_{D_h} \dashrightarrow r_{G_e} > S_{D_h} \dashrightarrow r_{G_d}.$$

4. Under hunger conditions S_{D_h} (#3),

$$S_{G_e} > S_{G_d}.$$

5. By logic similar to #3 and #4 it might be shown that under thirst conditions (S_{D_t}),

$$S_{G_d} > S_{G_e}.$$

6. Therefore steps #1, #3, and #4 would yield the following theoretical inequality:

$$\left.\begin{array}{c} S_{x_R} \\ S_{D_h} \\ S_{G_e} \end{array}\right\} \dashrightarrow R_{Rt} > \left.\begin{array}{c} S_{x_R} \\ S_{D_h} \\ S_{G_e} \end{array}\right\} \dashrightarrow R_{Lt.}$$

7. And from steps #2 and #5 we have the theoretical inequality:

$$\left.\begin{array}{c} S_{x_L} \\ S_{D_t} \\ S_{G_d} \end{array}\right\} \dashrightarrow R_{L_t} > \left.\begin{array}{c} S_{x_L} \\ S_{D_t} \\ S_{G_d} \end{array}\right\} \dashrightarrow R_{Rt.}$$

From the preceding considerations we arrive at our next theorem:

THEOREM 31. *If an organism operates on a T-maze when satiated with both food and water, consistently finding food at the end of one arm of the T and water at the end of the other arm of the T, this training will so reinforce the responses of turning into the respective arms of the maze to the visual and related traces of looking into those arms that later when under the food drive or water drive only the organism will have a slight tendency to choose the appropriate arm of the T.*

During the last ten years much careful experimental work performed exclusively with albino rats has been devoted to the matter of latent learning. Among the important studies may be mentioned those of Spence and Lippitt (*21*), Spence, Bergmann, and Lippitt (*20*), Walker (*24*), and Kendler (*11*). While these investigators disagree among themselves to some extent, the impression one receives from studying their reports is that there probably is a very slight positive tendency to latent learning. The weakness of this effect is rather surprising in view of the fact that we humans in performing one task ordinarily observe things unrelated to it which we later recall and utilize when some other task presents the need for the information. No doubt this anthropomorphic analogy has strongly fostered this belief regarding rats. The apparent fact that the tendency is so strong in humans and so weak in the rat presumably means that some subvocal speech mechanism not possessed by the rat is primarily responsible for the difference.

Summary

There is reason to believe that both goal and subgoal reactions become reinforced to stimulus traces and other persisting stimuli. These stimuli generalize throughout their period of persistence. This generalization has been especially obvious in connection with the stimulus trace and goal reactions. These give rise to the concept of fractional antedating goal reactions (r_G) and the consequent proprioceptive stimuli, s_G. Now the goal reaction, in whatever form, is believed to be mildly reinforcing. It thus comes about that through the mediation of r_G secondary reinforcement would logically occur, a matter of fact long known empirically.

These antedating reactions apparently can be both positive and negative. Consequently in a molar behavioral sense they become *foresight*, or what the philosophers have called *cognition*, though not necessarily with the speech accompaniment operative in humans. This negative expectancy, coupled with I_R, yields both experimental extinction and the possibility of learning to perform very long series of unreinforced acts which are consistently reinforced at the ends.

The analysis of delays in reinforcement series shows that r_G presumably becomes reinforced to the stimulus trace at the end of the series and generalizes to the series beginning where it reinforces the S $\rightarrow$ R connections there present, yielding a gradient of delay in reinforcement (iii B). Something like this gradient, but probably not the same thing (iii A), arises within a single behavior chain, though this is complicated by the type of chain involved.

The antedating goal reaction appears to explain the Kendler-Spence double-drive problem, and to give a supplementary explanation of the Hull-Leeper double-drive problem. It also gives some promise of clarifying the long-standing controversy regarding latent learning and of throwing light indirectly on the still longer-standing uncertainty regarding the molar aspect of reinforcement itself.

TERMINAL NOTES

FORESIGHT, FOREKNOWLEDGE, EXPECTANCY AND PURPOSE

Suppose that a hungry organism proceeds through a maze with food at the end. The various responses, including especially the goal or eating response (R_{G_e}) at the end will occur as indicated in this chapter. The fact that the fractional goal reaction (r_G) occurs in an antedating manner at the beginning of the behavior chain or sequence *constitutes on the part of the organism a molar foresight or fore-knowledge of the not-here and the not-now*. It is probably roughly equivalent to what Tolman has called "cognition" (*22*).

Now this r_G is behavior of peculiar significance. It does not itself produce any change in the external world; neither does the act itself bring the organism any nearer to the food. What the act does is to produce the goal stimuli which evoke responses by the organism that tend to lead it to food, a mate, or whatever the goal or terminus of the action sequence at the time may be. In short, its function is strictly that of producing a critically useful stimulus in biological problem solution (*5*, p. 515); i.e., it is a *pure-stimulus act*.

When an organism begins to respond to a situation which does not yet exist but is impending, we say informally that the organism anticipates or expects the event to occur. Since time out of mind the ordinary man has used the words *expect, expectation, expectancy,* and *expectative* in a practically intelligent and intelligible manner. Around 1931, Tolman put forward the term *expectation* in a technical sense as "an immanent cognitive determinant aroused by actually presented stimuli" (*22*, p. 444). Moreover, Tolman insisted that none of his technical concepts should lend support to any sort of "ultimately teleological and ultimately mentalistic interpretation of animal . . . behavior" (*22*, p. xii). Were it not for the fact that his writings at the time and since appear to be strongly opposed to an approach resembling the one here presented, we might suppose that the s_G cited above might be a concrete case of Tolman's imminent cognitive determining stimulus mediating the expectation, i.e., $r_G \rightarrow s_G$ as the covert expectancy, and $S_G \rightarrow R_G$ as the thing expected.

Now, human beings manifest this undoubted behavior much the same as do animals (4). When the incipient tendencies to $r_G \rightarrow s_G$ arise in their bodies these as stimuli may evoke verbal responses such as, "Dinner will soon be ready." Presumably such verbal reactions, even incipient ones as symbolic, i.e., pure-stimulus, acts, may make great differences in the dynamics of the situation. In order to avoid the ambiguity of confusing two things which are very different, we recommend that antedating situations with potential speech accompaniment, as in humans, be called *expectative*, and that antedating situations in lower animals without potential speech be called merely *anticipatory*. In that way we may help protect ourselves from inadvertently committing the fallacy of anthropomorphism and from implicitly but falsely assuming the dynamics of speech in animals not possessing such powers.

Another undoubted aspect of behavior which Tolman (22, pp. 12 ff.) has emphasized earlier, is *purpose*. This term has a bad metaphysical history but represents an undoubted aspect of mammalian behavior. We often know what we are about to do before we perform an act, sometimes long before. There is reason to believe that an organism's far antedating foreknowledge of its own goal and subgoal acts is mediated by subvocal speech pure-stimulus acts. If we define purpose as *far antedating foreknowledge*, or an organism's cognition of its own acts, this would presumably limit strictly purposive behavior to humans.

A SOMEWHAT MODIFIED HYPOTHESIS AS TO THE CRITERION
    OF RE.NFORCEMENT

Upon reexamining an earlier version of Postulate 4 (8, p. 178 and related sections of that work, notably pages 80 and 98), it may be seen that there is some inconsistency in the statements. The formal postulate states that reinforcement is the result of the diminution of a need or D. On the other hand, the formulation on page 80 states that reinforcement is due to the reduction in S_D. For example, on page 80 it is stated in italics:

> Whenever an effector activity occurs in temporal contiguity with the afferent impulse, or the perseverative trace of such an impulse, resulting from the impact of a stimulus energy upon a receptor, and this conjunction is closely associated in time with the diminution in the receptor discharge characteristic of a need . . . there will result an increment to the tendency for that stimulus to evoke that reaction.

Now ordinarily a reduction in a need implies that a reduction will soon follow in the drive stimulus and a reinforcement as well. This doubtless was the reason for the looseness of the preceding phraseology. In this connection it may be noticed that the present postulate (III) has taken the reduction in S_D rather than of the need or D as the essential criterion of reinforcement.

Sheffield and Roby appear to have presented a critical case in point (*17*). They showed that hungry albino rats are reinforced by water sweetened by saccharine which presumably is not at all nourishing, i.e., it does not reduce the need in the least. It may very well be that the ingestion of saccharine-sweetened water reduces hunger tension S_D for a brief period sufficient for a mild reinforcement, much as the tightening of the belt is said to do in hungry men, thus reinforcing that act. On the other hand it may be that Sheffield and Roby are right in their suggestion that the critical factor in learning is the act of ingestion, i.e., R_{G_e} and r_{G_e}. Indeed it may very well be that all the critical facts are not even yet fully known. A slight adaptation of the above equations should fit this hypothesis.

And finally we may note the role of $r_G \rightarrow s_G$ as a secondary reinforcing agent. A judicious exploration of these possibilities is likely to give a rather different picture of learning from that usually held at present.

REFERENCES

1. Blodgett, H. C. The effect of the introduction of reward upon the maze performance of rats. *Univ. Calif. Publ. Psychol.* 1929, *4*, 113–134.
2. Crespi, L. P. Quantitative variation of incentive and performance in the white rat. *Am. J. Psychol.*, 1942, *55*, 467–517.

3. Grice, G. R. The relation of secondary reinforcement to delayed reward in visual discrimination learning. *J. Exper. Psychol.*, 1948, *38*, 1–16.

4. Hilgard, E. R. *Theories of learning.* New York: Appleton-Century-Crofts, Inc., 1948.

5. Hull, C. L. Knowledge and purpose as habit mechanisms. *Psychol. Rev.*, 1930, *37*, 511–525.

6. Hull, C. L. Goal attraction and directing ideas conceived as habit phenomena. *Psychol. Rev.*, 1931, *38*, 487–506.

7. Hull, C. L. Differential habituation to internal stimuli in the albino rat. *J. Comp. Psychol.*, 1933, *16*, 255–273.

8. Hull, C. L. *Principles of behavior.* New York: D. Appleton-Century Co., Inc., 1943.

9. Keller, F. S., and Schoenfeld, W. N. *A systematic text in the science of behavior.* New York: Appleton-Century-Crofts, Inc., 1950.

10. Kendler, H. H. The influence of simultaneous hunger and thirst drives upon the learning of two opposed spatial responses of the white rat. *J. Exper. Psychol.*, 1946, *36*, 212–220.

11. Kendler, H. H. An investigation of latent learning in a T-maze. *J. Comp. Psychol.*, 1937, *40*, 265–270.

12. Leeper, R. The role of motivation in learning: a study of the phenomenon of differential motivational control of the utilization of habits. *J. Genet. Psychol.*, 1935, *46*, 3–40.

13. Pavlov, I. P. *Conditioned reflexes* (trans. by G. V. Anrep). London: Oxford Univ. Press, 1927.

14. Perin, C. T. The effect of delayed reinforcement upon the differentiation of bar responses in white rats. *J. Exper. Psychol.*, 1943, *32*, 95–109.

15. Perkins, C. C., Jr. The relation of secondary reward to gradients of reinforcement. *J. Exper. Psychol.*, 1947, *37*, 377–392.

16. Seward, J. P. Secondary reinforcement as tertiary motivation: A revision of Hull's revision. *Psychol. Rev.*, 1950, *57*, 362–374.

17. Sheffield, F. D., and Roby, T. B. Reward value of a nonnutritive sweet taste. *J. Comp. and Physiol. Psychol.*, 1950, *43*, 471–481.

18. Skinner, B. F. *The behavior of organisms.* New York: D. Appleton-Century Co., Inc., 1938.

19. Spence, K. W. The role of secondary reinforcement in delayed reward learning. *Psychol. Rev.*, 1947, *54*, 1–8.

20. Spence, K. W., Bergmann, G., and Lippitt, R. A study of simple learning under irrelevant motivational-reward conditions. *J. Exper. Psychol.*, 1950, *40*, 539–551.

21. Spence, K. W., and Lippitt, R. 'Latent' learning of a simple maze problem with relevant needs satiated. *Psychol. Bull.*, 1940, *37*, 429.

22. Tolman, E. C. *Purposive behavior in animals and men.* New York: Century Co., 1932.

23. Tolman, E. C., and Honzik, C. H. Introduction and removal of reward, and maze performance in rats. *Univ. Calif. Publ. Psychol.*, 1930, *4*, 257–275.

24. Walker, E. L. Drive specificity and learning. *J. Exper. Psychol.*, 1948, *38*, 39–49.

25. Wolfe, J. B. The effect of delayed reward upon learning in the white rat. *J. Comp. Psychol.*, 1934, *17*, 1–21.

6. Simple Behavior Chains

Simple trial-and-error learning (Chapter 2) involves the competition of two or more reaction potentials, such as the tendency of an albino rat to press a horizontal bar downward or to push a vertical bar to the left. The process of learning consists in the gradual acquisition of dominance by one of the tendencies. The end state in simple trial-and-error learning is thus less complex than the beginning in that there is only one overtly functioning reaction tendency, instead of several.

Even from casual observation of the behavior of mammalian organisms, however, it is quite evident that not all learning results in simplification; in one way or another most learning eventuates in the complication of behavior. This is because such acts as the two just considered may be joined as links in a *chain* of reactions of greater or less length. For example, the situation may be such that *both* the downward pressure on the horizontal bar and the lateral pressure on the vertical bar must occur, and in that order, before food can be secured. This is called *terminal reinforcement*, because reinforcement occurs at the termination of the reaction chain. Or it may be that food will be delivered after each act, provided the acts in question are performed in a certain order. This is called *serial reinforcement*, because reinforcement occurs in a series throughout the chain.

Conditions under Which Simple Chaining and the Integration of Homogeneous Reactions May Occur

Consider a situation such as that set up in an investigation by Arnold (*1*), where a miniature car runs on a track very close to the

window of an albino rat's restraining chamber (Figure 40). Let
us assume that through previous training the rat has a reaction
potential well above the threshold of pressing a white button or
disk, placed on the side of the car facing the window, to secure a
pellet of food. On this side of the car there are also placed at equal
intervals three duplicates of the white button, making a total of
four identical stimuli, B_1, B_2, B_3, and B_4; B_2 does not appear in the
drawing.

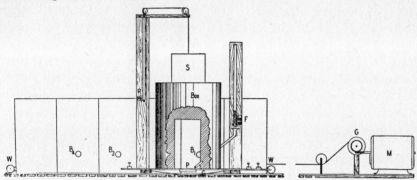

FIGURE 40. Diagram showing the essential structure of Arnold's apparatus. The four
button manipulanda B_1, B_2, B_3, and B_4 were mounted on a car which could be drawn
to the right by a windlass (G) operated by the motor (M). The wheels of the car are
shown on the track at W. The rat was placed in the celluloid cylinder labeled "Box"
and had access to the buttons through a window in the cylinder when the shutter (S)
was lifted as shown in the drawing. When the animal pressed button B_1 the car moved
forward, exposing B_2 (obscured in the drawing by the cylindrical box) to the animal.
When this button was operated the car moved forward, exposing B_3, and so on to B_4.
When B_4 was operated the magnet (R) released the shutter closing the window. At the
same time the magnet at F released ten pellets of food into the pan, P, which gave the
animal primary reinforcement. The car is shown as if in motion, the animal having just
pushed B_1, with B_2 moving up into position. Reproduced from Arnold (7).

At the beginning of the learning sequence the shutter rises,
exposing B_1. The rat sees this and presses it as he has been trained
to do, but he receives no food. Instead, the motor at once moves the
car forward, exposing B_2. Presently the animal presses B_2 and the
car moves forward, exposing B_3. Again the animal receives no food
but at length he presses this button and again the car moves forward, exposing B_4. Experimental extinction has not advanced very
far with this rat, so that after a short delay he presses B_4 also. This
pressure automatically lowers the shutter and at the same time ten
pellets drop into the food-pan, giving the animal primary terminal

reinforcement. The initial performance of a four-link behavior chain has now occurred. Because the several acts of the chain are substantially alike, this is called a *homogeneous* behavior chain.

It is evident that the stimuli which evoke the successive action links of this chain come from without the organism, i.e., the stimuli are exteroceptive. However, the chain does not become fully integrated until the proprioceptive stimuli arising from the animal's own muscles in the performance of one behavior link serve, at least in part, to evoke the succeeding behavior link, and so on to the end of the four-link chain. Thus further integration of the behavior chain is effected by the repetition of its performance with the terminal reinforcement of ten food pellets. Let us assume that this occurs once every 24 hours for 25 days.

We may now proceed to consider some of the more obvious behavior principles involved in the chaining integration process and their characteristic behavioral implications.

Terminal Reinforcement and the Goal Gradient

On the first evocation of the response chain the reaction potential will be approximately equal to that which obtained following the last individual reinforcement, except for extinction effects. Let us suppose that this reaction potential is 2.0σ in amount. However, following the reinforcement at the end of chaining trial 1 there will begin to develop a different set of reaction potentials, those resulting from the goal or terminal reinforcement (delay). We shall assume that this gradient of reinforcement after a number of trials is represented roughly by the equation,

$$\Delta_s E_R = 10^{-.07t},\tag{49}$$

and that the four delays (t) in reinforcement at links

I   II   III   and   IV

respectively, are:

9″   6″   3″   and   0″.

Substituting these values successively in equation 49, we have the following reaction potentials:

.234   .380   .617   1.000.

Unfortunately for the ease of understanding the quantitative aspects of behavioral chaining, the gradient of reinforcement suffers several quantitative distortions, so that to superficial observation it is at the end hardly recognizable. The first distortion occurs in the summation of the four reaction potentials with the separate initial flat reinforcement, which is assumed to amount to 2.0σ. Accordingly we combine $(+)$ 2.0σ from the original training with the series of reaction potential values, to secure the final reinforcement gradient. This gives us, respectively,

$$2.16 \quad 2.25 \quad 2.41 \quad 2.67.$$

Stimulus Generalization

The next step in this quantitative modification or distortion of the gradient of reinforcement arises from the principle of stimulus generalization (*12*). Since all the exteroceptive stimuli for the four responses of the chain are as alike as they can be made, the generalization would be nearly perfect except for the influence of certain stimulus-trace intensities. However, these traces evidently become reinforced to the response with ease, and generalization presumably takes place *jointly on the two bases*.

At this point we must recall that in respect to stimulus traces there are two distinct types of generalization: generalization (1) toward the maximum on the subsident phase of a trace, and (2) toward the fading termination of the trace. Moreover we recall (Figure 31) that from a given point on the subsident phase of the trace to which a response has been reinforced, generalization toward the trace origin tends to rise for some time rather than fall, as it does in simple generalization (p. 104 ff.); i.e., other things constant, generalization toward the maximum on the subsident phase of a stimulus is more intense than that toward the fading termination (Theorem 21 C).

A somewhat detailed but rough representation of the various traces involved is given in Figure 41. Here we see that at IV the reaction potential to R_4, as indicated by the oval, rises from a strong (young) trace of s_4, from a not so strong (older) trace of s_3, from a weaker trace of s_2, and from a still weaker trace of s_1. Now, R_4 will tend to generalize backward (to the left) along all four of these traces as continua. But at III the trace from S_4 is lacking, which will weaken the generalized $_sE_{R_4}$; at II both S_3 and S_4 are lacking, which will weaken the generalized $_sE_{R_4}$ further; and at I, S_2, S_3, and S_4 are all lacking, which will weaken the generalized $_sE_{R_4}$ from IV still more below the slight rise theoretically to be expected of a trace generalizing toward its maximum (Figure 31). Accordingly it is to be expected that in the stimulus chaining situation the gradient for the evocation of R_4 will be a falling one from IV to III, to II, and to I, descending in that order.

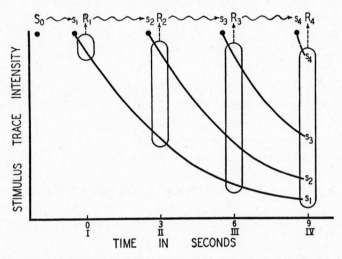

FIGURE 41. Diagram of the several perseverative stimulus traces involved in the stimulus-response chain here under consideration. The ovals indicate the traces conditioned to each reaction shown by the arrows. The intensities of the traces themselves are to be regarded as only *relatively* realistic. For example, the R's are supposed to follow the s's at once rather than after the comparatively long delay required by our diagram to show that s and R are distinct.

On the other hand, R_1 is reinforced to s_1 alone at I. This trace will weaken at II through the mere passage of time; it will weaken more at III, and still more at IV. We have seen (Figure 31) that this fading type of trace presumably yields a rapidly falling generalization, though the fact that other connections are added from II to IV will also weaken the generalized trace progressively.

Too many unknown principles and constants are involved in the generalization situation for us to attempt a detailed deduction of the exact gradient at the present time. It is evident, for example, that there are present in unknown amounts both qualitative and intensity elements which are believed to depend on different equations. For present expository purposes, accordingly, we have chosen to use the qualitative equation of Postulate X A, with the constant parts of the exponent at .15 and .30 respectively for the two directions of generalization. We take as the equation for the larger generalization, i.e., the less rapid generalization fall toward I,[1]

$$_s\underline{E}_R = A10^{-.15d}, \tag{50}$$

and for the weaker generalization, i.e., the more rapid generalization fall toward IV,

$$_s\underline{E}_R = A10^{-.30d}, \tag{51}$$

where A represents the value of the gradient of reinforcement at the origin of the generalization. These values appear in bold-faced type in Table 13.

Intimately connected with these exponents is the matter of the d values. As the generalization difference between III and IV, we take 1; as that between II and III, we take 2; and as that between I and II, we take 4. We have chosen this much larger difference or d value between I and II because the difference between the trace evoking response I (the shift from the living-cage to the apparatus box) and that evoking response II (the continuation of the apparatus box plus the proprioception of response I) is probably much greater than the difference between the traces evoking II and III which are to a large extent a continuation of the trace evoking II, and so are less different. This means that the d between I and III (or III and I) is $4 + 2 = 6$; between I and IV (or IV and I), it is $4 + 2 + 1 = 7$; and between II and IV (or IV and II), it is $2 + 1 = 3$. Thus the generalization from I to III would be:

$$\begin{aligned} _s\underline{E}_R &= 2.16 \times 10^{-.30 \times 6} \\ &= .03. \end{aligned}$$

We are now in a position to observe how stimulus generalization operates. The details of this are explained in Table 13, where the

[1] Presumably this slower apparent generalization fall toward I is due to the greater stimulus intensity (V) of the early part of the stimulus trace, which, strictly speaking, is not generalization at all. Equations 50 and 51 are coarse molar makeshifts which we will use until we know more about V and related matters.

four values of the final gradient of reinforcement appear in bold-faced type in the separate lines, and the dependent generalization values of each are in ordinary type in the same line. It will be noted that the first of the four gradient reinforcement values (**2.16σ**) can generalize only toward IV and that the fourth (**2.67σ**)

TABLE 13. The steps used in computing the theoretical mean reaction latencies at the response points of a four-link homogeneous response chain. The theoretical stimulus generalization reaction potentials ($_sE_R$) are calculated from the gradient-of-reinforcement values, the latter of which are shown in bold-faced type.

d values	4	2	1	
Response number	I	II	III	IV
Based on 9″ delay	**2.16**	.14	.03	.02
Based on 6″ delay	.57	**2.25**	.57	.28
Based on 3″ delay	.30	1.21	**2.41**	1.21
Based on 0″ delay	.24	.95	1.89	**2.67**
Behavior sums (+) of $_sE_R$	2.82σ	3.54σ	3.78σ	3.46σ
Reaction latencies ($_st_R$)	3.51″	2.19″	1.91″	2.30″

can generalize only toward I, whereas the second (**2.25σ**) and the third (**2.41σ**) can generalize in both directions.

Behavioral Summation of Homogeneous Reaction Potentials

At this point we note that not only are all of the four responses in this homogeneous series alike, but that the stimulus at I, say, evokes the primary reinforcement gradient reaction of 2.16σ and that the generalization values of .57σ, .30σ, and .24σ are all evoked simultaneously. It follows that all four summate behaviorally (+). This means that equation 11 will be applied first to two of the numbers in column I, 2.16 and .57 (which yields 2.52); then to 2.52 and the next number .30 (which yields 2.69); and finally to 2.69 and .24 (which yields 2.82) as recorded in Table 13 at the foot of column I. The behavioral summations of the other three columns are recorded in a parallel manner in the same row. An examination of these values will show what remains of the gradient of reinforcement at the end of the chain process. The gradient would be unrecognizable except for the relative size of the two extreme values at I and IV taken by themselves, and of the two middle values also taken by themselves. Still, as in the gradient of reinforcement, IV > I and III > II.

Chaining Reaction Latency

Finally, these summated reaction potentials must be converted into the corresponding reaction latencies, in order that we may have a directly observable empirical indication of the validity of our theoretical derivation. Gladstone *et al.* (7) have suggested the general nature of the relation between $_sE_R$ and $_st_R$. But their equa-

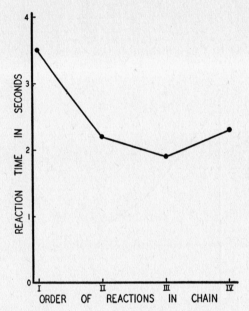

FIGURE 42. Graph showing theoretical reaction latency at the four reaction points of a homogeneous chaining process with terminal reinforcement.

tion was for a different response and evidently yields too small values. However, an adaptation,

$$_st_R = \frac{30}{_sE_R^{2.07}},\qquad (52)$$

will serve temporarily as a first approximation. The substitution one at a time of the values in the next-to-last row of Table 13 yields the rough theoretical latency values in seconds appearing in the last row. In Figure 42 a graphic representation of these values shows that the gradient slopes upward at each end. Table 13 and Figure 42 both give the latency at IV as less than at I, and that at III as less than that at II. Presented formally these four critical relationships are:

$$I > IV, \quad II > III, \quad I > II, \quad IV > III.$$

The preceding considerations lead us to our next theorem:

THEOREM 32. *The latencies of the responses in a simple four-link homogeneous reaction chain with terminal reinforcement show on the average the following fairly stable relationships: $I > IV$, $II > III$, $I > II$, and $IV > III$.*

We turn now to the question of the empirical validation of this deduction. Arnold (*1*) performed the experiment described above

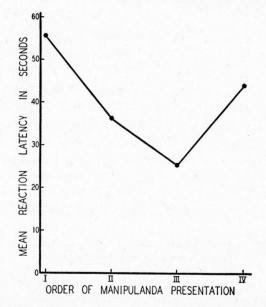

FIGURE 43. Empirical mean reaction latency curve for homogeneous response chaining under food reward and terminal reinforcement, based on trials 2–10. Adapted from Arnold (*1*, p. 356).

based on food reinforcement, and, using a separate group of animals, a parallel experiment in which the reinforcing agent was the cessation of a weak electrical shock to the rat's feet. A graphic representation of his food-reinforcement results appears in Figure 43. There we see that the four reaction latencies in the chain decrease in the order I, IV, II, and III, as in the theoretical deduction (Table 13). However, a comparison of Figures 42 and 43 indicates that the deduction is not exact; our constants are probably incorrect, though the general relationship evidently holds. This degree of agreement between experiment and theory is, perhaps, as close as may reasonably be expected in the present early stage of the science. Probably the most significant outcome of the analysis is an understanding of the detailed reasons for the characteristic transformation which the gradient of reinforcement undergoes (a reduction in the latencies of II and III as compared with those of I and IV) through the influence of stimulus generalization. As a matter of fact, this same general picture is seen in the results of Arnold's electric shock experiment already mentioned (1), as well as in other evidence to be presented later (p. 174).

Heterogeneous Response Chains with Terminal Reinforcement

At this point in our exposition we turn to a modification of the food-reward experiment just described. In this investigation Arnold used the same apparatus as that shown in Figure 40 except that in place of the four identical press buttons there were four manipulanda, each one different in appearance from the others and each one involving largely different response behavior (2). These were: a high horizontal bar, a low horizontal bar, a vertical bar, and a watch chain suspended from above (8). Now, since the reactions to these manipulanda are essentially different from one another their traces will be essentially different. Because of this the d value between what evokes I and what evokes II will be 4, the same as before, but the values between II and III, and III and IV, are both assumed to be larger than in homogeneous chains, and to be equal at 3. These values are formally shown in the first line of Table 14.

Generalizing on these and some earlier considerations (p. 161), we arrive at the following theorem:

THEOREM 33. *The generalization-difference* (d) *values in four-link homogeneous chaining follow a progressive decrease from the beginning to the end of the chain, whereas in four-link heterogeneous chaining the differences begin with the same relatively large value as that in homogeneous chaining, and, following a slight early fall, remain constant thereafter.*

The empirical verification of Theorem 33 must be indirect and rather slow in becoming clearly positive or negative.

Substituting these d values and the gradient-of-reinforcement values appropriately in equations 50 and 51, we calculate the generalization values shown in Table 14. But instead of summating,

TABLE 14. The steps of computing the theoretical mean reaction latencies at the response points of a four-link heterogeneous response chain with terminal reinforcement. The theoretical gradient-of-reinforcement values are in bold-faced type. The generalization ($_sE_R$) values related to each are shown in the same lines in ordinary type.

d values	4	3	3	
Response number	I	II	III	IV
Based on 9″ delay	**2.16**	.14	.02	.002
Based on 6″ delay	.57	**2.25**	.28	.04
Based on 3″ delay	.21	.86	**2.41**	.30
Based on 0″ delay	.08	.34	.95	**2.67**
$_sE_R$ interference values (∸)	1.55σ	1.25σ	1.50σ	2.47σ
Reaction latencies ($_st_R$)	12.11″	18.90″	12.96″	4.62″

these generalized reaction potentials are all assumed to be different and therefore to interfere (∸) with one another.

Accordingly all the theoretical gradient-of-reinforcement values of Table 13 will hold for the present project, but the generalization values are for the most part different because they are usually based on different d's. And, necessarily, the modes of determining the joint $_sE_R$'s of the various columns of data are quite different; the several generalized values are withdrawn (∸) from the basic gradient-of-reinforcement value because presumably different reaction potentials interfere rather than summate. Consider column I as an example. Using equation 13, we have,

$$2.16 \doteq .57 = 1.76$$
$$1.76 \doteq .21 = 1.61$$
$$1.61 \doteq .08 = 1.55$$

Similar computations were performed for each of the other three columns of Table 14, the results of which appear as the next-to-last row of values in that table. Then these reaction potentials were converted into reaction latencies by means of equation 52; they appear as the last row of Table 14. There it may be seen that I > IV and that II > III, which is all that remains of the gradient of reinforcement. It may also be noted that II > I and that III > IV.

From the preceding considerations we arrive at our next theorem:

THEOREM 34. *The latencies in a simple four-link heterogeneous reaction chain with terminal reinforcement will present the following stable quantitative relationships: I > IV, II > III, II > I, and III > IV.*

One empirical test of the soundness of the above theoretical deduction is furnished by an experiment performed by Arnold (2). The relevant empirical latency results are:

I	II	III	IV
4.24″	5.16″	3.56″	1.92″

It may be seen at a glance that here also,

I > IV,   II > III,   II > I,   and   III > IV.

The relationships specified in Theorem 34 hold, but one unspecified relationship, that between I and III, does not. We note, moreover, that all of the values in the theoretical deduction are much larger than the corresponding ones in the empirical findings. It is clear from this that something is defective; presumably this is with the constants utilized in the deduction. On the other hand, the close agreement of the general shapes of the functions when represented graphically, especially regarding relationships specified in the theorem, suggests that important elements in the theory correspond to fact. Other relevant data bearing on this type of chaining will be presented later (pp. 175 ff.).

Homogeneous Response Chains with Serial Reinforcement

Our theoretical analysis of behavioral chaining now turns to the form we have called serial reinforcement. In this situation, it will be remembered, the animal receives food immediately following *each* of its four responses. If a separate gradient of reinforcement is set up at each reward point it is evident that there will be four of these gradients, though several will be incomplete; and that they will summate, presumably as shown in Table 15. *This will yield a gradient of serial reinforcement.* The last row of Table 15 shows that the summation gradient of serial reinforcement is convex upward, and that its value at I is larger than that at IV—an almost complete reversal of the four gradients of reinforcement from which it is derived.

TABLE 15. Derivation of the gradient of serial reinforcement from the summation (+) of the four gradients of reinforcement produced by the feeding after each act in a four-link chain.

Points of reinforcement	I	II	III	IV
1st reinforcement	1.000			
2nd reinforcement	.617	1.000		
3rd reinforcement	.380	.617	1.000	
4th reinforcement	.234	.380	.617	1.000
Gradient summation (+)	1.96	1.80	1.52	1.00
+ initial 2.0 σ reinforcement	**3.31**	**3.20**	**3.01**	**2.67**

Generalizing on the preceding considerations, we arrive at our next theorem:

THEOREM 35. *When reinforcements follow each of the successive responses of a behavior chain a series of overlapping gradient-of-reinforcement sections are generated, the summation of which produces an upward-sloping and upward-arching serial-reinforcement gradient.*

We proceed now to calculate as before the generalized reaction potentials based on the serial gradient. These also are found by means of equations 50 and 51. The values are given in Table 16. Summating (+) the values in the respective columns we have the reaction potentials in the next-to-last line. Substituting these $_sE_R$'s in equation 52, we secure an approximation to the theoretical reaction latency values. The theoretical latencies, in the last line of Table 16, show the same upward sloping of the two end sections

TABLE 16. Steps in the computation of the theoretical mean reaction latencies at the response points of a four-link homogeneous response chain when integrated by serial reinforcement. The serial-reinforcement gradient values are in bold-faced type, as taken from Table 15. The generalization values related to each are shown on the same lines in ordinary type.

d values	4		2		1	
Response number	I	II	III	IV
Based on 9″ delay	**3.31**	.21	.05	.03
Based on 6″ delay	.80	**3.20**	.80	.40
Based on 3″ delay	.38	1.51	**3.01**	1.51
Based on 0″ delay	.24	.95	1.89	**2.67**
Behavior sums (+) of $_sE_R$	3.91σ	4.30σ	4.23σ	3.69σ
Reaction latencies	1.78″	1.47″	1.52″	2.01″

as appears in Figure 42. But the present results differ from the computations from which Figure 42 was derived, as is to be expected from the fact that they are based on distinct types of gradient in the general slope downward from IV to I.

From the preceding considerations we arrive at our next theorem:

THEOREM 36. *The latencies in a simple four-link homogeneous reaction chain with serial reinforcement will show the following stable relationships between the extremes of the chain and the links adjacent to the extremes: IV > I, III > II, I > II, and IV > III.*

Turning to the matter of empirical validation, we have another relevant investigation by Arnold (4). Since this experiment was performed at the University of Nebraska, the apparatus used in Arnold's earlier investigations was not available. Accordingly he carried out this later work on a very different apparatus, to superficial appearance at least. This was mainly a Skinner type of box in which there was a shutter shielding a single manipulandum—a bar which when pressed upward delivered a pellet and at once automatically withdrew through the wall of the chamber. The shutter was lowered while the rat was eating the pellet. Then the shutter was raised for the next trial, and so on to the fourth trial. It is clear that these external stimuli were by no means similar to those of the three experiments previously performed by Arnold with the car arrangement, though obviously this experiment involved homogeneous serial reinforcement. Unfortunately we do not know enough about chaining and behavior generally to say what effects these changes in apparatus and technique would produce.

Arnold's comparable experimental results were:

I	II	III	IV
1.72	1.63	2.18	2.39

Despite certain deviations in the experiment, as noted above, its outcome was fairly close to the theoretical expectation indicated in Table 16. An inspection of the above data shows that all four of the relationships specified in Theorem 36 hold,

IV > III,   III > II,   I > II,   and IV > III,

though one other, that between I and III, does not. For some unknown reason the theoretical values are in general much nearer the comparable empirical values in size than has been the case in several such comparisons. Fortunately there is other relevant empirical evidence on homogeneous serial reinforcement (p. 180).

Heterogeneous Response Chains with Serial Reinforcement

Our fourth and final case of simple four-link response chains concerns a heterogeneous behavior chain with serial reinforcement. From the preceding three presentations we have all of the quantitative accessory elements which will be necessary for the derivation of this one. We have already considered both heterogeneous response chains and serial reinforcement gradient values in Tables 14 and 15 respectively, and the d values also in Table 14. We now combine them appropriately in the computations of the values for Table 17. As usual in such tables, the critical reaction latencies are given in the last line. Here we see the latencies generally increasing

TABLE 17. Steps in the computation of the theoretical mean reaction latencies at the response points of a four-link heterogeneous response chain when integrated by serial reinforcement. The serial reinforcement gradient values are in bold-faced type. The generalization values related to each are shown on the same line in ordinary type.

d values	4	3	3	
Response number	I	II	III	IV
Based on 9″ delay	**3.31**	.21	.03	.003
Based on 6″ delay	.80	**3.20**	.40	.05
Based on 3″ delay	.27	1.07	**3.01**	.38
Based on 0″ delay	.08	.34	.95	**2.67**
Residual $_8E_R$ ($\stackrel{.}{-}$)	2.71σ	2.25σ	2.18σ	2.41σ
Reaction latencies ($_8t_R$)	3.81″	5.60″	5.98″	4.86″

from I to IV and from II to III, which shows the influence of the serial reinforcement gradient, with the two middle values higher than the extreme ones. This means that the two end sections of the series slope downward as in Table 14, demonstrating the general influence of the interfering heterogeneous generalizing values.

Formulating our general conclusions from the preceding theoretical computations, we arrive at our next theorem.

THEOREM 37. *The latencies in a simple four-link heterogeneous behavior chain with serial reinforcement will tend to have the following four relationships between the extremes of the chain and the links adjacent to those extremes: IV > I, III > II, II > I, and III > IV.*

A study by Arnold (3) supplies empirical verification of this theoretical deduction also. Fortunately in this experiment Arnold's original apparatus (Figure 40) was used. His relevant results were as follows:

I	II	III	IV
2.55"	8.59"	9.13"	4.18"

A comparison with Table 17 shows a reasonably close agreement, including all the points specified in Theorem 37, i.e.,

IV > I,   III > II,   II > I,   and III > IV.

The theory in so far is substantiated. Other verifying evidence will be presented later (pp. 180 ff.).

A Form of Trial-and-Error Behavior Chaining

In the preceding pages of this chapter we have considered four types of very simple four-link behavior chaining. Now it will be our task to observe not only that there exist behavior chains of various numbers of links from short up to very long series, but that there exist chains involving the greatest variety of behavior and circumstances of evolution. This form of behavior chaining is one which in its acquisition demands a conspicuous element of trial-and-error learning. In the considerable amount of experimental investigation which has been devoted to it this has sometimes been called *compound trial-and-error learning* (21).

A four-link linear rat maze with four choices at each choice point was used in several studies specifically concerned with compound trial-and-error learning (6, 9, 13, 14, 21). This maze is shown in Figure 44. At each choice point pressure from the animal's body easily pushed up one of the four sloping doors and permitted locomotion down the passageway to the next choice point, and so on to the end of the maze at F. Electrical contacts at all the maze doors recorded on the polygraph not only the doors actually passed under but, in proper order, all the doors erroneously attempted.

At the beginning of such learning the probability of the correct door being tried is in general a matter of chance, i.e., one in four, but as learning continues the proportion of false to correct choices becomes progressively less. Moreover, the nature of the three types of error is clearly indicated and in some cases may be very significant. Thus the phenomena which will mainly concern us in this type of learning pass from response latencies, the only criteria available in the validation of theoretical deductions involving simple chaining, to the nature of the responses themselves, i.e., whether they are adaptive (right, R) or unadaptive (wrong, $\overline{R}$).

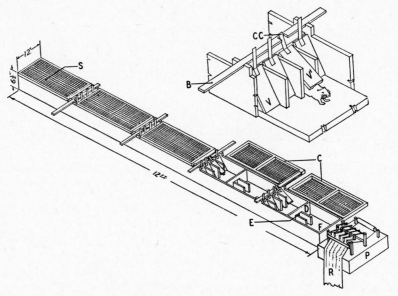

FIGURE 44. The rat maze used in studying compound trial-and-error learning (lower figure), and one choice point in detail (upper figure). Lower diagram: S, starting box; C, wire-mesh frames covering each section of the maze; D, partition midway in each section; E, aperture to force rat to middle of maze; F, food compartment; P, constant-speed polygraph; R, waxed paper record. Upper diagram: B, bar to block incorrect doors (V); CC, correct contact in slot which allows correct door (V') to be opened by pressure in goalward direction. From Hill (9, p. 568).

As might be expected this marked difference in the type of phenomenon to be taken as an indicator of the state of the chaining process involves the use of different methods of quantification.

Homogeneous Linear Maze Chaining with Terminal Reinforcement

We saw above (p. 169) that Arnold was able to carry out experiments on simple chaining with two very different types of apparatus. Now we shall observe that all four types of the chaining there considered may occur in the linear maze shown in Figure 44.

For example, we have *homogeneous* chaining with terminal reinforcement if we permit the animal to pass only through door 1,
say, at all four choice points with food (F) reinforcement at the end.
This passageway, projected on the floor plan of the maze, is shown
in Figure 45. There it may be seen that when running the true
course the rat must make the same type of turn before it advances
in the maze, since each time it must pass through the short alley
of the partition preceding and following each choice point. Considered as a whole the locomotor behavior at I, from the first to
the second partition, is the same as that at II, from the second to
the third partition, and so on to the end. In the present coarse
analysis these four locomotor sections may be considered as

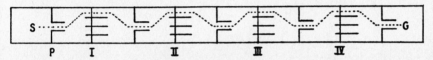

F I G U R E 45. Diagrammatic representation of the floor plan of the compound trial-and-
error learning rat maze. The animals were placed in the maze at S. P represents the
partition in each section of the maze with a 2.5-inch passageway in its center forcing the
animals to make their choices of doors at choice points I, II, III, and IV from a comparable position in the runway. The doors are numbered from 1 to 4 from the top down.
The animals were fed upon reaching G. The dotted line represents the correct pathway
through the maze for an animal whose learning task was to choose door No. 1 at each
choice point between S and G and to make the same reaction (homogeneous) at each
choice point. Analogous pathways were followed by animals whose task was to learn to
choose doors No. 2, 3, and 4 respectively. From Sprow (*21*, p. 198).

homogeneous even though at first considerable more or less random
trial-and-error behavior usually intervenes between the passage
through the partition and the successful door choice at a given
choice point.

As learning progresses the various $\bar{R}$'s involved in the trial-and-
error process will gradually "short circuit" (Theorem 23 B) and
drop out of the sequence, and the traces of the stable or uniform
acts of the sequence as required by the apparatus will gradually
become reinforced to the acts in question, quite as in Arnold's
parallel experiment. This means that we shall again find the
generalization of responses and their summation ($+$) as in simple
chaining, exactly as shown in detail in Table 13. It is believed that
habituation of the animals to the maze preceding the actual training, and the consequent secondary reinforcement, gave the equiva-

lent of the initial 2.0σ reinforcement operative in Arnold's simple chaining experiments.

But in order to calculate verifiable theoretical results from the $_sE_R$ values of Table 13, we must convert them into equivalent error or $\bar{R}$ values. Fortunately Sprow (21) published an equation formulated by H. G. Yamaguchi, which purports to give $\bar{R} = f(_sE_R)$. Transposed, this is:

$$\log \bar{R} = .914 - \left(\frac{_sE_R}{3.48}\right)^{1.25}. \tag{53}$$

Substituting the next-to-last row of theoretical values in Table 13 one at a time in equation 53, we have the following theoretical error ($\bar{R}$) values:

I	II	III	IV
1.396	.780	.638	.834

An examination of these results shows that as usual,

$$I > IV, \quad II > III, \quad I > II, \quad \text{and } IV > III,$$

which is the substance of Theorem 32, though in a strikingly different activity as superficially viewed.

Turning to the matter of an empirical check of this theoretical deduction, we find Sprow (21, p. 203) reporting errors ($\bar{R}$) as follows:

I	II	III	IV
1.305	.845	.720	.970,

which shows that:

$$I > IV, \quad II > III, \quad I > II, \quad \text{and } IV > III.$$

Thus Theorem 32 receives further confirmation on all four points.

There is another bit of incidental evidence regarding this deduction. This comes from an experiment by Montpellier (20), originally designed to solve a rather different problem. The apparatus consisted of three essentially similar six-link linear mazes with two choices at each link. Montpellier gave one trial each day to a total of 42 blinded albino rats divided into groups of roughly equal numbers, on these mazes, the ground plan of one of which is represented in Figure 46. Calculating the weighted averages for the mean number of trials required to eliminate the erroneous entrances at each of the six choice points, we secure the following values:

I	II	III	IV	V	VI
5.01	3.84	3.26	2.59	3.33	3.67

The outcome of this experiment when represented in a way parallel to our previous custom shows the two ends of the series tilting upward like Figures 42 and 43, and that:

$$I > VI, \quad III > IV, \quad I > II, \quad VI > V.$$

Thus in all respects these results from a fairly conventional form

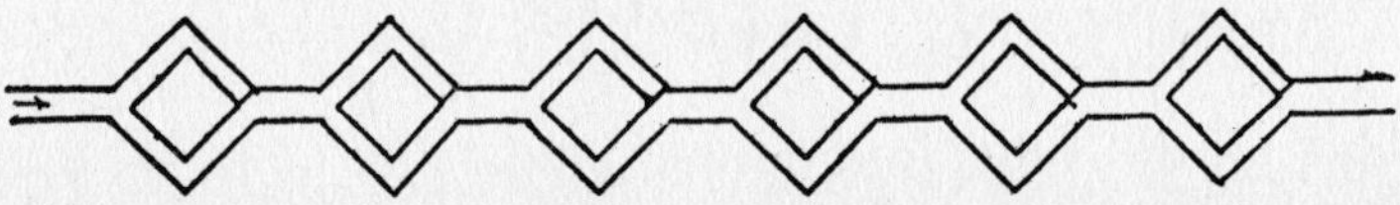

FIGURE 46. The pattern of a typical diamond linear rat maze used by Montpellier (20). The food reward was given in the animal's living cage which was attached for this purpose to the right-hand extremity of the maze. Note that all the correct reactions are right-turning.

of linear maze turn out to follow and thereby empirically to verify still further the secondary law presented in Theorem 32.

Heterogeneous Linear Maze Chaining with Terminal Reinforcement

The apparatus shown in Figure 44 was also used in *heterogeneous* chaining with terminal reinforcement. This differs from homogeneous chaining only in that the correct pathway through the maze involves passing through a different door at each choice point, which of course means that the correct *turning* act before going under the door at each point is different, much as in the corresponding experiment by Arnold. Following the general expository logic of the preceding section, we find the theoretical analysis of this type of chaining the same as that displayed in Table 14.

But in maze chaining each of the values of Table 14 appearing in the rows with bold-faced type has a distinctive, observable meaning in the outcome of the experiment, either as a correct response or as one of three different types of erroneous responses. The point is that in this procedure each type of generalization tends to produce erroneous reactions of a distinct form. This means that instead of simple interferences pooled (÷), we must convert each of the different reaction potentials into an approximation to the equivalent probability of the occurrence of each type of response. We do this on the analogy of the computations of the statistical probability of differences between means. Here we shall make the simple provisional assumption that the standard deviation of all four $_sE_R$ values in each column is 1.0. It follows that the standard deviation of each difference between these values must be $1.0 \times \sqrt{2}$, or 1.414. Taking the first pair of values of column I, Table 14, 2.16 and .57, we find the difference to be 1.59. The ratio of this to its standard error is,

$$\frac{1.59}{1.414} = 1.124.$$

Looking up this value in a normal probability table, we discover that with two forces of 2.16σ and $.57\sigma$ opposing each other, the 2.16σ will dominate 86.96 per cent of the time, and the $.57\sigma$ will dominate 13.04 per cent of the time.

But there is yet to be considered the simultaneous competition in this column of the $.21\sigma$ and the $.08\sigma$, with the two values just considered. This is a little more complicated. Calculating the probabilities of the separate dominations of 2.16σ and $.21\sigma$, and of 2.16σ and $.08\sigma$, we find that the first yields the probabilities of 91.61 and 8.39, and the second yields the probabilities of 92.94 and 7.06. Now within sampling limitations, the ratio of 86.96 to 13.04 will hold even when additional competitions enter. We accordingly have the probabilities:

$$86.96 \text{ vs. } 13.04,$$
$$91.61 \text{ vs. } 8.39,$$
$$92.94 \text{ vs. } 7.06,$$

all based on 2.16σ. But the probability corresponding to 2.16σ is different in each case. Therefore the 8.39 and the 7.06 do not correspond to the 13.04. This is rectified by the following proportions:

$$91.61:8.39::86.96:x.$$
$$92.94:7.06::86.96:x.$$

Solving these proportions, we find the respective x values to be

7.96 and 6.61. We now have the following four probability values all in their true proportions:

$$86.96$$
$$13.04$$
$$7.96$$
$$\underline{6.61}$$
Total 114.57

But the total probability, however many possibilities exist, must always amount to 1.00. This means that the values are too large. Accordingly we divide each of the four values by 1.1457 to reduce them to the proper size. As a result of this division we have:

$$75.90$$
$$11.38$$
$$6.95$$
$$\underline{5.77}$$
Total 100.00

We now see that at I there are 75.90 chances in 100 that the correct response will be evoked at that choice point; that there are 11.38 chances in 100 that the response proper at II will be evoked at I; that there are 6.95 chances in 100 that the response proper at III

TABLE 18. The theoretical per cent of correct response evocations (bold-faced type) and the per cent of erroneous response evocations of the three forms in four-link heterogeneous linear maze chaining with terminal reinforcement. Derived by computation from Table 14.

Choice points	I	II	III	IV
Responses correct if given at I	**75.90**	5.33	3.68	2.75
Responses correct if given at II	11.38	**73.30**	5.45	2.92
Responses correct if given at III	6.95	14.25	**77.16**	4.42
Responses correct if given at IV	5.77	7.12	13.71	**89.91**
Total per cent erroneous responses at each choice point	24.10	26.70	22.84	10.09

will be evoked at I; and that there are 5.77 chances in 100 that the response proper at IV will be evoked at I.

We make similar computations from the data in the second, third, and fourth columns of Table 14, and record all these theoretical values in Table 18, with the correct probabilities set in bold-faced type and the error probabilities in ordinary type. The total erroneous response per cents at the several choice points are given in the last row of values of this table. A glance at these values reveals that theoretically in maze learning the score in error per cents is:

$$I > IV, \quad II > III, \quad II > I, \quad \text{and } III > IV,$$

exactly as was deduced for simple chaining (Theorem 34).

Turning now to the question of the empirical soundness of the deduction, we find a study exactly on the point. An inspection of Hull's relevant published figures (13, p. 123) shows that,

$$I > IV, \quad II < III, \quad II > I, \quad \text{and } III > IV,$$

which agrees with Theorem 34 on three of the four points. It must be noted that the disagreement, which involves choice points II and III, is with the first-choice errors but not with the total errors. Moreover, exactly the same disagreement between theory and empirical fact is found in an experiment by Hill (13, p. 119), so that the inconsistency can hardly be due to sampling. Up to the present time we have not made any detailed distinction between total errors and first-choice errors in our deductions. It is probably too early to press the theory to that amount of detail.

Generalization in Linear Maze Heterogeneous Trial-and-Error Chaining

The fact that separate heterogeneous generalization gradients in terms of response probability have just been deduced in some detail permits us to make some additional comparisons with empirical fact. For example, an inspection of the row of response probabilities correct if given at IV (antedating generalizations, Table 18) shows that the fall of this gradient from IV to I is progressively less at each choice point; i.e., that the gradient curvature is in general concave upward. The same may be observed in the row of theoretical response probabilities correct if given at I (perseverative generalizations). Both have been tacitly assumed in our theoretical deductive procedure.

Turning now to the relevant experimental results (13, p. 127), we find that the corresponding generalization data are:

Antedating generalizations:	12.8,	19.1,	37.1,	**65.9.**
Perseverative generalizations:	**57.9.**	11.1,	9.1,	9.6.

Thus the theory is validated for the most part in regard to the curvature of the two types of generalization gradient.

A second examination of the rows of responses which would be correct if given at I and if given at IV of Table 18 will show that the figures in the first or perseverative row of theoretical erroneous generalization values are much smaller than those in the last row of theoretical erroneous antedating generalization values (correct if given at IV). This also was tacitly assumed by our choice of the exponents in equations 50 and 51. Glancing again at the two rows of corresponding empirical generalization values given in the preceding paragraph, we see that the antedating error values are distinctly larger than are the corresponding perseverative error values. Thus our original assumptions as represented in equations 50 and 51 appear to be fully substantiated.

A third theoretical matter here concerns the progressive influence of the learning process on the slope of a given generalization gradient. Consider, for example, the antedating gradient correct when the response is given at IV. This is really a discrimination gradient positively reinforced when the response is given at IV and not reinforced, i.e., partially extinguished, when it is incorrectly given at I, II, and III. It follows that with practice the gradient will rise at IV and will fall relatively at III, II, and I. Empirical evidence on this point is available in the study already cited. The empirical values just mentioned were the average results from a total of 50 trials. Computations from the published tables (*13*, p. 124) show that the corresponding mean antedating generalization gradients for the first and second ten trials respectively are:

	I	II	III	IV
First 10 trials:	20.42	21.11	23.47	**36.81**
Second 10 trials:	14.31	21.67	39.58	**63.47**

These results indicate that increase in the training raises the value at IV from 36.81 to 63.47, and lowers that at I from 20.42 to 14.31, which verifies the theoretical expectation.

Homogeneous Linear Maze Chaining with Serial Reinforcement

The experimental technique of the homogeneous linear maze chaining with serial reinforcement was exactly the same as that of homogeneous linear maze chaining with terminal reinforcement, except that a pellet of food was found by the animal at once after it had passed through the door at *each* of the four choice points (Figure 45). This means that the main theoretical analysis presented in Table 16 will also hold in the present situation. There is this difference, however: we must convert the reaction potentials in the next-to-last line into errors ($\overline{R}$) instead of latencies ($_s t_R$). To do this we must again use the Yamaguchi-Sprow equation (53) (*21*). This yields the following values:

$$
\begin{array}{cccc}
\text{I} & \text{II} & \text{III} & \text{IV} \\
.572 & .408 & .434 & .689
\end{array}
$$

which, as usual, yield the following inequalities:

$$
\text{IV} > \text{I}, \qquad \text{III} > \text{II}, \qquad \text{I} > \text{II}, \qquad \text{and IV} > \text{III}.
$$

This experiment was performed by Gladstone (*6*). His corresponding empirical $\overline{R}$ values were:

$$
\begin{array}{cccc}
\text{I} & \text{II} & \text{III} & \text{IV} \\
.528 & .244 & .356 & .776,
\end{array}
$$

i.e.,

$$
\text{IV} > \text{I}, \qquad \text{III} > \text{II}, \qquad \text{I} > \text{II}, \qquad \text{and IV} > \text{III}.
$$

Accordingly Theorem 36 appears to be validated for homogeneous linear maze chaining with serial reinforcement.

Heterogeneous Linear Maze Chaining with Serial Reinforcement

We perform the theoretical computations for heterogeneous linear maze chaining with serial reinforcement from Table 17 by the methodology described in connection with the construction of Table 18. The critical theoretical error values as thus derived are given in the last line of Table 19. An inspection of these values shows that,

$$
\text{IV} > \text{I}, \qquad \text{III} > \text{II}, \qquad \text{II} > \text{I}, \qquad \text{and III} > \text{IV},
$$

as in the theory and in Arnold's empirical findings for simple chaining (*3*).

Turning now to the empirical evidence concerning this phase of linear chaining, we find a study by the present writer reporting that for the first 50 trials the total empirical errors at the respective choice points were, on the average, as follows (*14*, p. 20):

$$\begin{array}{cccc} \text{I} & \text{II} & \text{III} & \text{IV} \\ 41.2 & 54.5 & 58.4 & 48.3 \end{array}$$

An inspection of these values shows that,

$$\text{IV} > \text{I}, \qquad \text{III} > \text{II}, \qquad \text{II} > \text{I}, \qquad \text{and III} > \text{IV},$$

quite in accordance with theoretical expectation. However, the predicted values are much smaller than are the experimental ones.

TABLE 19. The theoretical per cent of correct response evocations (bold-faced type) and the per cent of erroneous response evocations of the three different forms, heterogeneous chaining with serial reinforcement. Derived by computation from Table 17.

Choice points	I	II	III	IV
Response correct if given at I	**73.74**	1.58	1.96	2.73
Response correct if given at II	3.69	**90.07**	2.97	2.95
Response correct if given at III	1.50	6.36	**88.16**	4.97
Response correct if given at IV	1.06	1.99	6.90	**89.35**
Total per cent erroneous responses at each choice point	6.25	9.93	11.83	10.65

Here again both theory and empirical fact permit the distinction of the different types of erroneous responses as related to chaining generalization. All the theoretical expectations to be verified in the case of heterogeneous linear maze chaining have been observed in this situation, but with one curious addition. It will be noticed in row I of Table 19 that the generalization falls to 1.58 at II, then rises to 1.96 at III, and to 2.73 at IV. Glancing at a figure published in the study referred to above (*14*, p. 21) we see that the tendency for an upward tilt of this generalization gradient as expressed in percentages is anticipated by theoretical expectation. But this is too fine a point to be elaborated in detail at the present immature state of the science.

Difficulty in Heterogeneous Chain Learning as a Function of the Length of the Chain

At this point in our analysis of forms of heterogeneous behavior chain learning with serial reinforcement, we consider a new aspect. This concerns the ease or difficulty of the learning as dependent on the length of the chain. Because of its relative simplicity we shall consider the difficulty or ease involved in learning a three-link chain. Table 20 shows the response behavior characteristic of this form of learning. The series gradient is the same as that used in Tables 17, 18, and 19 except that it has only the first three links. The generalizations are based on the same exponents but the values in Table 20 differ somewhat because some of the numbers involved come in different combinations. Finally, the last two rows of the table give respectively the equivalent correct and erroneous per cent of responses at each of the three choice points.

TABLE 20. The error characteristics of a three-link heterogeneous behavior chain with serial reinforcement.

d values		4	3
Choice points	I	II	III
Response correct if given at I	**3.20**	.20	.03
Response correct if given at II	.76	**3.01**	.38
Response correct if given at III	.24	.95	**2.67**
Per cent of correct responses	94.10	90.72	91.94
Per cent of erroneous responses	5.90	9.28	8.06

First it will be noticed that in erroneous responses:

$$III > I, \quad II > I, \quad \text{and } II > III,$$

just as we expect from such chaining theory. But our present concern is mainly with the number of errors made in the performance of the three-link chain as compared with a four-link chain. We find this by comparing the last row of Table 19 with that of Table 20. A glance will show that at comparable points of the chain many more erroneous responses are associated with the four-link chain than with the three-link chain. One obvious reason for this is that the generalization from the extra link of the longer chain increases the competition given the correct responses.

Generalizing on the preceding considerations, we arrive at our next theorem:

THEOREM 38. *As heterogeneous behavior chains increase in length, the amount of learning remaining constant, they become progressively more prone to evoke erroneous responses.*

A further comparison of Tables 19 and 20 will show that the difference between the per cent erroneous responses at the initial choice points of the two chains is,

$$6.25 - 5.90 = .35,$$

whereas the difference between per cent erroneous responses at the final choice points of the two chains is,

$$10.65 - 8.06 = 2.59.$$

But,

$$2.59 > .35.$$

Generalizing on these considerations we arrive at our next theorem:

THEOREM 39. *As heterogeneous behavior chains increase in length, the amount of learning remaining constant, the per cent of erroneous responses at the posterior end of the chain increases more rapidly than does that at the anterior end.*

Turning to the question of the empirical verification of Theorems 38 and 39, we find that no evidence exists of the sort with which we have hitherto concerned ourselves. For this reason we introduce a relatively new consideration. This is that *rote learning is a form of*

TABLE 21. The number of repetitions required to learn different lengths of nonsense syllable series. Data from Meumann (*19*).

Number of syllables in series	Repetitions
8	5.2
12	10.4
16	17.0
18	21.5
24	30.0
36	32.5

heterogeneous serial chaining, the reinforcement in this case being of the secondary variety. This arises from the subject's discovery of the correctness or incorrectness of his response soon after it has been made.

Theorem 38 is substantiated by great amounts of experimental work on rote learning. Relevant data are found in studies by Ebbinghaus (*5*), Meumann (*19*), Lyon (*18*), and Hovland (*10*). Table 21 gives an example from Meumann.

Theorem 39 is substantiated by Hovland's rote learning results shown in Figure 47. Despite a certain amount of irregularity evidently due to sampling limitations, it is clear that the posterior ends of the three curves differ more from each other on the average than do the anterior ends.

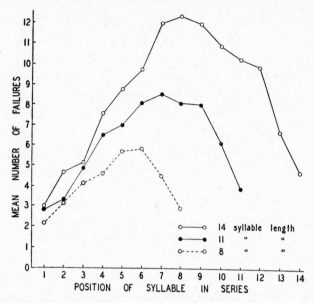

FIGURE 47. Mean number of failures in the various syllable positions during the learning of 8-unit, 11-unit, and 14-unit lists to a criterion of one perfect recitation. Data from Hovland (*10; 15*).

A Mixed Form of Behavioral Chaining—the Double Alternation Experiment

Up to now we have analyzed a single relatively pure type of chaining at a time, either homogeneous alone or heterogeneous alone. It is obvious, however, that in a single behavior chain the two types of responses (as well as the different types of reinforcement) may be combined in the greatest variety of ways. We have space here for the analysis of but one form of mixed behavioral chaining. Because it was one of the earliest forms intensively investigated we have chosen what Hunter (*16*) called *double alternation*. By this is meant the combination of two two-link homogeneous chains as A A and/or B B into a four-link chain, A A B B, the B responses being different from the A's. For example, we might perform the double alternation experiment on the linear maze of Figure 44 by requiring the rat to go through the first door at I and at II, and through the fourth door at III and at IV. The combination of choosing the first and fourth doors of the maze constitutes the heterogeneous element in the chain.

We proceed in this analysis on the basis of terminal reinforcement, the form usually employed. The first two d values will be

T A B L E 22. The theoretical analysis of the mixed form of joint homogeneous-heterogeneous behavioral chaining with terminal reinforcement, known as double alternation.

d values	4	2	3	
Response number	I	II	III	IV
Response reinforced at I	**2.16**	.14	.03	.004
Response reinforced at II	.57	**2.25**	.57	.07
Response reinforced at III	.30	1.21	**2.41**	.30
Response reinforced at IV	.12	.47	.95	**2.67**
I + II	2.52	2.34	.60	.07
III + IV	.41	1.59	2.98	2.84
Per cent correct responses	93.22	70.21	95.38	97.49
Per cent incorrect responses	6.78	29.79	4.62	2.51

4 and 2, as of the homogeneous series, and the third will be 3, the difference in stimulation resulting in the change of response at III, as at this phase in the heterogeneous series. The gradient of reinforcement values and the generalization exponents are the same as those previously employed. Table 22 was generated on these assumptions. Since in this case there are two distinct types of response, each column of $_sE_R$'s is summated in two portions; these are shown in the rows I + II and III + IV respectively. The $_sE_R$ summations determine the theoretical per cent of correct or of erroneous responses (shown by a probability table) at any given choice point, as calculated by the procedure described above (p. 177) for the simpler situation of only two alternative responses. The percentages are given in the last two lines of Table 22.

A glance at the series of theoretical error values shows that there is a sharp increase in the number of errors at II, the terminus of the first group of homogeneous links of the chain. In the body of the table we see that this is due to the relatively large generalization values in rows III and IV, which summate to 1.59σ as compared with the summation of 2.34σ for the correct reaction tendency. The fact that the error maximum falls at II rather than III is evidently due in the last analysis to the principle of greater strength of antedating generalization tendencies as compared with perseverative generalizations.

Generalizing on the preceding considerations, we arrive at our next theorem:

THEOREM 40. *In a mixed homogeneous-heterogeneous four-link linear maze chaining situation, A A B B, the learning task is more difficult for albino rats to master than that in either the pure homogeneous or the pure heterogeneous situation, the maximum difficulty lying definitely at choice point II where it exceeds that of the pure heterogeneous chaining situation, the relationships of the errors being I > IV, II > III, II > I, III > IV.*

The empirical work on double alternation or alternate repetition is fairly extensive. The most comprehensive single quantified study as well as the most recent one was reported by Woodbury (*22; 23; 24*). He employed a linear maze with four choice points constructed on the same general principle as the maze shown as Figure 44 except that there were only two gates at each choice point. At trials 41–50 his animals made the following per cent of errors:

I	II	III	IV
11.3	41.3	12.0	2.0,

i.e.,

$$I > IV, \quad II > III, \quad II > I, \quad \text{and } III > IV,$$

which constitutes a formal confirmation of Theorem 40.

It is important to observe that earlier, Hunter investigated this problem very extensively in a number of different experiments, perhaps the most original and significant of which were those using his temporal mazes. One form of this arrangement was an elevated maze in the shape of a longish rectangle with a path through its middle making two squares. The double alternation behavior sequence consisted in the rat's traversing the middle section, then following around the right-hand square up the middle section and around the right-hand square a second time, up the middle section a third time and around the left-hand square, up the middle section a fourth time and around the left-hand square a second time and back to the starting point where food was now found. In a linear maze such as that used by Woodbury there is a possibility of some difference in the stimuli at the various choice points, but in the temporal maze all of the choice points constitute the identical spot spatially. However, rats are believed to be very sensitive to tracking odors. On this hypothesis the choice point after one traversal around the right-hand square and up the cross-piece will have the odor of the first track, and after the traversal of the square twice this choice point will have an even stronger odor from the two tracks. This more intense stimulus might lead the animal to turn in the opposite direction and go around the left-hand square twice. Then of course there is the factor of the semi-circular canals; clearly there is a difference in the function of these organs when the animal repeatedly passes through the same point in space as distinguished from when it performs the same act twice and then a somewhat different act twice, as in Woodbury's experiment.

Hunter's double alternation temporal maze is obviously not identical with Woodbury's double alternation linear maze. The former is probably more difficult for animals to master than is the latter. As a sample of Hunter's remarks, we have (*16*, p. 528):

> Rat 1 had run the tridimensional l l r r maze 14 times in succession when it was started on the l l r r temporal maze. It was given 109 trials on the temporal maze, but never made a single correct trial. At no time did the animal respond l l l l. With but few exceptions the responses were l r r r or r r r r.

Summary

In summarizing briefly the preceding pages we must emphasize that any forms of behavior links whatever may, and do, constitute simple behavior chains. The restriction in choice of the types of chains discussed above is due to the limited number of those experimentally studied in a quantitative manner so far; and this in turn is due to the limitation in the characteristics of the chains which make them simple enough for quantitative interpretations to be feasible. Even so, we have cited results on the following types: isolated acts (Arnold); the compound trial-and-error chaining of the linear maze (Hill), with terminal reinforcement (Sprow), and serial reinforcement (Gladstone); the homogeneous chain (Arnold); the heterogeneous chain (Hull); the mixed homogeneous-heterogeneous chain (Woodbury); the temporal maze (Hunter); and the rote learning of nonsense syllables (Hovland). Much chaining in ordinary life is verbal and so is related to rote learning such as that of memorized words: poetry, songs, rituals, prose, and so on. Obviously these chains may be as short as two words, as in the association experiment; or they may extend to very large numbers of links, as in elementary numerical counting.

As we have shown, the detailed derivation of the several secondary laws of behavioral chaining involves a certain amount of complexity, but the chaining laws that have emerged so far are moderately simple even if the modes of their manifestation are fairly varied. Stated in terms of errors in four-link chains these laws are:

1. Homogeneous chains tend strongly to the formula: $II > I$ and $III > IV$.

2. Heterogeneous chains tend strongly to the opposite formula: $I > II$ and $IV > III$.

3. Both homogeneous and heterogeneous chains when given terminal reinforcement tend strongly to the formula: $I > IV$ and $II > III$.

4. Both homogeneous and heterogeneous chains when given serial reinforcement tend strongly to the opposite formula: $IV > I$ and $III > II$.

5. Mixed behavior chains composed of homogeneous and heterogeneous subchains of equal length, when given terminal reinforcement, follow the formula: $I > IV, II > III, II > I$, and $III > IV$, with the magnitude of II relatively greater than that found in pure heterogeneous chaining. The mixed form of chaining with serial reinforcement has not yet been investigated either theoretically or empirically, though the primary principles utilized above offer a ready means for this on the theoretical level.

TERMINAL NOTES

THE SIMPLE LOCOMOTION OF RATS TO A TERMINAL GOAL

Another bit of evidence which seems to bear on the above theoretical deduction of homogeneous chaining comes from an experiment which to superficial appearance is very different from those discussed in the preceding pages. This experiment investigated the speed of locomotion of rats in the approach to food through straight 20-foot and 40-foot runways (*11*). Typical results thus secured by five-foot sections of the runways were:

	I	II	III	IV	V	VI	VII	VIII
8-section runway:	6.32″	3.33″	2.57″	2.30″	2.48″	2.33″	1.77″	2.42″
4-section runway:	2.31″	2.08″	1.86″	1.99″				

The relevancy of this experiment to the homogeneous terminal reinforcement problem lies in the fact that each cycle of locomotor activity is like every other and corresponds to the cycle or behavior link of pressing the disks in Arnold's experiment of this type. The mean time required to traverse each five feet of the 20-foot runway was as shown in the 4-section line of data given above. This shows the same tilt-up at section IV as do Figures 43 and 44: 1.86″ vs. 1.99″. Similarly, the 8-section runway shows a tilt-up at the final section: 1.77″ vs. 2.42″. It is clear, however, that some factor not yet known is involved here. This is indicated by the fact that the point of minimum latency tends with continued reinforcements to approach the middle of the series, though upon partial extinction or satiation it again returns to the penultimate response.

The Lack of Homogeneity Within Each Link of a Behavior Chain

Throughout the present chapter we have considered the matter of homogeneity and heterogeneity in terms of the behavior of the links of a chain as such, without analyzing the homogeneity within the links themselves. Thus it is possible to have the links of pressing the disk repeated (as in Arnold's homogeneous experiment, pp. 156ff.). even though the movements in the early phase of pressing the disk, such as reaching the paw forward toward the disk, are different from the terminal movements, such as withdrawing the paw. Similarly, the locomotion in a straight line discussed just above is homogeneous when treated as analogous to complete stepping cycles, even though different legs are involved in doing distinctly separate things at different parts of the cycle (*17*, p. 206). This means that there remains the task of considering the behavior principles involved in the integration process in smaller parts than those considered above. This will be the task of our next chapter.

REFERENCES

1. Arnold, W. J. Simple reaction chains and their integration. I. Homogeneous chaining with terminal reinforcement. *J. Comp. and Physiol. Psychol.*, 1947, *40*, 349–363.
2. Arnold, W. J. Simple reaction chains and their integration. II. Heterogeneous chaining with terminal reinforcement. *J. Comp. and Physiol. Psychol.*, 1947, *40*, 427–440.
3. Arnold, W. J. Simple reaction chains and their integration. III. Heterogeneous chaining with serial reinforcement. *J. Comp. and Physiol. Psychol.*, 1948, *41*, 1–10.
4. Arnold, W. J. Simple reaction chains and their integration. IV. Homogeneous chaining with serial reinforcement. *J. Comp. and Physiol. Psychol.*, 1951, *44*, 276–281.
5. Ebbinghaus, H. *Memory* (trans. by H. A. Ruger and C. E. Bussenius). New York: Teachers College, Columbia Univ. Press, 1913.
6. Gladstone, A. I. Reactively homogeneous compound trial-and-error learning with distributed trials and serial reinforcement. *J. Exper. Psychol.*, 1948, *38*, 289–297.
7. Gladstone, A. I., Yamaguchi, H. G., Hull, C. L., and Felsinger, J. M. Some functional relationships of reaction potential and related phenomena. *J. Exper. Psychol.*, 1947, *37*, 510–526.
8. Herbert, M. J., and Arnold, W. J. A reaction chaining apparatus. *J. Comp. and Physiol. Psychol.*, 1947, *40*, 227–228.
9. Hill, C. J. Goal gradient, anticipation, and perseveration in compound trial-and-error learning. *J. Exper. Psychol.*, 1939, *25*, 566–585.
10. Hovland, C. I. Experimental studies in rote-learning theory. VII. Distribution of practice with varying lengths of lists. *J. Exper. Psychol.*, 1940, *27*, 271–284.
11. Hull, C. L. The rat's speed-of-locomotion gradient in the approach to food. *J. Comp. Psychol.*, 1934, *17*, 393–422.
12. Hull, C. L. *Principles of behavior*. New York: D. Appleton-Century Co., Inc., 1943.
13. Hull, C. L. Reactively heterogeneous compound trial-and-error learning with distributed trials and terminal reinforcement. *J. Exper. Psychol.*, 1947, *37*, 118–135.

14. Hull, C. L. Reactively heterogeneous compound trial-and-error learning with distributed trials and serial reinforcement. *J. Exper. Psychol.*, 1948, *38*, 17–28.

15. Hull, C. L., Hovland, C. I., Ross, R. T., Hall, M., Perkins, D. T., and Fitch, F. B. *Mathematico-deductive theory of rote learning.* New Haven: Yale Univ. Press, 1940.

16. Hunter, W. S. The sensory control of the maze habit in the white rat. *J. Genet. Psychol.*, 1929, *36*, 505–537.

17. Keller, F. S., and Schoenfeld, W. N. *A systematic text in the science of behavior.* New York: Appleton-Century-Crofts, 1950.

18. Lyon, D. C. The relation of length of material to time taken for learning, and the optimum distribution of time. *J. Educ. Psychol.*, 1914, V, 1–9; 85–91; 155–163.

19. Meumann, E. *The psychology of learning* (trans. by J. W. Baird from the third German edition). New York: Appleton, 1913.

20. Montpellier, G. de. An experiment on the order of elimination of blind alleys in maze learning. *J. Genet. Psychol.*, 1933, *43*, 123–139.

21. Sprow, A. J. Reactively homogeneous compound trial-and-error learning with distributed trials and terminal reinforcement. *J. Exper. Psychol.*, 1947, *37*, 197–213.

22. Woodbury, C. B. Double, triple, and quadruple alternation in the white rat. Ph.D. thesis, Yale Univ., 1948.

23. Woodbury, C. B., Double, triple, and quadruple repetition in the white rat. *J. Comp. and Physiol. Psychology*, 1950, *43*, 490–502.

24. Woodbury, C. B. Theory of double, triple, and quadruple repetition. *Psychol. Rev.*, 1951, *58*, 18–29.

7. Learning within the Individual Behavior Link

Simple trial-and-error learning, considered in Chapter 2, was described as a process whereby one response (R_+) of two fairly distinct ones evocable by the same stimulus combination is progressively strengthened, whereas another (R_-) is extinguished. At each trial only one act occurs, and it is immediately reinforced (R_+) or not reinforced (R_-).

Again, in the learning of reaction chains by heterogeneous compound trial and error and terminal reinforcement, say, as presented in Chapter 6 (p. 165 ff), several behavioral links of the sort that are mentioned in the preceding paragraph often are involved in a chain and all are reinforced at the end of the sequence by a single event (feeding). In the linear maze there considered a given true response simply cannot be performed until that of the preceding link has been correctly performed, and at the entrance to each section of the maze a trial-and-error process of door selection must occur before the animal can continue its forward locomotion. This means that there is a checking of forward movement at every wrong response, and at least a secondary reinforcement (based on the subsequent forward locomotion) at every correct response. From a behavioral point of view we must conclude that apart from the differences between one act and the next it is this interruption by the occurrence of errors in progress toward the goal that separates behavior chains into distinct links. This, it is believed, is largely what mediates the trial-and-error learning of behavior links as totalities.

In the present chapter we shall consider the associative organization *within* the separate act involved in simple trial-and-error learning (Chapter 2) and the behavior link, as distinguished from the organization of numerous total links into a chain as a whole (Chapter 6). Thus the units of our present analysis at once become smaller than those considered heretofore. From dealing with the entire behavior link as a unit, we shall now be concerned with the fractional action phases of numerous distinct muscles that occur simultaneously with nicely graded intensity contractions and synchronizations so as to bring about a state of affairs which *as a whole* is reinforcing or not reinforcing. In this way the reinforcement operative within behavior links is *all or none* in nature. Also, our analysis will concern the phenomena of what may be said to be minute behavior, behavior which ultimately will become so slight in extent as to be quite unobservable by the present-day methodologies of behavior investigation. At the same time the analysis itself will still be on a molar basis, as are all our analyses, in the sense that we shall not attempt an ultimate physiological interpretation. Accordingly we shall speak of this as a *micro-molar* approach, and in the following pages we shall adopt a manner of exposition rather different from that of the preceding chapters.

Micro-molar Analysis of Contraction-Intensity Selection by the All-or-none Type of Reinforcement

In order to save ourselves from becoming lost in a maze of expository details, it will be necessary for us to strip the theoretical situation down to the barest essentials; by this device we should be able to take up the six progressively more complex theoretical cases which are to follow without inflicting on the reader undue difficulty of comprehension. Moreover the computational methodologies which we have used heretofore, on the coarser analyses, will now be ignored for the most part because the detailed outcome cannot be checked easily on such minute phenomena.

CASE I. Let us assume, then, the joint action of only two muscles, A and B, occurring simultaneously over an instant of time, and followed immediately by reinforcement or non-reinforcement. Further let us assume that each muscle has available but two contraction intensities. We shall number these contraction intensities I and II. We shall also assume that these contraction intensities initially are equally likely to occur. There are thus in our simple theoretical situation the following contraction possibilities:

Correct
combination

A I   A II
B I   B II

Now let us assume that the contraction-intensities A I and B I will each be reinforced when they occur jointly, but that none of the other combinations will be. Finally let us assume that a single reinforcement will add 4 points to the habit strength of each muscle-contraction phase involved, and that each reaction evocation, whether correct or not, will add .2 of a unit of inhibition to each muscle-contraction phase involved. Accordingly we shall have the possible combinations shown in Table 23, together with the numer-

T A B L E 23. The theoretical reinforcement and inhibitory combinations together with a summary of the net effect on each reaction intensity involved in one evocation of each combination possible within a single behavior link.

Reinforced combination: $A I = +4.0 - .2; B I = +4.0 - .2$
Non-reinforced combination: $A I = -.2;$ $B II = -.2$
Non-reinforced combination: $A II = -.2;$ $B I = -.2$
Non-reinforced combination: $A II = -.2;$ $B II = -.2$
  In summary of A I's: $4.0 - .2 - .2 = 4.0 - .4 = 3.6$
  In summary of B I's: $4.0 - .2 - .2 = 4.0 - .4 = 3.6$
  In summary of A II's: $.2 - .2 = -.4$
  In summary of B II's: $.2 - .2 = -.4$

ical results of the consequent reinforcement or lack of reinforcement shown in the four summary lines. This means, of course, that the two correct reaction intensities on a single set of equally likely trials have both gained 3.6 net points despite one failure combination of each, and that the incorrect phase of each muscle has lost .4 of a point from the two failures. Thus in this sample set of trials there is a net advantage of a correct phase, such as A I, over the competing incorrect phase, A II, since A I gains strength as A II loses. It is evident that while this seemingly indiscriminate reinforcement or non-reinforcement alike of all contraction phases involved within a given behavior link on a given occasion is somewhat different from the trial-and-error learning of behavior links as a whole, it is perfectly consistent with the gradual but ultimate selection of the correct contraction phase combination.

Generalizing from the preceding considerations, we arrive at our next theorem:

THEOREM 41. *Other things equal, the all-or-none type of differential reinforcement of the joint outcome of the simultaneous contraction-intensity of each of several muscles involved in a simple behavior link will, within the limits of the normal oscillation range, result in the gradual elimination of the maladaptive phase combination and its gradual replacement by the adaptive phase combination.*

CASE II. We proceed next to the slightly more complex situation where everything is assumed to be the same as in Case I except that *two* sequential alternative contraction-intensity phases are involved in each of the two muscles. Adding Arabic numerals to indicate the order of the sequential contraction phases involved, we have:

	Correct combination	
First contraction phases:	A I 1	A II 1
	B I 1	B II 1
Second contraction phases:	A I 2	A II 2
	B I 2	B II 2

Taking the various possible of the equally probable combinations yielded by chance, and assuming the same amounts of reinforce-

TABLE 24. The various combinations of equally probable contraction intensities in Case II, together with the resulting increment of reinforcement and inhibition for each evocation.

Correct combination:
A I 1 = +4.0 − .2; B I 1 = +4.0 − .2; A I 2 = +4.0 − .2; B I 2 = +4.0 − .2

Incorrect combinations:
A I 1 = −.2; B I 1 = −.2; A I 2 = −.2; B II 2 = −.2
A I 1 = −.2; B I 1 = −.2; A II 2 = −.2; B I 2 = −.2
A I 1 = −.2; B I 1 = −.2; A II 2 = −.2; B II 2 = −.2

A I 1 = −.2; B II 1 = −.2; A I 2 = −.2; B I 2 = −.2
A I 1 = −.2; B II 1 = −.2; A I 2 = −.2; B II 2 = −.2
A I 1 = − 2; B II 1 = −.2; A II 2 = −.2; B I 2 = −.2
A I 1 = −.2; B II 1 = −.2; A II 2 = −.2; B II 2 = −.2

A II 1 = −.2; B I 1 = −.2; A I 2 = −.2; B I 2 = −.2
A II 1 = −.2; B I 1 = −.2; A I 2 = −.2; B II 2 = −.2
A II 1 = −.2; B I 1 = −.2; A II 2 = −.2; B I 2 = −.2
A II 1 = −.2; B I 1 = −.2; A II 2 = −.2; B II 2 = −.2

A II 1 = −.2; B II 1 = −.2; A I 2 = −.2; B I 2 = −.2
A II 1 = −.2; B II 1 = −.2; A I 2 = −.2; B II 2 = −.2
A II 1 = −.2; B II 1 = −.2; A II 2 = −.2; B I 2 = −.2
A II 1 = −.2; B II 1 = −.2; A II 2 = −.2; B II 2 = −.2

ment and inhibition at each reaction evocation as in Case I, we have the results shown in Table 24.

If, now, we cast up the aggregate reinforcements and inhibitions of the above single set of equally probable correct and incorrect contraction-intensity phases involved (as shown in Table 24), we have Table 25.

TABLE 25. Summary of the theoretical net reinforcement and inhibitory results of one complete set of equally probable reaction evocation combinations on the eight possible contraction phases.

$$A I 1 = 4 - .2 - .2 - .2 - .2 - .2 - .2 - .2 - .2 = 4.0 - 1.6 = 2.4$$
$$B I 1 = 4 - .2 - .2 - .2 - .2 - .2 - .2 - .2 - .2 = 4.0 - 1.6 = 2.4$$
$$A I 2 = 4 - .2 - .2 - .2 - .2 - .2 - .2 - .2 - .2 = 4.0 - 1.6 = 2.4$$
$$B I 2 = 4 - .2 - .2 - .2 - .2 - .2 - .2 - .2 - .2 = 4.0 - 1.6 = 2.4$$

$$A II 1 = -.2 - .2 - .2 - .2 - .2 - .2 - .2 - .2 = -1.6$$
$$B II 1 = -.2 - .2 - .2 - .2 - .2 - .2 - .2 - .2 = -1.6$$
$$A II 2 = -.2 - .2 - .2 - .2 - .2 - .2 - .2 - .2 = -1.6$$
$$B II 2 = -.2 - .2 - .2 - .2 - .2 - .2 - .2 - .2 = -1.6$$

Thus we see that the four correct contraction intensities all show a net gain of 2.4 points, whereas the incorrect contraction-intensity phases all lose 1.6 points. This makes a *relative* gain for the correct one of each pair of competing contraction intensities, which indicates that whenever correct and incorrect contraction-intensity phases occur anywhere in the combination making up a behavior link, by the all-or-none method of reinforcement an effective selection of the correct from the incorrect contraction-intensity phases is quite possible.

Generalizing on the preceding considerations, we arrive at our next theorem:

THEOREM 42. *In the all-or-none type of reinforcement of simple acts the elimination of faulty alternative successive contraction-intensity phases of the same muscle and the stabilization of adaptive contraction-intensity phases within a behavior link will gradually occur.*

It may be added that this section has given an account of an important aspect of behavior commonly called *skill*.

Learning Based on Correlated Reinforcement Intensities

It is to be observed that within each behavior link in the acquisition of motor coordination, each successful act usually results in a combination of stimulation which forms part of a generalization continuum, the other portions of which may not be directly associated with reinforcement. Now the portion of this continuum which is consistently associated with success (reinforcement) automatically acquires (Corollary ii) the power of secondary reinforcement (4, pp. 84 ff.). Moreover, the power of secondary reinforcement itself (4, pp. 183 ff.) presumably generalizes to other portions of the continuum according to the principle of stimulus generalization (X). Also it will be recalled that stimulus generalization operates as a negative growth function, the maximum point of the generalization being at that point of the stimulus continuum which is directly associated with reinforcement (5, pp. 18 ff.).

It thus comes about that acts which on certain trials fail of primary reinforcement of the all-or-none variety but approach more or less closely to the conditions necessary for such reinforcement, will receive *secondary* reinforcement as an increasing function of the approximation to the conditions necessary to primary reinforcement. Accordingly the joint behavioral outcome of the several muscular contraction-intensity phases which occur in any act will both yield and receive a functionally graded amount of (secondary) reinforcement. For example, in archery practice if the arrow hits the edge of the target more success is indicated than if it does not strike the target at all, and the smaller the ring it enters, the greater is the success, the very center of the target indicating the greatest success of all and so generating the greatest reinforcement. Similarly, the more pins a bowler knocks down with his ball, the greater will be the reinforcement of his act; the louder the laughter at the telling of a joke, the greater will be the reinforcement received by the comedian; the closer the approximation of a letter to the form of the copy, the greater will be the reinforcement to him who is learning to write; the more words typed per minute by the commercial student, the greater will be her reinforcement; the shorter the time required to run one hundred yards, the greater will be the reinforcement to the sprinter; the more rapidly the pile of work pieces increases, the greater will be the reinforcement to the piece worker; and so we could go on endlessly. All of these reinforcements, be it noted, are secondary in nature. Reinforcement by gradation according to the approach of the reaction to perfection will be called *correlated reinforcement intensity*.

Generalizing from the preceding considerations, we formulate our next theorem:

THEOREM 43. *When a reaction evocation has been reinforced one or more times in the presence of some phase of a stimulus continuum, subsequent evocations, whether the latter are maximally correct or not, will tend to receive graded secondary correlated reinforcement by generalization from other phases of this stimulus continuum.*

We are now ready to proceed to the consideration of Case III.

CASE III. At the end of the preceding section involving the learning of simple motor coordinations within a behavior link, we considered only two degrees of contraction intensity at any contraction phase of a given muscle. We must now recall, in the interest of realism, that according to the principle of response oscillation ($_sO_R$) there are an infinite number of gradations in the possibility

TABLE 26. The amounts of reinforcement and inhibition resulting from a single response involving each of the different response-intensity combinations in a theoretical behavior-link situation of the all-or-none type of correlated reinforcement (Case III).

A I and B I: $1 + 1 = 2$ units of reinf. and .2 unit each of I_R
A I and B II: $1 + 2 = 3$ units of reinf. and .2 unit each of I_R
A I and B III: $1 + 3 = 4$ units of reinf. and .2 unit each of I_R
A II and B I: $2 + 1 = 3$ units of reinf. and .2 unit each of I_R
A II and B II: $2 + 2 = 4$ units of reinf. and .2 unit each of I_R
A II and B III: $2 + 3 = 5$ units of reinf. and .2 unit each of I_R
A III and B I: $3 + 1 = 4$ units of reinf. and .2 unit each of I_R
A III and B II: $3 + 2 = 5$ units of reinf. and .2 unit each of I_R
A III and B III: $3 + 3 = 6$ units of reinf. and .2 unit each of I_R

of contraction intensity of any given muscle at any instant. These contraction intensities, moreover, are not distributed evenly over the total range, as assumed above, but presumably are distributed approximately according to the normal law of chance (4, p. 319). However, since it is impracticable in the present immature state of the science to work out an illustrative example involving a great range of gradations of contraction intensities, we shall as usual assume an artificially simplified situation which involves one at a time a single reaction phase of each of two muscles, A and B, acting simultaneously, each muscle having *three* intensities of contraction: I, II, and III; and each of the degrees of joint contraction intensity having a different degree of reinforcement. We shall further assume, in harmony with the principle of correlated reinforcement, that A I and B I contribute to the joint reinforcing state of affairs as a whole one point each; that A II and B II contribute 2 points each; and that A III and B III contribute 3 points each. Using the same notation as before, we have the following contraction-intensity possibilities *with parallel reinforcements:*

$$
\begin{array}{ll}
\text{A I 1} & \text{B I 1} \\
\text{A II 2} & \text{B II 2} \\
\text{A III 3} & \text{B III 3}
\end{array}
$$

This yields in the various possible combinations the amounts of joint reaction potential and of extinction effects listed in Table 26. An inspection of that set of summated values shows that the outcome of the joint contraction-intensity combination yields a graded set of net reinforcement results which is nicely correlated with the reinforcement differences. By sorting out the three reinforcement values of each response intensity, and averaging, we find that:

A I and B I each averages a reinforcement intensity of 3;

A II and B II each averages a reinforcement intensity of 4;

A III and B III each averages a reinforcement intensity of 5.

This insures, as practice continues, a progressive dominance, i.e., a progressive increase in the evocation of the more strongly reinforced contraction-intensity phases A III and B III as contrasted with the other two contraction intensities, especially A I and B I, even though both contractions of each combination receive equal reinforcement at any given evocation.

Generalizing from the above considerations, we arrive at our next theorem:

> THEOREM 44. *Other things equal, the correlated reinforcement of simple variable acts is favorable to the selection of response intensities which are more strongly reinforcing rather than of those which are less strongly reinforcing.*

Micro-Molar Analysis of Response-Intensity Generalization

CASE IV. At this point we must notice explicitly the entrance of the principle of response generalization (4, pp. 316–319). In a completely logical presentation this would, except for expository difficulties, have been introduced as involved in Case III. The principle of response generalization states in effect that every habit increment of response intensity oscillates more or less symmetrically (*4*, pp. 304 ff.) about a central response intensity. This means that as the habit strengths of A III and B III just cited grow strong, they will begin to generalize and therefore to vary about this new center of oscillation (xiii). This generalization will create a new group of evokable reaction-intensity phases, A IV and B IV. But as soon as A IV and B IV occur, they will be reinforced. Also, as a result the first group of reinforcements A I and B I will gradually weaken relatively, and possibly drop out of the competition.

If, now, the principle of correlated reinforcement is continued, A IV and B IV jointly yielding a reinforcement of 6 units, it is clear that in the course of time A IV and B IV will come respectively to be new centers of oscillatory response generalization, exactly as described above for A III and B III, thus:

$$
\begin{array}{ll}
\text{A II 2} & \text{B II 2} \\
\text{A III 3} & \text{B III 3} \\
\text{A IV 4} & \text{B IV 4}
\end{array}
$$

Generalizing from the preceding considerations, much as we did from Table 26, we arrive at our next theorem:

THEOREM 45. *Other things equal, response intensities will gradually be shifted an indefinite distance along any reinforcement continuum as long as the reinforcement increment continues to be positively correlated and the increment of extinction results remains relatively constant.*

This is believed to be a major molar mechanism responsible for the acquisition of *precise motor coordinations and skills.*

CASE V. But what may be expected to occur with simultaneous reinforcement throughout a behavior link if both muscles continue to respond as before but B III now combines less efficiently with the A's than before so that the joint action has the same reinforcement as B I? This means that so far as the B muscle is concerned the contribution of B II is now at its maximum, and from there the contribution slopes off in both directions to B I and to B III. In that case, neglecting previous learning, we shall have the reinforcement increments shown in Table 27.

TABLE 27. The various combinations of equally probable contraction intensities of two muscles, in one of which (A) the reinforcement gradient continues to rise as in Table 26, but in the other of which (B) the gradient ceases to rise with further shift in reaction intensity. The table shows the increments of reinforcement and extinction resulting from each combination.

A I and B I: 2 units of reinforcement and .2 unit each of I_R
A I and B II: 3 units of reinforcement and .2 unit each of I_R
A I and B III: 2 units of reinforcement and .2 unit each of I_R

A II and B I: 3 units of reinforcement and .2 unit each of I_R
A II and B II: 4 units of reinforcement and .2 unit each of I_R
A II and B III: 3 units of reinforcement and .2 unit each of I_R

A III and B I: 4 units of reinforcement and .2 unit each of I_R
A III and B II: 5 units of reinforcement and .2 unit each of I_R
A III and B III: 4 units of reinforcement and .2 unit each of I_R

Sorting out the total reinforcements and inhibitions of all the A combinations which contain A I, A II, A III, B I, B II, and B III, we have the results given in Table 28.

TABLE 28. A summation of the detailed reinforcements and inhibition increments as presented in Table 27.

$$A\ I\ \ \ = 2 - .2 + 3 - .2 + 2 - .2 = \ 7 - .6 = \ \ 6.4$$
$$A\ II\ \ = 3 - .2 + 4 - .2 + 3 - .2 = 10 - .6 = \ \ 9.4$$
$$A\ III\ = 4 - .2 + 5 - .2 + 4 - .2 = 13 - .6 = \mathbf{12.4}$$

$$B\ I\ \ \ = 2 - .2 + 3 - .2 + 4 - .2 = \ 9 - .6 = \ \ 8.4$$
$$B\ II\ \ = 3 - .2 + 4 - .2 + 5 - .2 = 12 - .6 = \mathbf{11.4}$$
$$B\ III\ = 2 - .2 + 3 - .2 + 4 - .2 = \ 9 - .6 = \ \ 8.4$$

An examination of these combined incremental and inhibitory results shows that, quite as one would expect intuitively, contraction-intensity phase A III has emerged as dominant over both A II and A I, with which it is in competition, whereas B II has emerged as dominant over both B I and B III, with which it is in competition. In the case of the first muscle the increased reinforcement has led to a further shift in reaction intensity from that at the first reaction evocation, but in the case of the second muscle the change (*decrease*) in the amount of joint reinforcement beyond B II has led to the stabilization of the contraction intensity which yields the optimal amount of net reinforcement. It is to be expected that sooner or later muscle A will reach a contraction intensity such that its advance oscillatory generalization will decline, as has been assumed in effect to be the situation in the case of muscle B. At that point its progressive shift in reaction intensity may be expected to become stabilized. Both muscles will then have become as fully coordinated as possible.

Generalizing from the above considerations, we arrive at our next theorem:

> THEOREM 46. *Other things equal, each muscle in a group involved in an act which permits of varying amounts of reinforcement according to the net effect of the joint activity, will gradually shift its individual contraction intensity in the direction of that intensity which when joined with the contraction intensities of the other muscles will yield a maximum of reinforcement, and will there become stabilized.*

Micro-molar Analysis of the Role of a Work Differential in the Coordination within a Response Link

In the preceding sections we have indirectly introduced the factor of work into the discussion by recognizing the influence of reactive inhibition. Now we shall recognize explicitly the influence of a *differential* work (W) factor (*4*, p. 279) on the acquisition of skilled coordination. Our exposition of the role of the differential amounts of work involved in the process of the acquisition of skill will employ a numerical example analogous to the one used in the preceding section.

CASE VI. Let it be assumed, then, that we have the artificially simplified situation of only two muscles involved in an act, and that each muscle has only three contraction-intensity phases, all of which at the outset are equally likely to occur. However, in this example all possible reaction combinations will be assumed to yield the same reinforcement, e.g., the same amount of food; and each reinforcement will be assumed to produce an increment of two units of habit strength. The amount of work, on the other hand, will be varied; A I and B I will each generate .2 of a unit of inhibition; A II and B II will each generate .4 of a unit of inhibition; and A III and B III will each generate .8 of a unit of inhibition from the movement in question:

$$
\begin{array}{ll}
\text{A I } 2 - .2 & \text{B I } 2 - .2 \\
\text{A II } 2 - .4 & \text{B II } 2 - .4 \\
\text{A III } 2 - .8 & \text{B III } 2 - .8
\end{array}
$$

Taking the various contraction-intensity combinations on this basis, we have Table 29. Summarizing these effects, we have Table 30.

An examination of these values shows that in the case of both muscle A and muscle B the series of reaction evocations have resulted in a definite net advantage in favor of contraction phase I, which involved the least amount of work and which therefore generated the least amount of inhibition for both muscles.

TABLE 29. The reaction and inhibitory potential increments generated by one response evoked by each combination of the conditions of Case VI where reinforcement is constant but the amount of work (W) (and so the amount of I_R generated at reaction evocation) varies (Case VI).

A I and B I: A I $= 2 - .2$ and B I $= 2 - .2$
A I and B II: A I $= 2 - .2$ and B II $= 2 - .4$
A I and B III: A I $= 2 - .2$ and B III $= 2 - .8$

A II and B I: A II $= 2 - .4$ and B I $= 2 - .2$
A II and B II: A II $= 2 - .4$ and B II $= 2 - .4$
A II and B III: A II $= 2 - .4$ and B III $= 2 - .8$

A III and B I: A III $= 2 - .8$ and B I $= 2 - .2$
A III and B II: A III $= 2 - .8$ and B II $= 2 - .4$
A III and B III: A III $= 2 - .8$ and B III $= 2 - .8$

TABLE 30. A summation of the detailed learning and inhibition increments presented in Table 29.

A I $= 2 - .2 + 2 - .2 + 2 - .2 = 6 - .6 = 5.4$
A II $= 2 - .4 + 2 - .4 + 2 - .4 = 6 - 1.2 = 4.8$
A III $= 2 - .8 + 2 - .8 + 2 - .8 = 6 - 2.4 = 3.6$

B I $= 2 - .2 + 2 - .2 + 2 - .2 = 6 - .6 = 5.4$
B II $= 2 - .4 + 2 - .4 + 2 - .4 = 6 - 1.2 = 4.8$
B III $= 2 - .8 + 2 - .8 + 2 - .8 = 6 - 2.4 = 3.6$

But as contraction phase I becomes dominant and phase III is partially extinguished, the center of oscillation will shift from III to II, with the result that oscillation or response-intensity generalization (4, pp. 316, 319) will spread to the next weaker contraction phase (I), which involves a still smaller amount of work. This progression will obviously go forward until a point is reached at which the original positive reinforcement begins to diminish either in amount or in probability of occurrence, or in both. At that point the migration of contraction-intensity phases will begin to stabilize itself. Final stabilization will occur at the point at which the maximum net reaction potential ($_s\overline{E}_R$) is attained. The locus of this point will be determined, of course, jointly by (1) the slope of the amount of inhibition as a function of work (W), and (2) the falling of the reaction potential as a function of the reduced muscular contraction. We do not know enough about the parameters involved to make such an attempt at the present time.

Generalizing on the basis of the above considerations, we arrive at our next theorem:

> THEOREM 47. *Other factors being equal, the various contraction-intensity phases of every muscle involved in the performance of a simple behavior link will gradually shift until they involve less work, eventually reaching a minimum where they will stabilize.*

At this point we may consider the *joint* effect of varying amounts of reinforcement on the one hand (Theorem 45) and of varying amounts of work in performing an act (Theorem 46) on the other, each originally treated separately. This *joint* coordination represents the maximum of adaptive efficiency and the maximum of attainable skill.

Generalizing from the above considerations, we arrive at our next theorem:

> THEOREM 48. *Other things equal, the repeated performance and reinforcement of simple behavior links tend to shift the contraction-intensity phases of the several muscles in such a way as to attain the maximum of reinforcement which is consistent with a minimum of work.*

Response Generalization and the Micro-molar Analysis of Restrictive Reinforcement of Response Intensity

At this point we must inquire in a little detail into the acquisition of a particular aspect of motor adjustments in separate behavior links. We have recognized above that the principle of behavioral oscillation formally yields response generalization. Now we face specifically the problem of restrictive reinforcement.

Let us assume that we have an animal in the presence of a bar attached to a recording spring dynamometer which will yield a pellet of food when the bar is pressed downward to the extent of 20 grams or more, but will not yield food for pressures of less than 20 grams. When the animal chances to press the bar to the extent of 26 grams, say, food will be delivered and the reaction will be reinforced. This increment in reaction intensity will generalize on the basis of the proprioceptive stimulus intensity and the oscillation function.

As practice continues, some of the response intensities will fall below the 20-gram limit and will begin to suffer extinction. This will not only attenuate still further the weak response itself, but through the stimulus-intensity generalization of inhibition it will cause adjacent stronger reaction tendencies to lose strength even at intensities above the limit of reinforcement. This in turn will remove the competition from the low level, permitting responses from the higher levels to be evoked. These responses will, of course, be reinforced, which will still further strengthen the tendencies at the higher levels and also increase the *generalized* reaction potentials at the levels consistently extinguished. As a result a small number of responses below the lower reinforcement level will continue to occur.

Generalizing on the above considerations, we arrive at our next two theorems:

THEOREM 49. *Where response intensities are given reinforcements restricted at the lower limit only, the frequency of the responses below the limit will gradually diminish, but a few responses below this level will continue to occur.*

THEOREM 50. *If the lower limit of restricted reinforcement is raised, the whole distribution of reaction intensities will be raised, many responses now occurring which have never previously been reinforced.*

Suppose, now, that we impose a second or *upper* restriction on the reaction intensities which will be reinforced, such that the new restriction falls appreciably below the level of response intensities made under the lower restriction when acting alone. A case in point would be to impose an above-30-gram restriction on a set of responses previously set up under a 20-gram lower limit. It is at once evident that all those responses falling above the 30-gram limit will tend to be extinguished, and that this inhibition will, by the principle of stimulus generalization, generalize especially upon the upper portion of the reaction intensities within the range really reinforced. This will gradually reduce the frequency of responses not only above the upper reinforcement limit but also in the upper portion of the intensities really reinforced.

Generalizing from these considerations, we arrive at our next theorem:

> THEOREM 51. *When an upper restrictive reinforcement limit is placed on a reaction intensity distribution set up under a lower restrictive limit, and the upper limit falls appreciably below the range already occurring, (a) the distribution will be narrowed, (b) its central tendency will shift downward, and (c) it will present a larger range below the lower limit of reinforcement than it did under the lower limit alone.*

At this point we must recall a principle already employed. This is to the effect that where we have a work gradient, as here, there will be a greater amount of extinctive inhibition generating from each response *above* the upper reinforcement limit (because of more work there) than from each one *below* the lower reinforcement limit. The generalization of this greater amount of inhibition above the upper reinforcement limit will depress, and so compress, the upper response range more than will the generalization of the inhibition below the lower response range.

Generalizing from these considerations, we arrive at our final theorem of this series:

> THEOREM 52. *When a double restrictive reinforcement limit is placed on reaction intensities, the range of the unreinforced distribution below the lower limit will exceed the range of unreinforced distribution above the upper limit, and the point of maximum reaction-intensity frequency will fall closer to the lower limit than to the upper limit.*

Empirical Data Relevant to the Validity of the Preceding Micro-molar Analysis

Now at the conclusion of our micro-molar analysis of the acquisition of simple adjustment learning within behavior links, let us see how far the preceding theoretical deductions are substantiated by empirical evidence. At the outset of this search it must be confessed that as yet there has been no direct experimental verification of the theory regarding the elimination of faulty intensity-of-contraction phases of individual muscles. Presumably such an experiment could be performed by cutting the muscle attachments of all but the major muscle on an animal's leg, and then recording the movement intensities of the part of the leg primarily involved in the activation of this one muscle. After the wounds incidental to the operation had healed and the animal had become habituated to the experimental conditions, a recording dynamometer could be attached to the moving member and the animal when hungry would be reinforced for such intensities of contraction as the experiment would require, but not for others. Until some such experiment is performed we can only make inferences from analogical studies involving the normal joint action of numerous muscles as observed in intact organisms.

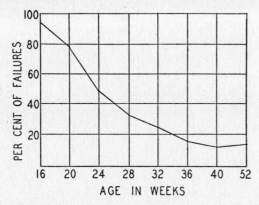

FIGURE 48. Graph showing mean per cent of failure of twelve or more infants of differ-ent ages to reach a red one-inch cube placed on a plane wooden surface in front of them. Adapted from Halverson (*3*, p. 161).

Fortunately, several fairly pertinent investigations of the latter type are now available.

Empirical verification of Theorems 46, 47, and 48 is furnished by the fact that the initial awkward and angular movements made while an act is being learned gradually become linear where rein-forcement conditions permit, and tend to follow smooth curves where changes of direction are required. This is because sharp changes in direction or other sudden stops and starts in movement require work to overcome the momentum in deceleration and the inertia in subsequent acceleration. An illustration of this at a very primitive level is reported in a meticulous study by Halverson con-cerning the acquisition by infants of the power to reach and grasp. The results from one part of this investigation are summarized as follows (*3*, p. 273):

Three forms of [reaching] approach appear: the backhand sweep; the circuitous, which includes, besides the angular and scooping sweeps, the less circuitous reaching; and the direct (straight) approaches. Infants from 16 weeks to 28 weeks of age employ either the backhand approach, or the very circuitous approach in reaching. Infants of 32 and 36 weeks use a less circuitous form of approach in reaching for the cube and infants of 40 and 52 weeks usually employ the direct approach. *Similarly, the backhand and circuitous approaches straighten out into the direct approach.* [Italics ours.]

And again (*3*, p. 274):

From 16 weeks to 24 weeks, infants often raise the hand, thrust it forward circuitously, and lower it in a manner which suggests that the approach consists of three individual acts. *At 40 weeks no trace of these separate acts is discernible; they are incorporated into one fluent reaching movement.* [Italics ours.]

A precise indication of the progress of young children in the acquisition of this primitive type of skill is given by the graph reproduced as Figure 48. Unfortunately for its illustrative value here, the learning involved in Halverson's study is believed by him to be complicated to a considerable but unknown degree by maturation (*3*, p. 258).

General verification of Theorem 48 is found in the universally observed fact that at the beginning of learning, simple cyclical acts requiring precision of performance are carried out awkwardly, slowly, uneconomically, and with poor success. This is evidently due to the fact that the contraction phases of the several muscles involved are not effectively coordinated by associated stimulus traces. However, with continued practice the unnecessary movement phases are gradually eliminated, pauses between movement segments disappear, and movements from point to point necessary in the operation become either straight lines or gentler curves. This is nicely illustrated by the record made by the Gilbreths (*2*) of the left-hand movements of a man relearning to operate a drill press after 25 years of no practice. Stereoscopic photographs were made of the path of a small electric light attached to the man's left hand. From these photographs three-dimensional wire models were made of typical behavior cycles at four stages of practice. These wire movement models were photographed and have been

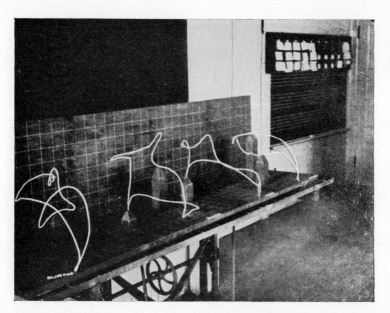

FIGURE 49. Three-dimensional models of the path of the left hand of a man re-learning to operate a drill press, at four different stages of training, the final stage being at the right. Unfortunately for the evidential value of this illustration, the learning represented occurred under specific instructions to eliminate waste motions. Its relevance here lies in the theoretical expectation that uninstructed practice would tend in time spontaneously to produce much the same kinds of movement simplification, though not so quickly and not so markedly as under the Gilbreth type of instruction. Reproduced from Gilbreth and Gilbreth (2, pp. 90–91).

reproduced as Figure 49. A study of these models shows a steady and marked simplification, shortening, and smoothing of the segments making up the action cycle from an early stage of practice, at the left, to a late stage, at the right. The success or precision of skilled action in industry is reflected in the usual increase in payment with length of training.

A second series of studies of a quite different type was begun by Hays and Woodbury who used an apparatus which was essentially a Skinner box with recording dynamometer. Their study shows (4, p. 305) the distribution of bar-pressure intensities of an albino rat. The mechanism was so set that all pressures above a 21-gram minimum were reinforced by a small cylinder of specially prepared food, and pressures below 21 grams were not reinforced. After several hundred trials of this restricted reinforcement had been given, a distribution of the responses showed (1) that most of the reaction intensities exceeded the 21-gram minimum, some of them by as much as 20 grams, and (2) that the distribution was approximately symmetrical. Thus Theorem 49 finds empirical verification.

We now approach a more complex problem. Hays and Woodbury shifted the critical reaction intensity from 21 to 38 grams. This change caused the distribution as a whole to move in the direction of greater reaction intensity, nearly half of the reactions under the new conditions exceeding the maximum reaction obtained under the first conditions. This is the main point of the empirical illustration: differential reinforcement of certain contraction intensities of a variable response causes the distribution to shift away from the unreinforced reaction intensities in the direction of the reinforced ones (4, p. 305). Thus Theorem 50 also finds empirical verification.

An experiment which considerably extended the Hays-Woodbury study was performed by Arnold (7). The apparatus used was the same as in the former study except that after the animals had learned to obtain food by receiving reinforcement only when their pressure exceeded 30 grams, it was modified in such a manner as to yield food only when pressures were made within an arbitrary range falling between 30 grams and 40 grams. The distributions of the reaction intensities of three typical animals at the last hundred of 800 trials are shown in the upper portion of Figure 50. Here we see that most of the reactions fall considerably above the minimum

marked by the broken vertical line. The lower portion of this
figure shows the distribution of pressures on the last hundred of
300 trials after the upper limit was imposed. It may be seen in this
graph that following the introduction of the upper limit there is a
marked reduction in the number of strong-intensity reactions.
Secondly, there is a shift of the distribution as a whole, somewhat
in the weak direction. Thirdly, there appears to be a net narrowing
of the amount of variability. In a word, these three facts furnish

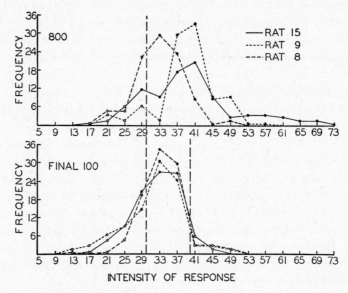

FIGURE 50. Figure showing (upper graph) the distribution of reaction intensities by
rats on a recording dynamometer where responses are reinforced by food only when they
exceed 30 grams in pressure, and (lower graph) when they fall between 30 grams and
40 grams. Adapted from a figure published by Arnold (7).

empirical verification to parts a, b, and c of Theorem 51. Finally
it may also be noted by inspection of the lower portion of Figure 50
that the spread beyond the lower reaction-intensity limit is appreciably greater than that beyond the upper reaction-intensity limit,
and that the maximum frequency falls closer to the lower limit
than the upper one, which furnishes empirical substantiation to
Theorem 52.

    As an example of the remarkable lengths to which training may
be carried through the progressive shifting of response intensities
by means of judicious reinforcement of small oscillatory variations

in a favorable direction, we have a striking experiment performed a few years ago by Skinner (6; 7). He trained an ordinary albino rat to lift a rather heavy steel ball in its paws and drop it into a tube which projected approximately a centimeter above the floor of the apparatus. The falling ball made an electric contact lower in the tube, which caused a magnetic food-vending device to deliver a pellet of food to the animal, thereby reinforcing the act. On the basis of the maxim that "an act must first occur before it can be reinforced," such an achievement in training would be impossible because the acts which occurred late in the training did not occur at all at its beginning. However, the technique employed by Skinner when taken in conjunction with the principles elaborated in this chapter make the feat perfectly intelligible. He first induced the rat to roll the ball a little in any direction whatever, giving food reinforcement after each response. Later, whenever this act varied in a favorable direction, e.g., when the ball was rolled toward the tube, it was reinforced, but it was not reinforced when the ball was rolled in any other direction. At the beginning the tube was lowered so that it represented only a hole in the floor. Thus the rat had only to roll the ball to the hole, and as it fell in the act was complete. The last and critical stage was to raise the tube ever so slightly above the floor of the apparatus. When the slight variations of preceding behavior necessary to overcome this obstacle were fixed by trial and error and differential reinforcement, the tube was raised slightly again, and some of the small variations of the motor coordination previously formed were sufficient to overcome the new obstacle. As practice was continued the tube was progressively raised and the rat's behavior gradually adapted to it until at the end of the training the animal was lifting the ball a full centimeter.

The exceedingly gradual progress of human skills and inventions, when viewed in historical perspective, rather suggests that a mechanism somewhat similar to that described above may be involved in addition to the advantage which the possession of language undoubtedly gives to man. In the latter respect men differ from rats in their ability under favorable circumstances to advance by larger steps in the direction of behavior novelty. The reason for the fact that the higher forms of non-speaking organisms possess greater power to acquire complex skills and coordinations than do the lower forms, probably lies mainly in their greater capacity for differential secondary correlated reinforcement (*4*, pp. 84 ff.); and this presumably arises from a greater capacity for differentiating (discriminating) more precisely the movements which lead more closely or less closely to states of affairs uniformly associated with primary reinforcement.

Summary

Ordinary behavior analysis is based on the reaction chain as a whole where success at a link is reinforced (secondarily) by progress toward a point of primary reinforcement or goal, and where errors at once produce a frustrating interruption in progress toward the goal. Such coarse divisions of behavior are not available for the selective process within the individual behavior link where the occurrence of an erroneous response does *not* cause a behavior interruption before the end of the link. At that time all reaction phases entering into the link are alike reinforced or not reinforced according to their joint results, regardless of the potential reinforcement virtues of the separate response phases when in other combinations. This form of learning is accordingly said to have an all-or-none type of reinforcement.

The preliminary micro-molar analysis of acts or links which we have called "simple" reveals a situation which is far from simple. Behavior links within themselves appear to constitute essentially a flux of action. Upon closer examination this proves to be made up of a series of overlapping strands of muscular contractions, each strand consisting in a flux of contraction-intensity phases of an individual muscle taking part in what is called the behavior link.

This picture of simple behavior links at once raises a number of serious questions. For example, according to the principles of trial-and-error learning based on reinforcement (as outlined in Chapters 2 and 3), how can such acts be selected from these more or less overlapping sequences of undifferentiated contractile phases? Another question concerns the simultaneous contraction-intensity phase selection in the several muscles. The answer to this is particularly important in view of the fact that most contraction-intensity phases of all the muscles involved in a given act must alike suffer reinforcement or extinction effects based on the outcome of the joint action of all. This is the so-called all-or-none type of reinforcement or extinction. There seems to be no *separate* trial-and-error learning for the muscular contractions within a behavior link.

An analysis of a pair of simple examples brings us to the conclusion that the all-or-none type of differential terminal reinforcement is capable of the effective selection of the more adaptive contraction-intensity phases from the less adaptive contraction-intensity phases of each muscle at each stage of an act.

A further analysis of the learning of simple acts or skills leads to the view that reinforcement is often not only all-or-none, or primary, but is secondary in nature; it is correlated or graded according to the nature of the joint outcome of the act. On the basis of the working out of an example we conclude that adaptive variations arising in accordance with the principle of behavioral oscillation $(_sO_R)$ can be selected from less adaptive ones quite effectively by correlated secondary reinforcement.

But granted that a sequence of parallel contraction-intensity phases which will approach a maximum correlated reinforcement can be selected, there remains another dimension in the reaction picture—that of the economy of energy consumption. By means of a simple example it is shown how those oscillatory variations which chance to reduce the work factor will, other things equal, gradually lead to more rapid and also to less fatiguing performances of uncomplicated repetitive acts. This is in conformity with the molar law of less work (*4*, p. 293).

In a still more minute examination of the acquisition of the motor coordination of behavior links and skill, the process of response generalization has been analyzed. It was found that the oscillation factor superposed upon the generalization on the stimulus dimension produces the phenomenon of *response intensity generalization* to which the response is attached (*4*, p. 316). From this it follows that differential reinforcement above a critical intensity of response will push the whole distribution of stimulus intensities upward; that putting on an upper limit will push the distribution of stimulus intensities downward; that a double (upper and lower) restrictive reinforcement limit will narrow the range of reaction intensity; that in such a case the reactions beyond the lower limit will extend farther than those beyond the upper limit; and that the mode of the response intensity will fall closer to the lower limit than to the upper limit. All of these latter theoretical deductions are supported by empirical observations.

And finally it may be pointed out that the principles of behavior oscillation and correlated reinforcement as stated in the preceding paragraph have yielded an understanding of how *needed novel acts never previously performed may come into existence* so that their reinforcement may occur in the conventional manner, a problem that has greatly disturbed some theorists.

REFERENCES

1. Arnold, W. J. An exploratory investigation of primary response generalization. *J. Comp. Psychol.*, 1945, *38*, 87–102.
2. Gilbreth, F. B., and Gilbreth, L. M. *Applied motion study.* New York: Macmillan Co., 1919.
3. Halverson, H. M. An experimental study of prehension in infants by means of systematic cinema records. *Genet. Psychol. Monogr.*, 1931, *10*, 107–286.
4. Hull, C. L. *Principles of behavior.* New York: D. Appleton-Century Co., Inc., 1943.
5. Hull, C. L. *Essentials of behavior.* New Haven: Yale Univ. Press, 1951.
6. Skinner B. F. Rat works slot machine for a living. *Life Magazine,* May 31, 1937, 80–81.
7. Skinner, B. F. *The behavior of organisms.* New York: D. Appleton-Century Co., Inc., 1938.

8. Behavior in Relation to Objects in Space

All behavior must necessarily occur in space. To be adaptive, however, much behavior, though by no means all, must take place in certain relationships to one or more specific *objects* in space. Behavior in relation to objects and points in space has definite characteristics. Except in the recent past, students of behavior have for the most part not explicitly recognized approach and avoidance behavior as a division of psychology requiring special and distinctive treatment. In the present work we ourselves have so far avoided the explicit consideration of this important phase of behavior theory. Now, however, we have reached a point in our exposition at which we can give it the somewhat detailed consideration which its importance and complexity require.

At first glance it may seem that behavior toward objects in space involves no special problems beyond those encountered in any other phase of behavior. To an anthropomorphic psychology the reaction to objects in space presents no special problems because the actual situations present no personal problems to normal humans. We are prone, therefore, naively to pass such situations by without raising the theoretical question of how non-orientational behavior differs from those forms involving the reaction directly to objects in space. At the very outset of the present chapter we must divest ourselves of this natural but fatal complacency regarding approach and avoidance phenomena.

Preliminary Qualitative Theoretical Analysis of Adience and Abience

Let us suppose that an organism is in a state of need (S_D) caused by its being subject to a temperature below the optimum, and that a short series of random locomotor movements will lead it to a region in which the temperature is such as to reduce the S_D. Through the principles of behavior chaining and compound trial-and-error learning (Chapter 6) the drive stimulus reduction will result in a reinforcement of the response which preceded it, especially the final segments of that response, to the stimuli which were acting while the behavior took place. Approach behavior of this kind we shall call *adience* or *adient behavior*, and the object approached will be called the *adient object*.

Next let us suppose that an organism is in close proximity to a heating unit of high temperature; that as a result of this proximity the organism has an S_D caused by its being subject to a temperature appreciably above the optimum; and that a random set of loco-motor movements will lead to a withdrawal from the superheated object, which is followed at once by a reduction in the S_D. This drive reduction will result in a reinforcement of the avoidance behavior, whatever its nature, to the stimuli which accompanied it, especially the stimuli which accompanied the maximum reduction in the drive. Withdrawal behavior of this kind we shall call *abience* or *abient behavior*, and the object from which withdrawal occurs will be called the *abient object*.

Up to the present time we have tacitly assumed that organisms automatically receive stimuli of various kinds, and that theoretical problems are concerned only with adaptive response. At this point it must be noted that not all stimulus reception is automatic; that some receptor adjustments are almost always necessary to enable the organism to receive the stimuli optimally, or even at all. For example, in order for an organism such as a rat to learn the size of a newly found hole, it must bring its vibrissae into contact with the hole's margin; for an organism to discover the temperature of a heating unit, it must approach close enough for its skin to feel the heat; to hear faint sounds, the organism must turn its better ear toward their origin; to identify an odor by its smell, the organism must sniff the air; and to see an object, the organism must open its eyes and direct its eyeballs toward the object so that the image will fall on corresponding points of the retina.

Now this receptor adjustment for optimal stimulation requires certain muscular activity which must be based initially on the automatic stimulus reception. This implies that the receptor adjustment is itself based on a general habit formation which precedes ordinary instrumental habit action. In the chapters on chaining (6) and behavior-link acquisitions (7) we have seen how this type of learning takes place.

Intimately connected with receptor adjustment is the matter not only of stimulus reception, but of *perception*. The specific question of *space* perception, for example, especially concerns us here. As we shall see, this very frequently depends on stimulus intensity. Other things equal, the more intense the vibrissae stimulation becomes, the shorter will be the distance to the redolent object; the more intense a radiant heat becomes, the shorter will be the distance to the hot object; the louder a sound becomes, the closer will be the sounding object. In the case of an object seen by the eye, the larger the image on the retina becomes, the closer will be the object and the more the two fixating eyes will converge; i.e., the greater the tension on the internal recti becomes, the closer will be the object.

How does the animal acquire a knowledge of these space relationships? A great deal of light has been thrown on this subject, at least so far as higher organisms are concerned, by Riesen's classical study of chimpanzees which lived in darkness from birth until the age of sixteen months (*15*). With these animals, apparently, space perception is learned, and the learning is acquired rather slowly through an indefinitely large amount of trial and error in which the complex stimuli of visual space are closely associated with manualmotor and locomotor space movements. For example, as an object in the hand is brought toward the eye its retinal image grows larger and the convergence of the optical fixation becomes greater; and the same thing occurs as the organism walks toward an object, though in this case the optical image of the whole surrounding landscape grows larger. Here we have a motor sense of space being associated directly with the corresponding visual cues. Riesen's study strongly suggests that in higher organisms these space cues normally receive an immense amount of reinforced practice during the first weeks of life. Lower organisms, however, require far less practice.

The most important characteristic common to adient and abient behavior is perhaps the extent to which they generalize, i.e., the extent to which what in some sense appears to be a new act may occur without specific practice. The pronounced generalization characteristics of orientational behavior arise from two major factors. The first of these is that behavior involving movement to any appreciable distance in space, either directly toward or away from objects, is largely locomotor in nature. In this connection it should be observed that *locomotion is a highly generalized form of behavior, since walking as such to one point in space does not differ from walking to any other point in space;* an organism that has learned to walk in unobstructed space to a point ten feet to the north needs no additional skill so far as walking is concerned to walk ten or twenty or forty feet to the east, west, or in any other direction. Thus locomotion is a prime example of response generalization (xiii).

We must now take note of the second major factor determining orientational behavior. All of these forms of distance reception, and especially those concerned with vision, constitute uninterrupted stimulus generalization continua which parallel the actual distance of objects within various ranges. It follows from this that *an object whose stimuli have been conditioned to a reaction at one distance will tend to evoke the reaction at any distance from which the stimuli may be received.*

In the case of adience, to food for example, the portion of the distance-reception continuum which is primarily conditioned to the object naturally is that which corresponds to a minimal distance, since the organism must make actual contact with food before it can eat. Even if the first reinforcement did not involve locomotion, sooner or later this will be the case, with the result that locomotion must inevitably become reinforced in connection with the increasing size of the visual image concerned. When the image is received later, even from a greater distance, this will initiate two processes: (1) optical fixation through habits of receptor exposure or adjustment previously learned, which will serve to orient the body as a whole toward the object, and (2) locomotion in the direction of the optical fixation. *In the case assumed, in which the distance is greater than in the original reinforcement, the activity will be qualitatively substantially the same as in the original reinforcement.* However, in order to cover the increased distance the organism must continue its locomotion for a greater length of time; this brings in the factor of response generalization (p. 199).

Thus it appears that adient behavior, in open space at least, must be highly generalized both as to direction and as to distance.

Generalizing from the above considerations we arrive at the following theorem:

THEOREM 53. *Organisms capable of distance reception and compound trial-and-error learning will display adient behavior which is highly generalized in respect to both direction and distance.*

In the matter of abience the reasoning is much the same, though an intriguing problem arises here. Despite the fact that adience and abience are exactly opposite in the sense of their behavioral and adaptive outcomes, in the case of appreciable distance they involve for the most part exactly the same activity—namely, locomotion. In a strictly objective theoretical system this presents a question. Why does a dynamically injurious situation lead to locomotion away from the relevant object or point in space rather than to locomotion toward it, or just to locomotion without any objective, i.e., mere foot and leg movements leading to no place in particular?

The answer is believed to lie in the fact that *the beginning of adience and abience ordinarily consists of an orientation movement*, i.e., a turning of the body as a whole in such a way that the object will be in front of the body in the one case or at the back of the body in the other. This orientational maneuver may be acquired by the process of chaining or compound trial-and-error learning, since orientational turning is a necessary preliminary to the success (reinforcement) of the activity as a whole. The point is that the responses of both adience and abience are patterned, as well as the stimuli in the situation. But once the turning or orientation of the body as a whole has occurred, the locomotion may continue much the same in the two cases.

Generalizing on the basis of the above considerations we arrive at our next theorem:

THEOREM 54. *Organisms capable of distance reception and compound trial-and-error learning will display abient behavior which is highly generalized in respect to both direction and distance.*

Theorems 53 and 54 are amply confirmed by universal observation of both human and lower animal subjects. Moreover, both theorems are supported by ingenious experiments by Brown (*13*, pp. 434 ff.).

Some Primary Quantitative Characteristics of Adience and Abience

At this point in our study of adience and abience we must take special note of an important quantitative relationship of the receptors to distant objects, already recounted, and the strength of the reaction potential evoked by other phases of these stimulus continua. We observe that with both adience and abience the

TABLE 31. A table showing the numerical values of supposititious adient (second column) and abient (third column) gradients of reaction potential as a function of the difference (d) between the distance stimulus continuum as received by the organism at various possible distances from the focal object, computed by means of the special forms of equation 1,

$$\text{for adience,} \quad +_s\underline{E}_R = 3.00 \times 10^{-.01d}, \tag{54}$$
$$\text{for abience,} \quad -_s\underline{E}_R = 4.00 \times 10^{-.02d}. \tag{55}$$

The approach (adience) values of reaction potential are arbitrarily marked plus, and the avoidance (abience) values of reaction potential are arbitrarily marked minus.

Values of d in j.n.d.'s	Values of $+_s\underline{E}_R$ in σ's (adience)	Values of $-_s\underline{E}_R$ in σ's (abience)
0	3.000	4.000
10	2.383	2.524
20	1.893	1.592
30	1.504	1.004
40	1.194	.634
50	.949	.400
60	.755	.252
70	.599	.159
80	.475	.100
90	.378	.063
100	.300	.040

point of primary reinforcement occurs when the receptor is in close proximity to the object. This means that the point of the stimulus continuum which receives the major reinforcement must be that portion which lies closest spatially to the object.

In this connection it must be recalled that stimulus generalization has a characteristic negative growth gradient, with its high end at the point of the continuum which was directly reinforced (X). Preliminary indications are that this relationship is approximately,[1]

$$_s\underline{E}_R = {}_s E_R \times 10^{-jd}, \tag{19}$$

[1] Because of the present uncertainties concerning the methodology of calculating the quantitative generalization gradient of stimulus intensity, and because of the labor involved and the similarity in outcome to the qualitative generalization gradient, the

where $_sE_R$ is the excitatory potential as conditioned, $_s\underline{E}_R$ is the effective or generalized reaction potential, d is the difference between the original conditioned stimulus and the evoking stimulus in j.n.d. units, and the exponent, j, is an empirical constant. This, taken in conjunction with the foregoing, means that in the case of adience the potentiality of the organism to approach the reinforcing object, if it is visible in open space, will have a characteristic gradient which will be approximately a negative growth function

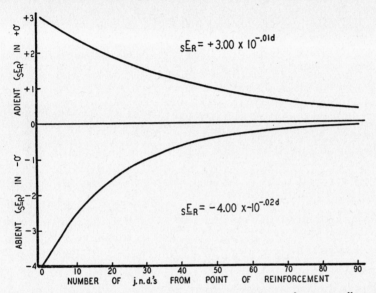

FIGURE 51. Graphic representation of the theoretical shape of a supposedly typical gradient of adient reaction potential (upper curve) and of a supposedly typical gradient of abient reaction potential (lower curve). The sign of the adient reaction potential is arbitrarily taken as positive. Note the negative growth nature of both functions and the steeper slope of the abient function. Plotted from Table 31.

of the reception continuum between the organism and the object, with the high end of the gradient at the object.

In the case of abience the potentiality of the organism to withdraw from an object will have a characteristic gradient which will also be a negative growth function of the reception continuum leading away from the object, the high end of the gradient again being at the object. A systematic series of illustrative numerical theoretical values, calculated by means of equations 54 and 55, are shown in Table 31. Graphic representations are presented in Figure 51. Thus

latter will be used here to open the various aspects of the problem to investigation. For further comments on the computational methodology, see final terminal note.

far the gradients appear to be the same as those related to the distance stimulus continuum, though the latter are not necessarily identical in the two cases. Moreover, the sign of the reaction potential ($_sE_R$), i.e., the direction of the locomotion, will be opposite in the two cases.

Generalizing on the preceding considerations we arrive at our next two theorems:

THEOREM 55. *Adient behavior will display a relatively weak reaction potential when the organism is far from the object, which will grow progressively stronger as the object is approached, the strength of the reaction potential being a negative growth function of the distance of the organism from the object.*[2]

THEOREM 56. *Abient behavior will display its maximum reaction potential close to the object, but this will decrease as a negative growth function of the distance of the organism from the object.*[2]

We must now note an obvious but highly important characteristic of the stimulus spatial continuum as related to adience and abience. This is that in free space this continuum extends in every direction equally. It follows that the gradients of adient and abient reaction potential in free space also extend in every direction. This means that even though at any given position of the organism there is but a single gradient of reaction potential, since the organism may occupy *any* point in free space, in a certain very real sense a genuinely comprehensive statement of the potentiality of adient and abient reaction must cover the *whole* of the space within the range of the distance stimulus continuum. For this reason we are here dealing with a two-dimensional *field* situation which radiates from the focal object. Geometrically, a model of this field would be a revolving figure produced by turning the curve representing the individual adient gradient, say, around the adient object as an

[2] Strictly speaking, we do not yet know the functional relationship between the distance of an object from the organism and either the adient or the abient generalization gradient in j.n.d.'s, so that statements in Theorems 55 and 56 regarding the shape of the gradient are especially dubious in that adequate grounds for their deduction do not exist. They are set down here more as a mark for experimentalists to aim at than anything else. Presumably the principle of stimulus-intensity dynamism (VI) will enter into this relationship, but its exact role is not known. Brown and Miller's work amply demonstrates the soundness of the general direction of the slope of the two gradients as stated in Theorems 55 and 56.

axis. Obviously this field of behavior potentiality, which operates on the principle of the inverse exponential or negative growth function, is not to be confused with electromagnetic or gravitational fields which operate on the principle of inverse squares.

Generalizing on the above considerations, we arrive at our next theorem:

THEOREM 57. *Both adient reaction potential and abient reaction potential in free space constitute plane fields of reaction potentialities.*

In continuing this account of some quantitative principles of adience and abience we must note that the type of stimulus generalization assumed is that characteristic of a strictly naive organism. By naivete in this context we mean the absence of discriminatory differential reinforcement. It will be recalled (*8*, pp. 267 ff.) that differential reinforcement produces a progressive diminution in stimulus generalization, i.e., a steepening of the net generalization gradient. Now in the case of strictly static stimulus objects, e.g., electrodes capable of delivering a moderate electric shock, no reinforcement whatever of abient reaction will occur at any distance from the object beyond actual contact, and the danger of shock even from accidental movements is zero when the organism as a whole is a relatively short distance away. It follows that as the organism is subjected to the sophistication of differential reinforcement in abient situations with static abient objects, the gradient of reaction potential will steepen (*8*, p. 267), tending ultimately to a zero asymptote at a relatively short distance from the object. The rate of the occurrence of this steepening sophisticated discriminatory process will obviously vary with circumstances, though this does not particularly concern us here. It is noteworthy that no such differential reinforcement takes place in the case of static objects yielding reinforcement to adient behavior in completely open space.[3]

---

[3] In 1944 Miller (*13*, p. 450) pointed out with admirable sagacity that the steepening in the slope of the gradient of reaction potential in the case of abience may also occur in special spatially restricted situations in the case of adience:

"If the individual is consistently rewarded for approaching near goals but not far ones, he should learn to discriminate on the basis of cues indicating distance and cease attempting to approach far goals. Such learning actually seems to occur in the case of adults, who will not attempt to reach through small openings for objects obviously more than an arm's length away. In these situations learning produces an approach gradient which falls off very steeply, in an almost step-wise manner at about the limit

Generalizing on the basis of the above considerations, we arrive at our next theorem:

THEOREM 58. *With sophisticated organisms operating in open space, the gradient of abient reaction potential to static objects at its point of maximum slope will be steeper than that of adient reaction potential at its point of maximum slope.*

On the side of empirical verification we are fortunate in having in Brown's experimental work certain critical results bearing on both adience and abience. For example, he trained hungry albino rats to run down a 200-centimeter alley to secure food. During the training each rat wore an ingenious little harness constructed of rubber bands, which when desired could be attached to a spring dynamometer in such a way as to determine how hard the animal would pull to get to the food. When the animals were well trained and 48 hours hungry, tests were made at distances of 30 centimeters and 170 centimeters. Graphs published by Miller (*13*, pp. 434–435) show that on the average the animals pulled approximately 58 grams at the near point and only about 42 grams at the far point. Thus our theoretical deduction as to the general nature of the slope of the adient gradient finds empirical verification, though that regarding its curvature remains unverified because Brown determined only two points on his gradient.

Brown then varied the above experiment by substituting with a different group of animals two brief electric shocks in place of the food. When subsequently placed in the alley at the end where they had been shocked, the animals naturally moved toward the opposite end. In this case the harness dynamometer trial showed that the pull was approximately 200 grams at 30 centimeters from the

---

of the subject's reach. Similarly, the principles of learning, backed up by casual observation, indicate that the steepness of the avoidance gradient should be subject to modification. If this analysis is correct, the relative slopes of the two gradients will depend upon whether or not the conditions of learning have been the same for both. In many situations approach is almost as likely to be reinforced when the subject is at a distance as when he is nearby; avoidance is not. Wherever such conditions are found they should tend to increase the relative steepness of the avoidance gradient."

It is also to be noticed that as early as 1931 Lewin (*10*, p. 92) stated, apparently as a matter of empirical inference based on general observation, that:

" . . . the *strength* of the field forces which correspond to the negative valence diminishes much more rapidly with increasing spatial *distance* than do the field forces corresponding to the positive valence."

point of shock. Thus our deduction regarding the general nature of the slope of the abient gradient finds experimental verification, though Brown's results throw no light on the nature of its curvature because, again, only two points on the gradient were determined. Finally, the steep slope of the abient gradient as compared with that of the adient gradient yields ample empirical support for Theorem 58.

As another pair of primary quantitative characteristics of adience and abience, we shall consider the relationships of approach and avoidance to primary motivation and incentive (VIII). The best evidence now available indicates that so far as primary motivation is concerned reaction potential is a monotonic function of drive multiplied by incentive, i.e., stimulus intensity and habit strength. This means that if the hunger involved in the adient generalization gradient shown in Figures 51 and 56 should be decreased so that the drive (D) falls $33\frac{1}{3}$ per cent, each value on the gradient would be reduced by one third. A general flattening of the gradient would, of course, result, together with a convergence of the gradients produced by the respective drives as shown by the broken-line curve of Figure 56.

Turning next to the matter of incentive, which is usually considered an aspect of motivation, we note the influence of increasing the amount of the food displayed as the adient object. Clearly, the larger the amount of food which is presented in the original reinforcement situation, the stronger will be the resulting reinforcement (8, pp. 131 ff.). By the above formula, the larger the amount of food (VII, VIII), the stronger will be the generalized $_s\underline{E}_R$ at any given distance. Thus the incentive, K, rather than the drive, D, is varied here. However, if the K is decreased by a third through a diminution in the food presented, it is evident that the resulting effect on the $_s\underline{E}_R$ will be the same as if the K were left constant and the D were reduced by one third. This means that owing to the multiplicative nature of the K and D relationship to $_s\underline{E}_R$, even though the details of the computations were different so far as the general characteristics of the gradient of generalized reaction potential are concerned, the two types of motivation modifications would result in exactly parallel outcomes.

Generalizing from the above considerations, we arrive at our next two theorems:

THEOREM 59. *Neither adient nor abient reaction potential will change the exponential constant of its gradient under various degrees of drive (D), but the height of the gradient at the focal object and throughout its course will be greater for strong than for weak motivations.* THEOREM 60. *Adient reaction potential will not change the exponential constant of its gradient under varying incentives (K), but the height of the gradient at the focal object and throughout its course will be greater for strong than for weak incentives.*

Excellent empirical evidence of the general soundness of Theorem 59 in regard to both adience and abience has been reported by Brown and Miller (*13*). The criterion of reaction potential employed in both cases was the strength of pull in rats as described above. The variation in the adient motivation was that produced by 48 hours of food privation as compared with one hour's privation. The variation in the abient motivation was the delivery of a 13.5 m.a. shock as compared with the delivery of a 1.0 m.a. shock. In both cases the stronger motivation yielded stronger pulls. No data bearing on the detailed shapes of the gradients are reported.

Theorem 60 finds partial empirical validation in a study by Fletcher (*3*), who reports evidence bearing on the amount of the incentive; no evidence, however, either positive or negative, has been found on the gradient of reaction potential as a function of the distance of the incentive from the organism.

As a final pair of quantitative characteristics of adience and abience we must consider the nature of the path that the organism takes (1) in approaching a positively reinforcing object, and (2) in avoiding a negatively reinforcing object. We shall first consider the path concerned with adience. A principle which has come down to us from Euclid is that a straight line is the shortest distance between two points. In the present context, this principle states that a straight line is the shortest path from an organism to an adient object. It follows that in free space, other things equal, a straight line is both the quickest and the least laborious path from an organism to an object. Moreover, in case some obstacle diverts the organism from a straight-line path it will at once turn back in a new straight course (toward the same object), since all adience converges toward the single point at which the image of the adient object is maximal. Within the limits imposed by the principle of the oscillation function, the principle of less work (8, p. 293) implies that a sophisticated organism will take a straight path to an adient object.

The situation concerning the abient path is much the same. The reinforcement, such as it is in the case of abience, tends also to favor a straight path. However, once an obstacle, or the chance effect of oscillation, has diverted the path from a straight line there will be no tendency for the organism to swing back to it, since abience paths diverge and every point of the compass satisfies the condition that the visual image of the abient object be minimal.

Generalizing from the above considerations, we arrive at our next two theorems:

> THEOREM 61. *Adience in free space, within the limits of the oscillation function* $(_sO_R)$ *will tend to a straight line toward the adient object.*
>
> THEOREM 62. *Abience in free space will tend to a straight line but irregularities from it due to the oscillation function or minor obstacles will tend cumulatively to produce deviation from a straight line more than in the case of adience.*

General observation indicates that both adient action and abient action tend to be linear, especially near the focal object where the reaction potential is relatively strong, though no empirical evidence has been found bearing on the presumably greater tendency for abience to deviate from a straight line.

The Interaction of Two Field Gradients of Adient Reaction Potential

Having considered the field gradients of adient and abient reaction potential when standing singly, we must now extend our examination to various natural complications. These complications involve the interaction under various conditions of (1) two adient gradient fields; (2) two abient gradient fields; and (3) an adient gradient field and an abient gradient field; they also involve the influence which the imposition of simple barriers has on these gradient fields. In the present section we shall consider the interaction of two adient gradient fields.

Let us suppose that an organism has received adient reinforcement to an object, that exact duplicates of the object, O_1 and O_2, are placed some distance apart in free space, that the organism is placed between the two objects at a point nearer O_1 than O_2, and that the relevant receptors are adequately exposed to both objects before the organism is given its freedom. In this situation the nearer object (O_1) will be closer to the origin of its generalization continuum; i.e., in equation 54 a smaller d will be substitutable in connection with O_1 than in connection with O_2. This will necessarily yield a larger reaction potential for O_1 than for O_2. Now, computational procedures based on equation 54 will show that there is a greater probability of the adient reaction being directed toward O_1 than toward O_2. By the same reasoning it follows that the more the distance between the organism and O_2 exceeds that between the organism and O_1, the greater will be the probability that the organism will choose O_1 rather than O_2.

On the other hand, in case the organism is placed exactly midway between the two objects, it does not follow that no reaction at all will occur. The principle of behavioral oscillation will very soon give one direction a slight advantage. As Miller (*13*, p. 442) has pointed out, this sets up a situation analogous to what in physics is called a state of unstable equilibrium. This initial advantage of one of the adient potentials will, according to equation 54, at once increase at a progressive rate the reaction potential of the one adient object and correspondingly decrease the reaction potential of the other adient object. However, since the initial advantage of the one reaction potential when the organism is placed midway between the adient objects results from the chance action of the oscillation factor, it follows that the reaction potential which acquires an advantage will arise purely from chance, i.e., it will be equal for both, or .5 for each.

Quantitative illustration of the situation just discussed may easily be presented by means of the numerical theoretical values given in Table 31. Let it be supposed that two adient objects are placed a certain distance apart and that an organism is placed on a line between them at a d distance on the distance-receptor continuum of 30 units for O_1, and of 40 units for O_2. By Table 31, O_1 will command a reaction potential of 1.504σ, and O_2 will command a reaction potential of 1.194σ. Utilizing the probability equation involving a difference, assuming that $\sigma_0 = 1$, we have,[4]

[4] Dr. Frank A. Logan, whose brilliant advice and criticisms have been of invaluable assistance to me in the final preparation of this volume, objects to the use of the process

$$\frac{D'}{\sigma_d} = \frac{1.504 \div 1.194}{1.414\sigma}$$

$$= \frac{1.504 \div 1.194}{1.414 \times 1}$$

$$= \frac{.3809}{1.414}$$

$$= .2673.$$

$$\therefore p_+ = .106 + .5000 = .606$$

$$p_- = 1.000 - .606 = .394.$$

Looking up the value of .2673 in Guilford's probability table B (4, p. 530), we find that it corresponds to a probability value (p) of approximately .106 + .500, or .606. This means that under the assumed conditions O_1 would be chosen 60.6 per cent of the trials, and O_2 would be chosen 100 − 60.6, or 39.4 per cent of the trials.

Unfortunately we do not yet know the functional relationship of distance in feet, say, to the d values of the stimulus distance continuum, so we cannot give a representation of p as a function of the various positions as stated in feet that a subject could take between two adient objects. This, however, should be made possible by means of future empirical investigation.

Generalizing on the above considerations, we arrive at our next two theorems:

THEOREM 63. *Other things equal, in a competing adient-adient situation in which the organism is placed midway between two duplicate focal objects with clear distance reception for each, the organism will be as likely to take a path leading to one object as to the other, but if placed nearer one object it will be more likely to choose that object.*

THEOREM 64. *Other things equal, in situations involving competing adient-adient reaction potentials to duplicate adient objects, the greater the disparity in distance from the organism to the respective objects, the greater will be the difference between the two choice probabilities.*

While many experiments have been performed on distance discrimination, one by Klebanoff has been found which has a real bearing on the validity of Theorems 63 and 64. At the outset of the

---

involved in $\div$ rather than the usual process of simple subtraction, in the computation of probability in the equation below. My own feeling regarding this is definitely uncertain. Even so, we are retaining the $\div$ process in order to call attention to the problem. As usual in such matters, a suitable experiment would decide the issue.

trial he made the adient objects clearly available to the distance receptors of the organism. According to Miller (*13*, p. 444),

> Klebanoff (1939) trained hungry rats to secure food by approaching whichever end of an alley was distinguished by a light and a buzzer. Then he placed them in an approach-approach competition by turning on the lights and buzzers at both ends of the alley. He found that, if the animals were started some distance away from the center, they always went directly to the nearest goal. If started at the center they went quickly to one goal or the other with little tendency to vacillate.

A second phenomenon, closely related to the matter of the probability of choice in competing adient-adient situations, is that of the reaction latency or choice time. Just as the probability of a given reaction dominating a given competitive situation is a function of the difference between the two competing reaction potentials (*8*, p. 163), it is here explicitly assumed that reaction latency is a decreasing monotonic function of the difference (d') between two competing reaction potentials. It follows that, other things equal, the farther apart the adient objects are, the farther will be the organism from each of them, and, by equation 54, the weaker will be the reaction potential to each and so the smaller the d' between the reaction potentials upon which a reaction latency can be based. Similarly, for constant distances between the adient objects the nearer the organism is to a point midway between them, the less the d' and so the greater the $_s E_R$. From these considerations we arrive at our next two theorems:

> THEOREM 65. *Other things equal, in an adient-adient competing situation involving duplicate objects, the greater the separation of the objects, the greater will be the reaction latency.*
>
> THEOREM 66. *Other things equal, in an adient-adient competing situation involving duplicate objects, the less the disparity in distance between the organism and the respective adient objects, the greater will be the reaction latency.*

Recalling Theorems 59 and 60 in connection with the competition of two adient reaction potentials, we obviously have at once a series of additional theorems concerning the probabilities and the latencies of reaction occurrences as dependent upon the amounts of (a) drive motivation (D) and (b) incentive motivation (K).

Generalizing on these and related considerations we arrive at our next two theorems:

> THEOREM 67. *Other things equal, in an adient-adient competitive situation involving duplicate objects, the greater the motivation, the greater will be the probability of the choice of the nearer adient object, and the less the latency ($_s t_R$).*
>
> THEOREM 68. *Other things equal, in an adient-adient competitive situation involving duplicate objects, the greater the incentive (K), the greater will be the probability of the choice of the nearer object and the less the latency ($_s t_R$).*

In the above adient-adient situations, the competition has been homogeneous in the sense that the adient objects have been duplicates. At this point we pass to the consideration of two adient-adient competitive situations which are heterogeneous; i.e., situations in which the adient objects are not duplicated. In all of these the organism is placed midway between the objects. However, in the first case one of the objects has a greater incentive (K') value than the other; e.g., it consists of a larger amount of food (VII; VIII). A second situation of this general nature is that in which the organism has a greater need up to a certain limit of inanition (ϵ) of the one or the other object (V B; VIII). It follows from Theorems 59 and 60 that the organism will choose that adient object which has the greater incentive value and the one for which it has the greater need.

Generalizing from these and related considerations we arrive at our next two theorems:

> THEOREM 69. *Other things equal, in a heterogeneous adient-adient competitive situation with the organism placed midway between the adient objects, one of which consists of a greater quantity of the reinforcing substance, the organism will tend to choose the direction of the object which has the greater incentive value.*
>
> THEOREM 70. *Other things equal, in a heterogeneous adient-adient competitive situation with the organism placed midway between the adient objects, for one of which the organism has a greater need or drive (D) than for the other, the organism will tend to choose the direction of the object involving the greater drive.*

As a final relationship in the present adient-adient series, we take the case in which one adient object is displayed at a certain stimulus continuum distance (d') from an organism and a duplicate adient object is displayed at a short distance beyond the first. It is evident that at the outset this is no competitive situation, but rather a summative one. There are numerous complex theoretical problems here related to afferent interaction with which we are not yet in position to cope. Assuming that the interaction effects are less in the aggregate than the original uncomplicated reaction potential of the more remote of the two objects, we may conclude that the joint reaction potential will be greater than that for the near object alone. It follows from this and the monotonic relationship of $_s t_R$ as a function of $_s E_R$ (Postulate XIV) that the reaction latency toward both O_1 and O_2 will be less than that toward either one alone.

Generalizing from these considerations we arrive at our next two theorems:

THEOREM 71. *Other things equal, when duplicate adient objects are placed on a line with and in the same direction from the organism, the adient latency ($_s t_R$) will be less than that for either object alone.*

THEOREM 72. *Other things equal, when an organism is presented with duplicate adient objects on a line with and in the same direction from the organism, the farther away the more remote object is from the organism, the greater will be the reaction latency.*

No empirical evidence bearing on the validity of Theorems 65 to 72 has been found, though the experimental procedures for performing such investigations are for the most part quite simple and straightforward.

The Interaction of Two Field Gradients of Abient Potential

At this point in our analysis of the behavior of organisms toward objects in space, we turn from the adient-adient relationships to the abient-abient relationships. Perhaps the simplest and at the same time one of the most interesting of the latter relationships is found in the experimental situation where the organism is enclosed in a long narrow space or alley, at each end of which is an abient object from which the organism has received some type of punishment, such as an electric shock. Let us assume that the organism has received the same number of shocks of equal intensity from each object; the height of the gradient of abient reaction potential is therefore at the same level at each end of the enclosure. If we take this level of reaction potential at 4.00σ in each case, the abient gradients being the same as the one shown in Figure 51, we shall

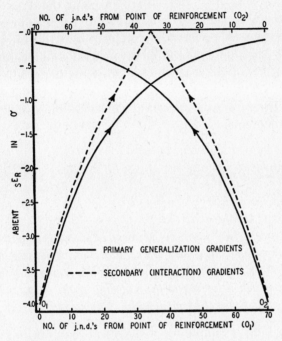

FIGURE 52. Diagrammatic representation of the interaction of two homogeneous abient gradients originating from points 0_1 and 0_2 respectively. Note that wherever the animal is placed it will move in accordance with the dominant difference in reaction potential (broken line) until a point is reached at which this difference is zero. Naturally this occurs where the two abient gradients intersect. Since the two abient gradients are symmetrical this intersection is at the mid-point of the enclosure, namely, a point 35 j.n.d.'s from each abient object. The differences were calculated by the ÷ equation (13).

have the interaction of the two gradients as they appear in Figure 52, where the two abient gradients are assumed to originate at points O_1 and O_2 respectively.

Now, wherever the animal is placed on the scale of j.n.d. distances from the points of reinforcement, with the exception of the midpoint, there will be an imbalance of reaction potential amounting to the difference (÷) between the two gradients. The difference is represented in Figure 52 by the broken lines. This means that if the animal finds itself 10 points from the right-hand extreme of the alley, there will be a net reaction potential of 2.525 ÷ .25 or 2.374σ to move toward the left. However, as the animal moves farther toward the left, the difference grows less and less until the two primary gradients cross, at which point the difference necessarily becomes zero. Here, then, the animal tends to cease moving progressively in either direction. Evidently at this intersection we have what has been called a point of stable equilibrium (*9*, p. 92; *13*, p. 436); i.e., a point at which the interacting gradients tend to produce no movement.

Generalizing from the preceding considerations we arrive at our next two theorems:

THEOREM 73. *When an organism is placed near one end of a restraining alley at each end of which there are duplicate abient objects, the organism will move to a point of equal reaction potential midway between the objects, where it will tend to cease systematic progressive movements toward either end.*

THEOREM 74. *When an organism is placed in a restraining alley at each end of which there are duplicate abient objects, the closer the organism is to one end when released, the greater will be the probability of action leading to the midpoint of the alley, and the shorter the latency of the act in question.*

This striking example of behavioral equilibrium is closely analogous to numerous cases of equilibrium in the physical sciences. Perhaps the best known of the latter is the case of a weight suspended from a string; whenever the weight is displaced from a point directly beneath the point of suspension it tends to return there through the action of gravity, with an intensity which grows progressively less as the angle of displacement becomes less (*13*, p. 442). However, despite this resemblance of behavioral to pendular equilibrium, the two cases are derived from quite different primary laws and therefore neither throws any real light upon the characteristics of the other. The fact that the phenomena of each must be derived from distinctly different equations is decisive; the science of molar behavior is not the science of molar physics.

However, even though the mean gradients of reaction potential are said to be equal at the midpoint of the restraining alley, it must be understood that this statement, even for an individual organism, necessarily holds only for the *average*. Actually the two reaction potentials still continue to compete. And since each is subject to its own individual and uncorrelated behavioral oscillation tendencies (*8*, p. 308) it is inevitable that the organism will not become immobile when it reaches the center of the alley. The momentum, both physical and behavioral, of the preceding movement will presumably carry the organism beyond the midpoint at first; this will tend to be corrected, which will cause further movements of a pendular nature. But quite apart from the pendular movements there will inevitably be irregular oscillating movements because of the principle of behavioral oscillation ($_sO_R$) as such.

Generalizing from the preceding considerations we arrive at our next theorem.

THEOREM 75. *Other things equal, when an organism is placed in a restraining alley at each end of which are duplicate abient objects, the organism even when at the midpoint will continue to oscillate short distances forward and backward from this point as a center.*

We are fortunate in having critical experimental evidence bearing on the validity of the above theorem. Miller (*13*, p. 445) reports an experiment by Klebanoff:

He trained another group of animals to escape an electric shock by running away from whichever end of the alley was distinguished by a light and buzzer, and then placed them in an avoidance-avoidance conflict by turning on the lights and buzzers at both ends of the alley. When released a considerable distance away from the center, all of the animals started by avoiding the nearest light. After running in one direction these animals stopped and turned back, remaining in conflict between the two lights. When released at the center, they started more slowly than the approach-approach animals, vacillated much more, and remained nearer the starting point.

Thus Theorems 73, 74, and 75 find empirical substantiation.

A reexamination of Figure 52 will show that the gradient which finally determines the abient movements occurring in the restricted abient-abient situation is that represented by the broken line of gradient differences ($\doteq$). It is also evident that deviations in reaction potential resulting from the oscillation factor must operate against this gradient, and that the steeper this difference gradient is, the more restricted the oscillatory movements must be. Now, it is easy to show that, other things equal, the nearer the abient objects are to each other, the steeper will be the two difference gradients.

From these considerations flow our next two theorems:

THEOREM 76. *Other things equal, an organism placed in a restraining alley with duplicate abient objects at either end will make, on the average, shorter excursions from the middle toward the respective ends the closer the abient objects are to each other.*

THEOREM 77. *Other things equal, an organism placed in a restraining alley with duplicate abient objects at either end will make, on the average, shorter excursions from the middle toward the two ends as the reaction potential at the abient objects increases, whether this is caused by increased primary motivation (D) or increased incentive (K').*

No empirical evidence bearing on the validity of Theorems 76 and 77 has been found, though the methodology of setting up such experiments is simple and obvious. The results of an experimental test of Theorem 77 would be of special interest because its validation depends in a critical manner upon the change in the intensity of the reaction potential as related to the parallel change in the oscillatory movements. This is a complex and uncertain matter because of our lack of knowledge concerning the empirical constants involved. An experimental investigation of this problem is likely to yield rich returns for the effort required.

The cases of interacting gradients of abient reaction potential employed in the present analysis have so far been homogeneous. We pass now to the consideration of a few cases involving heterogeneous abient reaction potentials. Let us assume, accordingly, that at one end of a restraining alley the abient object (O_1) has a maximum evocation potential of 4.000σ, whereas at the other end the abient object (O_2) has a maximum reaction evocation potential of 2.000σ. The respective abient gradients are shown in Figure 53, together with the resulting difference ($\doteq$) gradients in broken lines analogous to those in Figure 52. An examination of this figure shows that the point of the intersection of the two abient gradients, i.e., the point of zero difference in $_sE_R$, lies distinctly nearer the weaker of the two abient objects. Moreover, the slope of the difference ($\div$) gradient (broken line) has approximately the same steepness toward the weaker abient object as toward the stronger.

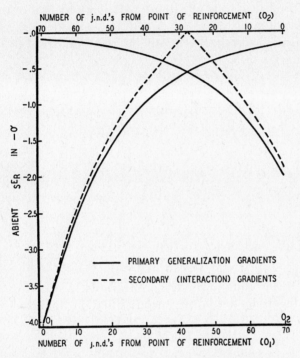

FIGURE 53. Diagrammatic representation of the interaction of two heterogeneous abient gradients originating from points O_1 and O_2, respectively. Note the asymmetry in the two abient gradients, but the relative symmetry, so far as they go, of the resulting difference gradients ($\div$) in reaction potential (broken lines).

It will be recalled that in the case of homogeneous abient gradients just considered, we found it easy to arrive at the determination of the point of zero reaction potential by construction methods. In the case of two abient gradients with different maxima it is still possible, as we have just seen in Figure 53, to arrive at fair approximations by means of graphic methods. For a precise determination of the point, however, as well as for a general statement of the law, we require an equation. This is not difficult to secure. Since at the point of zero difference in reaction potential both the opposing generalized reaction potentials ($_s\underline{E}_R$) are equal, we have, from equation 55,

$$_sE_R \times 10^{-jd} = {_sE_R'} \times 10^{-j(A-d)},$$

where $_sE_R$ is the maximum reaction potential of the stronger abient object, $_sE_R'$ is the maximum reaction potential of the weaker object, A is the distance between the objects in j.n.d.'s, and d is the distance between the organism and the stronger object. It follows that,

$$\frac{10^{jd}}{10^{j(A-d)}} = \frac{_sE_R}{_sE_R'}$$

$$jd - j(A - d) = \log \frac{_sE_R}{_sE_R'}$$

$$2d - A = \frac{\log \dfrac{_sE_R}{_sE_R'}}{j}$$

$$\therefore d = \frac{\dfrac{\log \dfrac{_sE_R}{_sE_R'}}{j} + A}{2}. \tag{56}$$

The use of this equation may be illustrated in a preliminary way by applying it to the homogeneous situation analyzed above, in which $_sE_R = {_sE_R'}$. This reduces $\log \dfrac{_sE_R}{_sE_R'}$ to zero so that equation 56 becomes,

$$d = \frac{A}{2};$$

i.e., d reaches a point half way between the two abient objects, which is a mathematical statement of Theorem 73.

As a second illustration of the use of equation 56, let us take the heterogeneous situation just considered, in which $_sE_R = 4.000\sigma$ and $_sE_R' = 2.000\sigma$. Substituting, we have,

$$d = \frac{\dfrac{\log \dfrac{4.000\sigma}{2.000\sigma}}{.02} + 70}{2}$$

$$= \frac{\dfrac{\log 2}{.02} + 70}{2}$$

$$= \frac{\dfrac{.301}{.02} + 70}{2}$$

$$= \frac{15.05 + 70}{2}$$

$$\therefore d = 42.53 \text{ j.n.d.'s,}$$

which agrees as well as could be expected with the graphic solution given in Figure 53.

Generalizing on the preceding considerations we arrive at the following theorem:

THEOREM 78. *Other things equal, an organism placed in a restraining alley with heterogeneous abient objects at the two ends will approach a point of equal reaction potential which will fall farther from the stronger adient object at a j.n.d. distance from it represented by the equation,*

$$d = \frac{\dfrac{\log \dfrac{_sE_R}{_sE_R'}}{j} + A}{2}.$$

The principle of the oscillation of reaction potential in this context brings us to our next theorem:

THEOREM 79. *Other things equal, when an organism is placed in a restraining alley with heterogeneous (abient) objects at the two ends, once its pendular reactions have become relatively stabilized at the point of zero reaction potential difference, the distribution of oscillatory reactions about this point will, within the limits of sampling errors and despite the asymmetry of the basic reaction potential gradients, be symmetrical to a close approximation.*

Recalling in connection with Theorem 78 our conclusions formulated as Theorems 57 and 60, let us suppose that in the situation just considered either the motivation or the (negative) incentive has been increased in the case of the dominant object from the 4.000σ assumed above to 4.5000σ. Substituting appropriately in equation 56, we have,

$$d = \cfrac{\cfrac{\log \cfrac{4.500}{2.000}}{.02} + 70}{2}$$

$$= \cfrac{\cfrac{\log 2.25}{.02} + 70}{2}$$

$$= \cfrac{\cfrac{.35218}{.02} + 70}{2}$$

$$= \cfrac{17.61 + 70}{2}$$

$$\therefore d = 43.81 \text{ j.n.d.'s.}$$

But $43.81 > 42.53$.

Generalizing from these considerations we arrive at our next theorem:

THEOREM 80. *Other things equal, with an increase in the primary motivation (D) or (negative) incentive (K') of one of two otherwise equal abient reaction potentials interacting in an organism placed within a restraining alley, the point of zero reaction potential difference will move to a point farther from the object which has the increased motivation or incentive.*

In our consideration of the interaction of adient fields of reaction potential we assumed completely open space, whereas in the consideration of the interaction of abient fields of reaction potential we have so far assumed that the organism was restrained within a narrow alley. We shall now consider the behavior potentialities in the interaction of two abient fields in completely open space; incidentally, we shall observe why in some sense it was necessary to assume the restraining alley in the formulation of Theorems 73 to 80.

In this renewed approach to the problems of abient-abient interaction, we shall accordingly assume that the organism is placed midway between the duplicate abient objects O_1 and O_2 represented in Figure 54 and that these are situated 30.1 j.n.d. units apart in free space. We shall further assume that where d = 0 each object has a reaction potential of 2.000σ. From appropriate computations by means of equation 55 it appears that at the midpoint between the two abient objects the actual reaction potential in each direction is 1.000σ. This means that every point on circles A and A' has a reaction potential or vector of 1.000σ in the direction away from its respective point of origin, which serves to emphasize

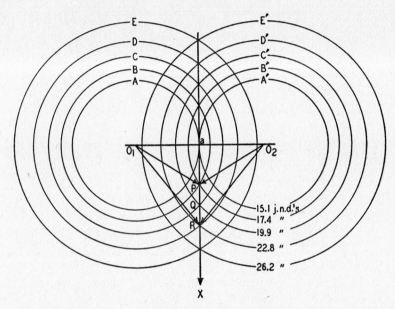

FIGURE 54. Diagrammatic representation of the interacting fields of theoretical reaction potential arising from the supposititious abient objects 0_1 and 0_2 in free space. The circles are drawn to represent loci of equal reaction potentials as follows: A = A' = 1.0σ; B = B' = $.9\sigma$; C = C' = $.8\sigma$; D = D' = $.7\sigma$; and E = E'. = $.6\sigma$.

the fact once again that we are here dealing with reaction potential fields or two-dimensional space rather than with mere linear reaction potential gradients.

Now since, according to Theorem 73, in the present situation the two opposing reaction potentials are equal, no consistent reaction tendency will occur toward either abient object. Because these opposed reaction tendencies are in an exact line they will completely neutralize each other so far as that factor alone is concerned. It follows that from this source there will be no lateral movement. However, the operation of the principle of behavioral oscillation may be expected to initiate from time to time small movements in all directions. Movements toward the two abient objects will meet with increasing opposition, but those at right angles to the line connecting the two objects will have no opposition.[5] Assuming as a first approximation that behavioral vectors in quite naive subjects operate roughly as physical vectors, even a small movement to one side of the line will unbalance the otherwise completely opposed reaction tendencies arising from O_1 and O_2, which will give rise to a combination vector away from the line O_1O_2 (Figure 54). This lateral or summational vector must grow larger as the angles aO_1P and aO_2P grow larger, say to aO_1R and aO_2R, depending on which side of the line O_1O_2 the first chance lateral movement occurs.

Finally we should observe that *the path of lateral movement must tend to fall at points where the two opposed zones or fields of reaction potential are equal.* Thus the organism will pass successively through those points where both the opposed fields have a reaction potential of $.9\sigma(P)$, thence through the points where they have $_sE_R$'s of $.8\sigma(Q)$, thence through the points where they have $_sE_R$'s of $.7\sigma(R)$, and so on. According to equation 19, the lines connecting P with O_1 and O_2 must at any given instant be equal, and the same must be true in the case of R. By ordinary geometry, PO_1O_2 is an isosceles triangle, and therefore the line Pa must cut line O_1O_2 at right angles. The same, of course, applies in the case of triangles QO_1O_2 and RO_1O_2, and at all other intersections of the circles of equi-reaction potential. It follows that the path an organism takes in flight from the line O_1O_2, when it is placed midway between the abient objects, will be at right angles to the line connecting them.

Since line Xa is perpendicular to line O_1O_2, lines O_1P and O_2P must be shorter than lines O_1R and O_2R. But the longer the lines O_1R and O_2R are, the greater must be the value of d in equation 19, and therefore the smaller must be both reaction potentials involved, with zero in each as the limit as d increases. Now, the summation of two vectors of zero reaction potential must be zero regardless of how great the angle aO_1R may be. It follows that in the supposed situation the vector summation must approach zero as a limit with continued flight from a. And since the course

[5] This means there will be no opposition here except for the inhibition arising from the amount of work of performing the locomotor movements necessarily involved.

started with a zero reaction potential it follows that the reaction potential must gradually rise to a maximum, after which it will gradually fall until it is less than the inhibition yielded by the locomotor activity involved; the organism will then cease responding to the abient objects in question.

Generalizing from these considerations we arrive at the following two theorems:

> THEOREM 81. *Other things equal, a naive organism placed midway between two duplicate abient objects in free space will tend to move in a direction at right angles to the line connecting the two objects.*
>
> THEOREM 82. *Other things equal, a naive organism placed midway between two duplicate abient objects in free space will have at the outset a zero mean lateral reaction potential vector at the line connecting the two abient objects. This potential will increase progressively as the angle from the organism to the abient objects increases, until this is over-balanced by the diminishing strength of abient potential with the increasing distance of the organism from the abient objects, after which it will gradually decrease and the organism will cease locomotion so far as these objects are concerned.*

Although no adequate evidence for the detailed validation of Theorem 81 is available, general observation tends roughly to confirm it. Moreover, Miller (*13*, p. 445) reports that Klebanoff's rats when in a situation substantially like the one here under consideration, "showed a definite tendency to try to escape to the side and up out of the alley." No empirical evidence whatever has been found bearing on Theorem 82, though the methods used by Miller and his associates would presumably, with a little adaptation, serve to secure it. Such evidence, particularly if based on data from extremely naive animals, might easily lead to a determination of the relationship between the mode of combination of behavioral vectors and that characteristic of physical vectors. It is tempting to assume the physical vector analogy in this situation, but such an assumption is extremely risky unless supported by convincing empirical evidence. However striking the analogy, it must never be forgotten that *molar behavior theory is not molar physics.*

We may add here that the principle stated in Theorem 81 has become quite well known through the work of Lewin (*10*), who seems to have been the first to put it forward. Lewin, however, apparently was relatively uninterested in the strictly spatial problems under analysis here; he gave more serious consideration to analogies of a non-spatial nature, such as the tendency of children to avoid where possible both an unpleasant task and parental disciplinary action, the latter being a normal alternative to the non-performace of the task. Evidently the principles derived above from strictly spatial considerations will apply with certainty to the purely analogical situation only by chance.

As a final case in the interaction of two abient field gradients, we take one in which the abient objects are again in completely open space, but are heterogeneous in nature, instead of homogeneous as in the situation just considered. We shall now assume that O_1 has an abient reaction potential at $d = 0$ of 2.000σ, whereas O_2 has an abient reaction potential at $d = 0$ of 4.000σ. Appropriate computations show that a reaction potential of 1.000σ surrounds O_1 at a distance of 15.05 j.n.d.'s, whereas an equal and opposing reaction potential surrounds O_2 at a distance of 30.1 j.n.d.'s. Accordingly a figure analogous to Figure 54 could be constructed on this basis, additional circles being drawn with each abient object as the center, which would show the j.n.d. distance between the organism and the object where reaction potentials of 1.0σ, $.9\sigma$, $.8\sigma$, $.7\sigma$, and $.6\sigma$ respectively would fall.

Now here, exactly as in the case of the homogeneous abient objects, the naive organism will at the outset have no particular tendency to go in either direction from the line O_1O_2, but due to the action of the oscillation factor small deviations from the line will spontaneously occur and once begun on one side or the other the imbalance of the vectors will evidently increase progressively quite as in the case of the homogeneous abient-abient open-space situation. In both cases the organism takes a path such that (1) both reaction potentials are equal and (2) both are at a minimum. This means that the organism's path follows the intersection of the circles possessing the same reaction potential. To facilitate the examination of such a figure, the intersections of the circles of equal reaction potential should be connected by a line. When this is done it may readily be seen (1) that this line is not perpendicular to line O_1O_2 as in Figure 54, but slopes perceptibly toward O_1; and (2) that the line is not exactly straight but curves slightly, also toward O_1.

Generalizing on the basis of the preceding considerations, we arrive at our next theorem:

> THEOREM 83. *Other things equal, in a heterogeneous abient-abient reaction situation in open space the organism will take a path to one side of the line connecting the abient objects, and the path will curve in the direction of the weaker object.*

No empirical evidence has been found bearing on the validity of Theorem 83, though it would be a relatively easy matter to set up an experiment for this purpose.

The Interaction of an Adient and an Abient Field Gradient

In the preceding two sections we have considered the interaction of two reaction potential fields of the same kind, either adient fields or abient fields. Now we must consider the interaction of two different kinds of reaction potential—that of an adient potential field with an abient potential field. There are two obvious situations where this is found.

Let us take as our first case of adient-abient interaction a situation in which O_1 is an adient object with a reaction potential (at $d = 0$) of 3.000σ, and O_2 is an abient object with a reaction potential (at $d = 0$) of 4.000σ. In addition we assume that the organism is placed as close as possible to O_2 on the line connecting the two objects. It is evident that under the assumed conditions the direction of the two reaction potentials, despite their different nature, will be the same, i.e., both will impel the organism in the direction of O_1. The magnitudes of the two reaction potential gradients are given in Table 31 and are shown in Figure 55 by the two continuous curves. Assuming that the summation is according to the summation principle (v, 11), and ignoring probable but unknown afferent interaction effects, as well as those of inertia, momentum, and so on, the combination of the two sets of reaction potentials (which operate in the same direction) yields the results represented by the broken line in Figure 55.

An examination of this broken line reveals a characteristic and striking situation. At the beginning (O_2) the reaction potential stands at a maximum of 4.2; it decreases to a minimum near the midpoint of the line from O_2 to O_1, after which it increases again to a secondary maximum of 3.08 at O_1. Unfortunately it is impossible to translate these summated $_sE_R$ values into speeds of locomotion because of the complication due to momentum and other

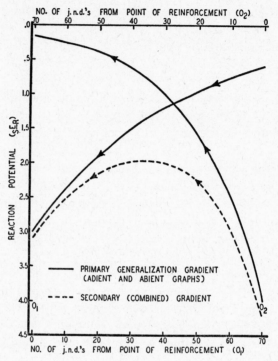

FIGURE 55. Graphic representation of an adient reaction potential gradient (shorter continuous line) and an abient potential gradient (longer continuous line), together with their presumptive summation ($+$) (broken line).

factors. With some hesitation, however, we venture to generalize from the preceding considerations and formulate our next two theorems:

THEOREM 84. *Other things equal, when an organism is placed on a line between an adient object and an abient object, it will move toward the adient object on this line, the two maxima of reaction potential will fall at the respective focal objects, and a minimum will fall at a point between the objects.*

THEOREM 85. *Other things equal, when an organism is placed on a line between an adient object and an abient object, the farther the objects are apart in j.n.d.'s, the smaller will be the minimal combined reaction potential and the more will this differ from the reaction potentials on the respective ends.*

Unfortunately we have here also no empirical evidence against which to check the above theorems, though as usual in this field the methods followed by Miller should render their validation relatively easy. Perhaps the most obvious method would be to place the organism at various points along the line joining O_1 to O_2 and measure the reaction latency of its locomotion, since reaction latency has a special inverse monotonic relationship to reaction potential (XIV).

Perhaps because of its somewhat dramatic issue, our second case of adient-abient interaction is relatively well known, having previously been discussed by Lewin (*10*, p. 92), Miller (*13*, p. 436), and the present writer (*7*, p. 288). It concerns a situation in which the adient and the abient objects, instead of being separate, occupy practically the same point in free space. In this way the two gradients, instead of summating as in the last case, oppose each other. In order to facilitate our exposition we shall use the two gradients presented in Table 31 and employed in other situations. In Figure 56, where these two gradients are represented, the abient gradient is placed below because its direction is opposite to that of the adient gradient. Since their two directions are opposite, the gradients combine by the withdrawal principle ($\div$, vii).

The resulting differences are represented by the broken line which appears between the other two lines. A second glance at Figure 56 will show that this difference line begins at the left with large negative (or abient) values, crosses the zero line at 12.48 j.n.d.'s, and then passes into a permanent phase of positive or adient values. It is evident that here, i.e., at the point where the difference value becomes zero, we have what is called a stable behavioral equilibrium; this means that except for the operation of the oscillation function, the organism will move neither toward the double or ambivalent goal object nor away from it.

It is a matter of some interest to know exactly what the theoretical distance of the point of zero difference in adient-abient reaction potential is from the two objects. This is easily found owing to the fact that at this point the two reaction potentials are equal. From

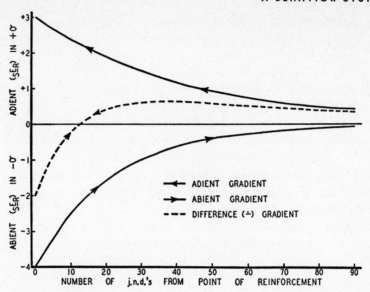

FIGURE 56. Graphic representation of an adient reaction potential gradient and an abient reaction potential gradient, together with their presumptive differences (broken line). It is to be noted that for d values less than 12.48 these difference values are negative, i.e., tending away from the two objects, that at a d value of 12.48 the difference is zero, and that at d values of more than 12.48 the difference is positive, i.e., tending in the direction of the double adient-abient object.

this and equation 20 we are able to write the equation,

$$_sE_R \times 10^{-jd} = {_sE_R'} \times 10^{-j'd},$$

in which the left-hand member represents the adient reaction potential and the right-hand member (with the primes) represents the abient reaction potential where it is assumed that,

$$_sE_R' > {_sE_R}$$

and that,

$$j' > j.$$

Accordingly we have,

$$\frac{10^{j'd}}{10^{jd}} = \frac{_sE_R'}{_sE_R}$$

$$j'd - jd = \log \frac{_sE_R'}{_sE_R}$$

$$\therefore d = \frac{\log \dfrac{_sE_R'}{_sE_R}}{j' - j}. \tag{57}$$

As an illustration of the use of this equation we substitute the relevant values involved in the preceding adient-abient interaction:

$$d = \frac{\log \dfrac{4\sigma}{3\sigma}}{.02 - .01}$$

$$= \frac{\log 1.333}{.01}$$

$$= \frac{.1248}{.01}$$

$$\therefore d = 12.48 \text{ j.n.d.'s,}$$

which agrees very well with the graphic solution represented in Figure 57.

Now, oscillatory movements will meet opposition whenever they are in a direction either toward the adient-abient object or away from it, but more when toward the object than when away from it, as shown by the steeper difference gradient toward the double focal object. This means that oscillatory movements toward the ambivalent goal object will be shorter than those away from it. Even though there will be present no forces opposed to lateral movements, and consequently lateral oscillatory movements may be expected to be greater on the average than either forward or backward movements, any considerable movement at right angles to the path originally taken toward the ambivalent goal object must move away from O_1O_2, which will oppose the positive or adient gradient difference. This is to say that lateral movements from the original path toward O_1O_2 must maintain such a distance that the adient-abient gradient difference will always be zero. Consequently, all lateral movements must tend to be circular, with a radius equal to the distance from the double object to the point of zero difference in reaction potential. The locus of such lateral movements is shown in Figure 57.

Generalizing on the above considerations we arrive at our next two theorems:

THEOREM 86. *Other things equal, with moderately sophisticated subjects, when an adient object and an abient object occupy nearly the same point in space and the maximum abient reaction potential is greater than the maximum adient potential, there will be a point of stable equilibrium at a j.n.d. distance from the adient-abient object amounting to*

$$d = \frac{\log \dfrac{_sE'_R}{_sE_R}}{j' - j}.$$

THEOREM 87. *Other things equal, when an adient-abient object occupies the same point in space and the maximum abient reaction potential is greater than the maximum adient, the oscillatory movements from the point of zero difference away from the object will be greater on the average than those toward the object, and those in a lateral direction will be greater on the average than either, the latter being generally in a circular course and the double object being the center with a radius equal to the distance from the point of zero difference.*

It is a matter of empirical observation that ambivalent situations of this kind, in which the abient reaction potential is greater at its

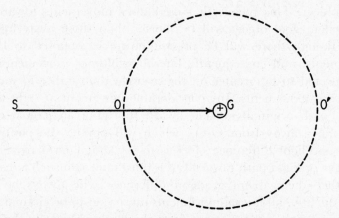

FIGURE 57. Graphic representation of the path that lateral movements must take under the conditions of equilibrium of adient and abient reaction potential at a point in free space. Reproduced from Hull (7, p. 290).

maximum than the adient reaction potential at its maximum, do present points of stable equilibrium, and that roughly circular oscillatory movements whose radius is the equilibrium distance tend to be made by naive organisms. Lewin considered this situation theoretically and came to the same conclusions (10, p. 96). Apparently he also made empirical observations on young children which agree with the theory. His concept of field vector here corresponds roughly to our spatially generalized reaction potential. Theorem 87 may accordingly be said to have some empirical substantiation.

Now let it be supposed that the motivation or the incentive of the adient reaction potential is increased. An increase in either of these will increase the value of the maximum reaction potential $_sE_R$ in equation 57. Let us suppose that this is changed from 3.0σ to 3.5σ. Substituting in equation 57, we then have,

$$
\begin{aligned}
d &= \frac{\log \dfrac{4.0}{3.5}}{j' - j} \\
&= \frac{\log 1.143}{.02 - .01} \\
&= \frac{.05805}{.01} \\
\therefore d &= 5.80 \text{ j.n.d.'s,}
\end{aligned}
$$

which, since $5.80 < 12.48$, indicates that the distance will be reduced.

In a similar manner, in case the adient motivation or incentive is reduced so that the reaction potential falls from 3.0σ to 2.5σ, we have,

$$
\begin{aligned}
d &= \frac{\log \dfrac{4.0}{2.5}}{j' - j} \\
&= \frac{\log 1.6}{.02 - .01} \\
&= \frac{.20412}{.01} \\
\therefore d &= 20.41 \text{ j.n.d.'s;}
\end{aligned}
$$

i.e., since $20.41 > 12.48$ the distance of the point of equilibrium will be increased.

In an analogous manner we find that if the abient motivation is increased, this will increase the maximum abient reaction potential from, say, 4.0σ to 4.5σ. Substituting in equation 57, we have,

$$d = \frac{\log \dfrac{4.5\sigma}{3.0\sigma}}{j' - j}$$

$$= \frac{\log 1.5}{.02 - .01}$$

$$= \frac{.17609}{.01}$$

$$\therefore d = 17.61,$$

which means, since $17.61 > 12.48$, that the equilibrium distance will be increased with an increase in the abient motivation.

In a similar manner, if the abient motivation is decreased, by Theorem 59 this will decrease its maximum reaction potential. Suppose this falls from 4.0 to 3.5σ. Then, by equation 57, we have,

$$d = \frac{\log \dfrac{3.5\sigma}{3.0\sigma}}{j' - j}$$

$$= \frac{\log 1.167}{.02 - .01}$$

$$= \frac{.06707}{.01}$$

$$\therefore d = 6.71 \text{ j.n.d.'s,}$$

which shows, since $6.71 < 12.48$, that the equilibrium distance will be decreased by a decrease in the amount of the abient motivation.

Generalizing from the above considerations we arrive at the following two theorems:

THEOREM 88. *Other things equal, when an adient object and an abient object are combined spatially and the maximum abient reaction potential is appreciably greater than the maximum adient reaction potential, an increase in the adient incentive (V) or primary motivation (D) or both will decrease the distance of the point of equilibrium from the objects, and a reduction of the adient incentive or motivation or both will increase the distance of the point of equilibrium.*

THEOREM 89. *Other things equal, when an adient object and an abient object are combined spatially and the maximum abient reaction potential is appreciably greater than the maximum adient reaction potential, if an increase is made in the abient motivation (D) there will be an increase in the distance of the point of equilibrium from the objects, whereas if a reduction is made in the abient motivation there will be a decrease in distance of the point of equilibrium.*

We are fortunate in having available convincing experimental results bearing directly on the preceding theorems. Miller, Brown, and Lipofsky (*14*) trained albino rats to perform an adient reaction in an enclosed alley by feeding them at an end of the alley marked by a small light. They then built up an opposing or abient reaction by giving the animals electric shocks while eating. The results of this training were recorded by means of a light-weight cord attached to a little rubber harness placed on the animals immediately preceding the tests, the latter being given without shock. In the tests, as in the training trials, the animals were always

TABLE 32. Summary of the outcome of the Miller, Brown, and Lipofsky experiment as reported by Miller (*13*, p. 437).

Change in motivation		Effect of motivation change on distance of point of equilibrium from adient-abient object
Adient motivation	Abient motivation	
increase	constant	decrease
decrease	constant	increase
constant	increase	increase
constant	decrease	decrease

placed at the beginning of the alley, i.e., the end opposite that at which they were fed. Four groups of animals were employed, in each group of which the intensity of one of the motivations was varied with the other intensities remaining constant. The several conditions, together with the effect on the distance of the point of equilibrium from the food-shock end of the alley, were as shown in Table 32. Thus Theorems 88 and 89 find complete verification so far as the primary motivation factor is concerned. The matter of incentive is left unverified.

Behavior Potential Fields, Barriers, and the Purely Spatial Habit-Family Hierarchy

In our account of abient-abient interaction we had occasion to assume a situation in which the organism was placed within a narrow alley. The organism could not escape from this hypothetical alley because it consisted of a complex enclosing barrier. Since in our further consideration of adience fields the matter of barriers will frequently be encountered, we shall now pause to consider the essential characteristics of barriers as such. Perhaps the most significant type of barrier with which to begin this discussion is that which is relatively transparent but impossible of penetration, such as a glass wall, a strong wire screen, a set of bars, or an obstacle over which an adient object may be seen, say, but which cannot easily be surmounted.

Consider, for example, the case of a naive organism moving toward an adient object seen for the first time through a glass barrier of rather limited area, perpendicular to the organism's line of vision. The stimulus complex relative to the adient object so received will be only slightly different from what it would be if the barrier were not present, so the afferent interaction will be relatively small. As a result, the adient locomotion will proceed in a straight line toward the object, though at a slightly reduced rate, until the glass is reached. If the organism is completely unsophisticated it will advance until its body impinges on the glass, which will (1) bring it to a halt and discontinue the progressive change in the stream of secondary reinforcing stimuli (e.g., the increasing size of the retinal image of the adient object), and (2) cause the occurrence or intrusion of a radically different set of cutaneous and even injurious stimuli. These latter stimuli (representing needs) will be reduced by the subject's reflex withdrawal from the barrier, which in turn will set up conditioned abient or withdrawal habits to the barrier as a stimulus. If the injury has been intense this abience may be considerable.

But, since the barrier is a static abient object and will cause no injury except that received from a considerable impact, it follows that with repeated stimulation (Theorem 58) the gradient of abience will become progressively steeper until ultimately it will be practically vertical; i.e., the barrier will be avoided only to the extent that accidental contacts do not occur, and even these may occur if the barrier is not such as to make mere contact injurious. This is why, generally speaking, organisms with normal sense organs avoid barriers on the basis of distance receptors and rarely come into physical contact with them, though the limiting abient distance is ordinarily minimal.

Generalizing on the preceding considerations we formulate our next theorem:

THEOREM 90. *Smooth and strictly static absolute barriers are abient objects, the reaction potential gradients of which normally attain early in the organism's interaction with them a practically vertical degree of steepness near $d = 0$.*

As the next step in our analysis of organismic behavior toward abient barriers, let us consider the organism's discrimination of the visual image of the adient object as it appears through the barrier, and the image as it appears without the intervention of the barrier. In this connection the reader will need to recall the fact of discrimination learning (Chapter 3) and especially the principle of pattern discrimination, which are here assumed without further comment. As a result of maximal stimulus pattern discrimination acquired in conjunction with the process known as compound trial-and-error learning (Chapter 6), the organism will halt its adient locomotion as soon as the distinction between the image of the adient object alone and that of the adient object seen through the transparent abient object (barrier) becomes great enough, since the combined stimulus pattern has become an inhibitory stimulus for that act. Moreover, such situations in the past have, through compound trial-and-error learning, set up exploratory receptor-exposure acts. These latter acts may reveal free space a little to one side of the barrier. Locomotor trial and error, originally occurring on the basis of the oscillation function, will lead the organism far enough to one side of the barrier for the reception of an unobstructed visual image of the adient object, whereupon a new adient gradient within the adient reaction potential field of the organism will evoke uninterrupted locomotion to the adient object and to consequent further reinforcement.

Generalizing from the above considerations we arrive at our next two theorems:

THEOREM 91. *When an adient object and an abient object are combined in the same situation and stimuli normally evoking adient or abient behavior in open space are conjoined with other stimuli which arise from an abient object (barrier), the resulting stimulus pattern will check the adient or abient behavior otherwise initiated or partially evoked and then give rise to visual and other exploratory behavior.*

THEOREM 92. *When an adient object and an abient object are combined in the same situation and a barrier stimulus pattern has given rise to exploratory behavior which reveals open space at one side of the barrier, trial-and-error behavior will lead to a detour, the unimpeded view which results from this activity serving as a secondary reinforcement of the detour behavior, after which the adient or abient behavior will continue from the new position at one side of the barrier.*

Since the field of adient behavior converges in general toward the adient object it is evident that after the detour the direction of the path will again turn toward the adient object. In the case of abience, however, since the latter field usually radiates in every direction *from* the abient object, the organism following a detour will not generally tend to return toward the path interrupted by the barrier but will take a direction which diverges from the one which it would have taken except for the barrier.

Generalizing from the above considerations, we arrive at our next two theorems:

THEOREM 93. *Once an organism showing adient behavior has rounded an abient object (barrier), the organism will, even before it receives an uncomplicated visual stimulus of the adient object, resume the normal adient linear approach to the adient object from that point beyond the barrier to which the abience of the latter has induced it to go.*

THEOREM 94. *Once an organism showing abient behavior has rounded an abient object (barrier to flight), the organism will resume the normal abient behavior on a path which is an extension of the line connecting the abient object and the organism at the point where the barrier's abience has forced it to go in rounding the barrier.*

Theorems 90 to 94 are all in agreement with general observation but no exact empirical evidence bearing on any of them has been found.

Next let us suppose that the transparent barrier encountered by the organism is at right angles to the latter's natural adient path as already assumed, and that this natural path intersects the barrier half as far from one end of it as from the other. As pointed out above, locomotor trial and error will, through the action of the oscillation function, lead the organism to perform the detour or *umweg*. From this, together with the principle of less work (*8*, p. 293) and of the gradient of delay in reinforcement (iii A or iii B), it follows that the organism will tend to prefer the alternative course or path involving the shorter distance of locomotion (and less work), and therefore will choose it more frequently than the longer path around the farther end of the barrier. An S ⟶ R diagram showing the behavior theory of the two paths is shown as Figure 58. Assuming that the short path is two seconds in duration and that the long path is five seconds in duration, the short goal gradient figures out, old style, at 3.155σ and the long one at 1.581σ. The reader will note that since the two alternative paths terminate at the same point in space, they constitute a special case of the habit-family; and since the shorter path is normally preferred to the longer one, the two constitute a hierarchy—the smallest number possible. We accordingly have here a special and limiting case of the *habit-family hierarchy*, a secondary principle of very wide application about which we will hear more presently.

Generalizing on the preceding considerations we arrive at our next theorem:

> THEOREM 95. *Other things equal, organisms which are presented with alternative paths in detouring about a barrier to an adient object will learn to prefer the one involving the shorter distance.*

The validity of Theorem 95 is attested by general observation.

At this point we must consider with some care a secondary principle of major behavioral importance. This is the principle of the habit-family hierarchy or motor equivalence to which we referred immediately above. The general concept of the habit-family hierarchy is this: when a single locomotor path habit is set up, it involves an infinite number of potential paths in free space, all terminating at the same goal point. Because of the principle of less work, the shortest and less laborious of these potential paths will be preferred to the others of the hierarchy. In case the first path found to a given goal is indirect, i.e., circuitous, the organism will naturally tend automatically to shift to the shortest or most preferred path available. Our present task is to try to understand how this automaticity comes about.

The discussion which led to the formulation of Theorem 95,

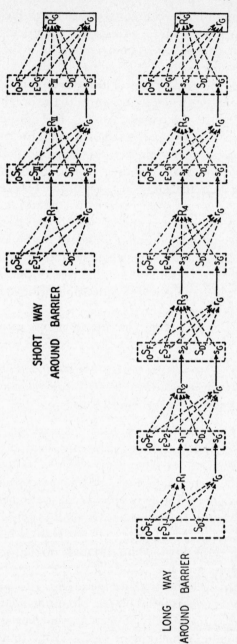

FIGURE 58. Diagrammatic representation of some of the details of the generation of the motor equivalence behavior described in Theorem 95. Note that: $_{O}S_F$ = optical fixation of the goal object, $_{E}S_1$, etc., = the external optical and other stimuli (with the exception of $_{O}S_F$), S_D = hunger drive stimulus, R_1, R_2 etc., and R_I, R_{II}, etc., are the locomotor acts of the respective paths, r_G is the fractional antedating goal reaction assumed to be common to the two paths, and s_G is the common goal stimulus.

and particularly to Figure 58, will aid materially in this understanding. A perusal of this figure and the associated discussion will suggest some of the principles which are operative in this situation. For one thing, optical fixation ($_oS_F$) is an important factor, as are the other external stimuli ($_ES_1$, $_ES_2$, etc.) both optical and otherwise. Riesen's classical study of visual perception (*15*) strongly suggests that the meaning of visual fixation stimuli is acquired, at least by anthropoids, very early in life. As a result, optical convergence in fixation yields an indication of the *distance* of seen objects. At the same time the size of the optical image in conjunction with the degree of optical convergence (distance) indicates the *size* of the object. Also the angle of the point fixated shows the *direction* of the goal. And the matters of image size and of the intensity of optical convergence introduce the principle of stimulus-intensity generalization. In addition to the above primary stimulus or perceptual principles, there is an important secondary principle known as the gradient of reinforcement, J, (iii A, or iii B). This has been utilized above (Chapter 5) through the mediation of the fractional antedating goal reaction, chiefly through stimulus generalization on the perseverative stimulus trace as a continuum. In the present situation the stimulus generalization is conceived to operate on the basis of optical fixation stimuli and their traces.

In considering the transfer of training from a long or indirect path to a short or direct one we present two main cases. They are represented diagrammatically in Figure 59 A and 59 B. We will first take up the simpler case seen in Figure 59 A. Let us assume that the original habit was set up in relatively free space substantially like the long sequence of Figure 58, and that the shortest path in this free space is a straight line normally requiring only one second to traverse; *this is considerably shorter than the short sequence of Figure 58.* Now this amount of delay in reinforcement would yield a reinforcement gradient value of 3.971σ, on the assumption that under the current reward conditions zero seconds' delay would yield 5.0σ. We also assume that the goal object was visible from the starting point but was not known to be a goal until after it was found and the reinforcing substance (K') was consumed. Under these conditions R_1 will have its full strength of 1.581σ, since all of its bonds at the outset of the five-second (longer) path (Figure 58) are operative.

On the other hand, one of the original three bonds leading to the short path (R_I) will be partially lacking, since from the starting point the stimulus of the view of the short path should be somewhat different from that of the view of the long path, which has been reinforced. This difference should reduce by an uncertain amount the generalization from $_ES_1 \dashrightarrow R_1$ to $_ES_1 \dashrightarrow R_I$. On the other hand, the generalization from $_OS_F \dashrightarrow R_1$ will be practically complete to $_OS_F \dashrightarrow R_I$, since the goal object will be the same except for size and the size will be larger on the transfer. Finally, the drive stimuli (S_D) will be strictly identical in the two cases.[6] If we assume that

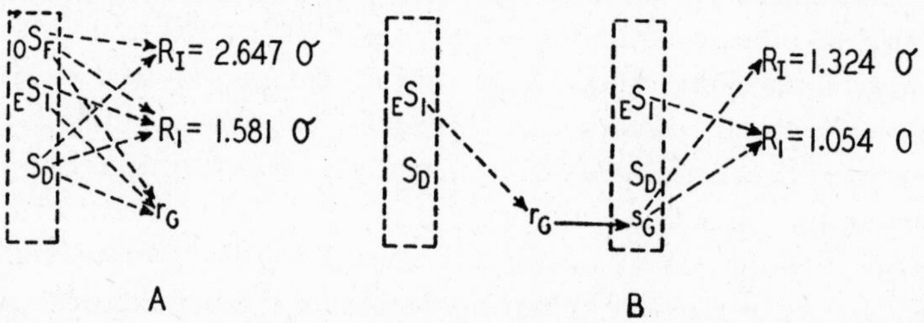

A   B

FIGURE 59. (A) Diagrammatic representation of the short path to an adient goal when the organism has transferred from it to the long path. The long path (R_1) has all of its three bonds, its full strength, or 1.581σ, at the outset, whereas the short or direct path has only two of its three original bonds, or roughly two-thirds of its original strength (3.971σ), or 2.647σ.
(B) Diagrammatic representation of the reaction potential to the competing paths to the goal when the organism has a different drive (S'_D) and no sight of the goal. In this case the short path (R_I) has one-third of the original bonds, or 1.324σ, and the long path has (R_1) two or two-thirds of the original bonds to R_1, i.e., 1.054σ.

the generalization from R_1 to R_I through $_ES_1$ will more than equal the slight loss of generalization from R_1 to R_I through $_OS_F$, we shall probably be very safe in letting the result stand as equivalent to the full short-path bond of $_OS_F \dashrightarrow R_I$. In a situation involving so many unknown values there is no point in attempting computation by the withdrawal technique (vii). Accordingly we shall figure the reaction potential to R_I by the simple proportion of the number of equivalent bonds remaining—two out of three as shown in part A of Figure 59. Two-thirds of 3.971 amounts to 2.647.

But $2.647 > 1.581$. It accordingly follows that under these con-

[6] Throughout this discussion we tacitly assume that the adient locomotor behavior generalizes about 100 per cent (Theorem 53).

ditions the short path, R_I, which has not yet been traversed or reinforced in this situation, will be preferred over R_1 which has been traversed and directly reinforced.

We next pass to the second and far more extreme situation of 59 B; here not only S_D is lacking but $_oS_F$ also is lacking, except for its appearance through secondary reinforcement as in Hebb's box-opening example (5, pp. 153–155). Assuming in this case that bond $_ES_1 \dashrightarrow r_G$ will be sufficiently strong to evoke r_G, s_G after a little delay will in turn tend to evoke both R_I and R_1. Now two full bonds to R_1 would yield 1.054σ, and one full bond to R_I would yield 1.324σ. Probably both values would be less than these figures indicate, though it is believed that the actual outcome would be in roughly the same proportion. But $1.324\sigma > 1.054\sigma$. Therefore once again the short path, R_I, which has not been traversed or directly reinforced in this situation, will be preferred to R_1, which has been traversed and directly reinforced.

Hebb seems to agree with this general approach to response variability, though he appears to feel that the variability in the stimuli presents a serious difficulty in the theory (5, p. 155). The oscillation function, it will be recalled, necessarily requires that the r_G of eating, which is the goal here, will vary over a small zone. But Hebb seems to forget that stimulus generalization should easily be able to bridge these small deviations in s_G. A very similar generalization bridge over oscillatory variability has been explained rather elaborately in another work (8, pp. 194–196).

Generalizing from the above considerations, we arrive at our next theorem:

> THEOREM 96. *When an indirect member of a locomotor habit-family hierarchy has attained a goal in a novel situation involving relatively free space, the learning then acquired is transferred to the initial segments of remaining members of the hierarchy without specific practice and on subsequent trials is manifested by the organism's spontaneous choice of the most direct path.*

General observation confirms the validity of Theorem 96 very fully. In addition, the classical maze work of Dashiell (2) confirms this theorem experimentally in an elegant manner (see Figure 66, Chapter 9).

The Angle That the Beginning of a Path Makes with the Direct Line to an Adient Goal and Its Influence on Initial Reaction Potential

At this point we turn to the question of the relative reaction potentials possessed by the various members of a naive organism's spatial habit-family hierarchy as based on the angle that the initial segment of a certain path makes with a direct line to an adient goal. Consider the starting point (S) and the goal point (G) in Figure 60.

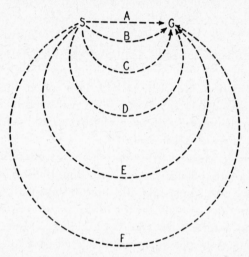

FIGURE 60. Diagrammatic representation of the typical mean lengths of various pathways belonging to a purely spatial habit-family hierarchy whose beginnings diverge by different amounts from a straight line between the starting point (S) and the adient goal object (G). Reproduced from Hull (7, p. 284).

Now, we may assume that from much goal seeking and from encountering various barriers to the goals in the past, normal locomotor organisms will have found by trial that as a rule paths which make an angle with the direct path, SAG, will require more locomotion and time to reach G by SBG and SCG than by SAG itself. Moreover, we assume in general that the greater the angle which the non-direct path of the habit-family hierarchy makes with the direct path, the more the path in question will exceed the direct path in locomotion distance and time. But by the principle of the gradient of reinforcement (6), the longer a given path is between S and G, the less will be the reaction potential at the beginning of such path. On this principle, coupled with that of stimulus generalization, we conclude that at the beginning the reaction potential to take each of the several paths between S and G in Figure 60 will be associated with the angular deviation of the initial segment of each possible path from a direct line to the goal. As a result of this previous habit formation, the organism will, without additional training, come to prefer the following hierarchy: path SAG, path SBG, paths SCG and SDG, and, last of all, path SFG.

From these considerations we arrive at our next theorem:

THEOREM 97. *Other things constant, the various possible alternative potential paths in free space from a starting point to an adient goal will tend without additional special training to create reaction potentials which are jointly a function of the strength of the reaction potential for the direct path and an inverse function of the magnitude of the angle that the beginning of each potential path makes with a straight line connecting the starting point and the adient goal object.*

Since reaction potential as such cannot be directly observed, at least by another organism, Theorem 97 cannot be tested experimentally. However, it should be possible to test it by means of the latencies (XIV) of the acts the organism performs in taking the several paths.

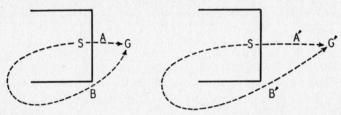

FIGURE 61. Diagrammatic representation of a detour or "*Umveg*" situation caused by a U-shaped barrier placed in the direct path of an organism at S with its goal at G. The goal object is supposed to be visible but the barrier, impassable (7, p. 281).

Let it be supposed, now, that an organism possessing this spatial habit-family hierarchy is placed behind the U-shaped barrier represented in Figure 61 in such a way that it can optically fixate the adient goal object, e.g., through bars, but cannot go directly to G by reason of the barrier. According to the habit-family hierarchy the excess of the reaction potential toward SAG over SBG will cause various exploratory movements into alternative paths or subpaths closely resembling SAG in general, in the order of the reaction potential of each path's initial segment. But since these much preferred members of the habit-family hierarchy do not lead to the goal they will gradually be extinguished (6, p. 139; 7, p. 278). When all have been extinguished to a point below the reaction potential of the first possible real path, SBG, this will be taken. But experimental extinction requires a certain amount of time (8, pp. 258 ff.).

From these considerations we arrive at our next theorem (7, p. 281):

> THEOREM 98. *Other things constant and no additional motivations present, a spatially naive organism oriented to a given goal will, when finding itself behind a U-shaped barrier in the direct path, spend some time in efforts to reach the goal by paths through the barrier deviating progressively more from a straight line to the goal before these tendencies are experimentally extinguished, when a really possible path around the barrier will be taken.*

No directly relevant empirical evidence bearing on this theorem has been found, though general observation makes its soundness highly probable.

Let it be assumed that an animal is placed behind one of two U-shaped barriers to a goal object, such as that shown at the left in Figure 61, except that the backward-turned arms of the U of one barrier are appreciably shorter than those of the other. Now, the shortening of the arms of the one U-shaped barrier will make smaller the angle drawn from the subject's stance to the tip of the barrier arm as seen in conjunction with the straight line SAG, than would be the case if the arms were longer. But, by Theorem 97, the greater the visual angle the initial segment of a potential path makes with a direct line to the goal, the weaker will be the $_sE_R$ to taking the potential path; and the weaker the reaction potential to the potential act is, the shorter will be the time required for the experimental extinction of the direct path down to the potential path level. Therefore the less will be the time required for a naive organism to extinguish the search for shorter and more favored paths to that goal.

From these considerations we arrive at our next theorem (7):

> THEOREM 99. *Other things constant and no additional motivation present, a naive organism oriented to a given adient goal, when finding*

itself behind a U-shaped barrier which it can see through but cannot surmount, will in general require a shorter time to detour this barrier successfully if the backward turning arms of the U are short than if they are long.

No direct empirical evidence bearing on this theorem has been found.

Let us assume further that each of two similar organisms finds itself behind a separate U-shaped barrier to the same goal. In the case of one organism, however, the barrier is appreciably closer to the goal than in that of the other, as shown in Figure 61. By Theorem 97, other things constant, the reaction potential at the beginning of SAG will, by reason of its comparative nearness to the goal, be greater than that at the beginning of SA'G' (iii). Also by Theorem 97, since the angle from the straight line at the beginning of the detour path to the goal is in both cases the same, the reaction potential to the detour path will constitute the same function of the direct path in the two cases. Suppose it is 40 per cent that of the direct path and that the two direct-path reaction potentials are 3.0σ and 1.0σ respectively. On these assumptions the initial segment of the detour path to G would have a reaction potential of $3.0\sigma \times .40 = 1.2\sigma$, whereas that to G' would have one of $1.0\sigma \times .40 = .4\sigma$. This leaves to be extinguished before the detour can be made a difference in reaction potential between the direct line and the detour path of

$$3.0\sigma - 1.2\sigma = 1.8\sigma,$$

in the case of G, whereas in the case of G' it will be,

$$1.00\sigma - .40\sigma = .60\sigma.$$

But, other things constant, it takes longer to extinguish a large amount of reaction potential than a small amount. It should therefore take longer to extinguish 1.8σ than $.60\sigma$.

Generalizing on the preceding considerations, we arrive at our next theorem:

THEOREM 100. *Other things constant, spatially naive organisms will require longer to choose a detour path around a U-shaped barrier to a seen goal when the latter is close to the barrier than when it is farther away from it.*

Köhler reports a case bearing on Theorem 100. A Canary Isle bitch was standing behind a wire fence which with an adjoining house wall made an obstruction much like that shown in Figure 61. We quote from Köhler (9, p. 14): " . . . over which food is thrown to some distance; the bitch at once dashes out to it, describing a wide bend. It is worth noting that when, on repeating this experiment, the food was not thrown far out, but was dropped only just outside the fence, so that it lay directly in front of her, separated only by the wire, she stood seemingly helpless, as if the very nearness of the object and her concentration thereon . . . blocked the 'idea' of the wide circle around the fence; she pushed again and again with her nose at the wire fence and did not budge from the spot."

Now let us assume that in the situation represented at the left of Figure 61 we have two groups of organisms; the first group has a strong drive for the goal object, e.g., food, and the second group has a weak drive. There is reason to believe that, other things constant,

$$_{s}E_{R} = {_{s}H_{R}} \times D.$$

Assuming that when the $_{s}H_{R} = .80$ the strong drive equals 3.00σ and the weak drive equals 1.80σ, we find by the above equation that these two drives yield the following reaction potentials:

$$_{s}E_{R} = .80 \times 3.00\sigma = 2.40\sigma$$
$$_{s}E_{R}' = .80 \times 1.80\sigma = 1.44\sigma.$$

Also, assuming that in all cases path SAG has three times the $_{s}E_{R}$ that path SBG has, it follows that on the average ($_{s}O_{R}$) something like two-thirds of the reaction potential of path SAG must be extinguished before path SBG can be chosen.
But,

$$\tfrac{2}{3} \times 2.40\sigma > \tfrac{2}{3} \times 1.44\sigma.$$

Moreover, as noted above, the extinction of a strong reaction potential requires a longer time and more work than that of a weak one, other things equal. Therefore, the extinction of $\tfrac{2}{3} \times 2.40\sigma$ will require more time and effort than will that of $\tfrac{2}{3} \times 1.44\sigma$.

Generalizing on the preceding considerations we arrive at our next theorem (4):

THEOREM 101. *Other things constant, the stronger the drive to a given goal object behind a U-shaped barrier, the more the time and work which will be required by a naive organism before the occurrence of sufficient extinction to yield the execution of a successful detour.*

Lewin gave some consideration to this problem and based his conclusions, apparently, on the observed behavior of young children. In this connection he stated (*10*, p. 83): "But if we continue to strengthen the valence, the solution of the task ceases to be facilitated and instead becomes more difficult. The strength of the attraction then makes it doubly difficult for the child to start in a direction opposed to the field force. Instead, the child will execute with all its energy, affective meaningless actions in the direction of the valence." We accordingly may say that Theorem 101 probably has empirical corroboration. It may be noted that Lewin's use of the expressions "valence" and "field force" corresponds roughly to our use of the expression "reaction potential," and that his expression, "restructuring of the field," corresponds in effect to the results of experimental extinction upon the preferred members of the spatial habit-family hierarchy.

Again, let us assume the situation represented at the left of Figure 61, with two equivalent organisms facing this barrier for the first time. With one organism the goal object has a K value of .80, and with the other organism the lure (e.g., a smaller goal object) has a K value of .40. Both are assumed to have a primary motivation (e.g., hunger) of 3.0σ, and a habit strength of 1.0. Now, by an earlier form of equation 8, these two situations yield different reaction potentials as follows:

$$_{s}E_{R} = 3.0\sigma \times 1.0 \times .80 = 2.40\sigma.$$
$$_{s}E'_{R} = 3.0\sigma \times 1.0 \times .40 = 1.20\sigma.$$

Here again we assume that the direct path SAG must be extinguished to about two-thirds of its reaction potential before the path SBG can be chosen.
But,

$$\tfrac{2}{3} \times 2.40\sigma > \tfrac{2}{3} \times 1.20\sigma.$$

Accordingly by reasoning exactly analogous to that leading to Theorem 101, we arrive at our next theorem (*6*):

THEOREM 102. *Other things constant and no other motivations present, the greater the incentive to action of the goal object behind a U-shaped barrier, the more the time and work which will be required before a successful detour will be executed by a naive organism.*

Lewin considered this problem also. He remarked, apparently with empirical behavior of young children in mind, " . . . the prospect of an especially intense reward . . . may impede the solution . . . " (*10*, p. 84).

Summary

All behavior occurs in space, but certain behavior, if it is to be adaptive, must take place in specific geometrical relationship to particular objects in space. From this point of view there are two primary but opposite relationships—that of approach or adience, and that of avoidance or abience. In situations in which approach must occur before reinforcement can take place, habits of approach behavior are in general set up through trial and error; and, likewise, habits of avoidance behavior are set up through trial and error in situations in which avoidance must occur before reinforcement can take place. Both adient and abient behavior are ordinarily locomotor in nature and are conditioned in part to objects and in part to distance reception continua. Because of the generalized nature of locomotion and the strong stimulus generalization characteristics of objects, of distance reception continua, and of the proprioception of primary orientation movements, adient behavior and abient behavior are highly generalized in respect to both direction and distance.

Adient behavior and abient behavior both have gradients of reaction potential which are high near the objects in question and decline with distance from the objects, probably roughly according to a negative growth function. This function is generally characteristic of both (1) stimulus generalization (*8*, p. 185) presumably operating mainly on the basis of distance reception continua, chiefly visual, where space is unobstructed, and (2) the gradient of delay of reinforcement (iii A and B) or goal gradient (*8*, pp. 135 ff.), presumably operating exclusively where the focal object is not available to any distance receptor. Owing to the process of discrimination, the exponent of the equation for abient behavior to static objects or stimuli is ordinarily steeper than that of the equation for adient behavior. Chiefly because of the principle of less work, the paths of both adience and abience will tend strongly to laterally straight lines.

The organism's approach to an adient object in free space may obviously occur from any or all directions; these several adient paths naturally converge. Withdrawal from an abient object in free space may obviously be in any direction and these several abient paths naturally diverge. Accordingly both adience and abience, which at first glance appear to be gradients with simple linear bases, actually when considered comprehensively involve areas, i.e., two-dimensional space at the least. The theory of adient and abient behavior thus involves examples of *bona fide* field theory, though this theory must not be confused with physical field theories, from which the present theory differs in most respects. The organism in behavior field theory corresponds to the particle subject to impulsion in physical field theories, and the energy involved in the transition in space arises in the main from the food eaten by the organism, rather than from the field.

Much of the available theory of adience and abience concerns the interaction of these behavior potential fields. In general, where two adient fields are in competition, the organism will choose the nearer adient object; and the greater the difference in the distances between the objects, the greater is this probability. In a clearly analogous manner, the choice time or reaction latency is likely to be greater, the less the difference in distance between the competing adient objects. Similarly, reaction latency is likely to be reduced by either an increased motivation (D) or an increased incentive (K), especially where one of the competitors is favored by the differential drive or incentive, though this is not a necessary condition.

The interaction of two abient fields of reaction potential has two main cases: that in which the organism is in a restraining alley with an abient object at either end, and that in which the organism is placed in free space on a line between the objects. In the case of the restraining alley with duplicate abient objects at either end, the organism tends to move from the neighborhood of either (abient) object to a point midway between them where the difference in reaction potential is zero. The closer the organism is to either abient object, the faster will be the movement toward the point of zero reaction difference, and the more certain the movement is to occur. In case one of the abient objects has greater drive than the other, the increased reaction potential of that gradient will cause a displacement of the point of zero reaction potential difference away from that end of the alley. In case the organism is placed at the point of zero reaction potential difference between two abient duplicate objects in open space, the action of behavioral vector summation based on small unbalancing movements due to the oscillation factor will generate a lateral movement to one side or the other at right angles to the line connecting the objects.

The interaction of an adient and an abient reaction potential field has two cases. When the organism is placed between an adient and an abient object, both reaction potentials lead to movement toward the adient object. The joint reaction potential is large close to each of the objects, but tends to sag to a minimum at a point between them. A second case of this type of interaction is seen where both the adient and the abient object occupy practically the same point in space. The interaction of the two fields ordinarily results in a zero reaction-potential difference, a state of so-called stable equilibrium, at a point some distance from the combined objects.

Static barriers encountered by organisms are abient objects for which the gradient has become maximal in steepness through differential reinforcement, so that the organism merely avoids rough contact with the object. The reactions of organisms to simple barriers in these adient and abient fields are complicated by stimulus pattern discrimination set up on the basis of compound trial-and-error learning. As a result of this process, sophisticated organisms will not attempt to surmount really impassable barriers but will detour them in otherwise free space by taking the shortest path either to the adient object or away from the abient object. The various alternative pathways to objects in space constitute habit-family hierarchies, the paths of less work being the preferred parts of the hierarchy.

Terminal Notes

HISTORICAL NOTE

The facts of adience and abience are so obvious in animal behavior that they cannot be overlooked. Adience has been widely employed by animal psychologists as an indicator of the results of learning in the greatest variety of situations. Unfortunately this has been done with little or no explicit recognition of the inherent complexities involved in the process itself. It is believed that this is the reason for some of the theoretical confusion regarding maze learning.

The first important publication in the field of the behavior of organisms toward objects in space was by Lewin in 1933. An amplification of substantially the same material was published as a book (10) in 1935. These works presented an exceedingly valuable analysis of the general field, and raised at a qualitative level a large number of the problems concerning behavior toward objects in space which have occupied the attention of subsequent workers, even though Lewin himself seemed not to have been much interested in the spatial problems as such.

In 1938 the present writer published a manuscript (7) written in 1934, which attempted to apply a quantitative mathematical analysis to some of these problems, in particular to those involving the goal gradient hypothesis. Since the manuscript was already written on the basis of the by-then-abandoned (7, p. 273) logarithmic formulation of the goal gradient, this form of the hypothesis appears in the published study. This article gave what is believed to be the first quantitative mathematical derivation of the problem of adient-abient equilibrium. It also gave quantitative analyses of several forms of the barrier problem. The author's present view is that these latter analyses are defective in that the principle of afferent stimulus interaction and stimulus patterning was not employed (8, pp. 349 ff.).

Around the year 1940, Neal E. Miller, in association with Judson S. Brown and several others, began an exceedingly sagacious and ingenious experimental attack on this series of problems, employing albino rats as subjects. Fortunately as early as 1942 Brown published in detail a part of this experimental work, together with the important germinal idea that the goal gradient principle is not the only factor operating in open space. He says (1, p. 209):

> It can be shown, however, that a number of these facts are also in accord with the concept of the *spatial generalization of conditioned responses*.

In the opinion of the present writer, the principle just quoted constitutes the most important single advance recently made in this field. As the reader has already seen, it has been exploited on a large scale in the foregoing chapter. While much of the work of Miller and his associates had not been published, owing to the participation of both Miller and Brown in the war effort, Miller was able in 1944 to include a summary of much of it in his chapter, "Experimental Studies of Conflict," which appeared in Hunt's *Personality and the Behavior Disorders* (*13*, pp. 431 ff.). Miller's theoretical analysis is essentially behavioristic in nature and, while technically qualitative in form, clearly advances the subject to a new high level. The experimental results are admirably quantitative.

THE MEANING OF THE EXPRESSION "FIELD THEORY"

The frequent use made in the present chapter of reaction-potential fields may quite naturally raise for the serious reader questions as to the relationship of these fields to the "field theories" and the "field forces" so extensively referred to in the literature of the Lewin branch of the *Gestalt* school. There is some uncertainty in this respect. This uncertainty has been increased by a late article by Lewin in which he proposed (*11*, p. 292) to make a final clarification of the subject from his point of view. In this connection he said (*11*, p. 294):

> Field theory, therefore, can hardly be called correct or incorrect in the same way as a theory in the usual sense of the term. *Field theory is probably best characterized as a method:* namely a method *of analyzing causal relations and of building scientific constructs.* This method of analyzing causal relations can be expressed in the form of certain general statements about the "nature" of the conditions of change.

In the present work the expression "field theory" definitely means a theory in the natural-science sense, and one which *is* either true or false in the usual meaning of the term. Moreover, field theory as here used is concerned with action potentialities in *space*. This, it is believed, is the ordinarily accepted use of the expression in works on physics such as that by Lindsay and Margenau, where various sorts of physical fields are dealt with and where, for example, we find the expression (*12*, p. 283):

> . . . a field of force, i.e., a continuous region of space at every point of which there is defined the force which would act on a standard particle placed there . . .

In the present behavioral field theory the organism corresponds to the particle, and it is supposed to move in true space, but there the analogy to the fields found in physics largely ends. The law connecting a particle to the source of a gravitational field is that of the inverse square of the distance measured in feet or miles. The law relating the organism to the adient or abient object, on the other hand, is presumably approximately of the form,

$$_s\underline{E}_R = {}_sE_R \times 10^{-id},$$

where d does not represent spatial distance as such, but instead represents j.n.d. values functionally based on distance.

REFERENCES

1. Brown, J. S. The generalization of approach responses as a function of stimulus intensity and strength of motivation. *J. Comp. Psychol.*, 1942, *33*, 209–226.

2. Dashiell, J. F. Direction orientation in maze running by the white rat. *Comp. Psychol. Monogr.*, 1931, 7.

3. Fletcher, F. M. Effects of quantitative variation of food-incentive on the performance of physical work by chimpanzees. *Comp. Psychol. Monogr.*, 1940, *16*, No. 82.

4. Guilford, J. P. *Psychometric Methods.* New York: McGraw-Hill Book Co., 1936.

5. Hebb, D. O. *The organization of behavior.* New York: John Wiley and Sons, Inc., 1949.

6. Hull, C. L. The concept of the habit-family hierarchy and maze learning. *Psychol. Rev.*, 1934. *41*, Part I, 33-52; Part II, 134–152.

7. Hull, C. L. The goal gradient hypothesis applied to some "field-force" problems in the behavior of young children. *Psychol. Rev.*, 1938, *45*, 271–299.

8. Hull, C. L. *Principles of behavior.* New York: D. Appleton-Century Co., Inc., 1943.

9. Köhler, W. *The mentality of apes.* New York: Harcourt, Brace and Co., Inc., 1925.

10. Lewin, K. *A dynamic theory of personality.* New York: McGraw-Hill Book Co., 1935.

11. Lewin, K. Defining the "field at a given time." *Psychol. Rev.*, 1943, *50*, 292–310.

12. Lindsay, R. B., and Margenau, H. *Foundations of physics*. New York: John Wiley and Sons, 1936.
13. Miller, N. E. Experimental studies of conflict. Chapter 14 in *Personality and the behavior disorders*, edited by J. McV. Hunt, Vol. I. New York: The Ronald Press Co., 1944.
14. Miller, N. E., Brown, J. S., and Lipofsky, H. A theoretical and experimental analysis of conflict behavior: III. Approach-avoidance conflict as a function of strength of drive and strength of shock. 1943, unpublished.
15. Riesen, A. H. The development of visual perception in man and chimpanzee. *Science*, 1947, *106*, 107–108.

9. Multidirectional Maze Learning

Having considered in the last chapter the subject of organismic behavior in free and partially barricaded space, we may now resume the study of compound trial-and-error learning with an increased capacity for understanding. Specifically, we propose to consider the learning of the ordinary maze—one of the classical problems of psychology. But before we proceed to the investigation of this major subject we need to examine one or two principles concerning a special type of problem which arises in the learning of what we shall call the alternative-path maze (*10*, p. 26).

A simple form of this type of maze consists of two distinct and symmetrical pathways extending from a common starting point (S) to a common ending point or goal (G) where, usually, food is found. This is illustrated in Figure 62. For purposes of exposition these pathways are divided into equal units of distance separated by broken lines; the shorter path, yy', thus has four units of length, whereas the longer path, xx', has eight units of length. Now it is known on the basis of an ample series of experiments, beginning with a study by DeCamp (*3*) and culminating with studies by Yoshioka (*31*) and Grice (*6*), that upon the whole if a hungry organism is given alternating rewarded trials on two paths of this general nature it will at length, when given free choices, come to take path yy', the shorter of the two. The experiments by Yoshioka and by Grice have also shown that the comparative ease with which the organism will learn to choose the shorter path is a function of the *relative* length of the two paths, rather than of the *absolute* difference between them. And Anderson has found that even with a period of delay substituted for the differential distance, the path involving the shorter delay will also come to be a preferential choice on a relative rather than an absolute basis.

These facts, among many others, have given support to the goal gradient hypothesis which the reader has had occasion to consider in numerous other but related connections in previous chapters

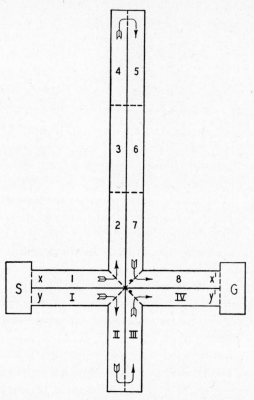

FIGURE 62. An alternative-pathway maze illustrating two goal gradients, x to x′ and y to y′. Since these two pathways both begin at the same point (S) and end at the same goal (G), they constitute a special type of habit-family hierarchy. The several sections of the pathway x to x′ are numbered in Arabic, and those of y to y′ in Roman numerals.

(pp. 39; 126; 158; 256). Moreover, an analysis of the Anderson data (*14*, pp. 148 ff.) has revealed a very considerable probability that the temporal goal gradient, at least, follows an exponential law backward from the point of reinforcement. In simple language this means that the strength of reaction potential at one unit of delay in reinforcement from the food-box will be less by a certain fractional amount than the strength of reaction potential at no delay; that the $_sE_R$ at two units of delay from the goal will have a similar fractional reduction below that at one unit of delay; and so on through as many units of delay in reinforcement as occur. For example (*14*, p. 163), if we take $_sE_R = 3.120\sigma$ as the strength of reaction potential at the limit of training with one unit of delay in reinforcement, and $\frac{1}{10}$ as the uniform factor of reduction (F), then the $_sE_R$ at one unit of delay would be:

$$3.120 - \frac{3.120}{10} = 3.120 - .312 = 2.808.$$

Similarly, the $_sE_R$ at two units of delay in reinforcement would be:

$$2.808 - \frac{2.808}{10} = 2.808 - .2808 = 2.527,$$

and so on. On this principle, at the limit of training the reaction potential to turn right at S (Figure 62), i.e., to choose path y four units from reinforcement, would be 2.047σ, whereas that to turn left, i.e., to choose path x eight units from reinforcement, would be 1.343σ. The difference between these two reaction potentials is,

$$2.047\sigma - 1.343\sigma = .704\sigma.$$

Now, assuming that the standard deviation of the $_sO_R$ at these two points is .3012, the standard deviation of the difference of the two would then be,

$$\sqrt{.3012^2 + .3012^2} = \sqrt{.18156} = .426.$$

Dividing the obtained difference, $.704\sigma$, by the standard deviation of the associated $_sO_R$, we have,

$$\frac{.704\sigma}{.426\sigma} = 1.652.$$

This value of 1.652 has a functional relationship to the probability of a correct choice being made at the limit of practice. Looking this up in an appropriate table of the probability integral we find that it corresponds to $.451 + .500 = .951$, or a little better than 95 short-path choices in a hundred trials, say. With this concrete example of the action of the goal gradient in a spatial learning situation before us, we may now begin the consideration of multi-directional maze learning.

The Goal-Gradient Principle and the Short-Circuiting of Multidirectional-Maze Blind Alleys

The ordinary maze is often called the Hampton Court maze because, historically, such a maze was laid out on the grounds of a place known as Hampton Court. The walls consisted of high hedges, and guests had the amusement of finding their way out through the intricate passages. In the hands of psychologists during recent years the maze has been adapted to the greatest variety of problems and has taken very many forms. In Chapter 6 we studied the phenomena associated with one of these forms, the linear maze as represented in Figure 44. Being linear, the true path of this maze necessarily extends as a whole in a single direction; such mazes may therefore be called *unidirectional*. But in the usual type of Hampton Court maze the true path may, and often does, extend in many directions; for this reason we shall call such mazes *multidirectional*.

Actually the latter type of maze is usually built on the right-angled principle. Such a maze may have as many as four paths emanating from any point. If one of these paths constitutes the entrance, there are three others which may serve as exits—right, left, and straight ahead. In order to simplify the matter of behavioral interpretation somewhat, the straight-ahead path is frequently eliminated, leaving a T-shaped path which at each choice point in the maze forces the subject to turn either to the right or to the left. Numerous T's joined together in various ways may make up a maze of any desired length and complexity. Such a maze, an adaptation of one used by Blodgett (1) in Tolman's laboratory, is represented diagrammatically in Figure 63. To simplify further the interpretation of maze behavior, valves are often placed in the true path to prevent retracing and the possibility of the subject's entering the same blind repeatedly. Also, curtains are often placed at each side of the choice point to prevent the subject from seeing in advance of choice what lies beyond them, e.g., the dead end of a blind alley.

When first put into a maze the animal, usually an albino rat, is apt to be very fearful, and ordinarily crouches quietly where first placed for some time. However, it will at length begin to explore the immediate vicinity, gradually extending the range of exploration, with frequent retracings to the starting point, until the entire maze is covered. For this reason the animal is often simply allowed to explore the maze for an hour or so on each of several days before the learning proper is begun and a record of behavior made. At that time the animal, usually very hungry, is placed in the maze at a given point such as that marked S in Figure 63, from which it wanders at will until at length it makes its way to the point marked G, where food is found and eaten. This constitutes a single trial.

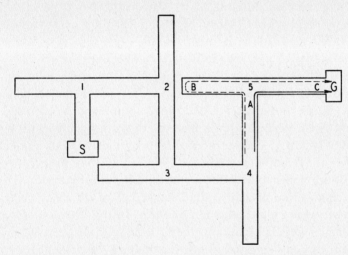

FIGURE 63. Diagrammatic representation of a fairly typical multidirectional maze made by combining five T's. Actually the true path in this case moves only north, south, and east, with no movement west. The five choice points are indicated by Arabic numerals in the order of the distance from the starting point (S). The true (shorter) path, AC, of the final or fifth section is represented by a continuous line; the long path, ABC, via the blind alley is represented by a broken line. Adapted from a drawing published by Blodgett (7, p. 117).

In doing this the animal will naturally enter many of the blind alleys. For example, instead of going directly from A to C and the food (Figure 63) the animal may go from A to B, turn 180 degrees and retrace its way back to A, and then go on to C and the food. This path is marked by the broken line. On successive trials the animal's behavior gradually takes on a more "purposeful" appearance, the speed of locomotion increases, the number and durations of pauses decrease, and the number of blind alleys entered also gradually decreases until with most mazes and most rats no false locomotion at all is made.

In the history of behavior theory much attention has been given to explanations of why animals cease to enter blind alleys during maze learning. Certain essentially qualitative principles such as recency, frequency, and intensity of associated stimuli, once much in vogue, were early put forward following the attempts of Hobhouse (*8*, pp. 174 ff.) and Holmes (*9*, pp. 164 ff.) to explain learning in general. An example of this is seen in Lloyd Morgan's famous chick and caterpillar combination and the concept of organic congruity and incompatibility. Watson proposed a clear but definitely inadequate theory of maze learning based on simple probability coupled with the principles of associative frequency and recency (*28*, pp. 256–269); Thorndike puzzled over how the pleasures (of success) are "able to burn in and render predominant the association which led to them," (*23*); and Peterson proposed a qualitative hypothesis based on "completeness of response" coupled with association. Thus as the quantitative theory of behavior began to emerge, it was seen by most serious students of learning that simple association alone as at that time conceived was not adequate to account for blind-alley elimination.

We shall show presently that a number of different principles operate in maze blind-alley elimination. In the interests of expository clarity we shall examine these principles one at a time. The first of these, as suggested in our introductory statement regarding the alternative-path maze, is the goal gradient (*10*) or the delay in reinforcement (iii A) hypothesis. On this analogy the blind alley ABC of the last T-unit in the multidirectional maze represented in Figure 63 corresponds in some sense to the long path in Figure 62, and the short path or true alternative (AC) corresponds to the short path in Figure 62; the former involves approximately three units of delay in reinforcement (and of work), whereas the latter involves only one unit. By means of computations exactly analogous to those given above for the alternative-pathway maze and summarized in the first line of Table 33, it may be seen that the short-circuit path from A to C will yield at the limit of training a reaction potential at A of 2.808σ for that choice of turn, whereas the long-circuit path from A to B to C will yield a reaction potential at A of 2.274σ for that choice of turn. The difference of $.534\sigma$ yields a ratio to $.426$ of 1.253. Reference to a table of the probability integral shows that this corresponds to the probability of a right-hand choice at A of 89.5 per cent at the limit of practice. Thus the short-circuiting of a maze blind alley is to be expected theoretically on the basis of the goal-gradient hypothesis alone.[1]

Generalizing on the basis of these considerations we arrive at our next theorem:

THEOREM 103. *Other things constant, the goal gradient will tend strongly to cause the short-circuiting of errors, i.e., to cause the elimination of the choice of blind alleys in maze learning to a suitable reinforcing agent.*

As already pointed out, the fact of blind-alley elimination was well known empirically long before the goal-gradient hypothesis was formulated.

TABLE 33. Systematic presentation of the theoretical probabilities of the correct over the incorrect choice at typical choice points throughout a 19-blind-alley maze on the assumption that the goal gradient is the only factor operating (which is not so) and that the oscillation factor (σ_{sO_R}) is .3012 (*14*, p. 163). But,

$$\sqrt{.3012^2 + .3012^2} = \sqrt{.18156} = .426.$$

No. of choice point counting from *goal*	Reaction potential to true path choice	Reaction potential to blind alley choice	Difference in favor of correct choice	Difference divided by .426, the square root of the sum of the two $_sO_R$'s squared	Probability of choice of correct path by table of the probability integral
1	2.808	2.274	.534	1.253	89.5
3	2.274	1.843	.431	1.012	84.4
5	1.843	1.492	.351	.824	79.5
7	1.492	1.209	.283	.664	74.7
9	1.209	.980	.229	.538	70.5
11	.980	.794	.186	.437	66.9
13	.794	.643	.151	.354	63.8
15	.643	.521	.122	.286	61.1
17	.521	.422	.099	.232	59.2
19	.422	.342	.080	.188	57.4

We next take up the question of whether the organism will learn to eliminate by means of the goal-gradient principle alone a long blind alley more easily than a short one. This problem may be solved by a procedure closely similar to that just followed. In the first problem a turn to the right was assumed to involve the travers-

[1] However, see the terminal note in the present chapter.

ing of one unit of distance between the choice and the attainment of the goal, and one second of delay in reinforcement, whereas a turn to the left involved traversing three units of distance and three seconds of delay in reinforcement. But suppose that instead the left turn entered a blind alley twice as long as the B choice shown in Figure 63, which would mean traversing five units of length and a delay of five seconds in reinforcement. By Table 33, a delay of five seconds will reduce the reaction potential to 1.843σ as compared with 2.808σ at one second. But $2.808\sigma - 1.843\sigma = .965$. Dividing .965 by the square root of the sum of the squares of the two standard deviations involved, we have $.965 \div .426 = 2.26$, which, by a table of the normal probability integral, yields an advantage of 98.8 per cent in favor of the shorter alternative path. But $98.8 > 89.5$.

Thus we arrive at our next theorem (*10*, p. 36):

> THEOREM 104. *Other things constant, the goal gradient will tend strongly to favor the elimination of a long blind alley as compared with the elimination of a short one.*

The first study we have been able to find on the relative ease of eliminating long versus short blind alleys was reported in a monograph by Joseph Peterson (*17*). On the basis of an ingenious study in which he used twenty-four rats he concluded that short blinds were more easily eliminated than long ones. Unfortunately, curtains in mazes were not used at that time so that Peterson's animals probably were able to see the ends of his short blind alleys without entering them. In his main experiment, moreover, six out of the ten blind alleys actually showed less errors on the shorter blinds. Six years later, White and Tolman (*29*) took up the same problem in a wholly convincing manner, using a simplified maze with relatively long blinds possessing right-angled turns so that the subject could not see the blind end from the entrance. They based their conclusions on the behavior of fourteen rats given five trials per day for four days. Every day of the experiment fewer entries were made by the group of subjects as a whole on the long alley than on the short one. And upon the whole the advantage of the elimination of the long alleys over the short ones increased as practice continued. The percentages of long versus short blind-alley entrances for the several days were: day 1, 48; day 2, 40; day 3, 23;

day 4, 36. Thus the theoretical deduction is believed substantiated by empirical fact.

Our third question concerns the relative ease of eliminating two blinds of the same length at the beginning and at the end of the maze respectively. This problem, again, is solved by methods quite analogous to those employed with the first problem. Consider the first and last blind alleys of the maze in Figure 63. Here, as in the case of the blind just considered, the difference in distance traversed and the delay in reinforcement between the blind-alley path and the shorter path is two units of distance and roughly two seconds in time. Thus there will be approximately five seconds of delay on the right turn and $5 + 2$ or 7 seconds by the blind. By Table 33, the true path would have a reaction potential to the right turn of 1.843σ, and one of 1.492σ to the left or incorrect turn. This yields a difference of $.351\sigma$, which corresponds to a choice probability of the elimination of the blind alley at the limit of practice of 79.5 per cent. But $79.5 < 89.5$. Thus we arrive at our next theorem:

THEOREM 105. *Other things constant, the elimination of a blind alley at the beginning of a maze is more difficult, by the goal-gradient principle alone, than at the termination (goal end) of a maze.*

Moreover, a glance at the probability-of-choice values in Table 33 at various distances from the terminus of a maze shows that elimination becomes progressively more difficult (*10*, p. 37). This yields the following theorem:

THEOREM 106. *Other things constant, the last blind alley of a maze will be eliminated first, by the goal-gradient principle alone, and the others progressively in a backward order, the first blind alley being eliminated last.*

The generally backward order of the elimination of blind alleys in maze learning was early noticed by experimentalists, among whom may be mentioned Carr and Peterson. Since 1917 many other investigators using various sorts of mazes have verified the original observation, especially with homogeneous mazes on which the interpretation is somewhat clearer. Spence (*21*), assembling data from twelve mazes of this type ranging from six to fourteen units in length, found that the mean ranks of the alleys from easiest to most difficult blind-alley elimination for the first, second, and third thirds of the mazes were 7.66, 4.36, and 3.58, with a satisfactory statistical reliability between all three pairs of differences. Since a small-numbered rank means easy learning, this shows upon the whole a backward order of blind-alley elimination, though other factors clearly enter.

But the number of trials required to complete the learning of a maze depends upon the most difficult single blind alley, and this (the first) depends upon the number of units following it in the maze. Thus by Table 33, a single-unit maze will yield at the limit of training 89.5 per cent correct choices, a five-unit maze will yield 79.5 per cent correct choices, an eleven- and a nineteen-unit maze will yield 66.9 and 57.4 per cent successful choices respectively.

Generalizing on these considerations we arrive at our next theorem (*10*, p. 37):

THEOREM 107. *Other things constant, long multidirectional mazes (with many choice points) will be more difficult to learn, by the goal-gradient principle alone, than short ones.*

For many years it has been known in a general way that long mazes are more difficult to learn than are short ones, though we have not been able to find any study where a strict comparison is made of the difficulty of learning multidirectional mazes differing only in the number of blind alleys. As a sample of the available evidence we take the mean number of non-retracing errors made

TABLE 34. The mean number of entrances into the first blind alley of five alternative-pathway mazes as a function of the length (number of blind alleys) of each. After Warden and Cummings (*27*).

Total number of blind alleys in mazes	Mean number of entrances into the first blind alley of maze
2	8.8
4	10.44
6	8.44
8	14.90
10	14.25

in a simple right-left alternative maze on the first blind as reported by Warden and Cummings (*27*). These are assembled in Table 34. It is well known that in alternation maze learning the alternation of early units is transferred more or less to the corresponding alternates of later units, which complicates interpretation from this point of view. Nevertheless it is evident that while the agreement is not precise, presumably in part because of the small number of animals used in each group, the tendency to agreement with the theory is clear.

Closely related to the above is the question of the shape of the curve of correct choices at the various points as a function of their

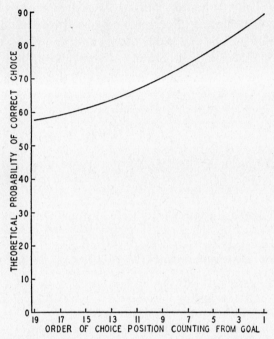

FIGURE 64. Graph representing the theoretically successful choices at the limit of training as a function of the delay in reinforcement, by the uncomplicated goal gradient as represented in column 6 of Table 33. Note that if they were counted from the anterior of the maze, the numbering of the maze units would be reversed.

distance from the point of reinforcement. We have secured this merely by plotting the probability values in the last column of Table 33 as a function of the blind-alley position values as given in the first column. This appears as Figure 64.

From an inspection of this graph we arrive at our next theorem:

THEOREM 108. *Other things constant, the per cent of correct choices at the several choice points of a maze progressively decreases under the influence of the goal gradient alone as the choice points are more remote from the point of reinforcement.*

So far as we can discover, the problem of the curve of successful choices as a function of the number of blind alleys between the goal and any choice point has never before been raised, either theoretically or experimentally. Moreover, other things never are constant in such series. For one thing such chains, if purely heterogeneous and plotted in terms of correct responses, will arch downward, and if purely homogeneous will arch upward (Chapter 6). Then of course there is the matter of spatial orientation, the frustration at the ends of the blinds (xvii), and so on.

Because of the general bearing of the relationship of reaction time to reaction potential, as represented by the empirical equation (5),

$$_st_R = \frac{8.71}{(_sE_R + .599)^{2.07}},$$

it follows from Table 33 that as the organism progresses in the reinforced trials during the learning of a maze, its speed of locomotion will progressively increase.

From these considerations we arrive at our next two theorems:

> THEOREM 109. *Other things constant, as an organism repeatedly traverses a maze with reward at the posterior end, the rate of locomotion will increase as a whole.*
>
> THEOREM 110. *Other things constant, i.e., apart from antedating and perseverative response-interferences, as an organism repeatedly traverses a maze with reward at the posterior end, the rate of locomotion through the later part of the maze will become progressively faster than that through the early part.*

Perhaps the simplest empirical evidence bearing on Theorems 109 and 110, even though it does not come from a situation involving a series of blind alleys, is presented by the speed of rats running in a plain 40-foot runway. This may be seen in Figure 65. The faster running of the animals on days 6 and 7 as compared with days 1 and 2 is clearly shown by the positions of the curves. Thus Theorem 109 is confirmed empirically. The tilting up of both curves at the posterior end is presumably due to the homogeneous nature of the path which positively generalizes the learning from both ends toward the middle where they summate positively (see Chapter 6). The goal gradient alone is therefore revealed by the relative position of the first section as compared with that of the last one, rather than by the positions of the intermediate sections. This is clearly shown by both curves of Figure 65. Thus Theorem 110 also is confirmed empirically.

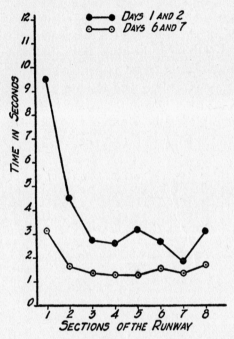

FIGURE 65. Graphic representation of the mean time required for fourteen albino rats to traverse the several segments of a straight 40-foot enclosed runway at two different stages of training, days 1 and 2 and days 6 and 7. From Hull (*12*, p. 404).

Goal Orientation and Maze Learning

In Chapter 8, Figure 60 illustrates a habit-family hierarchy with alternative paths in open space on a single side of a straight line from the starting point to the goal. We must here point out that according to the same theory (Theorem 107), other alternative paths in the same habit-family hierarchy exist in free space on the opposite side of the straight line; that an infinite number of paths of intermediate length pass *between* those alternative paths; and that at any given level of the habit-family hierarchy, *a very large number of alternative potential paths of equal length exist* which themselves do not constitute a complete hierarchy.

Consider, now, the behavior of an organism which has previously formed the visual habit-family hierarchies in open and relatively free space, on being placed in an enclosed maze. In traversing this maze from S to the goal or food box (G, Figure 63), the organism will form a locomotor habit corresponding to one of the grosser units of a habit-family hierarchy acquired in free space. Now in the past the organism has associated this sequence with directional movements such as those of the eyes, and with ordinary locomotion toward the goal object in space as performed at various points in its environment. Also, these associations have been followed by reinforcement, with the incidental action of the goal gradient. It accordingly follows that these guiding or pure-stimulus acts (r_G) will be evoked in the organism while it is in the maze situation, and

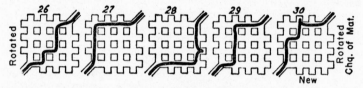

FIGURE 66. The heavy lines of these diagrams show five distinct pathways taken by the same rat through the open-alley maze on as many consecutive trials, numbers 26 to 30 inclusive. Reproduced from Dashiell (2, p. 25).

as stimuli will tend to arouse all of the responses characteristic of the habit-family hierarchy in free space.

Suppose, for example, that an animal finds itself in one of the open-alley mazes represented in Figure 66. The entrance is at the lower left-hand corner. Now in this maze there are twenty distinct pathways to the goal, all of equal and minimal length. These twenty paths constitute a given level of the habit-family hierarchy; all are of approximately constant value of reaction potential and, in view of the non-correlational nature of the oscillation function (14, p. 308), all are about equally likely to be chosen on different occasions.

Generalizing from the preceding considerations we arrive at our next theorem:

THEOREM 111. *Other things constant, organisms traversing an open-alley maze to a definite goal will tend to take, without special practice, numerous alternative paths to the goal.*

Ample empirical evidence bearing on Theorem 111 was published by Dashiell in 1930 (2). A total of 27 animals were run on substantially the same form of experiment with various controls. In general Dashiell found all these animals taking many distinct paths to the goal at all stages of the practice. He states, "Particularly worth noting are the trials numbered 22 to 42 inclusive of animal 11: in these 21 runs 13 different routes were included with only three cases of an immediate repetition. The eleven animals used in one series of 50 tests yielded an average of 7.5 distinct runs with either one or no error on each." A convenient concrete illustration of the tendency to take alternative pathways through the open-alley maze is represented in Figure 66, which shows the consecutive paths chosen by one rat on runs 26 to 30 inclusive, all of which are quite distinct. We therefore conclude that Theorem 111 is empirically substantiated.

In Chapter 8 we deduced the principle concerning the spatial habit-family hierarchy; i.e., the principle that when an organism finds its way to a goal by means of any member of a spatial habit-family hierarchy (11) this habit is at once transferred to every member of the hierarchy in that general situation, and that in such a hierarchy the maximum transferred reaction is to paths whose initial segment makes a zero angular deviation from a straight line connecting with the goal (13, p. 284) *at any given point where the organism chances to be.* From this principle a number of maze-behavioral laws follow at once. One of these concerns the tendency to enter goalward-pointing blind alleys (11, pp. 136 ff.).

Thus we arrive at our next theorem:

THEOREM 112. *Other things constant and no additional motivation present, spatially naive organisms which have been reinforced at a given goal in an enclosed maze will tend least to take blind alleys whose directions make an angle of 180 degrees with a straight line from the choice point to the goal, the chance increasing progressively to its maximum as this angular divergence decreases toward zero.*

Empirical evidence regarding the question of whether goal-pointing blind alleys do in fact have more entrances than those pointing away from the goal is unfortunately greatly complicated by other factors, especially by the goal gradient which plays a decisive role as already shown (Theorems 108, 109, 110). Ideally, to secure empirical proof we would desire a set of alleys in which the goalward-pointing blinds and those pointing away from the goal are evenly distributed throughout the maze, which would equalize the mean effect of the goal gradient. Actually such a situation probably never has existed. The set of published data (*25*) which we shall now discuss gives a mean rank for the goalward-pointing

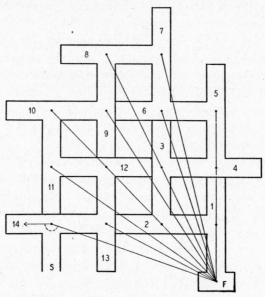

FIGURE 67. Diagram of the Tolman-Honzik maze (*24*, p. 43) with straight lines drawn from the goal box to each choice point. The blind alleys are numbered from the goal. The divergence of the blind alley direction from the direction of the goal or food-box was read off with a transparent protractor as is shown by the arrow and broken circle at choice point 14.

blind alleys of 5.2, whereas the mean rank of the non-goalward-pointing blinds is 8.6; this shows that the goalward-pointing blinds on the whole fall near the beginning of this maze and so have a mean excess of blind-alley entrances because of the goal gradient alone, and not necessarily because of the goal orientation principle.

Even so, the data in question are extremely valuable. They were based on the blind-alley entrances of 36 albino rats as secured by measuring the Tolman-Honzik published graphs. Now, blind alleys rarely point either directly toward or away from the food box. In order to secure the angular direction with respect to the goal, straight lines were drawn from the food box to the choice points of each of the fourteen blind alleys as shown in Figure 67. Then with a transparent protractor we measured the angular deviation of each line from the direction in which each blind alley was pointing.

Our next task was to secure some blind-alley entrance values which were not distorted by goal gradient tendencies. By judicious search we found in Figure 67 seven combinations of consecutive

TABLE 35. Table showing for a multidirectional maze, the goal gradient factor remaining relatively constant on the average, the tendency for blind alleys with a small angular divergence from a line to the goal (Figure 67) to have more entrances on the average than blind alleys with a larger angular divergence from a line to the goal. Based on the learning responses of 36 hungry animals on 17 reinforced trials. Compiled from measurements based on Tolman and Honzik (25, p. 250).

Distance from goal	Smaller angular divergence from goal direction			Distance from goal	Larger angular divergence from goal direction			Agreement with hypothesis
	Angular divergence	No. of errors	Mean no. of errors		Angular divergence	No. of errors	Mean no. of errors	
2	135	131.1	131.1	1	180	41.2	44.9	+
				3	154	48.7		
4	90	288.5	288.5	3	154	48.7	50.6	+
				5	180	52.5		
4	90	288.5	188.2	5	180	52.5	52.5	+
6	108	89.7						
6	108	89.9	76.8	7	166	101.2	101.2	−
8	117	63.7						
9	34	333.4	333.4	8	117	63.7	108.6	+
				10	135	153.6		
9	34	333.4	290.3	10	135	153.6	153.6	+
11	56	247.3						
11	56	247.3		10	135	153.6		
12	45	348.4	317.5	14	162	217.3	185.4	+
13	63	357.2						
Mean			232.3				99.5	

blind alleys, in each combination (usually three in number) of which (1) the two alleys at either side averaged the same number of steps from the goal as the alley lying between, and (2) either the middle alley or the two at its side showed considerable difference in the extent of goal pointing. These appear in detail in Table 35. For example, the first set of blind alleys chosen were respectively 1, 2, and 3 steps from the goal. The two extreme alleys (1 + 3 = 4 ÷ 2 = 2) average the same distance from the goal as the distance of the middle alley. Thus the goal gradient effect of the two extreme alleys will, upon the whole, average the same as that of the middle alley. Then the blind-alley entrance scores of the two alleys were averaged and compared with the blind-alley entrances of the middle alley. This procedure yielded, in the case of the three blinds here considered, the error value of 44.9 for the alley of larger angular divergence from the goal direction, and of 131.1 for the alleys of smaller angular divergence. Incidentally these results agree so far as they go with Theorem 112. Moreover, an examination of Table 35 will show that in all but one of the seven combinations the smaller angular divergence from a direct line to the goal has the larger number of blind-alley entrances.

The average number of blind-alley entrances of the large-angled group of alleys is 99.5, and that of the small-angled group is 232.3. These values yield what we shall call the *goal orientation* index (G.O.), which has a zero value for a zero effect and 100 for a maximum effect, thus:

$$
\begin{aligned}
\text{G.O.} &= 100 \left(1 - \frac{99.5}{232.3} \right) \\
&= 100(1 - .428) \\
&= 100(.572) \\
&= 57.2.
\end{aligned}
\tag{58}
$$

In this way we see that these data show a very considerable goal orientation effect. While this index probably will not hold for effectively comparing different mazes, it is believed to hold within sampling limitations for comparing the same maze under different conditions. Also it may be noted, incidentally, that the farther away from the goal the combination of alleys involved is situated, other things equal, the larger will be the number of entrances and the larger the difference; this is because the blind-alley entrances or error values far from the goal are ordinarily large, as is shown by Table 36. We conclude, then, that the widely held view set forth in Theorem 112, that the more goalward-pointing blind alleys definitely favor entrance by spatially oriented animals,[2] is substantiated by ample empirical evidence.

---

[2] Other very convincing evidence concerning the tendency to enter goal-pointing blind alleys, but of a somewhat different nature from the evidence here presented, is given by Dashiell's monograph (*2*). Tolman utilized the data of the Tolman-Honzik experiment, but in a different manner, to illustrate the principle just considered (*24*, pp. 119 ff.).

Through the goal-gradient principle it follows that the tendency to choose short but untried paths, angular divergence from the goal being held constant, will be an inverse function of the distance from the goal of the choice point in question (see Table 33, especially fourth column).

TABLE 36. The number of entrances into blind alleys as a function of the number of choice points from the goal, angular divergence from goal approximately constant. Based on the learning responses of 36 animals each given 17 reinforced trials. Compiled from measurements based on Tolman and Honzik (25).

	Greater distance of choice point from goal			Less distance of choice point from goal		Difference	
Angular divergence from goal	Distance from goal in choice-point intervals	Number of entrances	Angular divergence from goal	Distance from goal in choice-point intervals	Number of entrances	Difference in distance from goal in choice-point intervals	Difference in number of entrances
180°	5	52.5	180°	1	41.2	4	+ 11.3
135°	10	153.6	125°	2	131.1	8	+ 22.5
166°	7	101.2	153°	3	48.7	4	+ 52.5
117°	8	63.7	108°	6	89.9	2	− 26.2
162°	14	217.3	166°	7	101.2	7	+116.1
Means:							
152.8°	8.8	117.6	146.9°	3.8	82.4	5.0	35.2

Thus we arrive at our next theorem:

THEOREM 113. *With the angle of the entrance of a blind alley with a straight line to the goal constant, the farther a choice point is from the goal in choice-point intervals, the smaller will be the difference in favor of a correct choice and the greater will be the tendency to enter the blind.*

In a sense Theorem 113 represents the goal gradient when uncomplicated by the phenomena of goal orientation. The same Tolman-Honzik data from which Table 35 was derived yielded five pairs of alleys which had approximately the same goal-orientation angle but which stood at different distances from the goal. These data are assembled in Table 36. Four out of the five combinations show a greater number of blind-alley entrances as the distance from the goal becomes greater; the one exception had a choice-point difference of only 2. The mean distance from the goal is 5.0 maze units, whereas the mean number of blind-alley entrances is 35.2, yielding on the average an increase of about seven blind-alley entrances per choice-point increase.

The mean number of entrances of the same blind alleys near the goal is 82.4, and the mean number of those farther from the goal is 117.6. These two values, on the analogy of the goal orientation index, yield what we shall call the *goal gradient* index (G.G.), which has a zero value for a zero effect and 100 for a maximum effect, thus:

$$\text{G.G.} = 100 \left(1 - \frac{82.4}{117.6} \right) \tag{59}$$
$$= 100(1 - .70)$$
$$= 100(.30)$$
$$= 30.0.$$

The goal gradient index also is believed to hold within sampling limitations for the comparison of different conditions on the same maze, but not for different mazes. This, together with other evidence already introduced regarding the goal gradient (Theorem 105), definitely supports Theorem 113 empirically. It is noticeable that the G.G. index is smaller than the G.O. index (30.0 < 57.2). This seems to harmonize with the general weakness of the fitted weights of the gradient of reinforcement in four-link chains, as pointed out in Chapter 6.

Much evidence has accumulated indicating that the goal gradient is closely related to and dependent upon secondary reinforcement (*14*, pp. 84 ff.). Evidently secondary reinforcement is also closely related to and dependent upon goal orientation. Suppose, for example, that an organism traverses alternately two paths to a goal, the directions of which at first move away from the goal and then make a critical turn back toward it. Now, locomotor progress at a more favorable angle toward a goal is in general more closely associated with prompt reinforcement at the goal, and is therefore a stronger secondary reinforcing agent. For this reason, according to the goal-gradient principle, the closer this critical turn is to the point of choice, the stronger will be the learned reaction potential to the choice in question.

From these considerations we arrive at our next theorem:

THEOREM 114. *Of two equally long paths, each containing an angular turn toward the goal point, the one on which the goalward turn occurs earlier will come to be chosen over the other.*

In regard to the reward value of an early turn in the maze toward the goal as contrasted with a later turn of the same angle, the distance traversed remaining the same, we have empirical evidence from a study by Yoshioka (*30*). Working in Tolman's laboratory, Yoshioka trained 60 rats on two alternative pathways of approximately the same length. These pathways, shown in Figure 68, consisted of an outer triangular path with the turn at

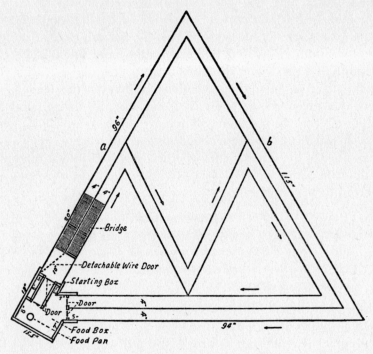

FIGURE 68. Reproduction of Yoshioka's alternative pathway maze giving the turn back toward the goal about four feet earlier on the pentagonal-shaped inner pathway than on the triangular-shaped outer one. Reproduced from Tolman (*24*, p. 123).

the top of the triangle 96 inches from the start, and an inner pentagonal path in which the same angular turn occurred as in the triangle, but approximately 48 inches nearer the choice point. After a certain number of "forced" alternating runs on the two paths with one of the two doors closed, the animals were given a large number of free choices. These trials yielded a significantly larger number of choices of the pentagonal path with the early turn toward the goal than of the triangular path with the later turn toward the goal. A series of additional related experiments by

Yoshioka (*32*) amply corroborate the same conclusions. Thus, despite the fact that the inner or pentagonal path is somewhat shorter and therefore preferred, Theorem 114 appears to be well substantiated.

Anticipatory Turning and Maze Learning

At this point we introduce a second principle, which was deduced much earlier and has already been utilized several times. This principle is to the effect that reactions which become conditioned to perseverative stimulus traces will, by the principle of stimulus generalization, be evoked by earlier and more intense phases of substantially the same stimulus traces; thus these traces yield anticipatory or antedating reactions. Wherever the tendency to turn at a given choice point is strong, e.g., at choice point 5 in Figure 69, and the preceding stimuli are similar, e.g., choice points 4, 3, 2, and 1, this same turning reaction will tend to occur at one or another of the latter points whether they lead into a blind alley or the true pathway.

From these considerations we arrive at our next theorem:

> THEOREM 115. *In mazes where a given turning choice is strongly conditioned to perseverative stimulus traces and where closely similar stimuli and stimulus traces are encountered at antecedent positions, the same turning-choice reaction will tend to occur in advance of the reinforced choice point.*

Moreover, in case the earlier choice points and the acts between them are alike, the stimulus situation close to the point where the turning act is reinforced (#5 of Figure 69) will be more like that evoking the reinforced reaction (#4) than that at choice points farther away (#3, #2, or #1). This, on the basis of the gradient of stimulus generalization, will lead to a falling gradient of the tendency to make anticipatory turns as a choice point recedes in distance from the point at which the particular reaction is reinforced.

Accordingly we arrive at our next theorem:

> THEOREM 116. *In mazes of the nature specified in Theorem 115, the tendency to make antedating turning reactions, often maladaptive, will be maximal near the point at which the turning reaction is reinforced, growing progressively weaker as the distance from this point increases.*

Empirical evidence concerning the tendency for subjects to make anticipatory turning errors in the Hampton Court type of maze is yielded by a maze designed by Spence and Shipley (22). A diagram of this maze is shown in Figure 69. Cases of entering the right-hand blind alleys instead of the opposite ones, or going straight ahead, constituted anticipatory errors. Because of the position of the food-box in this maze the factor of goal orientation was also involved, but in such a way that it could be distinguished from the anticipatory turning tendency in a manner which presumably revealed their relationship. Spence and Shipley reported that during the first nine trials on this maze a perfect gradient of right-turning errors developed, the error maximum being at choice point 1 (the alley pointing directly to the goal), and the gradient decreasing as the alleys approached choice point 5. Since the angular divergence these blind alleys make with a straight line leading to the goal increases as the choice points approach the A position, the above gradient is, of course, exactly what would be expected by the goal orientation principle (Theorem 112). How-

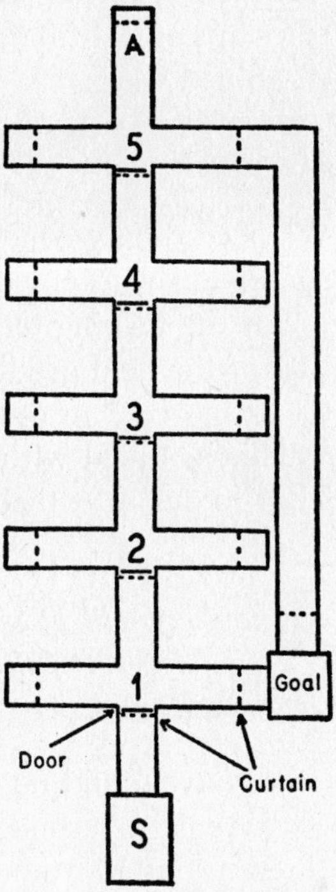

FIGURE 69. Diagram of the floor plan of the Spence-Shipley maze. The numbering of the right and left turns begins with the figure 1 at the lowest pair. The starting box is the rectangle at the bottom of the figure. Adapted from Spence and Shipley (22).

ever, as training continued the anticipatory-turning tendency apparently began to interact with the goal orientation factor. In any case the errors at the second choice point decreased and an antedating gradient leading to a high region at the final blind alley (choice point 4) developed. The four error values at this advanced stage of training were: 1 = 12.5; 2 = 7.5; 3 = 26.5; 4 = 53.5. The last three figures verify empirically Theorem 116.

Jones and Taylor (15) repeated the Spence-Shipley experiment except that with two groups of animals they placed their goal opposite the third choice point on the right side of the maze. With two more groups they extended the path down around the bottom end of the maze and up on the left side, leaving the food-box opposite the third alley. This study failed to reveal any tendency to orientation, but it did yield a very clear turning gradient which included the fifth point, the critical part of the gradient. The mean per cents of right-hand turns made by all four of their groups when combined were:

#1 = 53.4;   #2 = 70.9;   #3 = 77.7;   #4 = 86.1;   #5 = 90.1.

We accordingly conclude that Theorems 115 and 116 are both in agreement with empirical fact.

But the turning tendency itself will naturally be a positive function of the goal gradient; i.e., it will be a function of the distance the reinforcement of the reaction in question is from the goal.

This, coupled with the considerations leading to Theorem 115, leads to our next theorem:

> THEOREM 117. *Other things constant, the antedating turning tendency will be weaker the farther away from the goal the point of reinforcement of the original turning movement in question is by direct measurement.*

We have found no empirical evidence bearing on this corollary.

There is a second sort of antedating reaction of a somewhat different nature from the type just considered. Returning to Figure 63 let us take, for example, the case of an animal which is in the process of eliminating the blind alley B from its path to the food. The coordination of acts constituting the turning movement will become conditioned to the perseverative traces of the acts preceding it in the series. By generalization this turning complex of muscular contractions will gradually come to be evoked by an earlier phase of these stimulus traces, which will then be reinforced by the reward, the latter strengthening a new connection to the response at an earlier phase of the stimulus traces. This will cause a still earlier turning, also reinforced, and will finally result in a turning at the very entrance to B. Here the goal gradient on the correct path will coalesce with the shortened entrance, converting the turning into first a mere pause and then only a slight slowing down of locomotion on the true path. Finally even this will disappear.

From these considerations we arrive at our next theorem:

THEOREM 118. *Organisms which frequently enter a given blind alley will, on the average, enter less and less deeply as practice continues, later merely pausing or slowing down, and finally running the true path without interruption.*

Peterson gave special attention to the depth of entrance into blind alleys as learning progresses. In regard to this he stated (*17*, p. 32):

> The elimination of entrances to blind alleys does not come about mainly by a decrease in the *number* of entrances, but principally, especially in the case of the longer *cul de sacs*, by a gradual decrease in the degree, or the distance, of entrance.

An illustration of this is found in two detailed records reported by Peterson as presumably typical of blind-alley entrance elimination in a difficult maze having a total of 124 blind alleys. This

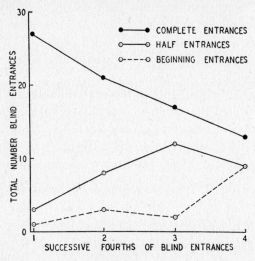

FIGURE 70. Graphic representation of the progressive shortening of the distance entered into blind alleys as training continues. Plotted from computations based on Peterson's published data from two typical rats on the same blind alley (*17*, p. 28).

may be seen graphically in Figure 70, which shows that the number of complete entrances decreased as training continued, the number of partial entrances increased up to the third fourth of the errors made and then decreased, the number of mere head and forefeet entrances increased to the fourth fourth of the errors made, and after this errors of all sorts ceased. On the basis of the above results, counting a partial entrance as one-tenth of a complete entrance, the mean depths of entrance of all the errors were respectively, 92.2 per cent, 81.6 per cent, 74.8 per cent, and 59.3 per cent. These data, together with completely confirming results published by Reynolds (*18*), abundantly substantiate Theorem 118 empirically.

The Experimental Extinction of Blind-Alley Entrance

Ordinarily the most direct path to a spatial goal is the one which will receive reinforcement. However, it may happen that only an indirect or long way to a goal will be reinforced. Mazes of this sort were used by Higginson (*7*), Valentine (*26*), and Gengerelli (*4*). A diagram of a modified form of Valentine's maze, used by Reynolds, is reproduced as Figure 71. The solid-line pathway in this figure represents the most direct path to the goal, whereas the broken line represents the only path which was reinforced. The door at X was closed until the animal had passed at least its head and forepaws over the line at Y before proceeding back through E; then the door at X was opened, permitting access to G and the food.

According to the principle of the spatial habit-family hierarchy, it is to be expected that after successfully completing the long path to the food at G in Figure 71 a very few times, the organism would make persistent attempts to go directly to G by the short path. On the basis of these considerations we arrive at our next theorem:

> **THEOREM** 119. *When a naive organism reaches the goal in a maze a number of times by first traversing what would ordinarily be a "blind alley," it will begin to show a marked tendency to short-circuit the long path even though the short path has never before been taken as such.*

Reynolds reported that in the situation represented by Figure 71 the animals attempted to take the short-circuiting path by turning into the opening at E which led directly to the food (*19*), even though in previous training they were always reinforced after taking the long path. The animals also attempted very persistently, in traversing the long path, to turn around before reaching the line at Y, requiring a very large number of trials to eliminate these tendencies entirely (xvii). Reynolds reported similar results from a second investigation (*20*, p. 275), in which her eight animals took on the average 231 trials to reach her training criterion. This was a truly enormous number of trials for learning such a simple habit. Thus Theorem 119 appears to be empirically substantiated.

Where experimental extinction is occurring by massed practice, which is followed by a period of no-practice, (*20*, pp. 279 ff.) the

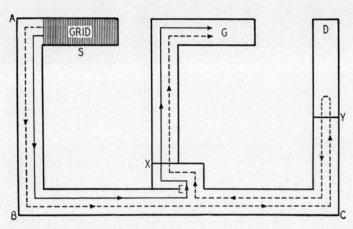

FIGURE 71. Diagram of the second Reynolds maze. The grid was removed from the maze except on the runs in which shocks were to be used for purposes of disinhibition. Reproduced from Reynolds (*20*, p. 274).

no-practice will be associated with spontaneous recovery of the reaction tendency.

Generalizing on these considerations we arrive at our next theorem:

THEOREM 120. *When naive organisms are trained by massed practice to traverse the "blind alley" of a maze in order to reach the goal, the tendency to attempt short-circuiting will undergo experimental extinction during the massed practice and a period of no-practice will produce spontaneous recovery.*

Miss Reynolds carried out her learning experiments by massed trials. In the one best illustrating the present theorem, twenty consecutive trials were given each day on the apparatus represented in Figure 71, the grid being removed. During the first ten trials the animals made a mean number of 25 attempts to go first to G by turning in at X before going up to Y;[3] during the second half of the trials that same day the mean number of such attempts was 9; during the first ten trials on the following day, after some 23 hours of no practice, the mean number was 18. Now, the fall of the second ten trials below the first ten on day 1 looks definitely like experimental extinction, and the rise of the curve at the first ten trials on the following day presents the picture of spontaneous recovery, because animals do not show anything like this amount of ordinary forgetting in 23 hours. This in turn indicates that the original loss was, in the main, not ordinary learning but genuine experimental extinction. We accordingly conclude that Theorem 120 has an empirical substantiation.

The introduction of an unusual or startling stimulus will cause the disinhibition (20, p. 278) of the internal inhibition which produces the experimental extinction just reported. Generalizing on this consideration, we arrive at our next theorem:

THEOREM 121. *When naive organisms are trained to traverse the "blind alley" of a maze in order to reach the goal, an unusual or startling stimulus introduced just at the entrance to a short-circuiting path will tend to produce a resumption of a previously extinguished tendency to short-circuit the "blind alley."*

In the three experiments based on the maze represented in Figure 71, Reynolds investigated the question of the disinhibition of extinction effects (19; 20). The disinhibiting agent in two of the experiments was a shock to the animal's feet from an electric grid placed on the floor of the maze, and in the third (and best experiment from this point of view) it was a curtain hung between B and E on the disinhibiting trials only. Reynolds reported that in all three studies nearly all of the animals turned in at E on the first trial on which they encountered the disinhibiting agent, and most of the remainder turned in at the next trial or the one following. Since it was inhibition that was lost, the process was one of disinhibition. We accordingly conclude that Theorem 121 is empirically substantiated.

[3] In a sense, Reynolds' technique made the path up to Y a part of the true path even though it has the form ordinarily used for a blind alley, and the short path from E to X on the way to Y (Figure 71) is the actual blind alley. To avoid confusion, when referring to the D-arm of this apparatus we shall set the term "blind alley" in quotation marks.

It is well known that the effect of disinhibition is a relatively transitory phenomenon (*16*, p. 65). From this and the preceding considerations we arrive at our next theorem:

THEOREM 122. *When naive organisms are trained to traverse a "blind alley" of a maze in order to reach a goal, and disinhibition of an extinguished short-circuiting tendency is produced by an unusual stimulus, the tendency to omit the "blind alley" will be spontaneously lost soon after the disinhibiting stimulus ceases to operate.*

This question also was considered by Reynolds. In the experiment in which a curtain served as a disinhibiting agent, all of the seven animals used chose the long path without attempting to turn in at E (Figure 71), immediately after the disinhibiting process had occurred. Tendencies to this type of spontaneous recovery also appeared when an electric shock was used as the disinhibiting agent, though here the recovery was much longer delayed and was less complete. This apparently substantiates Theorem 122.

Summary

An analysis of multidirectional maze learning involves the operation of several major principles: the goal gradient, the spatial habit-family hierarchy together with goal orientation, anticipatory turning in the maze, and experimental extinction.

The goal-gradient principle contributes to this learning by giving a special additional strength to the reaction potential of the shorter of every set of alternative paths. By the same action this principle mediates the elimination of long blind alleys more easily than short ones; the elimination of the last blind more easily than the first blind; and in general the backward order of the elimination of blind alleys. It also mediates the easier learning of short mazes as compared with long ones; the rise of the speed-of-locomotion gradient in passage through a maze; and the increase in the rate of rise in the curve of probability of correct choices from the beginning to the goal end of the maze. In general, all of these deductions agree with observation except the last, and appropriate empirical test data of this have not been found.

In multidirectional maze learning we also find a special case of the spatial habit-family hierarchy principle, one major sub-principle of which is the preference of the shortest available path to any goal; this in turn is in conformity with the goal-gradient principle. If several equally long paths are available, as in the Dashiell open-alley maze, they all, according to this principle, become practically equivalent. Moreover, through the oscillation principle ($_sO_R$) any slight advantage the previously reinforced use of any one of these paths may have given it over the others is distorted in such a way as to yield free and continuous shifting from one path to another from trial to trial. The preference of the organism for the shortest path available, practically regardless of previous practice, is the substance of goal orientation. This leads to the preference, other things equal, for that path at a given choice point whose beginning makes the smallest angular deviation from a straight line to the goal. This in turn causes the marked and long-known tendency of rats to enter with special frequency and persistence blinds pointing directly toward the goal. Indeed, this preference for goal-pointing paths is so great that under certain circumstances it apparently may serve as a secondary reinforcing agent.

Reactions become conditioned to perseverative stimulus traces as well as to stimuli themselves. Since the strength of the trace is a decay phenomenon, it is stronger at the anterior section of a maze than at the point where the conditioning ordinarily takes place. As a result of this principle and that of stimulus generalization, a turning response on trials following a certain amount of training tends frequently to be evoked at an earlier point in the sequence than at the point where reinforcement occurs. This produces, among other things, the frequently maladaptive tendency to make anticipatory turns. Following the course of the generalization gradient, the gradient of these antedating errors is highest near the point of reinforcement and tapers off as the distance from this point increases. But in some cases the tendency to anticipatory action is adaptive; when coupled with experimental extinction this brings it about that the 180-degree turn involved in an exit from a blind alley occurs on the whole earlier on successive withdrawals, until finally entrance is not made at all.

So many factors, such as the goal gradient and the habit-family hierarchy, are operating in maze learning that the action of a third important principle, that of experimental extinction, is not easy to prove. Nevertheless its presence and action were demonstrated by Henry Etta Reynolds. She found (1) that a tendency to enter a special type of blind alley pointing toward the goal decreased with massed practice; (2) that there was in part a spontaneous recovery of the tendency with 23 hours of no practice; (3) that when completed after long training the extinction underwent disinhibition as the result of a slight but novel stimulus; and (4) that this disinhibition disappeared on an immediately following trial. This combination of phenomena conforms exactly to the classical Pavlovian picture, thus making doubly convincing the interpretation that experimental extinction contributes to maze learning.

TERMINAL NOTES

THE VALUE OF $\sigma_{s^0_R}$ USED IN TABLE 33

Since the value of $\sigma_{s^0_R}$ is the unit by which reaction potential is measured, in such situations it should be 1.00. Actually the value chosen in the present exposition, e.g., on p. 277 and in Table 33, is .3012. The reason for taking this marked deviation from the theoretical value of $\sigma_{s^0_R}$ is that a value of approximately this magnitude had to be used in order to secure something like usual blind-alley elimination scores while using the present indications of maximum $_sE_R$, i.e., M and the factor of reduction $(F = \frac{1}{10})$. The cause of this necessity probably is, as pointed out earlier in this chapter, that the goal gradient is only one of several factors operative in the process of blind-alley elimination. An additional factor of major importance not taken into consideration in the computations in question is believed to be that of experimental extinction.

REFERENCES

1. Blodgett, H. C. The effect of the introduction of reward upon the maze performance of rats. *Univ. Calif. Publ. Psychol.*, 1929, *4*, 113–134.
2. Dashiell, J. F. Direction orientation in maze running by the white rat. *Comp. Psychol. Monogr.*, 1931, *7*.
3. DeCamp, J. E. Relative distance as a factor in the white rat's selection of a path. *Psychobiology*, 1920, *2*, 245–253.
4. Gengerelli, J. A. Preliminary experiments on the causal factors in animal learning. *J. Comp. Psychol.*, 1928, *8*, 435–457.

5. Gladstone, A. I., Yamaguchi, H. G., Hull, C. L., and Felsinger, J. M. Some functional relationships of reaction potential ($_sE_R$) and related phenomena. *J. Exper. Psychol.*, 1947, *37*, 510–526.

6. Grice, G. R. An experimental study of the gradient of reinforcement in maze learning. *J. Exper. Psychol.*, 1942, *30*, 475–489.

7. Higginson, G. D. Visual perception in the white rat. *J. Exper. Psychol.*, 1926, *9*, 337–347.

8. Hobhouse, L. T. *Mind in evolution.* New York: Macmillan, 1901.

9. Holmes, S. J. *The evolution of animal intelligence.* New York: Henry Holt and Co., 1911.

10. Hull, C. L. The goal gradient hypothesis and maze learning. *Psychol. Rev.*, 1932, *39*, 25–43.

11. Hull, C. L. The concept of the habit-family hierarchy and maze learning. *Psychol. Rev.*, 1934, *41*, Part I, 33–52; Part II, 134–152.

12. Hull, C. L. The rat's speed-of-locomotion gradient in the approach to food. *J. Comp. Psychol.*, 1934, *17*, 393–422.

13. Hull, C. L. The goal-gradient hypothesis applied to some 'field-force' problems in the behavior of young children. *Psychol. Rev.*, 1938, *45*, 271–299.

14. Hull, C. L. *Principles of behavior.* New York: D. Appleton-Century Co., Inc., 1943.

15. Jones, F. N., and Taylor, F. E. The relative effects of goal orientation and direction of the last turn on maze learning in the rat. *J. Comp. Psychol.*, 1938, *26*, 19–26.

16. Pavlov, I. P. *Conditioned reflexes.* (Trans. by G. V. Anrep) London: Oxford Univ. Press, 1927.

17. Peterson, J. The effect of length of blind alleys on maze learning. *Behav. Monogr.*, 1917, iii, No. 4.

18. Reynolds, B. A repetition of the Blodgett experiment of "latent learning." *Amer. J. Psychol.*, 1945, *35*, 504–516.

19. Reynolds, H. E. The disinhibiting effect of an electric shock upon the maze performance of the white rat. *J. Comp. Psychol.*, 1936, *22*, 187–197.

20. Reynolds, H. E. Further disinhibition phenomena in the maze behavior of the white rat. *J. Comp. Psychol.*, 1939, *27*, 271–282.

21. Spence, K. W. The order of eliminating blinds in maze learning by the rat. *J. Comp. Psychol.*, 1932. *14*, 9–27.
22. Spence, K. W., and Shipley, W. C. The factors determining the difficulty of blind alleys in maze learning by the white rat. *J. Comp. Psychol.*, 1934, *17*, 423–436.
23. Thorndike, E. L. *Animal intelligence: experimental studies.* New York: Macmillan, 1911.
24. Tolman, E. C. *Purposive behavior in animals and men.* New York: D. Appleton-Century Co., Inc., 1932.
25. Tolman, E. C., and Honzik, C. H. Degrees of hunger, reward, and non-reward, and maze learning in rats. *Univ. Calif. Publ. Psychol.*, 1930, *4*, 241–256.
26. Valentine, W. L. Visual perception in the white rat. *J. Comp. Psychol.*, 1928, *8*, 369–375.
27. Warden, C. J., and Cummings, S. B. Primacy and recency factors in animal motor learning. *J. Genet. Psychol.*, 1929, *36*, 240–257.
28. Watson, J. B. *Behavior. An introduction to comparative psychology.* New York: Henry Holt and Co., 1914.
29. White, A. E., and Tolman, E. C. A note on the elimination of short and long blind alleys. *J. Comp. Psychol.*, 1923, *3*, 327-331.
30. Yoshioka, J. G., A preliminary study in discrimination of maze patterns by the rat. *Univ. Calif. Publ. Psychol.*, 1928, *4*, 1–18.
31. Yoshioka, J. G. Weber's law in the discrimination of maze distance by the white rat. *Univ. Calif. Publ. Psychol.*, 1929, *4*, 155–184.
32. Yoshioka, J. G., A further study in discrimination of maze patterns by the rat. *Univ. Calif. Publ. Psychol.*, 1930, *4*, 135–153.

10. The Problem-Solving Assembly
of Behavior Segments

In our progressive analysis of adaptive behavior we shall now consider the concrete problem-solving behavior of non-speaking mammalian organisms. We have seen how chance variation ($_sO_R$) in combination with reinforcement and experimental extinction gives rise to trial-and-error behavior, and how trial and error in turn gives rise to behavior chains (pp. 156 ff.). With the exception of the conditioned reflex in a pure form, all types of behavior which mediate learning constitute problems for the organism, in one way or another. The problem consists in securing food, or a mate, or in avoiding nocuous stimuli, and so on.

Moreover, these behaviors normally display a kind of direction, in the sense that they are not purely random but are more or less restricted in various respects. This restriction arises from the limitation in the generalization range of the stimuli involved. Two types of stimuli are worthy of special note in this connection: (1) the drive stimulus (S_D) and its generalization (xii), characterized by a kind of over-all limitation or direction; and (2) the goal stimulus (s_G) and its generalization, characterized by a more specific limitation or direction. Both kinds of behavioral limitations mediate adaptive conclusions in excess of pure chance because of the limiting nature of reinforcement and generalization. The behavior in question must be more or less like what in the past produced the goal stimulus (s_G) and reduced the drive stimulus (S_D). We must also recall the fact that as life goes on the elements or units in the trial-and-error process increase in complexity; i.e.,

308

they begin as simple conditioned reflexes and later extend to behavior chains of various lengths with definite goals (r_G's) and goal
stimuli (s_G's) (2).

The Problem of Locomotor "Insight" Posed

At this point there arises a critical question in behavior theory
which has been debated for thirty years or so. Is there a single and
distinct behavioral element variously called *insight* or *intelligence*,
which aids in the orderly assembly of chain segments beyond the
limitations of chance suggested above? This is to ask whether there
is a peculiar mechanism called insight, or intelligence, which has
the power of joining, i.e., spontaneously organizing, two behavior-
chain segments previously learned on separate occasions so that
together they will solve a problem faced by the organism at a later
time (9, p. 46). For example, let us suppose that in a maze such as
that represented in Figure 72 an organism has learned on one
occasion the path J to L, with a large food reward; on a separate
occasion, the path H to J, with a small food reward; and on a third
occasion, the path H to N with a similarly small food reward.
Following this preliminary training, the hungry animal is placed
at H. Will the animal go (1) to N and get a small amount of food?
Or will it go (2) to J, get a small amount of food, and thence to
L where it will find considerably more food? In terms of behavior
chain segments, will the fact that the animal possesses the heavily
rewarded behavior segment JL add weight to the choice of the
path HJ versus the path HN beyond the normal or chance per
cent of choices? In the experimental investigation of such a problem
it would, of course, be necessary to determine with care the per
cent of the particular subject's choices of paths HJ and HN before
beginning the training on JL.

It is perfectly obvious that normally intelligent humans would
choose path HJL rather than path HN. How far down in the animal
scale this capacity extends remains to be determined experimentally. We are at present far from knowing enough about
individual and species differences (XVII) to speak with any
confidence on this matter from the theoretical point of view. However, the organism's performance of the sequence HJL, particularly
at points H and J, may vary greatly; it may range from a smooth
(rapid) unified act to a very slow and halting series of acts, depend-

ing upon the capacity of the organism in question to join independently acquired behavior segments into novel wholes. This
implies that the well unified type of response combination will be
comparatively strong; i.e., that the chance of the HJL choice will
be around 100 per cent, and that of the HN choice will be near zero
per cent. Such choices would be easy enough to distinguish either
statistically or by inspection. But in the case of a feeble but genuine

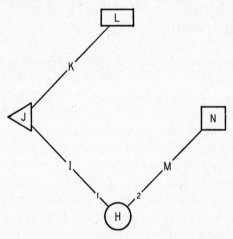

FIGURE 72. Diagrammatic representation of three locomotor paths suitable for use in
the Maier type of experiment for evidence of behavioral insight. It will be noticed that
each of the boxes H, J, L, and N has a different shape for the distinctive visual stimulation of the subject. Each box, especially L, is also supposed to have a characteristic
floor surface to yield distinctive cutaneous and proprioceptive stimuli.

tendency for the HJL path to dominate (say 57 per cent) a statistical methodology is indispensable. It follows that any experimental test for the presence of "insight" should provide a neutral
alternative comparison or control response. The main point is that
except in an organism which possesses an extremely strong tendency
to "insight" we do not have the clear alternative of such a phenomenon versus the trial-and-error learning process, as has often
been supposed (7; 8); rather, we have ordinary trial and error
(possibly) supplemented more or less strongly or feebly by a distinct insight or intelligence factor.

Theory of Insightful Learning in the Assembly of Spatial Behavior Segments

The reader should understand at once that in the solution of the
"insight" problem represented in Figure 72, the organism (an

albino rat, for example) first thoroughly forms the locomotor habit JKL with a very large food reward at L; then on a different occasion, say 24 hours later, it forms the locomotor habit H_1IJ with a comparatively small food reward; and finally, on a third occasion, it forms the locomotor habit H_2MN for a similar small food reward. After these three habits are formed the animal is placed at H and observation is made as to whether it goes to H_2MN or to H_1IJKL. Insight, of course, would lead to the choice of H_1IJKL and the much larger reward (K') at L, as compared with H_2MN.

Secondly, it must be noted that in spite of the fact that the locomotor habits H_1IJ and JKL were formed independently, they have box J in common. But this common box J makes possible the functional or dynamic junction of the two habit segments by means of the two fractional antedating goal reactions (2). The fractional goal response $r_{G_{ee}}$ (in Figure 73) first moves from L back toward J and then is evoked by J itself. Then when habit H_1IJ is formed this $r_{G_{ee}}$, now attached to J, becomes a part of J and is brought forward to path H_1. Thus a functional connection is established between the two related habit segments, and becomes the basis of their subsequent unity.

Some of the theoretical details of this process are given by the three $S \rightarrow R$ diagrams of Figure 73. Diagram I shows the antedating goal reaction at L, ($r_{G_{ee}}$), the two e's of the subscript indicating the very large reward. Diagram II shows the same tendency for the antedating goal reaction to come forward in series H_1IJ. But since both r_{G_e} (indicating the small reward) and $r_{G_{ee}}$ are already at J by the antedating tendency of series JKL, there are here *two* antedating reactions—one leading to J and one ultimately leading to L. Finally, Diagram III shows the stimulus-response sequence set up on the less adaptive locomotor series H_2MN.

And now we come to the test for the presence of insight. The animal, 24 hours hungry, is placed at H and allowed to choose. Which bonds lead toward MN, i.e., to H_2 and a small amount of food, and which to IJKL, i.e., to H_1 and several times as much food? Consider the learned reaction tendencies leading to R_{H_1} and to R_{H_2} in theoretical Diagrams II and III respectively. An inspection will show that in II five bonds lead to R_{H_1} and in III only four lead to R_{H_2}. All the bonds present in III are presumably the same as the comparable bonds in II. This would imply that the advantage of R_{H_1} is due to the additional presence of $s_{G_{ee}}$. There is of course the presumptive presence (not shown in the diagram) of the stimuli arising from the distinctive floors of the boxes, especially L, and

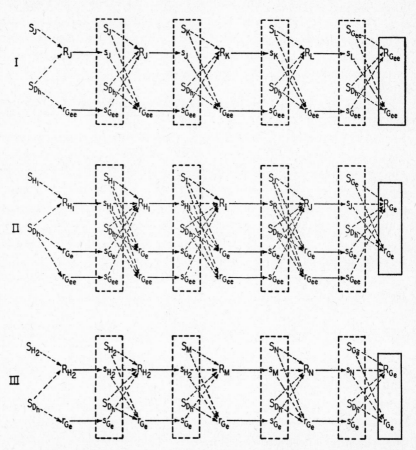

F I G U R E 73. Diagrammatic representation of theoretical stimulus-response sequences I, II, and III, which correspond to paths JKL, H_1IJ, and H_2MN respectively in Figure 72. Most trace tendencies are not represented. Note that sequence II (H_1IJ) is represented as having two sets of antedating goal reactions, r_{G_e} (small reward) and $r_{G_{ee}}$ (large reward).

from a series of *sub*goal antedating reactions drawn forward by the antedating goal reactions from I, J, K, and L in support of R_{H_1}, and from M and N in support of R_{H_2}; this constitutes four as against two such reaction stimulations. Thus on two counts we find the theoretical expectation that $R_{H_1} > R_{H_2}$. Such behavior is regarded as a rather simple form of *concrete insight*.

Generalizing on the preceding considerations, we arrive at our next theorem:

THEOREM 123. *If two separately formed spatial locomotor habit segments possessed by an organism would yield, when operating consecutively, a major goal, there would be a distinct tendency for them to so operate on the first occasion that offers.*

A second point at which the insightful mechanism of the antedating goal reaction stimulus ($s_{G_{ee}}$) operates (Figure 72) is at box J. From H to I and from I to J there are connecting reinforced traces, as there are from J to K and from K to L. But in the case considered above there can be no directly reinforced perseverative trace connection between I and K through J. The presence of such contiguously reinforced stimulus traces in a control group of organisms trained with reinforcement to go directly from H to L would imply that the locomotor process through box J will be somewhat slower in a group being tested for insight.

Generalizing on the preceding considerations, we arrive at our next theorem:

THEOREM 124. *On the first execution of an insightful behavior sequence involving two newly assembled behavior segments, there will be a longer latency at the junction point than in a control situation in which the locomotor sequence has previously been complete and reinforced.*

However, once the animal has made a few rewarded runs from H_1 to L, the rewarded stimulus-trace connections will be added to the insightful connection, making the response latency at point J approach that of a control experiment in which the subjects have received rewarded runs continuously from H_1 to L from the beginning of training (3, p. 232).

Generalizing from this and the preceding considerations, we arrive at our next theorem:

THEOREM 125. *In the course of a few normally rewarded response evocations of the insightfully joined habit, the reaction latency at the point of junction will be progressively shortened.*

At this point we may make an observation which has an important bearing on the relationship between insightful behavior and trial-and-error learning. In case the insight mechanism is not very strong, the $_sO_R$ principle may occasionally override it, though not usually. This would yield a minority of the trials for insight occurring without reinforcement, though the majority of the responses would be reinforced. But this choice element is the substance of trial-and-error learning. These trial-and-error responses will naturally supply the reinforced stimulus traces originally lacking in strength in the insight mechanism. Thus, while the two processes may be contrasted and must be distinguished, they evidently supplement each other as indicated in the above theorem.

This consideration leads us to our next theorem:

> THEOREM 126. *Reinforced trial-and-error learning, following locomotor insightful behavior, tends to make good the natural weakness at the junction of the two segments.*

Let us suppose a slightly different experimental arrangement, one in which an animal, after many distributed rewarded runs from J to L, is permitted to live freely in the joined sections of the maze from JIHMN. Because of the antedating reaction $R_{G_{ee}}$, the animal would tend to remain at J more than at other places, once its exploration had found this point, especially before experimental extinction had set in.

This leads to our next theorem:

> THEOREM 127. *After the posterior habit segment only of a potential insightful combination has been well rewarded many times, and the animal is then permitted the freedom of the joined spaces of (1) the maladaptive path and (2) the initial segment (only) of the adaptive path, it will spend more of its time at the posterior end of the initial segment of the insightful path than in the segments of the maladaptive path.*

If an animal is well reinforced in segment JKL as before and then is permitted to run freely in region JIHMN only long enough to demonstrate spontaneously a preference for J and not long enough to generate experimental extinction, in passing without food reward from H_1 to J it will receive secondary reinforcement from the antedating goal reaction $R_{G_{ee}}$ (xv), at J, which will weakly tend to reinforce that activity. But the animal's spontaneous explorational passage without food reward from H_2 to N will *not* produce this secondary reinforcement. It therefore follows that under these circumstances if later the hungry animal is placed at H and allowed a free choice, it will weakly tend to choose H_1 rather than H_2. This would be a case of feeble insightful behavior.

Generalizing on the preceding considerations, we arrive at our next theorem:

THEOREM 128. *If the final posterior habit segment of a potentially insightful behavior combination has alone been well rewarded and then the animal is permitted to run freely in the remaining two regions, a suitable test given a short time later will reveal a weak tendency to insightful behavior.*

Consider an additional change in the two supposed forms of behavior discussed above. Let it be supposed that after the two types of preliminary training, but just before the test for insight, the animal is placed at L and allowed to eat a little of the food there. This is known as *prefeeding*. The perseverative after-effects of this food consumption duplicates to a considerable degree the original feeding at L, making it much stronger than the anticipatory $r_{G_{ee}}$ normally transferred to H by the stimulus trace generalization. From this it follows that this stronger $r_{G_{ee}}$ (despite some loss from stimulus-intensity generalization) should yield a stronger difference in favor of H_1J over H_2N.

Generalizing on these considerations, we arrive at our next theorem:

THEOREM 129. *In the case of a situation favoring spatial locomotor insight, a small prefeeding at the goal will increase the probability of an animal's insightful behavior.*

The preceding considerations regarding insight have been based on two habit segments. We must now take up the question of whether *three* previously independent habit segments will spontaneously integrate themselves in such a way as to evoke concrete problem-solving behavior in an organism such as an albino rat.

Following the derivation of Theorem 123, the antedating mechanism there elaborated presumably could be extended to three habit segments as follows. The terminal segment including $r_{G_{ee}}$

would be formed as before. The middle segment would overlap the anterior end box of the terminal segment. This would transfer $r_{G_{ee}}$ to the anterior end of the middle segment. The posterior end of the initial segment would overlap the anterior box of the middle segment. This in turn would transfer the $r_{G_{ee}}$ to the anterior end of the anterior segment, thus completing the very tenuous but presumably genuine insightful integration of three habit segments in a concrete problem situation.

Generalizing on the preceding considerations, we arrive at our next theorem:

THEOREM 130. *Three or more independent habit segments may be assembled in orderly sequence for problem solution, but the mechanism will be progressively more tenuous than will that of the assembly of two habit segments for the same function.*

At this point the reader must recall the principle of the spatial habit-family hierarchy (Chapter 8). This states in effect that if a goal is located at any point in free space, all conceivable paths from an organism's position at the time to the goal point tend to become activated as reaction potentials, their strength being the reverse of their potential length, other things equal. So far as the habit-family hierarchy is concerned, therefore, the path in Figure 72 starting with H_1IJ is equal to H_2MN, and both would be weaker than a straight path directly from H to L. It follows from this that both H_1IJ and H_2MN have very definite tendencies to action when considered absolutely. As a consequence any test for insight involving paths must have for comparison a neutral control path.

Generalizing from the preceding considerations, we arrive at the following general principle:

All experimental tests for concrete spatial locomotor insight should be accompanied by neutral control paths in which the habit-family hierarchy factor is equalized.

Finally we must raise the question as to what molar factor is mainly influential in creating the difference between an organism possessing a high level of insight and one possessing a low level of insight. It must be confessed that our knowledge concerning the molar mechanisms underlying individual differences has hardly begun to develop. Looking toward such a development in the future, a few suggestions may be made here. On the basis of the preceding analysis, it would seem that molar insight is mainly dependent upon the organism's capacity to transfer antedating goal reactions from one temporal situation to another. Then of course there is the problem of the assembly of the habit segments once they have been strung together on the thread of $r_{G_{ee}}$. A little such speculation shows quite clearly that the present type of analysis demands a far more minute quantitative molar knowledge of behavior than we have at present.

Turning now to the question of the empirical validity of Theorems 123 to 130, we must say that despite the fact that two experimental studies have been published on the subject, no evidence bearing exactly on any of our theorems has been found. In a study (8) which very roughly approached the conditions of Theorem 123 but which employed too few subjects for conclusive results, Maier claimed to have attained positive evidence of concrete spatial locomotor insight in albino rats; the statistical reliability must have been utterly unsatisfactory.

One of three experiments (experiment #2) by Wolfe and Spragg (10), who used many more animals and report a closer approximation to the conditions of our Theorem 128, yields some evidence rather favoring concrete spatial locomotor insight in albino rats. However, the statistical reliability of these results also was not satisfactory.

No experiments bearing even remotely on Theorems 124, 125, 126, 127, 129, and 130 have been found. For this reason these latter theorems have the status of genuine theoretical predictions.

Spontaneous Tool-Use Acquisition

The major portion of what is now to be presented concerns insightful behavior in relation to the acquisition of the use of instruments or tools. This subject is inserted here because many have assumed that tool-using behavior involves insight (1; 3; 8). It accordingly becomes necessary to give an elementary account of one form of simple tool-use acquisition, though the case we shall consider here involves a problem of prime importance in its own right. The use of tools is so natural and universal with humans that we are likely to pass this problem over without a thought, or to consider it too unimportant to merit serious consideration. A greater mistake could scarcely be made.

The organism whose behavior we shall examine is the chimpanzee, and the instrumental use to be acquired by this superior animal is the power of intelligently reaching beyond the arm's length. Consider, then, a young chimpanzee which in spontaneously attaining certain goals is obliged to perform various manipulations of its environment, such as grasping a banana in its hand. But suppose that the banana lies a little out of arm's reach, through the bars of the chimpanzee's cage. If the hoe-like stick shown in Figure 74 were present, it would be used by a human in such a situation as a tool to drag the banana near enough to be reached by the hand. But apparently the chimpanzee will not do this until it has first learned the instrumental use of the stick. The point is

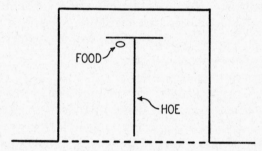

FIGURE 74. Diagram of a stick-hoe placed in position for use by the chimpanzee in dragging food close enough to be reached by the hand. Adapted from Birch (1, p. 372).

that manipulation of the stick involves grasping and other muscular activity rather different from simply reaching for a banana and eating it. Moreover, there is no appropriate food goal seen as yet in this stick activity; also there are no subgoal reactions, and of course no fractional antedating goal and subgoal reactions. These goal reactions can only be produced by reinforcement resulting from previous responses which have been successful (1). In our consideration of the junction of the two locomotor habits, we have already seen the important role of goal reactions of various types in this relatively simple case of insight.

But under what conditions will a chimpanzee spontaneously learn to use a tool as such, e.g., a simple stick? It happens that we have two clear experimental reports of this, the first by Jackson (5) and the second by Birch (1). The experimental technique of this training consisted merely in giving the chimpanzees a few sticks to play with at time intervals totalling a few hours. It is probably significant that the drives in play are very mild and that the goals are equally mild. *Both processes appear to be largely concerned with manipulation.* Now it happens that with this casual manipulation, the stick was simultaneously associated with the instrumental use of the hand which held the stick in reaching toward objects. In this connection Birch remarks (*1*, pp. 374, 375):

> However, in the course of this reaching, the animals, after having established manual contact with the object, sometimes poked at and touched it with the stick. . . . The object was not reached for with the stick but with the hand with the stick appearing to play no functional role in the reaching-contacting pattern. . . . [At a later] observation period of the first day the animals were seen to reach out and touch distant objects, usually another of the chimpanzees, with the stick. By the end of the first day during which the sticks were available to them, every one of the subjects had on several occasions used the stick as a functional extension of the arm. That is, they had all been observed *to reach out with the stick* and touch some animal or object distant from themselves. . . . During the second [day of stick play] the animals were observed to be using the stick more frequently as an arm extension, and several times fights were started when one chimpanzee poked another sharply with a stick.

Thus we appear here to have an account of *the shift from manipulative play with the stick to instrumental use of the stick,* a change of the greatest theoretical importance. At the end of this period presumably a considerable variety of goals have become fairly well attached to stick behavior. Let us consider how this could occur.

It must be recalled in this connection that the basic mechanism underlying response generalization (*4*, pp. 316, 319) is found in $_sO_R$ deviations which are relatively small individually, and that these deviations which chance to move in a fortunate direction, i.e., in a direction favorable to the manual goal dominant at the moment, will be reinforced. In short, this response generalization will consist of a kind of trial-and-error learning. The reinforcement will serve as a new basis for further oscillatory deviations (xiii, A and B) which also will be reinforced; and so on. The empirical observations show that once the instrumental use of the sticks had begun, the extension of this use, while definitely gradual, was rapid.

Two factors in this stick play should be carefully noticed here. The first is that when casual manipulative behavior receives even feeble reinforcement, the reinforced acts become goal reactions or subgoal reactions with the accompanying tendency to the fractional antedating of the original occurrence, the resulting guiding stimuli, and so on.

The second factor to be noticed in connection with this stick play is that the movements, especially as seen, and the associated cutaneous stimuli are rather similar to those involved in touching objects with the fingers. The fingers are seen as an extension of the hand and arm, just as is the stick when it is held in the hand; when the hand is on its way to touch an object the visual distance separating the two decreases continuously, just as it does when by chance the stick held in the hand moves toward a touchable object; moreover, the resulting change in manual pressure coming indirectly through the stick resembles somewhat the pressure stimuli coming from a touch with the fingers. Also intertwined with the touch stimuli will be the touch anticipatory goal reactions mentioned as our first factor, coupled with their similarity to the strong manual subgoal reactions, especially when the latter are first frustrated by the fact of the touchable objects being a little out of reach.

It is believed that the similarity of these stick-produced stimuli to manual touch-produced stimuli will tend, through stimulus generalization, to evoke under certain favorable manipulative circumstances the arm movements normally associated with hand movements leading to touching. The occasional success of such stick movements, especially when the touchable object is out of reach of the hand alone, should rapidly fix this instrument or tool use of the stick. Even though the grasping of the stick was initially evoked in play, the act will become attached to the goal (R_G) by the principle of the delay in reinforcement (J), which in turn will come to initiate the grasping of the stick, the reaching with it to various goals through response generalization, and so on.

Generalizing on the preceding considerations, we arrive at our next theorem:

THEOREM 131. *When an anthropoid is led to manipulate freely in play a simple instrument like a stick, the random variability of $_sO_R$ coupled with stimulus and response generalization from previous hand*

and arm habits will lead the animal to substitute the stick as an extension of the arm for the manipulation of distant objects.

Theory of the Insightful Assembly of Tool-Using Behavior Segments

Before giving the chimpanzees the sticks to play with, both Jackson, with one animal (*5*), and Birch, with five animals (*1*), made a thorough test to see whether they would use a stick-like tool in an "insightful" way to drag in food which was out of reach. The tool in both cases was a stick with a piece across its end making a kind of hoe, as represented in Figure 74. These tests definitely failed to yield insightful behavior. The several hours of free play with simple straight sticks then followed as just described. After the acquisition of the basic instrument-using skill or habit segment, the test for insightful behavior was repeated as given in the first place. All the animals grasped the stick-like tool either at once or almost at once and pulled in the food, picked it up in the hand, and ate it. In other words, after the establishment of the habit segment of lengthening the reach of the arm and hand by means of a straight stick, the junction of the two habit segments took place and the out-of-reach food was promptly secured and eaten. How shall we explain the occurrence of this supposedly insightful behavior?

We have already considered the relatively simple case of loco-motor insight as based on the conditions of Figure 72. Let us now try the same analogy on this case of supposed tool-using insight. Control path H_2MN corresponds to the futile stretching of the hand and arm toward the out-of-reach food. As a matter of fact, in reporting the unsuccessful trials for insightful behavior preceding the learning of the basic instrumental use of the stick, Birch states that each of the animals futilely reached out toward the food many times (*1*, p. 373); this shows that reaching corresponded rather well in fact to path H_2MN as a neutral control habit segment. Similarly, path JKL quite evidently corresponds closely to picking up the food, carrying it to the mouth, and eating. To complete the analogy in detail we must say that path H_1IJ corresponds to grasping the tool, to extending it a little beyond the food, and to dragging the food nearer by means of the tool. But this analogy is not so close. One point in the theoretical analogy which is here lacking from our original derivation is that in the space insight problem *the end of segment H_1IJ terminated with food, whereas the stick-play be-*

havior had never been associated with food. How shall this discrepancy be met? The recast deduction involves several steps as follows:

It will be recalled by consulting sequence I of Figure 73 that even though the subgoal reaction (R_L) precedes the goal reaction (R_G) in a behavior sequence, the fractional antedating goal reaction (r_G) as a stimulus (s_G) actually *precedes* the subgoal reaction. It accordingly follows that the antedating goal stimulus (s_G) is reinforced to subgoal response (R_L). From this it follows that when an anticipatory goal reaction is initiated by the sight of food, even though at a little distance beyond the cage bars, the various subgoal responses of the original series tend to be evoked more or less in their usual sequence.

Generalizing on these considerations we arrive at part A of our next theorem:

> **THEOREM** 132. *In the acquisition of simple tool-using behavior by chimpanzees:*
> A. *The fractional anticipatory goal stimuli (s_G) are reinforced to all the subgoal responses ($R_{G'}$) of the series by the reward received at the end of the behavior series.*

It happens that in the tool-using situation here under consideration the animals had reached through the bars for the food without success ($\bar{R}_G$) many times. This would naturally set up appreciable amounts of inhibition which would tend to become conditioned to the accompanying stimuli. On the other hand, in the (subgoal) play activity with the sticks which involved stretching to distances beyond reach of the hand, touching, poking, and so on, $R_{G'}$ had been uniformly successful. Here, therefore, we have a situation resembling that of trial and error in which a given set of stimuli is connected in such a way as to evoke two incompatible responses, one of which (reaching with the hand) has been weakened, but not abolished, by experimental extinction, and the other of which (reaching with the stick) even though originally considerably weaker, is now dominant.

Generalizing from these considerations we arrive at part B of Theorem 132:

> **THEOREM** 132 B. *The antedating goal stimulus (s_G) released by the sight of food at a distance tends to evoke two subgoal responses, the*

false one of which ($\bar{R}_{G'}$) has been weakened by experimental extinction to the local stimuli (increased size of retinal images, greater binocular convergence tension, and so on) below the other, the latter being the true, tool-using one ($R_{G'}$).

But since, by Theorem 132 B, ${}_sE_{R_{G'}} > {}_sE_{\bar{R}_{G'}}$ it follows that $R_{G'}$ will be evoked rather than $\bar{R}_{G'}$.

Generalizing on this we arrive at part C of Theorem 132:

THEOREM 132 C. *The successful subgoal $R_{G'}$ ultimately will be evoked rather than the unsuccessful subgoal $\bar{R}_{G'}$.*

But it must be remembered that the critical stimuli involved in reaching with the tool are those coming from the stick-like handle (Figure 74). Now the stick-hoe as a whole is a little different from the play-sticks, but its handle is similar to them, especially at the near end. By the principle of qualitative stimulus generalization (XA) this stimulus similarity will be sufficient to evoke a grasping of the handle of the stick-hoe.

Generalizing on these considerations we arrive at part D of Theorem 132:

THEOREM 132 D. *The similarity of the new tool is close enough to evoke the first part of the dominant subgoal response ($R_{G'}$), that of grasping.*

But after the grasping of the handle of the hoe there remains the task of using the hoe to drag in the food. This is probably the most critical part of the act of insight. The stick cannot grasp the food as a really elongated hand might do. In this connection it appears that the first act in a novel situation is to *touch* the goal object. The animal has learned to do this from its stick play.

This leads us to part E of Theorem 132:

THEOREM 132 E. *Once the tool is grasped, it is first used to touch the goal object.*

The position of the hoe in Figure 74 shows that probably on first touching the food with the hoe the organism moved it slightly nearer. Reports of chimpanzee behavior show that they are very quick to be reinforced by a favorable direction of slight movements of the goal object. This reinforced reaction will be generalized to other appropriate muscular activities by the principle of response generalization (xiii A and B), which will promptly bring the food within reach.

From the preceding considerations we arrive at part F of Theorem 132:

> THEOREM 132 F. *Secondary reinforcement and response generalization of the acts which gave an approaching movement to the goal object will rapidly lead to the dragging forward of the object and the reinforcement of the act as a whole.*

Theorem 132 F appears to complete the deductions of the insightful use of a simple tool. This is to say that after the stick play the chimpanzees, following a slight delay, would take the equivalent of the joint behavior segments H_1IJKL rather than the unrewarding segment H_2MN (Figure 72). No strictly unique principle has been used in the theoretical derivation of this process. It is true that a small element of trial-and-error learning was assumed, but many other factors were also assumed in the deduction. Moreover, the stick play resulted in much learning which had an element of trial-and-error throughout. Indeed it seems likely that a meticulous series of carefully controlled experiments on this problem will reveal substantially the same elements of insight in the progressive stick play as we have described in our deduction of the several parts of Theorem 132.

In addition to using sticks as tools, there is much evidence that anthropoids throw objects as missiles; this again is a kind of extension of the arm and hand, but here contact is withdrawn. Unfortunately no carefully conducted experiments have been performed on this type of learning. On the basis of the discussion concerned with learning to use the stick-tool, it is to be expected that a knowledge of the use of throwing will turn out to be acquired in a manner significantly similar.

Summary

Certain types of problem-solving have, following the example set by Köhler (7), come to be known as *insight*. Birch has advanced the analysis by stating (7, p. 369): "In the interests of theoretical and expositional clarity it is essential that two aspects of the opposition to the doctrine be sharply distinguished one from the other. This can be done by dealing with the two distinct uses to which the term, *insight*, has been put, the one categorical, the other explanatory." Hitherto the major achievements associated with the term insight, have been categorical. Maier advanced the problem as a whole by a useful bit of analysis. He described the phenomenon of insight as "the ability to bring together spontaneously two elements of past experience without having them previously associated by contiguity" (*8*, p. 46), the elements in question being habit segments. This advances the categorizing factor, or identification, toward the explanatory. This chapter has been concerned primarily with an attempt to understand how the phenomenon of insight comes about; i.e., it has been concerned with the explanatory aspect of the problem.

Briefly stated, the novel behavior mechanism which is mainly instrumental in the unique behavior displayed in what we have called insight, is the antedating goal reaction which is characteristic of behavior segments. It is this identity of fractional antedating elements which bridges the gap left by the lack of associative contiguity mentioned by Maier. Thus we find ourselves reverting in a sense to association by similarity, proposed by William James (*6*) in his attempt to explain rationality some forty years ago.

In the case of tool-using insight the present analysis finds the central factor to be the antedating goal reaction together with the subgoal reaction, combined in a complex way with arm- and hand-reaching extension. This analysis greatly needs to be followed by a series of carefully controlled experiments on stick play which will reveal in some detail the manner in which the mechanism of response generalization operates when the animals shift from one goal-response with the stick to another. It is strongly suspected that the mechanism which we have described as insight in the use of the stick-hoe also operates when the simple stick is used in play.

REFERENCES

1. Birch, H. G. The relation of previous experience to insightful problem-solving. *J. Comp. Psychol.*, 1945, *38*, 367–382.
2. Hull, C. L. Goal attraction and directing ideas conceived as habit phenomena. *Psychol. Rev.*, 1931, *38*, 487–506.

3. Hull, C. L. The mechanism of the assembly of behavior segments in novel combinations suitable for problem solution. *Psychol. Rev.*, 1935, *42*, 219–245.

4. Hull, C. L. *Principles of behavior*. New York: D. Appleton-Century Co., 1943.

5. Jackson, T. A. Use of the stick as a tool by young chimpanzees. *J. Comp. Psychol.*, 1942, *34*, 223–235.

6. James, W. *Principles of psychology*. New York: Henry Holt and Co., 1910.

7. Köhler, W. *The mentality of apes*. (Trans. by E. Winter) New York: Harcourt, Brace and Co., 1925.

8. Maier, N. R. F. Reasoning in white rats. *Comp. Psychol. Monog.*, 1929, No. 29.

9. Maier, N. R. F. The effect of cortical destruction on reasoning and learning in white rats. *J. Comp. Neurol.*, 1932, *54*, 45–75.

10. Wolfe, J. B., and Spragg, S. D. S. Some experimental tests of 'reasoning' in white rats. *J. Comp. Psychol.*, 1934, *18*, 455–469.

11. Value, Valuation, and Behavior Theory[1]

Can Value and Valuation Be Treated Objectively?

As our final view of individual behavior in its quasi-social aspects, we shall consider some of the phenomena and problems associated with the theory of value and valuation. Actually we have been dealing with the behavioral substance of value theory throughout all the preceding chapters. We must now treat it specifically.

The relationship of valuation to behavior theory can be clarified by a concrete example. Consider an ordinary apple. Such an object may be approached from many different scientific angles. Physics may treat of the light reflected from its surface or consider its weight and density; chemistry may discuss the constitution of its juice; botany may present its relationship to other plant species; plant physiology may report its processes of growth and reproduction. This list could be extended almost indefinitely. But in addition to these types of approach there is another of a somewhat different nature; this lies in the fact that the apple has a market price, i.e., it has *value*.

Value theory has a long history, much of it complicated by subjectivism. In illustration of this, let us examine briefly the kind of theoretical tangle which the injection of metaphysical presuppositions into the subject will produce. This may be clearly seen in the following extract from Robbins (*11*, pp. 87–90), who believes that value and valuation are quite beyond the powers of an objective scientific methodology such as that already put forward. Note

[1] This chapter is based to some extent on an article by the author (*5*), several paragraphs of which have been transcribed with little or no change.

especially his total lack of comprehension of the role of symbolic constructs in natural-science theory:

> Scientific method, it is urged, demands that we should leave out of account anything which is incapable of direct observation . . . Valuation is a subjective process. We cannot *observe* valuation. It is therefore out of place in a scientific explanation. Our theoretical constructions must assume observable data. . . . [This] is an attitude which is very frequent among those economists who have come under the influence of Behaviourist psychology or who are terrified of attack from exponents of this queer cult.
>
> . . . The argument that we should do nothing that is not done in the physical sciences is very seductive. But . . . it is very questionable whether this can be done in terms which involve no psychical elements. . . . The idea of an end, which is fundamental to our conception of the economic, is not possible to define in terms of external behaviour only. If we are to explain the relationships which arise from the existence of a scarcity of means in relation to a multiplicity of ends, surely at least one-half of the equation, as it were, must be psychical in character. . . . But . . . the procedure of the social sciences which deal with conduct, which is in some sense purposive, can never be completely assimilated to the procedure of the physical sciences. It is really not possible to understand the concepts of choice, of the relationship of means and ends, the central concepts of our science, in terms of observation of external data. The conception of purposive conduct . . . involve[s] links in the chain of causal explanation which are psychical, not physical, . . .

With the background of the preceding chapters, the reader should have little difficulty in connecting the present approach with the subject of value and valuation. He should note at the outset that *valuation* is at bottom an aspect of behavior and in so far is capable of the same degree of objectivity in its treatment as we have observed in the preceding chapters. This means that many of the basic aspects of value from which humans regard a certain object are shared by the lower animals. For example, a young and hungry rat or chimpanzee as well as a child who values a given food

will *strive* to secure and eat it. Conversely, having smelled and
nibbled at a novel kind of nourishing food, these organisms will
come to value it, as is shown by their striving for it when hungry.
In short, value represents the *potentiality* of action. But action
potentiality in this system is represented by $_sE_R$. And the presence of
$_sE_R$ serves to introduce the whole series of factors upon which it
depends, as demonstrated by equation 8,

$$_sE_R = D \times V_1 \times K \times _sH_R,$$

together with their determining circumstances. We have selected
from the many possible forms of value the above example related
to food needs because of its general familiarity to the reader, its
simplicity, and its comparative lack of political and metaphysical
bias.

The Paradox of the Locus of Value

The quantitative systematization of the theory of value and
valuative behavior enables us to resolve certain paradoxes which
have commonly been associated with "theories" of value. A discussion of some of these besides being of interest in its own right
may have the further merit of introducing the reader to the natural-
science approach to this important set of phenomena.

One of the standard problems of this type concerns the essential
locus of economic value—whether it lies in the valued object or in
the valuing organism. In a certain sense the question is a false one
in that it implies that the locus must be exclusively in one or the
other. It is a little like asking whether the momentum of a falling
object is due primarily to its mass or to the time it has been falling;
the fact is that a knowledge of *both* is indispensable for the determination. The habit strength ($_sH_R$) *resides* in the state of the nervous
system of the organism. This in turn *results* from a certain historical
relationship between the organism and the object, situation, or
state of affairs which has value (K′) such that the former has
learned through reinforcement to strive for the latter.

In a special sense value, as distinguished from valuation, may be
said to lie in that characteristic (K′) of the substance or commodity
which makes it a reinforcing agent to that organism, but it is
equally true that the reinforcement process depends upon the

characteristics of the organism; hay will reduce the food need of an ox but not of a man. A substance will not be valued (striven for) by an organism until the process of reinforcement has occurred, i.e., until $_sE_R$ exists.

But suppose a substance having no power of need reduction chances to have a pattern of stimulation much like the substance which previously has reduced a need. This stimulus will, through stimulus generalization (X), evoke striving activity. Does this mean that the second substance has value for the organism? To assert this would be something like a play on words. One could properly say, however, that the organism values this second object or substance but that the object or substance in question has no value for the organism. The latter is demonstrated behaviorally by the fact that after striving reactions have been evoked a few times by the falsely valued object, experimental extinction (IX) will supervene and this particular stimulus complex will no longer evoke striving (ix, x, and xi).

A paradox not quite so easily resolved is that in which the striving has been generated through secondary reinforcement; i.e., where the reinforcement has been set up through the action not of a state of affairs which actually reduces a drive, but of a secondary reinforcing agent (II). A classical case of this is furnished by Wolfe's chimpanzees (*13*) which would work for, and treasure, poker chips that much later could be inserted in a slot machine which would then always deliver a grape for each chip. Here, of course, we approach on a very simple level fairly close to the psychology of money value. Since the chimpanzee strives for the poker chip, it may properly be said that the chip is valued. However, the chip has no capacity to reduce a primary need and therefore it may be said to have no intrinsic value. But since it is an indispensable *means* to the securing of grapes, which do reduce the primary need for food, the poker chip has an indirect but genuine value. It is a subordinate goal and as such possesses secondary reinforcing powers.

The Supposed Natural-Science Paradox of Behavioral Evaluative Choice

Wolfe reports (*13*) that a type of poker chip which would yield a grape when inserted in the slot machine was distinctly preferred by his chimpanzees to a type which would yield nothing. This illustrates at a coarse level the behavioral fact so prominent in the economic theory of price determination, namely, that individual men value certain goods more than other goods, and that these valuations in fact display a hierarchy from high to low valuation. This commonplace observation that

$$_sE_{R_1} > {_sE_{R_2}}$$

arises because,

$$_sH_{R_1} > {_sH_{R_2}},$$

or,

$$D_1 > D_2,$$

or,

$$K_1 > K_2.$$

This has been believed in certain quarters to give rise to problems, such as those of choice, which are quite insoluble by the methodology available to natural science.

The supposed problem of how and why the striving potentials for, or evaluations of, different objects, substances, or states of affairs displayed by a given organism vary from time to time is resolved quite simply by the present approach. This has been incidentally elaborated above in Chapter 2. If the two stimulating situations are presented simultaneously or in close succession in such a way that the acts of striving for one preclude the simultaneous performance of the acts involved in striving for the other, there arises a competition within the body of the organism and that reaction potential which is momentarily greater mediates the corresponding reaction (xiv). The laws governing the resolution of the competition of two reaction potentials are different from those involved in the dominance of the heavier of two weights on the pans of a balance, but the outcome is closely analogous; in the case of behavior competition the balance is the organism itself. In the one case the process is no less naturalistic than in the other, and no greater metaphysical mystery surrounds it. It is indisputable, of course, that the theoretical determination of the outcome of a choice situation is more complex than is the question of the dominance of the heavier of two weights on a balance, but the labor involved in the theoretical determination is not the matter at issue here.

Why Do Organisms Value the Same State of Affairs Differently on Different Occasions?

The question of the consistency and inconsistency of an organism in its valuation of various states of affairs is a matter of some importance to the logical foundations of value theory. For example, Robbins remarks (*11*, pp. 91–92):

> The celebrated generalization that in a state of equilibrium the relative significance of divisible commodities is equal to their price, does involve the assumption that each final choice is consistent with every other, in the sense that if I prefer A to B and B to C, I also prefer A to C . . .

From the point of view of the present approach, the consistency of organisms in making evaluative choices is not necessarily a syllogistic matter, as might possibly be supposed from the above quotation, since it is displayed by subhuman organisms which presumably do not syllogize. To syllogize involves the use of words or equivalent symbols (pure-stimulus acts), whereas subhuman animals do not employ language in any proper sense. Behavioral inconsistency in evaluative choices of both humans and lower animals is believed instead to be a function of the spontaneous oscillation of the reaction potential ($_sO_R$), (XII). Where two reaction potentials of equal strength are in competition, as in simple discrimination situations, each appears to dominate on fifty per cent of the occasions (instead of neither one occurring at all as would be the case with a coarse balance); this condition of equal reaction potential therefore yields a maximum of inconsistency in choice. However, as one of the potentials becomes stronger than the other (as in simple trial-and-error learning—see Chapter 2), its reaction will be evoked more than half the time. But since the respective reaction potentials oscillate independently the weaker of the two will occasionally chance at the moment of stimulation to be in a high oscillatory phase, whereas the generally stronger of the two may chance at the same time to be in a low oscillatory phase (*4*, p. 146). Indeed, complete consistency in reaction, i.e., complete dominance of the stronger potential, will occur on single trials only when the difference between the two has become so great that the lowest oscillations of the strong potential no longer are exceeded by the highest oscillations of the weak potential (*4*,

p. 327). Consistency is attained only by a very large group of organisms taken as a whole or by single organisms when very many trials are massed. It is only in this latter situation that Robbins' proposed consistency is attained. In economics it is attained through the pooled action of many individuals.

There is another type of apparent inconsistency in valuative choice behavior; the nature of this is well recognized by economists, among whom it is known as the Law of Diminishing Marginal Utility (*11*, pp. 136 ff.). This law formulates the familiar fact of satiation, that the more an organism has of a given reinforcing substance or commodity the less it will strive for an additional increment. In systematic behavior theory this general subject is called *motivation* (*4*, p. 226). A recent experimental study by Perin (*8*) indicates that, other things equal, the valuation, or K' which an organism places upon a bit of food is the product of an increasing function of the need or drive for food (D) multiplied by habit strength, $_sH_R$ (VIII). The product ($_sE_R$) is bound to rise or fall as D rises or falls. Recently both these functions have received preliminary empirical determination. Because of the oscillation of $_sH_R$ and its multiplication by D, the momentary variability of valuative behavior ($_sE_R$) in no sense indicates a lack of lawfulness in the primary behavior principles, since the oscillation function ($_sO_R$) itself is lawful (XII).

Still a third source of what appears superficially to be behavioral inconsistency or capriciousness in the sense of the lack of the operation of natural law in valuative behavior is brought about by the differences in the histories of the valuing organisms. If one organism in the past has had its food needs reduced exclusively by a diet presenting certain stimulus characteristics, and another has had the corresponding needs reduced exclusively by a diet presenting distinctly different stimulus characteristics, each organism will strive with maximum vigor for its accustomed food and not for the food of the other. This in no sense implies a breakdown of primary natural-science dynamic laws. It is true that the natural laws involved are not the laws of Newtonian mechanics. It is also true that behavior laws, owing to the principle or law of the oscillation of reaction potential ($_sO_R$), are molar in the sense that they hold strictly only for central tendencies calculated from numerous samples of carefully measured data. Nevertheless, in the molar sense just indicated there is strong reason to believe that all behavior, including that of evaluation, displays definite calculatable and predictable characteristics provided the habit structure ($_sH_R$) of the organism, the reinforcing characteristics (K) of the stimulating situation, the drive (D), and the stimulus intensity (V) are known. Alternatively, prediction may be made from a knowledge of the history of the organism and of the immediate stimulating situation because, theoretically at least, the characteristics of the habit strength may be calculated from a complete knowledge of the organism's history. Thus in the variations of evaluative behavior there is no evidence that a genuinely determinate behavioral dynamics is lacking.

Finally, a fourth source of evaluative differences, those between organisms with the same history, is due to different constants characteristic of different individuals, e.g., in the learning exponent (IV). Consequently one organism may follow the law of learning just as exactly as the majority even though more rapidly or more slowly depending on the learning parameter possessed by him (6). Such differences may thus be entirely consistent with a general lawfulness of valuative behavior.

The Natural-Science Status of Certain Classes of Values

The bearing of the present approach on several different types of generally recognized value and valuation will now be briefly and dogmatically indicated.

Economic value in one of its more obvious and primitive aspects involves the exchange of a certain amount of the potentially exchangeable commodity X possessed by person No. 1 for a certain amount of the potentially exchangeable commodity Y possessed by person No. 2. This type of behavior can come about voluntarily and continuously only on the condition that person No. 1 has a striving potential for the certain amount of Y which is greater than would be his striving potential for the amount of X when he no longer has that portion of X; and when person No. 2 has a striving potential for X which is greater than would be that for Y when he no longer has Y. *Thus the total striving potential of both persons is reduced by the transaction.*

In the case just considered, X and Y are conceived as primary reinforcing agents (K'), i.e., substances such as food which can mediate the reduction of specific primary needs. In the more sophisticated cultures, some substance which is more easily transported than most commodities, and which while usually not capable of *directly* mediating the reduction of any primary need is a dependable indirect *means* to a considerable variety of such need reductions, usually comes to be employed as a medium of exchange, i.e., money. This is possible because money, being an indirect means to need reduction, becomes a *secondary reinforcing agent* (ii).

According to the present analysis, economics appears to be a kind of hybrid science inasmuch as it has its source in the application of a number of different primary or pure sciences. For example, the pure-science aspects of psychology or behavior have been stressed above, but this by no means covers the whole discipline. There are also the scientific aspects of *production*. In the case of agricultural economics there is involved in production the additional primary science of plant growth, from which there flows the secondary or applied principle of diminishing crop yield of a plot of earth per unit of labor employed as the amount of labor spent upon it is indefinitely increased. This is the so-called Law of Diminishing Returns.

A second type of value and valuation of great significance is found in *truth*. In one sense a bit of truth may be specified as a statement whose symbols accurately correspond to their referents. Organisms strive for truth because it constitutes, or contains the means to, a dependable representation of selected portions of the environment. All organisms, particularly those with distance receptors, learn early in life to expose their receptors in such a way as to receive the most adequate impact of environmental stimuli at critical points of behavior sequences. These habits are largely organized by compound trial-and-error learning (Chapter 6) and maintained by means of the secondary reinforcement based on stimulus traces, the ultimate reinforcement being the goal attainment which in general cannot be achieved without the exposure of the receptors to the environment. For example, in case a marksman is at a place (or time) such that he cannot make the necessary receptor exposures for the appropriate observations, a parallel observation made by a second person more favorably situated can be conveyed to the first by means of language or symbols. Through the learned equivalence of stimulus patterns,

the stimuli resulting from the language are approximately substitutable for the needed but inaccessible stimulus pattern which
would result from direct observation, and thus a hit may be made.
This kind of truth may be called factual truth or information, as
distinguished from misinformation, error, or untruth. That truth
is valued is shown by the fact that it is widely striven for.

Alternatively, truth of the natural-science theoretical variety
may be defined as the characteristic symbolically formulated rule
or principle, e.g., an equation, which applies accurately to certain
types of relationship in such a way that when numerical values
based on relevant observations are substituted in the equation there
is secured a new quantitative value which agrees with fact. The
value secured may be an end in itself, i.e., the satisfaction of
curiosity; or it may lie in a subgoal, the final goal being the fulfill-
ment of some primary need. Truth is striven for originally because
it is a means to need reduction and so receives indirect, i.e., secondary, reinforcement (4, p. 84). In this way theoretical-truth value
is conceived to arise. Scientific truth is widely striven for.

A third class of values of a still more complex nature arises from
the fact that men usually live in fairly close association, and thus
the behavior of other people often becomes a matter of acute
concern to each individual. This concern has two contrasted
aspects, positive and negative. In the positive aspect one organism
(the *initiator*) may use a second organism (the *subject*) much as a
tool is used—as a means to the initiator's end, i.e., to a state of
affairs which will be either primarily or secondarily reinforcing
to the initiator. But to accomplish this through the behavior of the
subject *the initiator must himself somehow act in accordance with the laws
of motivation and reinforcement* (1) by supplying adequate motivation
and (2) by giving the subject something which will reduce the
latter's needs; otherwise the subject's behavior will not be as
desired or will suffer experimental extinction (IX). Thus a person
who has a supply of meat will induce another person to cook it by
promising some of the prepared food as potential reinforcement or
reward. In this way both persons receive nutriment and therefore
primary reinforcement from the transaction. This is an example
of the Law of Reciprocal Reinforcement which underlies all
social transactions. This law may be formulated as our final
theorem:

THEOREM 133. *Every voluntary social interaction, in order to be repeated consistently, must result in a substantial reinforcement to the activity of each party to the transaction.*

This formulation implicitly presupposes the setting of ordinary respectable economics which is based on exchange. There is, however, another side to the picture. The same principle operates in situations where the initiator organism, or group of organisms, has sufficient power to resort to coercion. In the one case the initiator will create a need, usually primary, which would not otherwise exist; in the other case the initiator will prevent the reduction of a need already or potentially existent in the subject. This ugly phase of the control of behavior leads to slavery and forced labor as a limiting case. It also appears currently in various forms of racketeering.

Through trial and error the subject organism often finds ways of preventing the occurrence of this type of behavior on the part of the initiator organism, or of terminating it if it is already under way. One of these involves return punishment—the causing of injury to the offending (initiator) organism. Such acts of counter-attack are frequently reinforced because they cause the offender to take flight, thereby terminating the need he was causing. Similarly, the flight reaction is reinforced in the offender because it is followed by the cessation of the injury (need) caused by the counter-attack. Here again we have a case of reciprocal reinforcement.

It happens that certain signs such as frowns and other kinds of threatening movements, as well as certain words (overt threats) through their association with attack, acquire the power of evoking incipient flight reactions (fear). Through trial and error, habits of performing these social "pure stimulus" acts are acquired by organisms, and they are used where effective in place of physical attack. Accordingly words acquire a certain real power to punish, and so to deter, transgressors. And since the statement that a person has transgressed in a certain way is associated with punishment and such a statement is a moral judgment, it comes about that the overt passing of an adverse moral judgment becomes a deterrent to forbidden acts. In a similar manner, the passing of a favorable moral judgment becomes a secondary positive reinforcing agent fostering desirable action. Because these effects are reinforcing, the passing of positive moral judgments becomes another example of reciprocal reinforcement.

It is clear from the foregoing discussion that natural-science methodology presumably will be able, ultimately, to deduce from its principles all kinds of behavior of organisms, whether generally characterized as good, bad, or indifferent. Moreover, since the passing of a moral judgment is itself a form of verbal behavior, either overt or covert, it is to be expected that natural-science theory will be able to deduce the making of moral judgments along with other forms of behavior.

Is a True Natural Science of Ethics Possible?

At the outset of this discussion we must recall to the reader a commonplace which has been implicit throughout the preceding chapters—the methodology of validating natural-science laws. Stated simply, the validation depends upon two factors: the *conditions* preceding an event and the principles or *laws* upon which the outcome is supposed to depend. The conditions are normally quantitative values such as the length of a pendulum suspension and the value of gravity; and the law in that case would be the equation,

$$P = 2\pi \sqrt{\frac{l}{g}}.$$

If the theory is sound the substitution of any length of suspension (l) at any point having a known gravitational value (g) will predict what the period (P) will be. The validation process is to observe whether the period of any concrete pendulum agrees with the computation. All natural-science laws and combinations of law must satisfy this type of validation test.

It is quite clear from the above summary statement of scientific methodology that there is no *a priori* impossibility of ultimately attaining a molar theory of organismic behavior which will cover all aspects of the striving of organisms. This includes what *human* organisms will do under all sorts of conditions. It should even be possible, ultimately, to predict the verbal reactions which people make, i.e., what they will *say*, overtly or covertly, regarding their approval or disapproval of the behavior of others as well as of their own behavior. Therefore, the methodology of science presumably will ultimately apply to moral behavior, even including the *moral judgment*. Moreover, it is equally clear that such a theory when worked out will be capable of being proved valid or invalid by the empirical test of observing what really happens in a behavior causal sequence following the occurrence of any dynamic conditions to which the theory applies (*4*, p. 12).

But here we encounter a critical question, one concerning which there is a great deal of current confusion among both scientists and ethicists. Is pure science's methodological capacity to mediate the *prediction* (the logical deduction) of the occurrence of an event under given conditions of behavior of whatever nature—whether moral, immoral, or unmoral—the same thing as the capacity to make a moral judgment, i.e., to *characterize* certain behavior absolutely as ethically good or bad? As so often happens, the clear posing of a problem furnishes us with valuable clues to its solution. The clue in the case of the present problem is the distinction between *prediction* and *characterization*. No ethical system known to the present writer attempts to *predict* the occurrence of any event whatever: the "laws" which are proposed are merely principles for characterizing acts as good or bad, as a basis for making moral judgments. A moral judgment, like any other act, may serve as a test of the validity of supposed behavioral law but it does not itself state a law any more than any other ordinary act does. *True natural laws have no exceptions.*

Does this difference between ethical theory and the theory of moral behavior mean that ethical principles inherently can never have the type of validity that the scientific theory of moral behavior may have? We believe that the considerations just outlined leave us no alternative. So long as ethical theory only mediates the *characterization* of events as good or bad, statements of what men ought or ought not to do, and never *predicts* the occurrence of anything on the part of the subject, there can be no objective scientific test of its truth or falsity; i.e., there is no scientific way of determining its validity.

But statements which cannot be tested for truth or falsity cannot be said to be either true or false. This means that such statements occupy a scientific no man's land; which is practically equivalent to saying that such statements are scientific nonsense. Probably this is the reason why men who are familiar with the techniques of science, by and large, are able in the course of time to attain substantial agreement in regard to scientific matters but as a rule make little progress toward agreement in regard to matters of moral judgment, where serious concrete issues are involved. It follows that the so-called science of ethics, so far as *ultimate* ethical values are concerned, is a pseudo-science.[2] Meanwhile this presents no impediment in the way of the development of a true natural science of moral behavior, including the moral judgment as an act that is concerned with events which may be predicted and publicly observed. Neither does it impede the application of science in the determination of the most effective means of attaining values of all kinds, ethical or otherwise.

By much the same reasoning we may show that the hope of somehow deriving ethical principles from the innate constitution of the "mind," on the analogy of the "self-evident" truths of logic and Euclid's approach to geometry, is also doomed to disappointment. This is because there probably is no such thing as a self-evident truth in Euclid's sense. The primary principles of logic and mathematics are believed to be those rules of reasoning (symbol manipulation) which have been found by trial to mediate valid conclusions. The formulation of these principles has taken centuries and is by no means complete even now. Scientific theory requires for the derivation of valid theorems (1) sound scientific principles and (2) sound logical rules for the mediation of the deductive process. Therefore each empirically verified scientific theorem tends to validate both the scientific principles employed in its derivation and the logical rules whereby the scientific principles were transformed into the theorem. Logical rules are validated in the same way and, indeed, at the same time as are scientific principles. We accordingly conclude that the innate constitution of the "mind" also fails to yield a dependable basis for the scientific validation of ultimate ethical principles.

An Objective Natural-Science Interpretation of Some Typical Approaches to the Theory of Value

It is inevitable that where conscientious and intelligent scholars from the same culture are giving an account of practically the

[2] The term *ethics* is employed here in the technical sense of the alleged science of what absolutely *is* good or bad, as distinguished from what particular individuals or cultural groups *say* is good or bad.

same phenomena there should be a very substantial identity in the several systematic outcomes. This seems to be true in the case of value theory. We believe that various current approaches to the theory of value are essentially alike in that each in turn takes its origin from a position which is substantially identical to one or another phase of the logico-causal hierarchy of the natural-science approach implicit in the preceding chapters. This approach may be summarized as follows, the Roman symbols in parentheses representing the relevant postulate of origin:

1. Original need (I; V).
2. Substance or state of affairs (K′) possessing power of mediating need reduction (VII).
3. Original need reduction (III).
4. Resulting habit formation ($_sH_R$) (IV).
5. Subsequent need or drive (D) (V).
6. Reaction (striving) potentiality ($_sE_R$) (VIII).
7. Actual striving or work (W) (objective valuative behavior) (IX E).

We shall begin our examination of the origins of various value systems by citing an interpretation of Bentham's pain-pleasure hypothesis, which goes back to 1780 (*1*, pp. 339, 353):

> Nature has placed mankind under the governance of two sovereign masters, *pain* and *pleasure* . . . pleasure, and what comes to the same thing, immunity from pain . . .

First, Bentham's concept of *pain* is equated substantially to our own concept of *need*. Secondly, Bentham's concept of pleasure is found in those situations in which need or anxiety (the learned antici- patory responses to the impending impact of a need) is in the process of reduction. But as shown at length in the preceding chapters, all the striving which is the immediate observable factor indicating valuation is derivable from $_sE_R$, i.e., ultimately from need reduction. Thus Bentham takes his point of departure approximately from level 2 of our logico-causal hierarchy. If he were writing today he might conceivably say that value, or K (2) becomes manifest under conditions of need (1) through its power of need reduction (3); that need reduction generates habit (4); that habit in conjunc- tion with subsequent need (5) generates striving potentiality (6), which generates actual striving (7) and which normally constitutes the objective evidence of evaluation. There accordingly appears to be substantial harmony between the present systematic approach and that of Bentham.

Next we consider a much more recent work, that of Urban. Urban's critical value concept is *feeling*.[3] He says (*12*, p. 22):

> Existence is perceived; truth is thought; value is felt . . .
> The feeling of value includes the feeling of reality.

Urban's basic postulate is not really very different from Bentham's, because for Urban feeling is affect. But affect is the pleasantness or unpleasantness aspect of stimulating situations, and pleasantness and unpleasantness are essentially pleasure and pain. Accordingly, Urban's theory of value may be regarded as taking its origin from substantially level 1 of our own development, exactly as may Bentham's, and for the same reasons.

We pass next to a group of writers among whom are found most modern economists. Their approach derives value from *wants* (*3*, p. 1). This notion, while somewhat vague, appears to be very nearly equivalent to need except that the emphasis is naturally placed on specific objects or commodities wanted, on the one hand, and on potential action to obtain the commodities on the other. When they say that a person wants bread it is equivalent to saying that he has a need which bread has the power of reducing, and by implication that he possesses an internal habit structure which under appropriate stimulation will lead to striving with bread (the eating of bread) as the goal. It is accordingly evident that this school sets out from a place in the natural-science logico-causal hierarchy extending from primitive needs to value and valuation, though it enters the hierarchy at a tabular level considerably below that of Bentham and of Urban—probably somewhere near level 6.

At approximately the same level in our logico-causal hierarchy from need to striving, we find Köhler (*7*), who derives value from "requiredness." To the best of our understanding, requiredness for Köhler is a phenomenological vector of a felt incompleteness or need. This vector corresponds to the subjective aspects or equivalent of reaction potential ($_sE_R$). Köhler's approach accordingly also finds its place rather definitely at level 6 in our natural-science logico-causal hierarchy. We therefore conclude that his requiredness vector, at least in so far as it is capable of giving rise to striving

[3] The same may be said of Reid (*10*), a more recent writer somewhat influenced by Urban.

for goals, is derivable by a process of learning which has its roots in need and need reduction.

Next in order we examine the approach of Perry. His key concept in value theory is *interest*. But Perry does not use this term as equivalent to attention. In this connection he remarks (*9*, p. 115):

> It is characteristic of living mind to be *for* some things and *against* others . . . It is to this all-pervasive characteristic of the motor-affective life, this *state, act, attitude, or disposition of favor or disfavor*, to which we propose to give the name of "interest" . . . That which is an object of interest is *eo ipso* invested with value.

In short, Perry uses *interest* as substantially equivalent to interested action, or striving. Thus he takes his point of departure from levels 6 and 7 of the present natural-science logico-causal hierarchy. It is to be noted, moreover, that Perry clearly recognizes that a process of habit formation does take place and that striving consequently has its roots in the history of the organism, though he makes no attempt at a precise derivation of striving from original biological needs.

The last systematic treatment of the problems of value and valuation which we shall consider is that of Dewey, who advocates a strictly natural-science approach. He states, for example (*2*, pp. 63, 64):

> The separation alleged to exist between the "world of facts" and the "realm of values" will disappear from human beliefs only as valuation-phenomena are seen to have their immediate source in biological modes of behavior and to owe their concrete content to the influence of cultural conditions. . . . A grounded theory of the phenomena of human behavior is as much a prerequisite of a theory of valuation as is a theory of the behavior of physical (in the sense of nonhuman) things. The development of a science of the phenomena of living creatures was an unqualified prerequisite of the development of a sound psychology.

It is evident from this quotation that Dewey's general approach to the problems of value and valuation is substantially the same as our own. He does not go into the specific details of behavior theory, but stresses the role of subordinate goals and the more complex processes of valuative procedures such as employ the pure-stimulus acts of verbal symbolism as mediating devices. His point of origin can scarcely be assigned a particular place in our formal natural-science hierarchy, since implicitly he recognizes the whole of it. By emphasis, however, he seems somewhat to favor the aspect of objectively observable action which we have listed as level 7.

TERMINAL NOTE

THE SYSTEMATIC STATUS OF INTROSPECTION IN THE
    NATURAL-SCIENCE APPROACH TO THE THEORY OF
    VALUE

There remain to be examined certain differences among the approaches to value theory just considered as to implicit or explicit methodology. All of the writers mentioned, with the exception of Dewey and the probable exception of Perry, take more or less the subjective, introspective, or phenomenological approach to the theory of value, one of them (Köhler) somewhat insistently so. From the present point of view the subjective states such as pain and pleasure are characteristic internal conditions and are observable by means of internal receptors. These receptors discharge into the nervous system quite as do the external receptors (such as the retina and the cochlea) and so in different combinations are able to evoke responses of various kinds, including those of verbal symbolism which constitute introspective reports and valuative judgments.

It would appear that the presence of internal conditions or neural organizations, such as habit structures ($_sH_R$) and reaction potentials ($_sE_R$), are also reportable. It is not clear, however, whether the verbal symbolic acts which constitute such reports are mediated by direct connections between the habit structures and the speech effectors, or whether the connections are between the effectors and the proprioceptive stimuli which arise from incipient tendencies to action mediated directly by the habit structures in question. At all events, verbal reports mediated in some such manner are frequently useful; e.g., in clinical situations where a precise and objectively metricized history of the ailing subject is lacking and where time or energy would not be available to make exact calculations concerning relevant habit structures even if an adequate history and suitable equations were available. Consequently, introspective reports concerning internal conditions are useful for rough qualitative purposes; nevertheless they become inadequate wherever primary quantitative laws are in the process of systematic formulation or precise validation. Fortunately, as we have tried to show above, in the formulation of natural law it is not necessary to depend on such unsatisfactory evidence. We can utilize symbolic constructs.

As quantitative behavioral symbolic constructs are gradually perfected and come into more general knowledge and use, the insistence of value theorists upon the logical primacy of introspection may be expected correspondingly to diminish. Then the theory of value will cease to be a division of speculative philosophy and will become a *bona fide* portion of natural science.

REFERENCES

1. Bentham, J. An introduction to the principles of morals and legislation. *British Moralists* (ed. by L. A. Selby-Bigge), Vol. I. Oxford, England: Clarendon Press, 1897.
2. Dewey, J. Theory of valuation. *International encyclopedia of unified science*, Vol. II. Chicago: Univ. Chicago Press, 1939.
3. Fairchild, F. R., Furniss, E. S., and Buck, N. S. *Economics*. New York: Macmillan Co., 1937.
4. Hull, C. L. *Principles of behavior.* New York: D. Appleton-Century Co., 1943.
5. Hull, C. L. Value, valuation, and natural-science methodology. *Philos. of Science*, 1944, *11*, 125–141.
6. Hull, C. L., Felsinger, J. M., Gladstone, A. I., and Yamaguchi, H. G. A proposed quantification of habit strength. *Psychol. Rev.*, 1947, 54, 237–254.
7. Köhler, W. *The place of value in a world of facts.* New York: Liveright Pub. Corp., 1938.
8. Perin, C. T. Behavior potentiality as a joint function of the amount of training and the degree of hunger at the time of extinction. *J. Exper. Psychol.*, 1942, *30*, 93–113.
9. Perry, R. B. *General theory of value.* New York: Longmans, Green and Co., 1926.
10. Reid, J. R. *A theory of value,* New York: Charles Scribner's Sons, 1938.

11. Robbins, L. *The nature and significance of economic science* (2nd ed.). London: Macmillan and Co., 1937.

12. Urban, W. M. *Valuation: its nature and laws.* London: George Allen and Unwin, Ltd., 1909.

13. Wolfe, J. B. Effectiveness of token-rewards for chimpanzees. *Comp. Psychol. Monogr.*, 1936, *12*, No. 5.

12. Concluding Considerations

In our final chapter we wish to emphasize three types of related conclusions which seem to flow from the preceding theoretical elaborations. These concern the joint automaticity and adaptivity of the behavior forms deduced in this volume, the scientific soundness of the detailed behavior forms, and the additional behavior forms which will probably be deduced from the same general system in the not too distant future.

Sample Automatic Adaptive Behavior Mechanisms

Throughout the preceding pages we have been so largely concerned with the informal deductions which make up the bulk of this volume that we have taken no space to present our view of the biological (adaptive) picture as such. Even so, the reader has seen by now that the organism is here conceived as a completely automatic entity; that in our approach to behavior theory there is no *entelechy*, no disembodied mind, soul, or spirit which in some way tells the various parts of the body how to cooperate behaviorally to attain successful adaptation, i.e., how to achieve survival.[1] When the various laws governing this behavioral automaticity are completely known they presumably will be presented in full detail. At that time these laws should be stated objectively at the outset,

---

[1] Munn (*4*, p. 190) states that where no one believes in disembodied ideas, the controversy regarding all behavior being made up of learned responses becomes merely one of whether these responses are simple or complex. It may be added that complex automaticity is quite as automatic and self-regulating as simple automaticity; that highly complex automaticity constitutes no more evidence concerning the existence of an entelechy, or reason for indulging in anthropomorphism, than does simple automaticity.

perhaps after the general manner of Chapter 1 in this volume. We are at present a long way from knowing these laws with precision, and some of those which we think we know almost certainly will later prove to be in error. Nevertheless it may help to fill out the reader's picture of the adaptive aspects of the present system if we sketch in a tentative manner typical aspects of its automaticity. This will consist in the brief presentation of eight examples of adaptive automatic behavior mechanisms.

Organic evolution has provided the normal organism at the beginning of its life with (1) receptor organs and (2) responding organs. The two types of organs are similarly connected by the nervous system to form unlearned stimulus-response connections or reflexes (Postulate I). These inborn response tendencies ($_sU_R$) are the body's *first major automatic mechanisms* for adapting to various types of emergency situations.

But the processes of evolution have definite limits. The organism has not been provided with ready-made reflexes for evoking adaptive responses to the infinity of complex situations in which it will find itself. To meet this type of emergency, evolution has developed a second automatic device. This is the primitive capacity to learn; to profit by past experience (III). Learning thus constitutes the *second major automatic adaptive behavior mechanism*, which provides a slightly slower means of adaptation to less acute situations.

Simple learning itself is seen in the conditioned reflex. A neutral stimulus (S) preceding a response (R) to an injury which is followed by a lessening of pain (S_D) tends to set up a learned habit S $\dashrightarrow$ R, i.e., $_sH_R$; S may be any stimulus, or set of stimuli. Now the S of the habit will normally resemble closely the situation-stimuli which shortly preceded the injury. According to the principle of stimulus generalization (X), therefore, the defense withdrawal action will on succeeding occasions occur earlier than on the first occasion, and so will reduce or eliminate the injury automatically. The learning law coupled with the stimulus-generalization law yields the *antedating defense reaction*, which is obviously adaptive. Here, then, we have our *third major automatic adaptive behavior mechanism*.

The inborn response potentiality ($_sU_R$) consists in a hierarchy of somewhat diverse response tendencies (I). Let us suppose that the strongest response potentiality of the hierarchy chances not to reduce S_D; we accordingly call it R_-. The fact that R_- requires work (W) and that work generates (I_R) naturally leads to experimental extinction, which ultimately reduces the potentiality of $_sH_{R-}$ to the response threshold ($_sL_R$). This may be called *negative response learning;* it protects organisms from exhausting themselves in performing useless acts. Thus we have our *fourth major automatic adaptive behavior mechanism.*

Now let us suppose as before that the dominant response of the $_sU_R$ hierarchy chances to be unadaptive (R_-), but that the second next strongest response potentiality is truly adaptive; we therefore call it R_+. Here enters the principle of behavioral oscillation ($_sO_R$), through which, with (or without) negative response learning, an irregular alternation occurs between R_- and R_+ resulting in *trial learning* (XII). This is the combined occurrence of negative and positive response learning in the same process; it is commonly known as trial-and-error learning; as the irregular alternation of the trials continues R_- grows weaker and becomes less frequent, while R_+ grows stronger and becomes more frequent. This trial-and-error learning constitutes our *fifth major automatic adaptive behavior mechanism.*

We now pass to a second form of joint positive and negative trial learning. Let us suppose that an adaptive response is conditioned to a given point on a stimulus generalization continuum, but that the stimulus at a different point on the continuum operates on the organism to evoke the same response, which in this situation is *un*adaptive. Here we have a case where a primary behavior law (generalization) produces a major but temporary maladaptivity. The same response will become R_+ or R_-, depending upon which part of the same stimulus continuum is operating. In order to avoid the superficial paradox of calling the same response both R_+ and R_-, according to the evoking conditions, we shall now attach the plus and minus signs to the stimuli, as S_+ and S_-.

This maladaptivity is easily and automatically remedied. The joint strengthening of $S_+ \dashrightarrow R$ at one point of the continuum and weakening of $S_- \dashrightarrow R$ at a different point on the continuum, together with the principle of stimulus generalization, will result in a tilt of the reaction-evocation power in favor of this section of the stimulus continuum for this particular response, which will finally reduce the $S_- \dashrightarrow R$ to the reaction threshold ($_sL_R$). This is properly described as *positive-negative* stimulus trial learning. It is usually known as *discrimination learning*. This tilting of the evocative power of the stimulus continuum by the organism's learning S_+ and S_- is obviously a *sixth major automatic adaptive behavior device*.

We next consider a stimulus continuum which we call the *stimulus trace* (s). This, through decay, has a natural tilt downward beginning soon after the stimulus is received and extending downward for some seconds. In this way a stimulus through its trace may be conditioned to a response some seconds after the physical stimulus has ceased to exist. This continuum yields generalized responses in both directions, but notably from the low subsident end of the trace toward the relatively high antecedent end. In these circumstances the response will antedate the conditions under which the habit was set up; i.e., this continuum and combination of circumstances yield a second type of *antedating defense reaction*. A defense reaction such as flight, which occurs before a dangerous event is encountered, clearly constitutes our *seventh major automatic adaptive behavior device*. (Incidentally this mechanism automatically spans time for the organism.)

Now we come to the behavioral mechanism known as the *fractional antedating goal reaction*, together with its proprioceptive stimulus correlate, $r_G \rightarrow s_G$. The r_G is a pure-stimulus act ($\textcircled{r}$) which tends to antedate all goals established by a given organism. It follows that the proprioceptive goal stimulus (s_G) will automatically precede each such goal, as well, of course, as the acts by which the goal has already been attained. Thus each s_G is a stimulus leading to the realization of its particular goal. Clearly the automatic (stimulus) guidance of organismic behavior to goals is adaptive in the highest degree. Further study of this major automatic device presumably will lead to the detailed behavioral understanding of thought and reasoning, which constitute the highest attainment of organic evolution. Indeed the $r_G \rightarrow s_G$ mechanism leads in a strictly logical manner into what was formally regarded as the very heart of the psychic: interest, planning, foresight, foreknowledge, expectancy, purpose, and so on. This, our *eighth major automatic adaptive behavior device*, concludes our list of sample mechanisms presented to exemplify the automatic self-maintenance of the mammalian organism.

The Test of a Sound Theory

At this point we pass to our second concluding consideration, that of the scientific soundness of the deductions yielded by the system. Two general types of procedure are followed by those who attempt to evaluate the validity of a theoretical system. The first method, representing the German philosophical approach (3, pp. 69, 684, 685), begins in a negative manner by marshalling *a priori* arguments designed to reveal the fallacies of potentially conflicting approaches; it then proceeds to defend the conclusions arrived at in the system being evaluated by showing their general harmony with some metaphysical principle or dogma. Our own method, on the other hand, is patterned after the objective procedures of the physical sciences. Those who follow this approach take the view that the basic criterion of the soundness of a theoretical system is the extent to which the deductions from the system correspond to empirical fact. In the present immature state of the behavior sciences, the importance of this method of evaluation cannot be too strongly stressed.

In scoring the various theoretical deductions of the system presented here, we have prepared a special summarizing table for each chapter which contains such deductions. A typical example of these tabulations may be seen in Table 37, which represents Chapter 2. This table gives the total number of theoretical propositions presented (in this table, 22), and indicates whether or not relevant empirical evidence has been found regarding the validity of each and in case it has, whether it is judged valid (+), uncertainly valid (?), or invalid (−). The opinions of individual scientists will, of course, differ in such matters; each scientist who knows the empirical field will wish to arrive at parallel judgments for himself.

The results of the validity tables of all the ten chapters thus scored were then combined. Of the *178* formal theoretical propositions contained in the volume, 93, or 52 per cent, were judged as having empirical evidence bearing on their validity (+), and 30, or 17 per cent, were judged as possessing approximate or indirect empirical evidence (±) as to their validity. Fifty-five, or 31 per cent, of the 178 theoretical propositions were judged as not covered by known relevant empirical evidence. Of the 123 propositions wholly or partially covered by empirical evidence, 106, or 86 per cent, were judged as substantially validated; 14, or 11 per cent, were judged as probably valid, though with considerable uncertainty; and one proposition (related to the Weber-Fechner law), or about 1 per cent, was judged as definitely invalid.

TABLE 37. A typical validity summarizing table for Chapter 2. This shows (1) whether definite (direct) empirical evidence exists (+), approximate (indirect) empirical evidence exists (±), or no empirical evidence (−) has been found bearing on the soundness of the theoretical deductions in question; and (2) whether the empirical evidence found is judged to support (+) or not support (−) the particular deduction. A question mark indicates special uncertainty of judgment. Similar tables were made for Chapters 3 to 11 inclusive.

Theoretical conclusions and/ or parts	Relevant evidence found bearing on empirical sound- ness of deduction	Judged empirical soundness of theo- retical deduction
Corollary XV A	+	+
" B	+	+
Theorem 1 A	+	+
" B	−	
" C	−	
" D	−	
" E	−	
" F	−	
" G	−	
" H	±	+
Theorem 2	−	
Theorem 3	−	
Theorem 4	±	+?
Theorem 5	±	+?
Theorem 6	±	+?
Theorem 7	+	+
Theorem 8	±	+
Theorem 9	+	+
Theorem 10 A	+	+
" B	+	+
" C	+	+
" D	+	+

The fact that only one proposition out of 123 was considered to be definitely contrary to empirical fact presumably reflects to some extent the writer's unconscious avoidance of problems which would not yield readily to his systematic approach. Even so, the reader will observe that the system has covered a fairly wide range of phenomena. Moreover, the 55 propositions presumably not yet covered by empirical fact will in the course of time be investigated. These are genuine predictions, and experimentalists seeking fertile fields for investigation will find in them challenging targets for research. It will be particularly interesting to see what per cent of validity the predictions will show as experiments gradually produce the relevant evidence.

They who know the history of theoretical psychology will understand that the present system is merely the most recent of a series of miniature systems evolved by the present writer. The coming generation of scientists will, it is hoped, present other theoretical systems, each succeeding one of a progressively more precise and quantitative nature.

Theoretical Behavior Challenges of the Near Future

We come now to our third concluding consideration—those behavior forms likely to be deduced soon. During recent years the physical sciences have been developing with a marked positive acceleration. Present indications are that the empirical behavior sciences are manifesting the same type of growth. One characteristic of this is that the theoretical or systematic development will follow with not too much delay the empirical growth. This means that we may confidently expect a number of obvious systematizations during the next fifty years or so. The successful development of the behavioral sciences will be hastened by the early solution of a few typical problems which we shall now consider.

One of the factors which retard both the empirical and the theoretical growth of a science is an inadequate vocabulary or set of signs by means of which the main concepts may be designated. The general technique of symbolic logic, when separated from its metaphysical entanglements, seems admirably adapted to this service. In the development of this technique much care must be devoted to the choice of the primary or undefined terms, so that the meanings can be made public and objective by simple sensory demonstrations and/or discriminatory differential reinforcements. With a satisfactory set of undefined terms available, all the other concepts of the system should be defined in those primary terms as the system develops. The point is that the terms or concepts of a system can, and should, be built up systematically much like the formal propositions or theorems.

Closely related to the terms upon which a system is built is the matter of the behavioral units employed. All scientific systems of importance must be quantitative; quantification requires units, and systematic quantification requires a most meticulous definition of the units in their various relationships. For example, it should be possible to convert ten units of one motivation into an equivalent number of units in any other of the numerous types of motivation, so that all will yield strictly equivalent amounts of potential, or real, adaptive action (R). This will be an exacting task, probably extending over a very long time. The small and tentative beginning made in the present system (σ) will serve mainly to call attention in a concrete manner to the problem.

The behavioral units employed are closely related to the matter of the quantitative equations representing the relation of the various behavior functions, such as ${}_sH_R$, ${}_sE_R$, D, ${}_sI_R$, and so on, in the present system, to the number of reinforcements (N), the length or amount of food privation (h), the number of extinction trials (n), and so on. In the midst of these problems is the critical series concerned with the numerical values of the constants or parameters which enter into these equations. The history of the physical sciences indicates that this presumably will be accomplished by a series of approximations, but that even though the problem is urgent it will be a very long time before a final stage is reached. Small beginnings have been made in this by the rough postulation of various constants in the present system; this, again, will serve mainly to call attention to the problem.

Passing to the more qualitative aspects of systematic behavior development, toward which we may look forward with considerable confidence, we turn first to that traditionally known as *perception* (*1*). Now, perception appears to be based on sensory stimulation (S), together with stimulus generalization, and the results of previous learning (${}_sH_R$), e.g., Chapter 8. The best makeshift we have been able to achieve so far has been to treat S and ${}_s\bar{H}_R$ separately. Perhaps one of the reasons why the failure to distinguish sharply between stimulation and perception does not interfere any more markedly with the validity of the present deductions is that the elements of both stimulation and generalization are explicitly included in the system.

Perception has ordinarily been reported by means of speech

symbolism. Perhaps because of this connection between speech and introspective reports, the *Gestalt* psychologists have specialized in this field, and have made notable contributions to it (*3*). In the present work it is conceived that the whole subject should be re-worked from a behavioral point of view, and that the various laws peculiar to perception should be deduced in terms of $_8H_R$, $_8\bar{H}_R$, D, S, R, and so on. Thus a real scientific unity would be attained (*1*). We are under the impression that several persons in various parts of the world are spontaneously considering undertaking this task. Publications by the following are suggestive: Kenneth W. Spence, of Iowa State University (*6*); James S. Taylor, of the University of Cape Town, South Africa; Harold Schlosberg, of Brown University (*5*), and Daniel E. Berlyne, of St. Andrews, Scotland (*1*).

A second division of individual psychology which urgently needs to be formally systematized and incorporated in the body of a behavior system is that concerning the emotions. Fortunately in the systematic work of Brown and Farber (*2*) we have an excellent groundwork for the scientific treatment of this hitherto elusive subject.

A third division of individual psychology which has occupied serious minds from the earliest ages is concerned with the detailed mechanisms of abstract reasoning. The expectation of an early and radical solution of this ancient group of problems lies in the study of speech movements considered as pure-stimulus acts ($_{(r)}$). On this assumption, logic would become a set of rules by which habits of manipulating verbal pure-stimulus acts eventuate into valid motor adjustments to various life conditions. The subject matter of Chapter 10 may be considered as a tentative gross-behavioral approach to this great subject.

And finally, the crowning achievement of all will be the creation of a really quantitative system of social behavior. Social psychology has its roots in individual psychology because the latter furnishes us with the skills which are employed in social intercourse and communication, and necessarily must precede to some extent. But world conditions are crying loudly for a really scientific system of the inter-organismic behavior of groups. It seems incredible that nature would create one set of primary sensory-motor laws for the mediation of individual behavior and another set for the mediation of group behavior. Presumably, then, the laws which are derived for social behavior will be based for the most part on the same postulates as those which form the basis of individual behavior. If this turns out to be true, we are even now an appreciable distance on our way toward the ultimate goal of integrating the individual-social sciences with the group-social sciences.

References

1. Berlyne, D. E. Attention, perception and behavior theory. *Psychol. Rev.*, 1951, *58*, 137–146.
2. Brown, J. S. and Farber, I. E. Emotions conceptualized as intervening variables—with suggestions toward a theory of frustration. *Psychol. Bull.*, 1951, *48*, pp. 465–495.
3. Koffka, K. *Principles of Gestalt psychology*. New York: Harcourt Brace and Co., 1935.
4. Munn, N. L. *Fundamentals of human adjustment*. New York: Houghton Mifflin Co., 1951.
5. Schlosberg, H. A note on depth perception, size, constancy, and related topics. *Psychol. Rev.*, 1950, *57*, 314–317.
6. Spence, K. W. Cognitive versus stimulus-response theories of learning. *Psychol. Rev.*, 1950, *57*, 159–172.

Glossary of Symbols

A = amplitude; a constant; distance between two objects in j.n.d.'s.

a = empirical constant; an incentive substance (water).

B = mean number of reactions in a response cycle; mean number of responses per alternation cycle; exponential constant.

b = empirical constant.

C = the larger habit strength in behavioral withdrawal, $C \doteq {}_sH'_R = {}_sH_R$; the larger reaction potential in behavioral withdrawal, $C \doteq {}_sE'_R = {}_sE_R$.

C_D = condition producing a drive.

D = drive; primary motivation; need; emotion; effective or gross drive; $D = D' \times \epsilon$.

D' = drive proper.

d = difference between two stimuli; difference between the logarithms of two stimuli.

${}_sE_R$ = reaction potential.

${}_sE'_R$ = some other ${}_sE_R$.

${}_sE_{R_+}$ = reaction potential of the "correct" reaction.

${}_sE_{R_-}$ = reaction potential of the "incorrect" reaction.

$+{}_sE_R$ = reaction potential of adient reaction.

$-{}_sE_R$ = reaction potential of abient reaction.

${}_s\underline{E}_R$ = generalized reaction potential; effective reaction potential; generalized superthreshold reaction potential.

${}_s\bar{E}_R$ = net reaction potential; ${}_s\bar{E}_R = {}_sE_R \doteq {}_sI_R$.

${}_s\underline{\dot{E}}_R$ = net discriminatory reaction potential; maximum reaction potential at the point of original learning.

${}_sE_R$ = superthreshold portion of reaction potential; ${}_s\dot{E}_R = {}_sE_R \doteq {}_sL_R$.

${}_s\tilde{E}_R$ = momentary reaction potential.

${}_s\dot{\underline{E}}_R$ = superthreshold reaction potential, ${}_s\dot{E}_R \doteq {}_sL_R$.

F = food reinforcement; uniform factor of reduction of reaction potential; mean number of uninterrupted sequences; mean number of responses per alternation.

f = an incentive substance (food); function of (   ).

G = goal; goal object.

G.G. = goal-gradient index.

G.O. = goal-orientation index.

${}_sH_R$ = habit; habit strength.

357

$_s\text{H}'_\text{R}$ = some other habit.

$_s\bar{\text{H}}_\text{R}$ = generalized habit strength; habit strength resulting from stimulus generalization.

h = hours of food privation; length or amount of food privation.

I_R = reactive inhibition.

I'_R = reactive inhibition remaining after a period of spontaneous recovery.

$\dot{\text{I}}_\text{R} = \text{I}_\text{R} + {_s\text{I}_\text{R}}$.

$\dot{\text{I}}_\text{R} = {_s\dot{\text{E}}_\text{R}}$; enough $\dot{\text{I}}_\text{R}$ to neutralize the superthreshold reaction potential.

$_s\text{I}_\text{R}$ = conditioned inhibition; inhibitory potential.

$_s\underline{\text{I}}_\text{R}$ = generalized inhibitory potential; generalized conditioned inhibition.

i = exponential constant.

J = the influence on reaction potential reduction caused by the delay in reinforcement represented by: $\text{J} = {_s\underline{\text{E}}_{\text{R}_\text{d}}} = \text{D} \times \text{V}_2 \times \text{K} \times {_s\text{H}_\text{R}} \times 10^{-.15\text{d}} \times \text{V}_1$; it also represents an earlier empirical fitted approximation $(\text{J} = 10^{-\text{jt}})$.

j = an empirical exponential constant.

j.n.d. = just noticeable difference; discrimination threshold.

K = component of reaction potential; incentive motivation.

K′ = the physical incentive or reward in motivation.

$_s\text{L}_\text{R}$ = minimum reaction potential evoking reaction; reaction threshold.

M = the learning maximum; maximum of reaction potential.

m = exponential constant.

N = number of reinforcements in general.

$\dot{\text{N}}$ = number of reinforcements from the beginning of learning, i.e., from absolute zero (Z).

$\underline{\text{N}}$ = number of superthreshold reinforcements.

n = number of unreinforced reaction evocations required to produce experimental extinction.

$\dot{\text{n}}$ = ordinal number of unreinforced reaction evocations at a given time.

$_s\text{O}_\text{R}$ = momentary behavioral oscillation.

p_+ = probability of occurrence of the correct response.

p_- = probability of occurrence of the incorrect response.

R = response; an act of some kind.

$\bar{\text{R}}$ = wrong or unadaptive response.

R_+ = appropriate, correct, or right response; a response that is reinforced.

R_- = inappropriate, incorrect, or wrong response; a response that is extinguished (by non-reinforcement).

R_G = consummatory response; reinforcing state of affairs; antedating goal reaction.

Ⓡ = pure-stimulus act in general.

r_G = fractional antedating goal reaction; a concrete pure-stimulus act.

S = stimulus; stimulus energy; stimulus intensity.

S' = theoretical stimulus intensity which is functionally equivalent to a given molar afferent impulse; equivalent stimulus trace intensity; another stimulus.

S_+ = a stimulus aggregate that precedes a reinforced reaction (R_+).

S_- = a stimulus aggregate that precedes an unreinforced reaction (R_-).

$\dot{S}_+$ = stimuli originally conditioned to the reinforced reaction (R_+).

$\dot{S}_-$ = stimuli originally conditioned to the unreinforced reaction (R_-).

$\dot{S}'$ = theoretical recruitment phase of molar afferent energy impulse.

$\underset{.}{S}'$ = theoretical subsident phase of molar afferent energy impulse.

S_D = drive stimulus; need; drive intensity.

S_{D_h} = drive stimulus due to hunger.

S_{D_t} = drive stimulus due to thirst.

S_G = goal stimulus.

s = neurophysiological afferent impulse evoked by S; the trace of the stimulus afferent impulse.

s' = theoretical molar afferent impulse corresponding to s; molar stimulus trace intensity; $s' = \log S'$.

$\dot{s}'$ = theoretical recruitment phase of molar afferent impulse.

$\underset{.}{s}'$ = theoretical subsident phase of molar afferent impulse.

$\check{s}$ = afferent impulse as modified by afferent interaction.

s_G = fractional goal stimulus; proprioceptive stimuli resulting from r_G; proprioceptive goal stimulus; fractional antedating goal stimulus.

t = time (usually in seconds); duration; delay in reinforcement.

t = time since the termination (or beginning) of a stimulation.

t' = time since the maximum of the recruitment phase of a stimulus trace; $t' = t - .450''$.

$_st_R$ = reaction latency; reaction time.

$_sU_R$ = unlearned receptor-effector connection.

V = stimulus-intensity dynamism; $V = 1 - 10^{-a \log S}$; adient incentive intensity.

V_1 = stimulus-intensity dynamism involved in original learning.

V_2 = stimulus-intensity dynamism which evokes the response.

W = work involved in a response (R).

w = weight of food incentive.

$$Y = \text{response cycle asymmetry; } Y = \frac{F_p - F_q}{F_p + F_q}.$$

y = distribution of momentary behavioral oscillation ($_sO_R$).

Z = absolute zero of reaction potential.

Δ = increment.

ϵ = inanition component of food privation drive; $\epsilon = \dfrac{D}{D'}$.

σ = the standard deviation.

$+$ = behavioral summation.

$\dotdiv$ = behavioral withdrawal.

$\dashrightarrow$ = acquired receptor-effector connection.

$\rightarrow$ = unlearned receptor-effector connection.

$\rightsquigarrow$ = causal relationship other than receptor-effector connection.

Index of Names

(Page numbers in bold-face type refer to the lists of references at the ends of the chapters.)

Anderson, A. C., 275, 276
Antoinetti, J. A., 62, 63, 64, 67, 74, 88, 89, **98**
Arnold, W. J., 156, 157, 164, 165, 169, 171, 172, 173, 174, 175, 180, 187, 189, **190**, 209, 210, **214**

Bentham, J., 341, 342, **345**
Bergmann, G., 137, 150, **155**
Berlyne, D. E., 355, **356**
Birch, H. G., 318, 319, 321, 324, **325**
Blodgett, H. C., 146, **153**, 278, 279, **305**
Brown, J. S., 67, 68, 69, 81, 82, 83, **98**, 219, 222, 224, 225, 226, 253, 271, 272, **273, 274**, 355, **356**
Buck, N. S., **345**

Carr, H. A., 283
Crespi, L. P., 141, 142, 143, 147, **153**
Cummings, S. B., 284, **307**
Czehura, W. S. (Stanley, W. C.), 118, **121**

Dashiell, J. F., 261, **273**, 288, 289, 292, 304, **305**
DeCamp, J. E., 275, **305**
Dewey, J., 343, 344, **345**

Ebbinghaus, H., 183, **190**
Euclid, 4, 226, 340

Fairchild, F. R., **345**
Farber, I. E., 355, **356**
Fechner, G. T., 89, 92, 352
Felsinger, J. M., **98, 122, 190, 306, 345**
Fitch, F. B., **14, 58, 191**
Fletcher, F. M., 226, **273**
Frick, F. C., 74, **98**
Furniss, E. S., **345**

Gengerelli, J. A., 300, **305**
Gilbreth, F. B. and L. M., 208, 209, **214**
Gladstone, A. I., **98**, 106, **122**, 163, 180, 187, **190, 306, 345**
Grice, G. R., 94, **98**, 132, **154**, 275, **306**
Guilford, J. P., 26, **57**, 229, **273**
Gulliksen, H., **98**
Guthrie, E. R., 118

Hall, M., **14, 58, 191**
Halverson, H. M., 207, 208, **214**
Hays, R., 61, 97, **99**, 209
Hebb, D. O., 261, **273**
Herbert, M. J., **190**
Higginson, G. D., 300, **306**
Hilgard, E. R., **122, 154**
Hill, C. J., 172, 178, 187, **190**
Hobhouse, L. T., 39, **57**, 280, **306**
Holland, G., 23, 30, 37, 38, **57**
Holmes, S. J., 39, **58**, 280, **306**
Honzik, C. H., 145, 146, 147, **155**, 290, 291, 292, 293, **307**
Hovland, C. I., **14, 58**, 66, 67, 69, **98**, 183, 184, 187, 188, **190, 191**
Hull, C. L., **14**, 51, **58**, 61, **98, 99**, 118, **122**, 136, 139, 140, 151, **154**, 178, 187, **190, 191, 214**, 250, 262, **273**, 287, **306, 325, 326, 345**
Hunt, J. McV., 272, **274**
Hunter, W. S., 184, 186, 187, **191**

Jackson, T. A., 318, 321, **326**
James, W., 325, **326**
Jones, A. W., 44
Jones, F. N., 297, **306**

Keller, F. S., 135, **154, 191**
Kendler, H. H., 139, 150, 151, **154**

Kimble, G. A., 38, **58**, 103, 116, **122**
Klebanoff, S., 229, 230, 235, 243
Koffka, K., 39, **58**, **356**
Köhler, W., 92, 93, 266, **273**, 324, **326**, 342, 344, **345**

Ladd, G. T., **58**
Lashley, K. S., 78, 92, 93, **99**
Leeper, R., 136, 139, 140, 151, **154**
Lewin, K., 224, 243, 247, 250, 267, 268, 271, 272, **273**
Lindsay, R. B., 272, **274**
Lipofsky, H., 253, **274**
Lippitt, R., 137, 150, **155**
Logan, F. A., 228
Lyon, D. C., 183, **191**

Maier, N. R. F., 325, **326**
Margenau, H., 272, **274**
McGeoch, J. A., 118, **122**
Meumann, E., 183, **191**
Miller, N. E., 222, 223, 224, 226, 228, 230, 235, 243, 247, 253, 271, 272, **274**
Montpellier, G. de., 174, 175, **191**
Morgan, L., 280
Muenzinger, K. F., 93
Munn, N. L., 347, **356**

Nissen, H. W., **122**
North, A. J., 115, 118, **122**
Nowlis, V., **122**

Pavlov, I. P., 59, 64, 67, **99**, 100, 119, **122**, 134, **154**, **306**
Pearson, K., 14
Perin, C. T., 132, 133, **154**, 333, **345**
Perkins, C. C., Jr., 132, **154**
Perkins, D. T., 14, **58**, **191**
Perry, R. B., 343, 344, **345**
Peterson, J., 280, 282, 283, 299, **306**

Raben, M. W., 67, 74, **99**
Reid, J. R., 342, **345**
Reynolds, B., 101, 102, 103, 116, **122**, 300, **306**
Reynolds, H. E., 300, 301, 302, 303, 305, **306**
Riesen, A. H., 122, 217, 259, **274**
Robbins, L., 327, 332, 333, **346**

Roby, T. B., 153, **154**
Rodnick, E. H., 119, 120, **123**
Ross, R. T., 14, **58**, **191**
Rowley, J. B., **99**

Saltz, E., **98**
Schlosberg, H., 355, **356**
Schoenfeld, W. N., 135, **154**, **191**
Seward, J. P., 133, **154**
Sheffield, F. D., 153, **154**
Shipley, W. C., 297, **307**
Skinner, B. F., 127, 135, 136, **154**, 169, 209, 211, **214**
Spence, K. W., **58**, 59, 78, 92, **99**, **123**, 127, 133, 137, 150, 151, **154**, **155**, 283, 297, **307**, 355, **356**
Spragg, S. D. S., 317, **326**
Sprow, A. J., 173, 174, 180, 187, **191**
Stanley, W. C. (see Czehura, W. S.)
Switzer, S. A., 119, **123**

Taylor, F. E., 297, **306**
Taylor, J. S., 355
Thorndike, E. L., 39, **58**, 280, **307**
Tolman, E. C., 93, **99**, 145, 146, 147, 151, 152, **155**, 278, 282, 290, 291, 292, 293, 295, **307**

Urban, W. M., 342, **346**

Valentine, W. L., 300, **307**

Walker, E. L., 150, **155**
Warden, C. J., **99**, 284, **307**
Watson, J. B., 39, 41, **58**, 280, **307**
Weber, E. H., 89, 92, 352
White, A. E`., 282, **307**
Wilcoxon, H. C., 61, **99**
Wolfe, J. B., 132, 133, **155**, 317, **326**, 330, **346**
Wolfle, D. L., **98**, **99**
Wolfle, H. M., 116, **123**
Woodbury, C. B., 186, 187, **191**, 209
Woodworth, R. S., **58**

Yamaguchi, H. G., **98**, **122**, 174, 180, **190**, **306**, **345**
Yoshioka, J. G., 275, 295, 296, **307**

Index of Subjects

Abient-abient conflict, heterogeneous, 236 ff., 244 ff., 269; homogeneous, 232 ff., 240 ff., 269

Abient barriers, and compound trial-and-error learning, 255; and pattern discrimination, 255, 270 ff.

Abient behavior, generalized nature of, 218 ff.; and gradient of reinforcement, 221 ff.; gradients of, 220 ff.; and incentive, 225 ff.; and limb movements, 219; and orientation, 219; path selection in, 226 ff., 256 ff; and primary motivation, 225 ff.; qualitative analysis of, 215 ff; quantitative characteristics of, 220 ff.; and role of barriers, 253 ff.; and stimulus generalization, 220, 223; and stimulus-intensity dynamism, 222

Adaptive behavior, 215; 357 ff.; versus non-adaptive behavior, 60

Adaptive responses, the antedating of, 110 ff.

Adient-abient behavior, as a function of primary motivation, 251 ff.; role of barriers in, 253 ff.

Adient-abient conflict, behavioral oscillation in, 249 ff.

Adient-abient field gradients, with objects occupying different places, 245 ff., 270; with objects occupying the same place, 247 ff., 270

Adient-adient behavior, and latency of reaction, 230 ff., 269; non-competitive, 232

Adient-adient competition, and behavioral oscillation, 228; and drive, 230 ff., 265; and incentive, 230 ff., 265; and latency of reaction, 230 ff., 269; heterogeneous, 231, 265; homogeneous, 227 ff.

Adient behavior, as a function of location of adient goal, 262 ff.; generalized nature of, 218 ff.; and gradient of reinforcement, 220 ff.; gradients of, 220 ff.; and incentive, 225 ff.; and limb movements, 219; and orientation, 219; path selection in, 226 ff., 256 ff.; and primary motivation, 225 ff.; qualitative analysis of, 215 ff.; quantitative characteristics of, 220 ff.; role of barriers in, 253 ff.; role of random behavior in, 215 ff.; and stimulus generalization, 220, 223; and stimulus-intensity dynamism, 222

Afferent stimulus interaction, and barrier problems, 271; Postulate XI, 11; and reversal learning, 115; and stimulus generalization, 94, 96; and the afferent impulse, 11; and the patterning of stimulus traces, 115; and the stimulus trace, 109

Alternation, definition and example of response, 42; definition of double, 184 ff.

Alternation cycle, asymmetry of, 42 ff., 46 ff., 52 ff.; defined, 42; responses per, 46 ff.

Alternation phase, defined and example of, 42; responses per, 46 ff.

Amplitude of reaction, reaction potential as a function of, 13

Antedating defense reaction, and adaptive behavior, 348 ff.

Antedating generalized tendencies, and double alternation, 185

Antedating goal reaction, and double drive problems, 150 ff.; and partial reinforcement, 134 ff.; and reinforcement theory, 148 ff., 150; secondary

363

reinforcement mediated by the, 150, 314; and the pure-stimulus act, 151

Antedating responses, adaptive significance of, 110 ff.; and delay learning, 112 ff.; in conflict with instrumental responses, 125; and persisting stimulation, 111; subgoal, 312; and the stimulus trace, 108, 110 ff., 350; and time of reinforcement, 116

Anthropomorphism, and behavior theory, 347

Anticipation, the frustration and realization of, 133 ff.

Anticipatory turning, in maze learning, 296 ff.; in maze learning and goal orientation, 297; in maze learning and stimulus generalization, 296 ff., 304; in maze learning and the goal gradient, 298; in maze learning and the perseverative stimulus trace, 296 ff., 301

Anxiety, and need, 341

Approach-avoidance behavior (see Adient-abient behavior)

Asynchronism, of reaction potential oscillation, 12, 235

Avoidance learning, 111 ff. (see also Abient behavior)

Barriers, their role in adient-abient behavior, 253 ff.

Behavior, abient (see Abient behavior); adaptive, 347 ff.; adient behavior and the role of random, 215 ff.; avoidance (see Abient behavior); challenges of the near future, 353 ff.; consistency of valuative, 332 ff.; evaluative, 333; evolution and unlearned, 348; flight reaction in social, 337; generalization of orientational, 217 ff.; in relation to objects in space, 215 ff.; insightful, 308 ff., 314 ff. (see also Insight); laws of mammalian, 1; minute, 193; moral, 339 ff.; non-orientational, 215 ff.; non-random, 308; non-social, 2; primary laws of social, 355 ff.; problem-solving, 308 ff.; pure-stimulus acts in valuative, 236, 343; purposive, 152; qualitative aspects in the development of systematic, 353 ff.; quantitative aspects in the development of system-

atic, 354 ff.; quantitative system of social, 355 ff.; random, 15, 215 ff.; role of barriers in detour, 253 ff.; science of molar, 2, 234; skilled, 192 ff.; social, 336 ff., 355 ff.; speech or symbolic, 4; stimulus generalization and orientation, 218; and the molar stimulus trace, 100 ff.; value in choice, 331 ff.

Behavior chains, 156 ff.; compound trial-and-error learning as a form of, 171 ff.; defined and example of homogeneous, 157 ff.; and delay of reinforcement, 7 ff., 126 ff., 158; double alternation as a form of, 184 ff.; generalization in, 178 ff.; and gradient of reinforcement, 158 ff.; heterogeneity within each link of, 189; in maze chaining, 172 ff., 175 ff., 179, 180 ff.; and latency of response, 162, 163 ff., 167 ff.; length of chain in determining the difficulty of learning heterogeneous, 181 ff.; locomotor "insight" in, 309 ff.; and proprioceptive stimuli, 158; serial reinforcement and homogeneous, 167 ff.; serial reinforcement and heterogeneous, 170 ff.; simple locomotion as an example of homogeneous, 188 ff.; stimulus generalization in, 159 ff.; stimulus trace intensity in, 160; terminal reinforcement and heterogeneous, 165 ff.; terminal reinforcement and homogeneous, 172 ff.; trial-and-error learning in, 156

Behavior functions, need of quantitative equations relating various, 354

Behavior link, delay of reinforcement and the, 7 ff., 126 ff.; empirical validity of theoretical analysis of learning within the, 206 ff.; learning within the individual, 192 ff.

Behavioral oscillation, and adient-abient competition, 249 ff.; and adient-adient competition, 228; asynchronism in, 11 ff., 235; changes in the concept of, 57; and contraction intensity, 198; in multidirectional maze learning, 288, 304; in valuative behavior, 332 ff.; and individual differences, 13; and interaction of heterogeneous abient reaction potentials, 239; and learning within the response link, 203; and locomotor trial-and-error learning, 255; and path selection, 227; Postulate XII, 11 ff.; and receptor adjustment acts, 93 ff.; recurrence of extinguished responses resulting from, 17; and response alternation, 41, 42; and response generalization, 12, 200, 319 ff.; standard deviation of, 305

Behavioral summation, of habit strengths, 8; of incentive substances, 9; of inhibitory potentials, 75 ff.; of reaction potentials, 8, 161, 162

Behavioral withdrawal, of habit strength, 8; of inhibitory potential from reaction potential, 70 ff., 77 ff.; of reaction potential, 9

Coercion, the role of drive in the maintenance of, 337 ff.
Cognition, 151 ff.
Comparison phenomena, 92 ff.
Compound trial-and-error learning, and abient barriers, 255; and behavior chaining, 171 ff.; and maze learning, 275 ff.
Condition of drive, 6, 7 (see Drive)
Conditioned defense reaction, 111 ff.
Conditioned inhibition (see Inhibitory potential), Corollary ix, 10; in discrimination problems, 71 ff., 91; in massed versus spaced learning, 36 ff.
Conditioned reflex, as a case of simple learning, 348; eyeblink, 101; and problem solving, 308
Conditioned responses, spatial generalization of, 271
Conditioning of inhibition, to the fractional goal stimulus, 133 ff.
Constructs, natural law formulation and symbolic, 345; natural science theory and the role of symbolic, 328

Delay, inhibition of, 113
Delay learning, example and analysis of, 112 ff.
Delay of reinforcement, and behavior chains, 7 ff., 126 ff., 158; changes in the treatment of, 4; Corollary iii, 7 ff.; equation of, 39 ff.; and fractional antedating goal responses, 150; in

maze blind-alley elimination, 280 ff.; in maze learning, 276 ff.; in stick problem solving, 320; reaction potential as a function of, 126 ff.; and receptor adjustor acts, 93; and role of motivation, 133; secondary reinforcement and the gradient of, 132 ff.; the amount of reinforcement and the gradient of, 132 ff.; and the constitution of reaction potential, 7 ff.

Differential reinforcement, in discrimination learning, 59 ff., 60 ff., 67 ff., 69 ff., 74 ff.
Diminishing marginal utility, law of, 333 ff.
Diminishing returns, law of, 335
Discrimination gradients, as a function of stimuli separation, 72 ff.
Discrimination learning, 59 ff.; and abient barriers, 255; and adaptive behavior, 349 ff.; based upon objective stimulus intensities, 84 ff.; defined, 94; delay learning as an example of, 112 ff.; and differential reinforcement, 59 ff., 60 ff., 67 ff., 74 ff.; discrimination gradients following, 70 ff.; example of simple separate-discriminanda presentation, 60 ff.; generalization gradients in, 63, 69 ff.; and generalization of reaction potential based upon stimulus intensities, 78 ff.; qualitative or subjective scales in, 69 ff.; and ratio of reinforcement, 67; role of incidental stimuli in, 64 ff.; stimulus selection and simple, 60; stimulus-intensity, 69 ff.; with objective stimulus intensities, 87 ff.; with three discriminanda presented separately, 75 ff.
Discriminatory trial-and-error learning, with joint stimulus presentation, 92 ff.; with single stimulus presentation, 90 ff.
Disinhibition, 302 ff., 304
Distributed trials, as distinguished from massed trials learning, 20 ff., 36; and law of habit formation in simple trial-and-error learning, 6
Double drive problems, 150 ff.
Drive (see Motivation), condition, 6, 7; and emotion, 133 ff.; experimental extinction and increasing primary, 114;

generalization of, 7; in detour behavior, 266 ff.; in double drive learning, 140 ff.; inanition component of, 6; latent learning and the role of, 140 ff.; maintenance of coercion by, 337 ff.; pleasure and reduction of, 341; Postulate V, 6 ff.; primary negative, 9; proper, 6; and secondary motivation, 6; and the constitution of reaction potential, 7 ff.; and unlearned behavior, 5

Drive intensity, generalization based upon, 11

Drive reduction, and a theory of value, 341; pleasure and pain as drive or, 342

Drive stimulus, drive condition and the, 7; fractional antedating goal reactions and the, 124 ff.; generalization and the role of the, 124 ff., 138; generalization continua and the, 124; in problem-solving behavior, 308 ff.; motivation or reinforcement and the, 5; reduction and reinforcement, 152 ff.

Dynamism (*see* Stimulus-intensity dynamism)

Economics, as a science, 327 ff.

Emotion, frustration and, 133 ff.; in behavior theory, 355

Emotional responses, and shifts in amount of incentive, 142

Entelechy, behavior theory and the, 347

Equations, *1, 2, 3,* 5; *4, 5, 6; 6, 7, 8,* 7; *9, 10, 11, 12,* 8; *13, 14, 15, 16, 17,* 9; *18, 19, 20,* 10; *21, 22, 23, 24, 25,* 11; *26, 27,* 12; *28, 29, 30, 31,* 13; *32, 21; 33, 34,* 26; *35, 36,* 39; *37,* 40; *38,* 42; *39, 40,* 43; *41,* 44; *42,* 45; *43,* 67; *44,* 79; *45, 46,* 103; *47,* 131; *48,* 140; *49,* 158; *50, 51,* 161; *52,* 163; *53,* 174; *54, 55,* 220; *56,* 238; *57,* 248; *58,* 292; *59,* 294

Ethics, a natural science of, 338 ff.

Evaluative behavior, 333

Evolution, adaptive behavior and organic 348

Expectancy, and the stimulus trace, 108, 120; and foresight, 151 ff., negative, 150

Experimental extinction, as a function of reaction potential, 13; delay learning and the generalization of effects of, 113 ff.; differential resistance to, 69 ff.; disinhibition of effects of, 302 ff., 304; and emotion, 134; and fractional antedating goal reactions, 135; generalization of the effects of, 54; in maze learning, 300 ff., 304 ff.; in separate-discriminanda presentation discrimination learning, 60 ff.; in insightful assembly of tool-using segments, 322 ff.; and incidental stimuli, 67; and increasing primary drive, 114; and inhibitory potential (Postulate IX), 9 ff.; and insightful behavior, 314 ff.; and negative expectancy, 150; and partial reinforcement, 120 ff., 134 ff.; and ratio of reinforcement, 134 ff.; and spontaneous recovery, 17; and valuation, 330

External inhibition, 20

Fear, as an incipient flight reaction, 337

Feeling, as Urban's value concept, 341 ff.

Field theory, and behavior in relation to objects in space, 250, 267, 269, 271 ff.

Foreknowledge, 151 ff.

Foresight, 151 ff.

Fractional action phases, within the behavior link, 193

Fractional antedating goal reactions, 124 ff.; and adaptive behavior, 350; as a function of the stimulus trace, 127; as a secondary reinforcing agent, 14, 125 ff., and delay in reinforcement, 150; and double-drive learning, 136 ff.; and drive stimuli, 124 ff.; and generalization of habit strength, 128; and insightful behavior, 311, 321 ff.; and latent learning, 148 ff.; and path selection, 259; and resistance to extinction, 135; and stimulus-intensity generalization, 315; the role of stimulus-intensity dynamism in, 131

Fractional goal stimulus, and the conditioning of inhibition, 133 ff.

Frustration, of an anticipation, 133 ff.; and reversal learning, 115 ff.

Galvanic skin reaction, 116 ff.

Generalization, based upon stimulus intensities, 78 ff., 84 ff.; examples of 100 per cent, 65; fractional antedating goal reactions and stimulus intensity, 315;

in limiting behavior, 308; in maze learning, 178 ff.; mediating temporary unadaptive behavior, 349; of abient or adient behavior, 217 ff.; of drive, 7; of fractional antedating goal reactions and stimulus traces, 125, 127; of habit strength and the fractional antedating goal reaction, 127; of inhibitory potential, 11, 20, 22 ff.; of inhibitory potential and the role of stimulus-intensity dynamism, 86; of inhibitory potential in triple discriminanda problems, 75 ff.; of inhibitory potential in trial-and-error learning, 20, 23 ff.; of orientational behavior, 217 ff.; of reaction potential in trial-and-error learning, 20; of secondary reinforcement, 197; of the effects of experimental extinction, 54, 113 ff.; on a black-white continuum, 63; path selection and stimulus, 263; perseverative, 185; response (see Response generalization); response-intensity, 199 ff., 204 ff., 206 ff.; role of the drive stimulus in, 124 ff., 138; spatial, 271; stimulus (see Stimulus generalization); the goal stimulus in, 308 ff.; the stimulus trace as a continuum for, 104 ff., 350

Generalization gradient, changes in the steepness of, 68 ff.; determination of the exponent of, 97; and discrimination learning, 69 ff.; discrimination learning and a post-discrimination, 61–64; discrimination learning and a theoretical, 70; in a three-discriminanda problem, 75 ff.; incidental stimuli affecting the, 64 ff., 70; mechanisms mediating the, 69 ff.

Goal gradient (see Gradient of reinforcement), anticipatory turning in maze learning and the, 298; hypothesis, 271 ff., 275 ff.; in maze blind-alley elimination, 280 ff.; in maze learning, 275 ff., 303 ff.; index, 294; spatial, 275 ff.; temporal, 276 ff.

Goal orientation, and anticipatory turning, 297; index, 292; and maze learning, 287 ff.; secondary reinforcement in, 294 ff.

Goal stimulus, 124 ff.

Gradient of reinforcement (see Delay of reinforcement), abient behavior and the, 221 ff.; adient behavior and the, 220 ff.; behavior chains and the, 158 ff.; delay in reinforcement and the, 126 ff.; double alternation and the, 185; path selection and the, 257 ff., 262 ff.

Habit-family hierarchy, defined, 257 ff.; example of, 256 ff.; in maze learning, 287 ff., 304; spatial, 253 ff., 267, 289, 303, 310 ff.; and "U"-shaped paths, 263 ff.

Habit formation, law of (Postulate IV), 6

Habit strength, behavioral oscillation of, 11 ff., 57; behavioral summation of, 8; behavioral withdrawal of, 8; drive intensity in the generalization of, 11; effect of additional practice upon, 66; effective, 11; fractional antedating goal reaction and the generalization of, 127; in the constitution of reaction potential, 7 ff.; introspective reportability of, 344; latent and manifest, 140 ff.; and stimulus generalization, 10 ff.; and the nervous system, 329; and theory of value, 340 ff.

Habituation, and secondary reinforcement, 173 ff.

Hierarchy (see Habit-family hierarchy), innate responses, 347 ff.; of responses, 5, 17; of valuation, 331

Incentive, and abient-adient behavior, 225 ff.; and Bentham's pleasure-pain hypothesis, 341; delay in the receipt of, 7 ff.; effects of shifts in, 140 ff.; and latent learning, 140 ff.; reaction potential as a function of delayed, 126 ff.

Incentive motivation, in detour behavior, 267 ff.; Postulate VII, 7

Incentive reinforcement, in the constitution of reaction potential, 7 ff.

Incentive substances, behavioral summation of, 9; and theory of value, 340 ff.

Incidental stimuli, 64 ff., 91

Individual differences, and evaluative behavior, 334; in the capacity for insight, 316; Postulate XVII, 13; and problem solving, 309; and specie; 3

Inhibition, and amount of work, 202 ff.; dissipation of reactive, 36; external, 20; and learning within the individual behavior link, 194 ff.; of delay, 113; the fractional goal stimulus and conditioning of, 133 ff.

Inhibitory aggregate, 9, 36

Inhibitory potential (*see* Conditioned inhibition), as a function of the number of responses, 10; behavioral summation of, 75 ff.; behavioral withdrawal of, 70 ff.; 77 ff.; and frustration, 133 ff.; generalization of, 11, 22 ff.; gradient of, 70; Postulate IX, 9 ff.; role of stimulus-intensity dynamism in the generalization of, 86; stimulus-intensity generalization of, 205; trial-and-error learning and the generalization of, 20; triple discriminanda problems and the generalization of, 75 ff.

Innate reaction tendency, and organic evolution, 18, 19, 348

Innate response hierarchy, 5, 347 ff.

Insight, assembly of tool-using behavior segments and a theory of, 321 ff.; experimental evidence of, 317; individual differences in the capacity for, 316; mediated by qualitative stimulus generalization, 323 ff.; problem of locomotor, 309 ff.; and response generalization, 323 ff.; and spontaneous tool-use, 317 ff.; theoretical diagrammatic representation of, 312

Insightful learning, theory of, 310 ff.

Intensity (*see* Stimulus intensity)

Interaction, afferent stimulus (*see* Afferent stimulus interaction)

Interest, and value theory, 343

Introspection, 344 ff.

j.n.d., scale of brightness, 63

Language, and expectative situations, 152; in latent learning, 150; in evaluative behavior, 332; prediction of verbal responses, 338

Latency of reaction, and adient-adient interaction, 232; as a function of incentive; 141; and behavior chaining, 162–165, 167 ff., 170 ff.; and generalization gradients, 68; in adient-adient behavior, 230 ff., 265; and insightful behavior, 313; and reaction potential, 13; and response strength, 17; and the galvanic skin reflex, 117

Latent learning, current aspects of the problem of, 148 ff.; in theoretical perspective, 140 ff.

Law(s), introspection in the formulation of, 344; methodology of validating natural-science, 338 ff.; natural-science and behavior, 333 ff.; of diminishing marginal utility, 333 ff.; of diminishing returns, 335; of habit formation, 6; of mammalian behavior, 1; of social behavior, 2; of value, 329 ff.; primary molar behavioral, 13; symbolic constructs and formulation of natural, 345

Learning, adient-abient (*see* Adient-abient behavior); based upon correlated reinforcement intensities, 196 ff.; chain (*see* Behavior chains); compound trial-and-error (*see* Behavior chains); discrimination, 59 ff. (*see also* Discrimination learning); double drive, 136 ff.; latent, 140 ff.; 148 ff.; maze (*see* Maze learning); of novel acts, 209 ff., 214; of the conditioned defense reaction, 111 ff.; rote, 117, 183; theoretical analysis of reversal, 114 ff., 120 ff.; trial-and-error (*see* Trial-and-error learning); within the individual behavior link, 192 ff.

Maze blind-alley elimination, 280 ff.; and the goal gradient, 303

Maze blind-alley entrances, as a function of the distance to the goal, 293 ff.; depth of penetration in, 298 ff.; experimental extinction of, 300 ff.; and goal direction, 289 ff.

Maze learning, and adience-abience, 270 ff.; anticipatory turning and the perseverative stimulus trace in, 296 ff.; anticipatory turning and stimulus generalization in, 296 ff.; anticipatory turning and the goal gradient in, 298; anticipatory turning in, 296 ff.; blind-alley elimination in, 280 ff.; experimental extinction in, 302 ff., 305; generalization in, 178 ff.; and goal orientation, 287 ff.; habit-family hierarchy in, 287 ff., 304; and incentive shifts, 140 ff.; and maze chaining, 172 ff., 175 ff., 180 ff.; multidirectional, 275 ff.; problem solving in, 309 ff.; pure-stimulus acts in, 288; reaction time in, 286 ff.; spontaneous recovery in, 302 ff.; and the goal-gradient principle, 278 ff.

Moral judgment, 337 ff.

Motivation (see Drive), delay in reinforcement and the role of, 133; incentive, 7; and law of diminishing marginal utility, 333 ff.; primary (see Primary motivation); secondary, 6

Need(s), and anxiety, 341; in energizing tendencies to action, 18; and pleasure-pain, 340 ff.; related to valuation, 329 ff.; the fractional goal stimulus in differentiating among, 125; and unlearned behavior, 5

Need reduction, a modification of the role of, 152 ff.; and a theory of value, 340 ff.

Objects in space, behavior in relation to, 215 ff.

Oscillation (see Behavioral oscillation)

Pain, Bentham's concept of, 340 ff.

Path selection, 226 ff., 256 ff.

Perception, learning of space, 217 ff.; of depth, 259; and receptor adjustments, 217; the reporting of, 354

Perseverative responses, in rote learning, 207

Perseverative stimulus trace (see Stimulus trace)

Pleasure, or pain as drive reduction or drive, 342

Postulates, I, II, 5; III, 5 ff.; IV, 6; V, 6 ff.; VI, VII, VIII, 7; IX, 9 ff.; X, 10 ff.; XI, 11; XII, 11 ff.; XIII, 12; XIV, XV; XVI, XVII, 13

Primary motivation (see Drive), and abient-adient behavior, 225 ff.; delay learning and an increase in, 114; Postulate V, 6 ff.; reaction potential and changes in, 225

Primary reinforcement, Postulate III, 5 ff.

Problem solving, ability and statistical methodology, 309 ff.; assembly of behavior segments in, 308 ff.; delay in reinforcement in stick, 320; in maze learning, 276 ff.; involving three habit segments, 315 ff.; of non-speaking organisms, 308 ff.; and tool use, 320

Proprioceptive stimuli, and behavior chains, 158

Pure-stimulus act, antedating goal responses as examples of the, 151; foresight and the, 151 ff.; in maze learning, 288; in valuative behavior, 337, 343; language, evaluative behavior and the, 332; the study of speech movement as a, 355

Purpose, 151 ff.

Purposive behavior, 152

Reaction (see Response), adaptive, 215, 347 ff.; antedating (see Antedating responses); defense, 110 ff., 118, 119; galvanic skin, 13

Reaction amplitude, and reaction potential, 13

Reaction potential, absolute zero of, 12; adience-abience and generalized, 220; as a function of delay in reinforcement, 126 ff.; as a function of incentive, 225; as a function of j.n.d. differences, 72 ff.; as a function of latency of reaction, 13; as a function of reaction amplitude, 13; asymptote of, 8; asynchronism of the oscillations of, 12, 235; and behavioral oscillation, 11 ff.; behavioral summation of, 8, 161, 162; behavioral withdrawal of, 9; and changes in primary motivation, 225; and delay in reinforcement, 7 ff.; drive intensity in the generalization of, 11; generalization of, 10 ff.; and generalization gradients (see Generalization gradient); incentive component of, 7; and incentive shifts, 140 ff.; incidental, 65, 67; introspective reportability of, 344; momentary, 12 ff.; net discriminatory, 72 ff., 75 ff., 84 ff., 204 ff.; reaction threshold and momentary, 12 ff.; stimulus intensity as a basis of generalization of, 78 ff., 84 ff.; superthreshold, 9, 92; the constitution of, 7 ff.; the interaction of two field gradients of adient, 227 ff., 269 ff.; the stimulus trace as a basis for generalization of, 104 ff.; and theory of value, 340 ff.; value represented by, 329 ff.

Reaction potentials, competition of, 12 ff., 20 ff., 30 ff., 111, 331 ff.

Reaction threshold, and absolute zero of reaction potential, 12 ff.; and delay in reinforcement, 8; drive and the, 7; and momentary reaction potential, 12 ff.; and response alternation, 57

Reasoning, abstract, 355 ff.

Receptor adjustment acts, 92 ff., 96, 216 ff., 255, 335

Reinforcement, all-or-none type of, 193 ff., 195, 196, 212 ff.; antedating responses and the time of, 116; cessation of pain as, 112; correlated, 200; criterion of, 152 ff.; delay learning and the role of, 112 ff.; delay of (see Delay of reinforcement); discrimination and the ratio of, 67; and drive stimuli, 124; experimental extinction and partial, 120 ff.; experimental extinction and the ratio of, 135 ff.; goal gradient and terminal, 158 ff.; gradient of delay in reinforcement and the amount of, 132 ff.; gradient of serial, 167 ff., 170; and habit formation, 6; and incentive motivation, 7; incidental non-, 63; law of reciprocal, 336 ff.; limiting nature of, 308 ff.; neutralization of incidental reaction potential by differential, 91; post-discrimination generalization gradients and differential, 60 ff.; primary, 5 ff.; secondary (see Secondary reinforcement); serial (see Serial reinforcement); terminal (see Terminal reinforcement); the anticipatory mechanism in partial, 134 ff.; theory and antedating goal reactions, 148 ff., 150; and value, 329 ff.

Reinforcement intensities, learning based on correlated, 196 ff.

Reminiscence, 37 ff.

Response(s) (see Reaction), competition of incompatible, 19, 20 ff., 30 ff., 111, 331; contraction-intensity selection of, 193 ff.; emotional, 142; evocation and reaction potential, 7; hierarchy of, 17 (see also Habit-family hierarchy); innate, 5, 19, 347 ff.; latency of reaction as an indication of strength of, 17; order of occurrence of, 17; relations type of, 94, 96; repetition of erroneous, 17; rote learning and perseverative, 207; short-circuiting of, 111, 173; the stimulus trace and the antedating of, 108, 110 ff., 350

Response alternation, characteristics of trial-and-error learning, 184 ff.; comparison of theoretical with empirical phenomena of, 49 ff.; and competition between reaction potentials, 41 ff., 55, 56; and spontaneous recovery, 57

Response alternation cycles, historical note on, 56

Response chains (see Behavior chains)

Response cycle, asymmetry of, 42 ff.

Response generalization and behavioral oscillation, 12, 199; Corollary xiii, 12; definition and example of, 200; in tool-using behavior, 320 ff.; and insightful behavior, 323 ff.; locomotion as an example of, 217 ff.; and response intensity, 204 ff.

Response intensity, as a function of incentive, 141; generalization, 199 ff., 204 ff., 206 ff.; learning within the behavior link, 193 ff.

Response oscillation, and contraction intensity, 198

Response selection, and trial-and-error learning, 60

Reversal learning, theoretical analysis of, 114 ff., 120 ff.

Rote learning, 117, 183

Satiation, and law of diminishing marginal utility, 333

Science, growth of empirical behavior, 353 ff.; of molar behavior, 2 ff., 234; and moral judgment, 339; of ethics, 338 ff.; theory of value and natural-, 340 ff.; truth and natural-, 336 ff.

Secondary motivation (see Drive)

Secondary reinforcement (see Reinforcement), affecting the gradient of delay in reinforcement, 132 ff.; Corollary ii,

6; and fractional antedating goal
reaction, 14, 125 ff.; generalization of,
197; and goal-pointing paths, 304; and
habituation, 173 ff.; in discrimination
learning, 67; in goal orientation, 294
ff.; in latent learning, 147 ff.; and
insightful assembly of tool-using behavior segments, 324; and insightful
behavior, 314; and the antedating goal
reaction, 150, 314; and the fractional
goal stimulus, 128; theoretical truth
value based upon, 335 ff.; and valuation, 330 ff.
Serial reinforcement, defined, 156 ff.; and
heterogeneous response chains, 170 ff.;
in heterogeneous linear maze chaining,
180 ff.; in homogeneous linear maze
chaining, 179 ff.; in homogeneous
response chains, 167 ff.
Skilled behavior, 192 ff.
Social behavior, flight reactions as
examples of, 337; systematization of,
335 ff.; valuation in, 336 ff.
Spatial habit-family hierarchy, 267, 289,
303, 310 ff.
Spontaneous recovery, in delay learning,
114; in maze learning, 301 ff.; recurrence of extinguished responses resulting from, 17; and response alternation,
57
Stimuli, discrimination learning and the
role of incidental, 64 ff.; incidental,
64 ff.; insightful assembly of tool-using
behavior segments and antedating goal,
322 ff.
Stimulus, equivalence, 59 (see also Stimulus generalization); fractional goal, 124
ff.; patterning, 115, 255, 270 ff.; reception, 5; secondary motivation based
upon a neutral, 6; selection and simple
discrimination learning, 60; trace (see
Stimulus trace)
Stimulus generalization, and abient-
adient behavior, 220, 222, 268 ff.; and
adaptive behavior, 349 ff.; and afferent
stimulus interaction, 94, 96; and behavior chains, 159 ff.; gradient of (see
Generalization gradient); in mediating
insightful behavior, 323 ff.; in tool-
using problem-solving behavior, 320;

and incidental stimuli, 64 ff.; and
orientational behavior, 218; and path
selection, 263; Postulate X, 10 ff.; and
rote learning, 117; and the defense
withdrawal reaction, 348; and valuation, 330
Stimulus intensity, discrimination learning, 69 ff., 84 ff., 87 ff.; discrimination
learning based upon objective, 87 ff.;
generalization, 11, 78 ff., 84 ff.; generalization and the fractional antedating goal response, 315; generalization and habit-family hierarchy, 257
ff.; generalization and response generalization, 204 ff.; and space perception, 217; stimulus-intensity dynamism as a function of the, 7
Stimulus-intensity dynamism, and adient
behavior, 222; as a constituent of reaction potential, 7 ff.; and conditions of
learning versus evocation, 102, 128;
fractional antedating goal reactions and
the role of, 131; and generalization of
inhibitory potential, 86; and generalization of reaction potential, 78 ff.; in
stimulus-intensity discrimination learning, 84 ff.; Postulate VI, 7; and stimulus
generalization, 11; and the molar
stimulus trace, 101; and the stimulus
trace as a generalization continuum,
104 ff.
Stimulus-response connections, diagrammatic representation of, 59, 92
Stimulus trace, and afferent stimulus
interaction, 109, 115; and antedating
reactions, 108, 110 ff., 350; anticipatory
turning in maze learning and the perseverative, 296, 303; as a generalization
continuum, 104 ff., 350; behavior and
the molar, 100 ff.; behavior chaining
based upon the, 159 ff.; comparison
phenomena dependent upon, 93; defined, 100; delay of reinforcement and
the, 126 ff.; delay learning and the, 112
ff.; derivation of the postulate on the,
101 ff.; distributed versus massed learning and the, 36; experimental validity
of the theorems relating to the, 116 ff.;
fractional antedating goal reactions as
a function of the, 259; generalization

of the fractional antedating goal reaction and the, 126 ff.; its role in adaptive behavior, 350 ff.; partial reinforcement and the, 120 ff.; reversal learning and the, 114 ff., 118 ff.; secondary reinforcement and the, 14; stimulus generalization based upon the, 159 ff.; stimulus-intensity dynamism and the, 7 ff., 101; stimulus reception and the, 5; tentative theorems regarding the, 107 ff.

Symbolic logic, and behavior science development, 353

Systematic behavior development, qualitative and quantitative aspects of, 353 ff.

Terminal reinforcement, defined, 156; and double alternation, 184 ff.; and heterogeneous response chains, 165 ff.; in heterogeneous linear maze chaining, 175 ff.; in homogeneous linear maze chaining, 172 ff.; and simple locomotion, 188 ff.

Theory, future challenges to behavior, 353 ff.; symbolic constructs and natural-science, 328; the test of a sound, 351 ff.

Threshold, reaction (see Reaction threshold)

Tool-use, acquisition of spontaneous, 317 ff.

Trace, stimulus (see Stimulus trace)

Trial-and-error, vicarious, 93

Trial-and-error learning, and adaptive behavior, 348 ff.; additional forms of, 56; an example of, 15 ff.; and behavior chains, 156; behavioral oscillation and locomotor, 255; by continuous trials, 38 ff.; by massed trials, 36 ff.; definition of and example of, 20 ff.; differentiated from discrimination learning, 59 ff.; joint-stimulus presentation discriminatory, 92 ff.; quantitative assumptions in, 20 ff.; and response alternation, 41–53; single stimulus presentation and discriminatory, 90 ff.; and space perception, 217; theoretical analysis of, 16 ff.

Valence, 267

Validation, rquirements for, 338 ff.

Value, valuation, and behavior theory, 327 ff.; distinguished from valuation, 329; ethics and, 338 ff.; in choice behavior, 330 ff.; interpretation of some theories of, 340 ff.; needs and, 329 ff.; objective treatment of, 327 ff.

Valuative behavior, consistency of, 332 ff.; and pure-stimulus acts, 343

Work, and amount of reward, 135; gradient, 206; habit-family hierarchy and the principle of less, 257 ff.; inhibitory potential as a function of, 10; path selection and the principle of less, 227; and secondary reinforcement, 112; and theory of value, 340 ff.

Work differential, learning within the behavior link and the role of, 202 ff.